Applications in Basic Marketing

Clippings from the Popular Business Press

2000-2001 Edition

Applications in Basic Marketing

Clippings from the Popular Business Press

2000-2001 Edition

William D. Perreault, Jr.
University of North Carolina

and

E. Jerome McCarthy
Michigan State University

Boston   Burr Ridge, IL   Dubuque, IA   Madison, WI   New York   San Francisco   St. Louis
Bangkok   Bogotá   Caracas   Lisbon   London   Madrid
Mexico City   Milan   New Delhi   Seoul   Singapore   Sydney   Taipei   Toronto

McGraw-Hill Higher Education

*A Division of The **McGraw-Hill** Companies*

APPLICATIONS IN BASIC MARKETING, 2000–2001

Published by Irwin/McGraw-Hill, an imprint of The McGraw-Hill Companies, Inc. 1221 Avenue of the Americas, New York, NY, 10020. Copyright © 2001, 2000, 1999, 1998, 1997, 1996, 1993 by The McGraw-Hill Companies, Inc. All rights reserved. No part of this publication may be reproduced or distributed in any form or by any means, or stored in a data base or retrieval system, without the prior written consent of The McGraw-Hill Companies, Inc., including, but not limited to, in any network or other electronic storage or transmission, or broadcast for distance learning.

Some ancillaries, including electronic and print components, may not be available to customers outside the United States.

This book is printed on acid-free paper.

domestic   1 2 3 4 5 6 7 8 9 0 QPD/QPD 0 9 8 7 6 5 4 3 2 1 0
international   1 2 3 4 5 6 7 8 9 0 QPD/QPD 0 9 8 7 6 5 4 3 2 1 0

ISBN 0075610310
ISSN 1099-5579

Publisher: *David Kendric Brake*
Sponsoring editor: *Rick Adams*
Coordinating editor: *Linda G. Davis*
Senior developmental editor: *Nancy Barbour*
Marketing manager: *Kimberly Kanakes*
Project manager: *Christine A. Vaughan*
Manager, new book production: *Melonie Salvati*
Director of design, Burr Ridge: *Keith J. McPherson*
Supplement coordinator: *Mark Sienicki*
Compositor: *Electronic Publishing Services, Inc., TN*
Printer: *Quebecor Printing Book Group/Dubuque*

INTERNATIONAL EDITION   0-07-118063-X
Copyright © 2001. Exclusive rights by The McGraw-Hill Companies, Inc. for manufacture and export.
This book cannot be re-exported from the country to which it is sold by McGraw-Hill.
The International Edition is not available in North America.

www.mhhe.com

Preface

This is the eleventh annual edition of *Applications in Basic Marketing.* We developed this set of marketing "clippings" from popular business publications to accompany our texts—*Basic Marketing* and *Essentials of Marketing.* All of these clippings report interesting case studies and current issues that relate to topics covered in our texts and in the first marketing course. We will continue to publish a new edition of this book *every year.* That means that we can include the most current and interesting clippings. Each new copy of our texts will come shrink-wrapped with a free copy of the newest (annual) edition of this book. However, it can also be ordered from the publisher separately for use in other courses or with other texts.

Our objective is for this book to provide a flexible and helpful set of teaching and learning materials. We have included clippings (articles) on a wide variety of topics. The clippings deal with consumer products and business products, goods and services, new developments in marketing as well as traditional issues, and large well-known companies as well as new, small ones. They cover important issues related to marketing strategy planning for both domestic and global markets. The readings can be used for independent study, as a basis for class assignments, or as a focus of in-class discussions. Some instructors might want to assign all of the clippings, but we have provided an ample selection so that it is easy to focus on a subset which is especially relevant to specific learning/teaching objectives. A separate set of teaching notes discusses points related to each article. We have put special emphasis on selecting short, highly readable articles—ones which can be read and understood in 10 or 15 minutes—so that they can be used in combination with other readings and assignments for the course. For example, they might be used in combination with assignments from *Essentials of Marketing,* exercises from the *Learning Aid for Use with Essentials of Marketing,* or *The Marketing Game!* micro-computer strategy simulation.

All of the articles are reproduced here in basically the same style and format as they originally appeared. This gives the reader a better sense of the popular business publications from which they are drawn, and stimulates an interest in ongoing learning beyond the time frame for a specific course.

We have added this component to our complete set of **P**rofessional **L**earning **U**nits **S**ystems (our **P.L.U.S.**) to provide even more alternatives for effective teaching and learning in the first marketing course. It has been an interesting job to research and select the readings for this new book, and we hope that our readers find it of value in developing a better understanding of the opportunities and challenges of marketing in our contemporary society.

William D. Perreault, Jr. and E. Jerome McCarthy

Acknowledgments

We would like to thank all of the publications that have granted us permission to reprint the articles in this book. Similarly, we value and appreciate the work and skill of the many writers who prepared the original materials.

Linda G. Davis played an important role in this project. She helped us research thousands of different publications to sort down to the final set, and she also contributed many fine ideas on how best to organize the selections that appear here.

The ideas for this book evolve from and build on previous editions of *Readings and Cases in Basic Marketing.* John F. Grashof and Andrew A. Brogowicz were coauthors of that book. We gratefully recognize the expertise and creativity that they shared over the years on that project. Their fine ideas carry forward here and have had a profound effect on our thinking in selecting articles that will meet the needs of marketing instructors and students alike.

We would also like to thank the many marketing professors and students whose input have helped shape the concept of this book. Their ideas—shared in personal conversations, in focus group interviews, and in responses to marketing research surveys—helped us to clearly define the needs that this book should meet.

Finally, we would like to thank the people at Irwin/McGraw-Hill, our publisher, who have helped turn this idea into a reality. We are grateful for their commitment to making these materials widely available.

W.D.P. and E.J.M.

Contents

Marketing's Role in the Global Economy and in the Firm

Keep On Truckin':

Muslim Town in Serbia Finds Riches and Risks On the Road to Kosovo

'Bosniaks' Dare to Deliver Where Many Fear to Go; Of Banditry and Bigotry

'We Have a Nose for Money'

By Robert Block

Staff Reporter of The Wall Street Journal

NOVI PAZAR, Yugoslavia — Once upon a time, this Serbian city was a crossroads on the Turkish caravan routes, a prosperous market town trading and trafficking in goods through the badlands of the Balkans.

Five centuries later, things haven't changed much.

Almir Bruncevic, a 25-year-old purveyor and transporter of counterfeit designer jeans, is proof that commercial traditions die hard in this part of the world. Several times a month, Mr. Bruncevic drives not a mule, but a silver Mercedes that is loaded with stacks of illicit denim bound for Kosovo.

Kosovo isn't as far away or as exotic as the casbahs of Turkey or the medieval cities of the Adriatic, but it's a lucrative market. And the trade, both legal and illegal, has given a new sense of purpose to this city.

"The goods are here in Serbia. The demand and cash are in Kosovo. We just connect the two," boasts Mr. Bruncevic, nursing a Coke made in Hungary and smuggled into town by local traders. The "we" are the Muslim Slavs of the Sandzak (pronounced SAND-jack) region of Yugoslavia, who over the past eight months have become the brokers and transporters of Serbian building materials, food and countless other products to Kosovo.

Supply and Demand

In the aftermath of the North Atlantic Treaty Organization's victory in Kosovo, ending years of Serbian repression, Kosovar Albanians want nothing to do with Serbs. With ethnic hatred and lust for revenge running rampant in Kosovo, Serbian businessmen and companies lost their Albanian partners, their shops and sometimes their lives. Nonetheless, after months of war, the demand for low-cost goods from Serbia is higher than ever.

Into this vacuum have stepped the Muslim Slavs from Novi Pazar, venturing where Serbs fear to tread, let alone trade. The business is risky: Many Serbs and Albanians in Kosovo resent what they see as the opportunism of the Sandzak Muslims. Drivers and businessmen from Novi Pazar have been threatened, beaten and, in at least one case, killed. But the lure of quick money keeps them on the road.

The Sandzakis, or Bosniaks as they prefer to be called, have been using their religion and their own history of problems with the Serbs as a passport to make deals with the mainly Muslim Kosovars, as well as with the NATO-led peacekeeping forces occupying the province.

Like the ethnic Albanians of Kosovo, the Muslim Slavs of Sandzak have been the victims of state repression under President Slobodan Milosevic, and the targets of sporadic bombings, kidnappings, torture and murders, especially in the early '90s. Many U.S. Balkan experts consider the region the target of a possible Milosevic offensive if the president feels his leadership is threatened.

The way the Muslim Slavs have managed to survive all this is through economic opportunism, and not resorting to the ethnic violence common in this part of the world. In the face of political harassment and the hardship of international trade sanctions imposed on Belgrade for its role in the breakup of Yugoslavia, the Muslims took refuge in pirate manufacturing industries, turning the country's pariah status to their advantage.

Novi Pazar, whose very name means money (either New Market or New Turnover, depending on the translation), is now home to about 600 factories that churn out counterfeit Levi's, Calvin Klein and other labels worth an estimated $100 million annually. The jeans, tops, shoes and accessories are shipped to markets as far away as Russia, making the city the unofficial denim capital of the Balkans.

The owners of the workshops know that Mr. Milosevic, desperate for infusions of tax and bribe money, is unlikely to crack down on them at the behest of Western officials griping about infringements of trademarks and licensing agreements.

Signs of Sandzak's latest business ventures are as conspicuous as a fleet of 18-wheelers in a front yard. The growth of opportunity in Kosovo just 50 miles away has sparked an explosion in the transport industry in Sandzak. Novi Pazar today looks more like a residential trucking depot than a city of 100,000 people. Cabs and trailers are everywhere — they jam the narrow streets and are parked outside houses like family cars.

"A year ago, there were about 10 people seriously involved in transport. Now there are hundreds," says Rasim Ljajic, a regional political leader. "All it takes here is one person to get an idea, and then everyone follows."

In the early morning hours, dozens of trucks roll toward the Kosovo border. Some truckers stop at roadside motels or cafes on the Serbian side of the frontier, waiting until a policeman they know, and can bribe, starts his shift. Serbia hasn't banned all trade with Kosovo, but it prohibits the export of food and livestock, which have become the favorite cargo of some drivers.

Dzemail Zutic, a k a "Zuti" or "Yellow" because of his blond hair, owns a fleet of 10 trucks delivering construction materials across Kosovo. In the building-supply business for a decade, Mr. Zutic decided to get into trucking when the conflict with NATO ended in June. "It was clear during the war that when it was over, there would be opportunity for us," Mr. Zutic says. "We have a nose for money and we are the only ones with clean hands in Kosovo."

Indeed, Sandzakis were happily left on the sidelines during the war. Unlike in the rest of Serbia, there was no mobilization here, since the Serbs didn't trust the Muslims. In 1998, at the height of the fighting between Albanian separatist guerrillas and Serbian security forces, at least 15 Muslim Slav police officers were fired for refusing to go to Kosovo to fight against their Muslim brothers.

But clean hands aren't a guarantee of trouble-free business. After dark, when the lights decorating the minarets of Novi Pazar's 19 mosques illuminate the city's skyline, a greasy spoon on the outskirts of town comes to life. Mr. Zutic and dozens of other truckers gather here at the Bife Bosna for coffee, juice and gossip. All of them trade in Kosovo, though few want to talk openly about it. Some fear the Serbian taxman, since their business is in German marks traded at black-market rates. Most, however, are anxious not to tempt ethnic extremists in Kosovo. Almost everyone has a story of someone they know getting robbed, hijacked, threatened or beaten up.

Sticks and Stones

"Every time you drive down there you never know what will happen," says Mr. Zutic over the din of Serbian folk music. "This is a high-risk business."

Kosovo Serbs accuse the Sandzakis of having sat out the war with NATO, waiting to make money. When traveling through Serbian enclaves in Kosovo, drivers say their trucks are stoned, and they are sometimes stopped at makeshift barricades and threatened for doing business with Albanians.

Some Albanians, on the other hand, see the Muslim drivers as wallets-on-wheels, ripe for the picking. Almost every day there are reports of trucks being stopped by armed gangs, the drivers forced to part with large sums of cash. "Most of the trouble is banditry. The Albanians know that on the way down, we're full of goods and on the way back loaded with money," says a driver who transports food to Kosovo and identifies himself only as K.G.

(Cont.)

Highway robbery is among the least of the drivers' worries. Since the end of the war, many Albanians have been gripped by fierce nationalism. Tens of thousands of non-Albanians, including Muslim Slavs, have been driven from their homes in Kosovo. Hundreds have been killed by Albanian extremists bent on creating an ethnically pure ministate. What makes life particularly dangerous for Muslim Slavs is that they speak Serbian, widely considered the language of Kosovo's oppressors.

Murder of a Cleric

According to Sefko Alomerovic, the president of the Helsinki Committee for the Protection of Human Rights in Sandzak, there have been at least seven reported cases of serious attacks by Albanians on Muslim Slav truck drivers, including the murder of Sefket Dragolovcanin, a Muslim cleric delivering milk to Kosovo. He disappeared last August. Three weeks later, his body was found in an Albanian village near Jablanica. The only crime he and the others committed, Mr. Alomerovic says, was speaking Serbian.

Drivers have since worked out ways to limit their risks. "Most of us have our Albanian business partners with us to help if the situation gets difficult," says Mr. Bruncevic, the jean dealer. "But it's 50-50. You never know who will give you trouble, the Serbs or the Albanians. The money makes it worthwhile, but your life is constantly on the line."

Mr. Bruncevic knows this better than most. In December, he was returning from Kosovo when he got a flat tire in the divided town of Mitrovica. The north of the town is a Serbian enclave. Mr. Bruncevic was stranded in the Albanian south side. A group of youths approached him, asking something in Albanian. Mr. Bruncevic explained in Serbian that

he was a Muslim from Sandzak. "That's when they started to hit me and smash my car," he recalls.

A NATO Rescue

Luckily, French peacekeepers were nearby. They fired into the air, scattering the attackers. "I have no doubts NATO saved my life, but my car was trashed. It cost me $3,000 to get it fixed," Mr. Bruncevic says.

The danger and unforeseen costs of doing business in Kosovo, however, haven't been much of a deterrent. If anything, they have added to the attraction, justifying a markup in shipping costs of as much as 300%.

For the Albanians, even with the additional costs, goods from Serbia are still cheaper than those from other countries. Kosovo, although run as a United Nations protectorate, is still technically part of Serbia, and there aren't any tariffs or duties. In addition, the Yugoslav dinar is constantly falling against the German mark, which has become the official tender in the province.

The result is that Kosovo groans with goods coming from Novi Pazar. "They are good quality. And people here are used to the things Bosniaks bring," says Shefki, an Albanian trader at Pristina's central market who didn't want to give his full name. "People also know Bosniaks are Muslim and have problems [with Serbs] maybe as much as we did."

Risks of the Middleman

Serbian companies, as well, appear happy with the arrangement. "Of course, since the war we can't deliver our products there," says Nikola Svilengacin, a spokesman for Polet Novi Becej, a building-supplies manufacturer in northern Serbia whose roofing tiles are hot sellers in Kosovo. "We sell directly to buyers in Novi Pazar. What they do afterwards with those products is none of our business."

Bearing the risk in all of this are the drivers and businessmen from Novi Pazar. They buy the goods from the Serbian producers and companies up front. They run the gantlet of bandits and threats. All business with Albanian buyers is done orally, on the honor system. There are no contracts, no deposits and no guarantees that they will get paid upon delivery. And yet, "we always deliver, and the Albanians always pay," Mr. Bruncevic says.

But how long before the business gets too dangerous or Mr. Milosevic decides to crack down? Mr. Bruncevic shrugs. "It could all end tomorrow. But right now there is money to be made and it's what we Bosniaks do best."

Reading the Tea Leaves, China Sees a Future for Coffee

BY IAN JOHNSON
Staff Reporter of THE WALL STREET JOURNAL

BAOSHAN, China — All the coffee in China is a trifling amount. But now, after long being kept at bay by Chinese politics and poverty, the drink is making two inroads into this nation of tea drinkers.

One is here, by China's lush southern border with Burma, where officials are telling farmers to stop growing tea and sugarcane and start planting coffee, which has greater potential for revenue — and tax dollars.

Meanwhile, in China's crowded cities, foreign coffeehouse chains are gambling they can buck tradition and create a coffee culture in the land of the teahouse.

The change won't come easily. While Beijing wants the coffee from Baoshan and the rest of Yunnan province to sell like Jamaica's high-priced Blue Mountain beans, production has been plagued by corruption, politics and chronic low quality. And while chains such as the U.S.'s Starbucks Corp. and Tully's Coffee and Japan's Manabe Kohikan open new coffee bars by the month, coffee sales have declined slightly over the past four years, according to market researchers. Future growth, they say, is likely to be in low-end instant coffees and presweetened coffee mixes.

But that's not the vision driving coffee's missionaries. Here in Baoshan, a major outpost on the old Burma Road, Mayor Yang Jingjian uses a barrage of statistics and rhetoric to persuade the local populace to switch to coffee, arguing that the hard-to-grow and harder-to-roast beans will make them — and his government — rich.

The region around Baoshan now has 5,000 acres of coffee, Mr. Yang says. He wants to double that within five years and make coffee the region's major cash crop. By then, he promises farmers, coffee will have nearly doubled their annual income.

From missionaries 100 years ago to reform-minded communists in the 1980s, many have been attracted by the bean's potential to earn money. But coffee, first condemned by nationalists as a foreign intrusion and later by communists as the "tail of capitalism," was politically incorrect — until recently.

"Politics and coffee have a long relationship," the mayor concedes. "Now the government is all for it."

Farmers may be another matter. At the bottom of a verdant valley planted with coffee, bananas and papayas, one of Mr. Yang's star coffee growers casually announces that he and many of his neighbors want to abandon coffee in favor of longans, a fruit resembling litchis. Mr. Yang shakes his head in frustration and, as though talking to a simpleton, bellows: "Don't talk to me about longan. You have to stick to coffee, understand?"

The man nods skeptically. He knows it's easier to yield to the pressure of local authorities. But he also knows that coffee plants take three years to mature and must be cut back after seven, while longans bring rich harvests almost immediately.

In fact, this desire for fast profits, widespread among Chinese farmers, has crippled China's coffee-growing aspirations, says Robert Tibbo, with Eastern Strategic Consulting Ltd. in Hong Kong. With most coffee plucked early and processed as cheaply as possible, Yunnan coffee remains inferior. At the end of a busy day touring the countryside, Mayor Yang proudly presents a visitor with what is purported to be a bag of choice green coffee beans. A quarter of these beans later turn out to be too low quality for roasting when inspected by a roaster in Beijing.

While the central government has budgeted funds for advanced processing and roasting equipment, local press reports say much of the money was siphoned off by corrupt officials. Last year, China produced 3,400 metric tons of coffee. Virtually none was fit for export, with almost all being ground into instant coffee. "It's a mess down there," Mr. Tibbo says.

Up north, in China's big cities, coffee has a slightly more promising hold, although the vast majority of people still measure their lives in sips of tea rather than coffee spoons. Most coffee is sold to hotels, and almost all the coffee sold at retail is instant.

Undeterred, gourmet-coffee retailers have moved aggressively into China. Starbucks opened its first coffeehouse last month in Beijing, promising to open up to another dozen by mid-2000. "We're going to create a market that may not exist currently," says Lawrence Maltz, chairman of Beijing Mei Da Coffee Co., which has been licensed to open Starbucks in China.

Starbucks's belief in China is based on a simple certainty: Coffee consumption is directly related to income. Following the pattern of other countries, China's rising income is supposed to mean growing coffee sales — as has been the case in Japan, where the tea

Planet Starbucks

The ubiquitous coffee chain gives a dash of international flair to its cafes in Asia

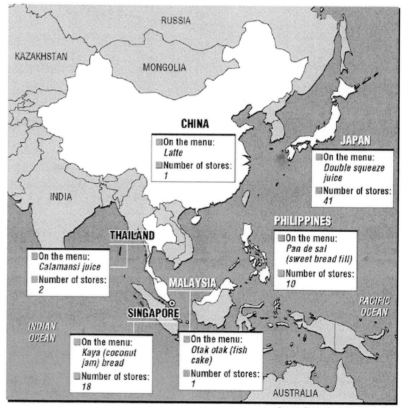

Source: Starbucks Coffee International

ceremony has taken a back seat to street-corner coffee vending machines.

To a degree, this is also true in China. Coffee shops have become popular meeting places and a $2 latte is a status symbol in China, which has a per-capita income of $750. Says Mr. Maltz: "We can't build our business on expatriates and tourists."

For the next few years, however, there may be no other choice. With income levels in China low, coffee consumption has stagnated over the past four years — reflecting a leveling-off in the number of expatriates working in China.

Besides income, a major hurdle is deeply ingrained views toward food and health in China. Traditional medicine views coffee as a "warming" beverage — something that holds true whether the drink is sold scalding hot or as one of Starbucks' iced frappuccinos. Thus, says Mr. Tibbo of Eastern Strategic Consulting, coffee has been slow to catch on in southern China's Guangdong province, the richest — and warmest — part of China. "It's a northern drink and pretty much only in the winter months," Mr. Tibbo says.

The dangers of overestimating China's eagerness to embrace coffee can be seen in its import statistics. When China's economic boom began to gather pace in the early 1990s, foreigners flocked to China and coffee sales began a modest expansion, growing between 5% and 8% a year. In 1996, as experts began predicting that China was the next big coffee market, government coffee traders imported 12,000 metric tons of coffee, almost six times the previous year's imports. That year, however, turned out to be the end of China's coffee-drinking growth period. "I think most of those beans are still sitting in Chinese warehouses, waiting to be roasted and ground," says a Beijing coffee roaster.

Dell Cracks China

No way, the skeptics scoffed, could Dell take its all-American model to China. So why is it being imitated? ■ *by Neel Chowdhury*

It's a wet morning in old Shanghai, and Dell salesman Peter Chan is selling hard. As the Yangtze River flows by the Bund district a few floors below, Chan is getting into a flow of his own. His subject: computers and the unique benefits of Dell's direct-selling model. His customer: Xiao Jian Yi, deputy general manager of China Pacific Insurance, a fast-growing state-owned insurance company. The audience: three of Xiao's subordinates.

China Pacific, a potentially big account, is in the process of computerizing its entire billing system. It already has about 400 desktops and about 70 servers, mainly from IBM and Hewlett-Packard. But Xiao needs more hardware. Much more.

Though Xiao's sleep-heavy eyes suggest he's heard it all before, Chan excitedly says that "direct selling" means China Pacific can order PCs directly through the Internet, the telephone, or salesmen like himself. At the mention of the Internet, still a rare marketing tool in China, the fustily dressed bureaucrat visibly perks up.

Chan goes on to explain that direct selling not only eliminates middlemen—saving Xiao and China Pacific a chunk of change—but also means that Dell can build China Pacific's computers to the firm's exact requirements, from the hardware on the outside to the software on the inside. A murmur of approval ripples through Xiao's subordinates. By the time Chan finishes with a description of Dell's convenient after-sales service, the rain has stopped and Xiao is smiling. "All salesmen from computer companies are aggressive," he says. Then Xiao whispers to FORTUNE: "But the Dell guys are even more aggressive."

That aggressiveness is beginning to pay off. Not only did Dell reel in the China Pacific account, but it is well on its way to becoming a major player in China. Last August, 34-year-old billionaire Michael Dell opened the fourth Dell PC factory in the world in Xiamen, a windswept city halfway between Hong Kong and Shanghai on China's southeastern coast. The point of Dell's push into China seems so obvious as to be a cliche: China is becoming too big a PC market for Dell, or anyone, to ignore. "If we're not in

what will soon be the second-biggest PC market in the world," asks John Legere, president of Dell Asia-Pacific, "then how can Dell possibly be a global player?"

China is already the fifth-largest PC market, behind the U.S., Japan, Germany, and Britain. But if PC shipments in China continue to grow at an average annual rate of 30%—as they have over the past three years—China's PC market will surpass Japan's in only five years. Not even the Asian crisis has slowed down this growth. While crisis-wracked Asian markets like South Korea saw a 46% decline in PC shipments in 1997-98, for example, PC shipments to China surged 48%.

Though the competition is intense, Dell is confident it has a strategy that will pay off. First, it has decided not to target retail buyers, who account for only about 10% of Dell's China sales. That way Dell avoids going head to head against entrenched local market leaders like Legend. "It takes nearly two years of a person's savings to buy a PC in China," notes Mary Ma, the chief financial officer of Legend. "And when two years of savings is at stake, the whole family wants to come out to a store to touch and try the machine." Dell just isn't set up to make that kind of sale yet.

Instead, the company thinks it can make big inroads by selling directly to corporations. Established American PC makers in China—Hewlett-Packard, IBM, and Compaq—depend largely on resellers. Because of the cost savings derived from cutting out the middleman, Dell believes it can sell computers at lower prices than its competitors can—and thus steal market share. Already the gambit seems to be working: At the end of last year Dell's market share tripled to 1.2%, while Compaq's fell from 3.5% to 2.7%.

The outlook wasn't always so rosy. When Dell set up its first Asian factory in Malaysia in 1996, there were serious doubts as to whether its direct-selling model would work. Skeptics fretted that Asia's low Internet penetration and the value Asians put on personal relationships with distributors would punish the Dell model. But in practice Dell has managed to pump up sales during one of Asia's worst economic crises. That has silenced

most of the critics.

In fact, the direct-selling model has almost certainly been a boon, not a barrier, to Dell's plans. "With low-priced, entry-level PCs shaving traditional profit margins, the direct-order model is gaining popularity across Asia," says Archana Gidwani, an analyst with the Gartner Group in Singapore. She figures that starting in 1998, direct sellers like Dell saw shipments in Asia jump 15%, while Hewlett-Packard, IBM, Compaq, and other PC makers that go through resellers saw shipments decline 3%. And she expects 40% of Asia's PC shipments to be ordered directly this year, up from roughly 30% last year. "Dell," she concludes, "is changing the way computers are being sold in Asia."

Though Dell started shipping computers in China only last August, it has already risen to become the country's eighth-largest PC maker; quarter-on-quarter sales are growing 50% on average, admittedly from a very low base. Dell will not say if its operations there are profitable yet.

More impressive is the fact that Dell is starting to rattle Chinese PC makers like Legend and Founder by nibbling into their most valuable client base: state-owned enterprises. These bureaucratic behemoths may seem an odd fit with Dell's fast-as-lightning direct model, but somehow it works. Two-thirds of Dell's corporate customers in China are state-owned enterprises, up from next to none ten months ago. The rest of Dell's customers are multinationals like Ericsson, Nortel, Motorola, and Ford. Dell hopes to keep signing up more Chinese companies—not easy, given the price-slashing tactics of the small shops that sell cheap PCs with bootlegged software. But if it does, then Dell will do something few U.S. companies in China ever manage to do: turn a profit without investing a fortune in manufacturing and without sharing the booty with a Chinese partner or middleman.

Why is Dell's direct model winning in China? First, look at the way Dell is selling to the Chinese. Shredding the myth that to sell in China requires padding the egos (and wallets) of capricious bureaucrats—usually during long and boring banquets—Dell is winning over the chief information officers of state-owned companies the American way: with speed, convenience, and service. "We don't have to change the formula," insists Dell salesman Peter Chan. "It will work in the U.S, China, India, or even in space."

At the heart of that "formula" is the simple tenet that the customer knows best. When Dell's Chan pauses for breath after his sales pitch at China Pacific, for example, the newly awakened Xiao peppers him with questions. How quickly will the computers arrive? Can Excel be loaded onto the hard drive? What kind of service does Dell offer? And, ahem, how much?

What is powerfully clear is that Xiao knows computers. He knows what he needs from Dell. He knows how much he wants to pay. Critically, Xiao knows enough that he does not need to see or touch the machine, or even raise a few glasses of Tsingtao beer with a honey-tongued distributor, before he orders it. All Xiao needs is a phone or, better yet, an Internet connection, to buy what he needs.

Such tech savviness and straightforwardness is increasingly common in China, and that is a terrific advantage for Dell, whose biggest perceived shortcoming was that it lacked the kind of service network that Hewlett-Packard or IBM has. These service networks can provide companies like China Pacific with technical advice and long-term system consultancy. But as Xiao makes clear, Chinese managers are growing more and more tech savvy on their own. They simply don't need that kind of babysitting—and they don't want to pay for it. "We may still need some consulting services, but in our front offices we know how to choose our equipment," says Xiao. "Dell provides exactly what we need, and with Dell we can choose exactly what we want."

In response, IBM, Hewlett-Packard, and other PC makers are changing tactics. Says Dennis Mark, Hewlett-Packard's computer-marketing director in Asia: "We're doing less with smaller local companies and focusing our resources more on big nationwide technology projects." For now, that gives Dell a clean shot at the low end of the PC market. But down the line Dell too may want to go after bigger, more complex sales. At that point competitors like Hewlett-Packard and IBM will have a considerable head start.

In the meantime, Dell will have its hands full in the direct-sales market. Chinese Internet use is spreading like a brushfire. Between 1997 and 1998, according to technical consultants at International Data Corp., the number of Internet users in China jumped 71%, to more than two million. But so far Dell sells

We're No. 8!

After only ten months in China, Dell has reached No. 8 in PC shipments.

1. **Legend**
2. **IBM**
3. **Hewlett-Packard**
4. **Founder**
5. **Compaq**
6. **Great Wall**
7. **Toshiba**
8. **Dell**
9. **NEC Japan**
10. **Acer**

FORTUNE TABLE/SOURCE: IDC PC ASIADAT BULLETIN

only 5% of its PCs in China through the Net, compared with 25% worldwide. Dell's telephone sales also represent just a small percentage of its total, even though the company advertises aggressively on billboards. Part of the problem is that the Chinese are uncomfortable with credit card sales.

For now, however, Dell's going to have to invest more time and money in door-to-door sales calls to Chinese companies than it might like. For example, Dell's two dozen or so young, gung ho salesmen in Shanghai usually make three to four sales calls a day and spend roughly one-third of their time on the road. Not an easy life, but they are well rewarded for it. Dell will not tell how much they make, but says its sales staff in China is paid salaries and commissions commensurate with those paid in Hong Kong and the U.S. That's expensive, and until China catches up to the West in terms of Internet penetration and credit card use, those costs will take a tidy chunk out of Dell's earnings.

To offset its higher-than-expected marketing costs, Dell is cutting out fat and boosting operational efficiency at its Xiamen plant. In fact, Dell's modest manufacturing operations are a paragon of financial restraint in a country like China, where land and equipment costs can spiral out of control.

In Xiamen the operation is lean and smart. The entire assembly process employs only about 200 workers and is housed in a modest, airy room about the size of a high school gym. Workers scrutinize sales sheets detail-ing the hardware and software specs of each computer, which is then built according to the buyer's taste (luckily for Microsoft, the Chinese version of Word for Windows is the leading software request).

After the "fully loaded" computer rolls off the line, it goes to Xiamen's sleek and spacious airport to be flown to wherever the customer is located. In China the time it takes for a Dell PC to reach a customer, from order to delivery, is nine days, about the same as in the U.S. "We're leading the entire Dell world in terms of keeping to our promised delivery date," boasts David Chan, president of Dell China.

Behind that boast, of course, is China's increasingly impressive infrastructure of roads, airports, and ports. Belying those horror stories of endless paperwork slowing the traffic of goods or bad phones or potholed roads, most of urban China is relatively well linked. Bureaucratic bottlenecks do arise from time to time, but Dell's just-in-time model is probably easier to execute in China than it would be in, say, the Philippines or India.

Getting the PC to the customer quickly also saves Dell a ton of cash. Because its just-in-time model forces Dell to keep its inventory levels low—about six days' worth of supply, compared with 40 for Chinese PC leader Legend—Dell saves time and money that would otherwise be wasted on warehousing. Shorter inventory cycles also give Dell a greater degree of control over price and profitability than its Chinese competitors have. "The sub-$1,000 PC has been driven by Chinese distributors who have to move obsolete products that have been lying around their warehouses," argues Dell's Legere. "We'll never be driven by those factors, because our inventory cycles in China are so short."

Also greasing the efficiency of Dell in China is money, or to be more precise, stock options. David Chan says the options scheme is meant to "instill a sense of ownership," but most Chinese workers are likelier to see a direct link between their output and the stock price—which is, after all, not a bad way to look at it. Around August every employee in Xiamen got roughly 200 shares of Dell, back when its stock was trading near $60. Three months later Dell's shares had shot up to $110, giving each employee a paper gain of about $10,000. That equals roughly one year's salary for the average Xiamen worker. "Then it dawned on me that they had no idea of the value of the paper in their hands," says Chan. After the worth of the options was explained at a workers' meeting, Chan noticed an uptick in productivity: "They were good before. Now they're better."

So what can go wrong? To some extent, Dell has had to deal with the traditional bugbears of factory life in China: idleness and

7

corruption. The concept of a job for life, though no longer a guarantee in today's China, still attracts workers who expect to spend hours drinking tea or reading the papers on the factory floor—and keep their jobs. Dell China executives acknowledge that at first a little "reeducation" was necessary in Xiamen so that workers understood that their jobs depended on their performance.

Corruption has been a trickier issue. Though Dell vehemently denies that it has ever paid a bribe to get a license or a sales order, David Chan admits he had to "terminate" two Chinese employees suspected of corruption. It's no coincidence, either, that Dell's top salesmen in China are not mainland Chinese but predominantly Overseas Chinese from Hong Kong or Singapore, where the sales culture is defined more by doggedness than by personal favors. Peter Chan, for example, is from Hong Kong.

The company must also grapple with the problem of software piracy. Microsoft estimates that over 95% of the software in use in Chinese corporations is stolen. In fact, setting up a factory in China was Dell's defense against pirates. Concerned that pirates would load bad software onto its machines, ruining its reputation, Dell now controls the process from beginning to end. That quality control is a relief to Dell, its customers, and Microsoft, which collects its Dell-related revenue reliably. But quality costs: No matter how frugal Dell's operations, it cannot compete on price with the small job shops that sell knockoff PCs equipped with bootleg software. Dell computers sell for about the same as in the U.S.—$1,200 to $1,500 each, depending on what is loaded.

Dell's biggest problem, though, is a product of its success: Because the Dell direct model is so simple, it can be copied. And that's just what Legend is doing. "Yes, we're using Dell's direct-selling model when we target Chinese government companies or multinationals in China," admits Mary Ma. For a start, Legend is aping Dell's cash-management model, reducing the time it takes to get payment from its distributors by half, to 30 days. It is also rapidly moving toward Dell's just-in-time delivery model, trying to sell directly to its corporate customers and shaving excess inventory. It is even offering stock options to employees. All these copycat moves will make Legend a more formidable company and should therefore have Dell worrying.

Another cause for concern is China's often nationalistic politics, which can quickly turn against U.S. corporations. Consider, for example, the rash of anti-American demonstrations that swept across China after NATO's accidental bombing of the Chinese embassy in Belgrade in mid-May. Not only were U.S. embassies pelted with eggs and stones, but so were Nike and McDonald's outlets. Given the billions at stake in the telecom and PC markets in China, high-profile U.S. companies like Motorola or Dell could be vulnerable to the ups and downs in Sino-American relations, though retail outlets, not tech factories, seem to be bearing the brunt of patriotic dudgeon so far. "It's not a given for U.S. companies, especially information technology companies, to come into China and grab the entire market," warns Dong Tao of Credit Suisse First Boston Securities in Hong Kong. "The Chinese government has made no secret of the fact that it wants to promote national industries like IT."

Where will Dell be in China five years from now? It will probably never be the No. 1 PC maker in China, or even No. 2, slots that are likely to be occupied by local manufacturers, which will always be able to sell more cheaply to China's masses. Ironically, that seems to suit Dell just fine. Grabbing market share, in the U.S., China, or anywhere else, has never been its highest priority. Profits are. Says John Legere of the estimated $25 billion in revenue that computer sales will generate in China by 2002: "Even if we get 1% of $25 billion, that's a lot. You don't need to be the market leader in China to be profitable."

One thing's for sure: The Dell model is working in China. And as long as China's PC market continues to grow, Dell is ready to grow with it—provided it sticks to that model and continues to execute it better than anyone else.

HOW LEGEND LIVES UP TO ITS NAME

The state-owned PC maker aims to become a Chinese IBM

The shiny new research center for Legend Holdings, China's leading PC maker, is teeming with activity. Young hipsters and nerds alike bustle down corridors or clack on keyboards. While two-thirds of the 120 researchers are designing new computers, the rest are testing everything from how smoothly they run software to what happens when they fall off a desk to how well they hold up in the 100F-plus sizzle of China's summer.

So far, Legend—and its PCs—are holding up just fine. Even though its research center can't match the resources of Compaq or IBM, it is Legend that's turning up the heat on those rivals and others. The $758 million Beijing-based computer company saw its sales grow by 106% last year, making it the biggest seller of PCs in the fastest-growing computer market on earth—a title that foreign rivals had hoped to capture. But with 15% of China's sales, Legend has twice the market share of its closest competitor, IBM. "We plan to be among the top 10 PC manufacturers in the world by 2000," vows Yang Yuan-qing, general manager of Legend Computer Systems Ltd. Legend's goal: to sell 1.5 million computers in 2001, up from 800,000 units today.

How did Legend dash the dreams U.S. PC makers had of dominating the Chinese market? Credit the company's low prices, broad product range, helpful software, and vast distribution network. Just as important have been Legend's strong links to the Chinese government, which accounts for 25% of Legend's sales, and the decision to push state-of-the-art PCs, not yesterday's models. That helped remove the stigma associated with buying a local computer. Consumers "stopped being ashamed of buying a Chinese brand," says Sean Maloney, senior vice-president for sales and marketing at Intel Corp., which urged Legend to sell the more powerful PCs. "Legend has become synonymous with high tech."

LOCAL HERO. The computer maker is also benefiting from China's love affair with the PC. Desktop-computer sales there are expected to swell 30% this year—double the growth that's forecast for the U.S. market. If this torrid pace keeps up through 2002, some 10.3 million PCs will be sold in China that year, making it the No. 3 market in the world following the U.S. and Japan. (Sales are higher in the U.S. and Japan.)

But Legend's ambitions go well beyond the PC. The company is aiming for nothing short of becoming China's version of IBM—a full-service provider of computers, software, and high-tech knowhow. In the past 12 months, Legend has parlayed its local savvy into development and marketing alliances with Microsoft Corp. and IBM, among others, to take the company into new markets, including software and systems-integration services for China's businesses. This month, Legend plans to sell in China a handheld computer that will challenge 3Com Corp.'s popular Palm computer. "As a local company, we have much more insight into the needs of Chinese customers," says Legend's Yang.

In China, hand-holding is need No. 1. After all, it is a population of PC newbies with only 1 out of every 175 Chinese currently owning a computer. Legend understands this better than foreign PC makers do. The company has developed a variety of software products for first-time customers that are bundled with its PCs, including tutorial programs on everything from using the World Wide Web to mastering home finances.

Legend will test just how well that formula works in a new market: palm-size computers. After one year of development work with Microsoft, Legend's palm-size computer, called Tianji, will appear this month running Microsoft's Windows CE software. As with PCs, Legend has tailored the product to the local market by including a stylus for entering Chinese characters and English letters and by installing a powerful English-Chinese dictionary. Legend and Microsoft also are working with 10 local software companies to develop applications for the product. And with a price of around $540 in China, the Tianji is $60 less than the price of 3Com's Palm computer.

HEMORRHAGE. Just two years ago, Legend might have been viewed as the least likely to survive. The company, founded in 1984, was hemorrhaging $25 million a year and lagging behind multinational rivals IBM, Hewlett-Packard, and Compaq. Then Legend launched a vicious price war, cutting prices three times in one year. With lower production and distribution costs than its foreign rivals, Legend now sells its desktop PC with a Pentium II chip for about $1,200, or 30% less than IBM or Compaq.

State-owned Legend, which is listed on the Hong Kong stock exchange, has something else going for it: a strong distribution network. That's what has stymied foreign competitors. In the past 10 months, Legend has added 800 distributors and now has close to 1,800 across China. It also has its own retail stores that sell Legend products, make repairs, and offer free training for China's often first-time users—including home visits. With 11 shops now open, Legend plans to have more than 50 by yearend. "They have an extremely well-developed distribution network," says Tony C. Leung, director of

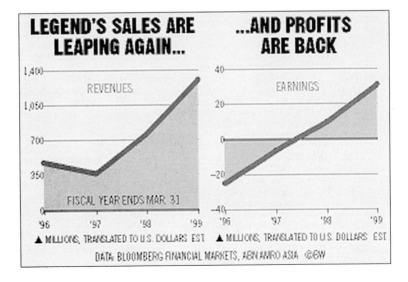

LEGEND'S SALES ARE LEAPING AGAIN...

REVENUES

1,400
1,050
700
350
0

FISCAL YEAR ENDS MAR. 31

'96   '97   '98   '99

▲ MILLIONS, TRANSLATED TO U.S. DOLLARS EST.

...AND PROFITS ARE BACK

EARNINGS

40
20
0
-20
-40

'96   '97   '98   '99

▲ MILLIONS, TRANSLATED TO U.S. DOLLARS EST.

DATA: BLOOMBERG FINANCIAL MARKETS, ABN AMRO ASIA ©BW

(Cont.)

Greater China marketing for Compaq in Hong Kong. "It will take a lot of time to catch up."

That's why no foreign company can afford to ignore Legend. Its superior distribution network and strong government connections spell opportunity. Last summer, Legend inked a deal with IBM to pre-install Legend PCs with IBM software, including a Chinese-language version of IBM's ViaVoice 98 speech-recognition software. IBM and Legend also are developing software for China's telecom, finance, and aviation sectors. "On the one hand, we compete with Legend," says D.C. Chien, general manager of distribution for IBM's Greater China Group. "But on the other hand, they are our second-largest partner in China."

ACHILLES' HEEL. Despite its standing in PCs, Legend needs foreign help to expand into corporate software and service. Last fall, for example, the company signed deals with Lotus Development Corp. and Oracle Corp. to resell groupware and database software to Chinese businesses. "They still are relatively weak in R&D and in software," says Jay Hu, managing director of the U.S. Information Technology Office, an industry association in Beijing.

For now, that is. In late November, Legend and Computer Associates International Inc. agreed to a $3.5 million software joint venture. First task: to create a software development tool to compete with Microsoft's Visual C++. The software will be available in the Chinese market this summer.

Legend isn't relying strictly on the kindness of foreigners to create a software stronghold. It recently invested $4.5 million to become the leading shareholder of Kingsoft, a Chinese software company. The two will develop Chinese word processing, dictio-nary, and game programs. And in November, the government announced it would send more than 400 researchers from the Chinese Academy of Sciences—a national think tank—to work at Legend's research labs. The move gives Legend much-needed brain-power in its quest to develop better software and more powerful computers.

With China's computer market the lone bright spot in a now-battered region, competition is bound to be intense. It will take more than frenetic nerds and hipsters to keep Legend on top.

By Dexter Roberts, with Joyce Barnathan, in Beijing and with Bruce Einhorn in Hong Kong

Foreign Rivals vs. the Chinese: If You Can't Beat 'em...

Humility is not a word normally associated with Compaq Computer Corp. After all, you don't get to be No. 1 in PCs by being humble. Yet when it comes to cracking the market in China, Compaq is conceding that it has a lot to learn. Having tried for five years to operate a joint venture with Beijing's Stone Group—in what is now one of the world's fastest-growing markets—the Houston-based company has little to show for its effort but an anemic 4% market share.

Now, Compaq is trying to reboot. As part of its new strategy, the company is cutting deals with personal computer manufacturers around the country—but it's making sure this time that partners will focus on improving Compaq's market share. In October, for example, Compaq signed an agreement to put its brand name on computers made by Dawn, a small PC maker in the grimy city of Shenyang in China's northeast, a part of the country better known for its hulking heavy industry than its high-tech prowess. No matter, says Tony C. Leung, Compaq's marketing director for Greater China. "We are working with someone who understands the market better than we do," he says.

CATCH-UP. Think of it as the Legend lesson. Foreign PC makers have discovered the hard way that local companies have established distribution networks, provide better service, and offer lower prices. Compaq is just one of many foreign PC makers playing catch-up in China. From IBM to Dell to Toshiba, companies that dominate other global markets are taking a second look at their strategy for the world's largest emerging PC market. Beijing's recent crackdown on smuggling has changed the landscape for foreign PC makers: They can no longer rely on producing low-priced machines in other parts of Asia that can then be brought into China by third parties. Now, PC makers are working more closely with Chinese partners and are decreasing their reliance on imports.

It wasn't supposed to happen this way. A few years ago, most analysts were convinced that the global powers would gobble up the Chinese market, with locals like Legend stuck in second-tier status—at best. Instead, the foreigners are trailing Legend (table). Moreover, the foreigners are steadily losing market share. Locals enjoyed sales growth of 65% in the first three quarters of 1998, far outpacing the meager 14% of major foreign players Compaq, Hewlett-Packard, and IBM. Indeed, the top four foreign PC makers command just 19% of the market, down from 21% the previous year. That compares with 23% for the top four local players, according to International Data Corp.

HIGH BARRIER. The grim numbers are making many foreign PC makers recognize the need for a change. Take Toshiba Corp. Like Compaq, the Japanese giant is expanding its ties with local partners. It recently announced a new joint venture with Chinese PC maker Tontru Information Industry Group Co., which is tied with Compaq for fourth place in the Chinese PC market. Meanwhile, IBM has expanded its joint venture with Great Wall Group in Shenzhen, increasing its stake to 70% from its original 51%.

Companies also are trying to break through one of China's biggest barriers: the distribution system. With China's notoriously inefficient transportation system, companies rely on a vast number of local distributors to get their computers to customers, who often turn to the distributor for help with service. Dell Computer Corp. figures that its trademark direct-sales model can help it overcome that disadvantage. It opened a manufacturing plant in the southern city of Xiamen last year and has 300 people working in China. Manufacturing locally, rather than importing machines from a factory in Malaysia, helps Dell compete better with Legend and other Chinese companies. Until Dell opened its Xiamen plant, it had to pay 17% import duty on all its computers sold in the country. Meanwhile, to overcome the idea that foreigners can't offer the kind of service that locals do, Dell also has set up toll-free hot lines to offer technical support. The company even started selling computers over the Internet in China.

For beleaguered foreign PC makers, moves like that may turn out to be the key to the China market.

By Bruce Einhorn in Hong Kong

Way Out in Front in China

Total 1998 estimated sales: 3.9 million units

	MARKET SHARE
LEGEND	13%
IBM	7
HP	6
COMPAQ	4
TONTRU	4

DATA: INTERNATIONAL DATA CORP.

Lost in the Shuffle

As the Telecoms Merge And Cut Costs, Service Is Often a Casualty

One Client's Internet Access Fails—Right After Lines To Its Call Center Go Out

A Bill, but No Repairman

By Rebecca Blumenstein and
Stephanie N. Mehta
Staff Reports of The Wall Street Journal

Torrid consolidation in telecom has created soaring stocks, sprawling empires and ever-advancing technology.

Then there's customer service.

One day last summer, the phones stopped working at the national reservations center of LOT Polish Airlines in New York's Queens borough. The airline called the phone company's problem line at about 9 a.m. Eleven hours later, after the reservations center had closed for the day, a repairman arrived. Before all was fixed, the center was without phone service for 33 hours.

Bell Atlantic Corp., which had taken over the service area after merging with Nynex Corp., and which is now merging with GTE Corp., says it followed procedure: It had to check that the problem wasn't in one of its switching facilities before dispatching a technician. Bruce Gordon, group president for Bell Atlantic's Enterprise business unit, says business-customer satisfaction is up since its merger with Nynex.

OK, these glitches happen. But just a few weeks later, Polish Airlines lost its Internet service, too. This time the provider was MCI WorldCom Inc., which, in the wake of one of the 65 mergers that have built it into a colossus, had agreed to sell its Internet "backbone" to another company. Unfortunately, MCI WorldCom neglected to make the transfer, sending the airline and some other business customers into cyberspace limbo.

'Making It a Mess'

A solution was offered, though, to the airline's telecom chief, Jeff Kilpatrick: Just buy an Internet service contract from yet another company with which MCI WorldCom had done a deal.

"MCI WorldCom is one company, but when you get down to the nitty-gritty of who runs things, mergers are making it a mess," Mr. Kilpatrick says. "These telecom companies are killing us. One domino falls and everything falls apart."

MCI WorldCom won't comment on the Internet incident, citing a lawsuit it faces over the matter from the company the accounts were supposed to be transferred to, Britain's Cable & Wireless PLC.

During the past three years, mergers and acquisitions valued at more than $500 billion have rearranged the telecommunications landscape. Phone companies say the corporate customers ultimately benefit: The mergers bring them the latest technology and provide one-stop shopping at the lowest possible prices.

But acquisitions also usually mean layoffs and other cutbacks as companies squeeze costs out of their newly acquired business. Customer-service centers, often seen as overlapping, are among the first operations to be pared. "The morale at the company that is being acquired immediately goes down. Everyone starts throwing their resume around," says Casey Letizia, communications manager for one business customer, Credit Guard of America in Fort Lauderdale, Fla. "At that point, we are orphans."

Business customers can find themselves shuttled between account managers or forced to make multiple phone calls to find someone who can solve their problems. Sometimes the human touch is almost completely lost. AT&T Corp. recently installed an online system that compels many of its business customers to report problems via the Internet.

Rick Roscitt, president of AT&T's Business Services unit, acknowledges that some businesses have expressed concern but says the move saves money and is part of the business evolution toward using the Internet. "We are choosing to keep service levels as high as we possibly can while we take the costs out," Mr. Roscitt says. "AT&T is now an e-enabled company."

It wasn't always like this. Before the consolidation frenzy, client representatives were assigned to take special, goldplated care of business customers. Of course, things were simpler then; one phone company provided local and long-distance calling, and few customers needed special systems for moving bits of data around the country.

And prices were higher. Thanks to competition, the prices on services such as long-distance calling have fallen. "If you are going to charge a nickel, you cannot keep the same cost structure as you did when you were charging 20 to 30 cents a minute," Mr. Roscitt notes.

To keep up with the competition — and to please an increasingly fickle Wall Street — phone companies are cutting fat, automating functions that humans used to provide, and abandoning white-glove services. "That's the old way," says William T. Esrey, chief executive officer of Sprint Corp., which has agreed to merge with MCI WorldCom. "If you do that, you don't get the cost down, and you don't get the ticket to play."

In slashing costs, telecommunications is doing what practically every other business is doing. But in some other businesses — say, a retail store or bank — the customers can manage by themselves if there are fewer people around to help. In the technical world of telecom, a customer without good customer service is helpless.

One reason the merger frenzy makes it harder to deliver good customer service is that companies that are combining don't always communicate with each other. Consider the case of a New York customer called Speedpay Inc. It contracted to get service from Teleport Communications Group, or TCG, a competitive local telephone company. But AT&T acquired that provider in 1998. Speedpay officials claim that since then, AT&T has disavowed responsibility for repairing the line but wants to be paid for it just the same.

Jeff Kilpatrick

"TCG was merged into AT&T, and AT&T is treating it as a separate company," says Darren Manelski, Speedpay's CEO. "Service has become a huge bureaucracy, and the customer is expected to navigate the bureaucracy without a roadmap."

AT&T says it can't discuss confidential customer accounts. But a spokesman, Don Ferenci, says the company tries to provide top service at the best value and adds: "Any company that cares about its customers wouldn't ask them to pay for service they didn't receive."

As the phone companies merge, they have to combine complex networks that often use different equipment and technologies. MCI WorldCom has built an extensive data network through its acquisitions. When the network failed earlier this year, in an outage unrelated to the one that crippled Polish Airlines, the problem shut down numerous bank

BREATHTAKING. This setup generates some very un-utility-like growth. AES should rake in net income of $377 million this year, up 21% from 1998, on 25% higher sales, according to a report from Donaldson, Lufkin & Jenrette Inc. Even that's down from its recent pace. Driven by a breathtaking string of power-plant acquisitions in developing countries, AES posted average annual earnings gains of 54% over the past three years. Its debt-to-capital ratio of 72% is in line with the industry. Meanwhile, shareholders have been rewarded with a more than 400% increase in the stock price, to about 58, since Jan. 1, 1996. That's about four times the gains generated by Enron Corp., another aggressive power producer. In March, AES was the only such company to make the Business Week 50 list of top corporate performers.

The shares would be worth more, some investors suspect, if Wall Street were more comfortable with the company's philosophy. Bakke and Sant, who headed up conservation programs for the old Federal Energy Administration back in the 1970s, wrote into their company's charter that it would put social responsibility ahead of profitability. AES contributes about 5% of its earnings to nonprofit causes, through "social responsibility" funds and matching employee donations. The company hasn't always lived up to its mission: It was fined in 1992 after Oklahoma workers falsified emissions reports, but executives cut their own bonuses afterward.

After leaving the government, Sant and Bakke built cheap-power plants and sold the electricity to lumbering utilities, which had to buy it under a 1978 federal law designed to increase generation. But the real growth was overseas. By the '90s, AES was buying assets in Argentina, India, Pakistan, and a dozen other countries as governments rushed to auction off electric plants.

Those acquisitions—financed with debt tied to each plant's cash flow—fueled the phenomenal growth. AES is often the only independent supplier in regions that are just beginning to power up heavy industry. And company executives have cultivated ties with local leaders, giving AES an edge when power needs grow. The stock price swooned last year, as investors worried about the company's exposure to volatile economies in Asia and Latin America. But it bounced back as AES diversified, capitalizing on Europe's belated move to deregulate. On Nov. 30, AES closed on its $3 billion purchase of Britain's massive Drax coal-fired plant, which will boost the company's energy output by 11%, to 42,000 megawatts.

If its consumer business in the U.S. takes off, AES should spread its risk further. In July, it paid $90 million for NewEnergy Inc. in Los Angeles, an aggressive retailer of electricity to businesses. And in October, AES completed its $886 million purchase of Cilcorp Inc., a Peoria utility. With the most ambitious energy retailers—Enron, Pacific Gas & Electric, and Duke Energy—concentrating on big industrials, NewEnergy is focusing on midsize customers in the West and Northeast. Its clients include MCI WorldCom and Macy's.

The idea to go after even smaller accounts bubbled up from within Cilcorp, which had tried and abandoned a retail project three years ago. After regulators in Pennsylvania and New Jersey improved competitive conditions, Cilcorp Senior Vice-President William M. Shay and AES Executive Vice-President Thomas A. Tribone proposed jumping back in. Their plan: buy power in bulk from local utilities and independent producers and sell it, over the utility's own lines, to homeowners and small businesses. In typical AES fashion, a memo describing the idea was distributed to other employees, sparking four

months of debate. "It was very controversial," Bakke says. Still, Shay and Tribone decided to go for it.

There are plenty of reasons to be skeptical. AES has to negotiate for enough cheap power that its customers don't suffer brownouts during peak usage. Meanwhile, local utilities have economies of scale and established customer relationships. Also, consumers have shown little interest in shopping around for such a plain-vanilla commodity as energy. Enron found that out three years ago when it tried creating a residential electricity business. It was launched with a $30 million national marketing campaign that included Super Bowl ads. But the efforts were greeted with a collective yawn, and Enron pulled the plug last year.

Power Direct, with only 3,500 subscribers so far, is cutting its risk by concentrating for now on a single region and running a bare-bones marketing effort that relies on the Internet and direct mail. So far, AES has spent less than $2 million. Shay, who is now Power Direct's president, hopes to pay less than $100 to attract each new customer, compared with a $300 industry average. Enron "went way overboard" on advertising, he says. "There wasn't a market to support that kind of cost."

Bakke is frank in hedging his own expectations. He acknowledges that AES is moving from its specialty, power generation, into what is basically a marketing business. "Do we know what we're doing? Are we really good at it? I have no idea," he says. But at this company, a strategy like that is too important for the CEO to take on alone.

By Lorraine Woellert in Arlington, Va.

Sales smarts rule Internet

Pocket protectors are out, marketing skills are in at tech start-ups

By Greg Farrell
USA Today

Forget the geeks and finance people: Marketers are the new rock stars of the Internet. Consider the case of Karen Edwards.

Five years ago, Edwards, a 32-year-old executive with a Harvard MBA, desperately wanted to join an Internet company as head of marketing. She got turned down everywhere for the same reason: She didn't know enough about technology.

Finally, she landed a job, as employee No. 17 at start-up Yahoo. At a time when dot-com companies didn't realize the importance of advertising, she led the way, transforming the search engine with the quirky name into one of the most recognized brands of the Internet economy.

Edwards says that if she were in the same spot with the same resume today as five years ago, she'd have a different problem finding work: "With the marketing background I had then, I wouldn't get my job today. No way!"

So it goes in the wacky world of the Internet economy, where technology smarts and financial acumen are still important, but not as important as a strong background in marketing. Venture capitalists are now insisting that the management team of a start-up include a marketing heavyweight. The result: Headhunters are combing the ranks of the Fortune 500, looking for men and women who know how to build brands.

These start-ups no longer need geniuses in technology and finance; they need people who can sell soap and soft drinks. Marketers are the new "it" people in Silicon Valley.

"This is an enormous position," says Peter Sealey, former head of marketing at Coca-Cola and now an adjunct professor at the University of California at Berkeley. "Companies that want to be the next eBay or Amazon know it's not the technology: It's the marketing position and strategy."

Five years ago, before the Internet was discovered by Wall Street and Main Street, only a few brave young souls like Edwards left comfortable marketing jobs to take a flier on the Web. Now it's a different story: Executives are leaving the biggest marketing jobs in Corporate America for the chance to build Web-based brands. Here are some recent bigwigs who defected:

▲ John Costello, the former head of marketing at Sears, who did a brief stint at AutoNation, joined MVP.com in December as CEO.

▲ David Ropes bolted his position as director of corporate advertising at Ford Motor in November to become head of marketing at zUniversity.com.

▲ Jim Ritts left his perch as LPGA commissioner last March to join the Digital Entertainment Network, where he's CEO.

▲ Michael Beindorff left the top marketing job at Visa last September to become chief operating officer of PlanetRx.

The Web was such an attractive lure for Beindorff that he turned down a job as head of marketing at McDonald's before joining PlanetRx. Of course, money might have had something to do with that decision. Beindorff joined the Internet company with a generous option package just before it went public in October.

"For marketing people, it's too exciting to say no," Beindorff says. "The money is attractive, but only one in 10 will pay out. The real attraction is the opportunity to take a blank sheet of paper and build a business. This is an opportunity that a traditional company can't offer you. McDonald's is a great company, but I've been there and done that."

William Razzouk, CEO of PlanetRx, knew that bringing a top marketer into his organization would help him build his business and impress Wall Street.

"Mike is a huge believer in brands and in how those brands get developed and made," Razzouk said in an interview at the time. "There's no time to waste here. We've got a chance to win."

"A marketer does add value to a company that's seeking funding," says David Powell, a recruiter in Silicon Valley.

"The CEO needs to know how to run a business. But somewhere in the organization you need to have someone who knows marketing."

The Godfather of all these marketers who have taken the plunge is Bob Pittman, president and COO of America Online, and the designated co-COO of the combined AOL Time Warner. Pittman, who helped launch MTV in the early 1980s, left his job as CEO of Century 21 to join AOL in October of 1996. At the time,

AOL was still in a horse race with other Internet service providers. Pittman's marketing skill helped AOL crush competitors to become the dominant brand in its space and one of the most valuable brands in the world.

Before Pittman came along, "I thought AOL was dead," Sealey says.

At the opposite end of the spectrum are young pioneers like Yahoo's Edwards. In 1995, despite the fact that her resume included stints at Clorox, Chevron and ad agency BBDO, Edwards got the cold shoulder in Silicon Valley.

"When I did encounter people at Cisco, At Home and Netscape, they said, 'You don't have enough technology background,' " she recalls. "Nobody was doing consumer marketing at any other consumer Web site I was visiting."

What's in a name?

Her success at Yahoo taught competitors a lesson: In a world with virtually no barriers to entry, a strong brand is the best defense against competition.

"I clearly believe that a brand is the strongest barrier to entry in anything related to consumer/technology product or service," Edwards says. "It's not technology, because you can leapfrog that or acquire it. At the end of the day, consumers are loyal to brands, not feature frenzy."

Edwards' success helped establish the importance of branding on the Internet, and drew a flurry of imitators. Other marketers crossed the divide; the pace of dot-com ad spending began to pick up; and now the trickle of marketers from soap companies to cyberspace has become a torrent.

"In the early days of the Internet, the search work was in infrastructure," says Jean Bagileo, a managing partner at Powell's recruiting firm. "The pipeline had to get laid.

"The content thing happened two years in, and now we seem to be in this branding phase. Now half my practice relates to young, emerging e-commerce companies looking for CEOs or vice presidents of marketing."

"I think brands will rule in the new decade," says Costello, the former Sears head marketer who's CEO of MVP.com. "Technology is important, but it's the means to an end. The key to success is building a brand that meets customer needs better than anybody else. I find many of the key components of brand building are similar in the Internet space, but taken to the nth degree. Customers are more demanding; competition is more intense; and speed to market has accelerated dramatically."

"The world is becoming this caldron of choices,"

says Ropes, who left Ford for zUniversity.com. "Because of this proliferation of choices, brands will win the day. Before, marketers and manufacturers had control, but the Web opens up more choices. For the first time in the history of marketing, the consumer is in control."

While many of the new e-commerce marketers were lured by stock options, there is heady appeal in shaping a new company in the new economy.

"Your touch probably doesn't change the trajectory of a Pepsi," says Gary Briggs, who helped launch the Aquafina water brand at Pepsi and who is now chief marketing official at Ourhouse.com. "But here, I have the opportunity to take something that had no definition in the consumer's mind and define it and have fun with it."

"Moving to a big, established firm wasn't as interesting as moving to a category on the verge of everything that's happening," says Len Short, head of advertising and brand management at Charles Schwab. "I wanted to be a part of that revolution."

It's in the budget

Perhaps the most alluring aspect of this brave new world is that these marketers don't have to fight to persuade management to increase the ad budget.

"A lot of this is being driven by the recognition that marketing is an investment," says Jerry Gramaglia, chief marketing officer of E-Trade, whose career included stints at Procter & Gamble, Taco Bell and Sprint. "The irony is that these investors are probably more in tune with the role and potential value of marketing than the guys at General Mills and P&G who wrote the book. They're still looking at marketing as a cost and a maintenance."

When Beindorff spoke at the Association of National Advertisers' annual conference in Florida last October, some members of the audience joked that if a marketer hadn't turned down at least one major offer from a dot-com start-up, his or her career was obviously going nowhere.

"This is an absolutely great time for people who have a real interest in marketing," says Paul Ray of Ray & Berenson, who specializes in placing marketing people in top positions. "It's similar to the early 1980s, when the energy business took off like a shot. Suddenly there was this huge demand for land men and geologists. That didn't last long, but this demand will sustain itself for a period of time."

Not for everyone

But for those who do make the leap, success is no guarantee. Most of the start-ups are doomed to failure, and not everyone can adapt to life at dot-com speed.

"I don't think that every person from the offline

(Cont.)

world can adapt," says Annie Williams, who left Conde Nast to become head of marketing at Cnet. "You have to be comfortable making decisions with 80% of the information that's available. The things that were valued in publishing, like what you wore, where you ate lunch and what your office was like — not one of those things mattered in this industry. We eat lunch out of a vending machine."

Even if you adapt to the new lifestyle, the competitive environment is fierce. At Yahoo, success hasn't made Edwards complacent.

"Every time I read one of the press releases about older men with white hair joining Internet start-ups as marketers, it makes us more aggressive," she says. "I'm young; we've got a young team; and we want to win."

UNCLE SAM WANTS YOU...TO HAVE FUN!

The military is hoping new ads will attract Gen Y recruits

Smack in the middle of New York's Times Square, James Sutton Jr. is surrounded by the enemy. The U.S. Air Force sergeant is charged with persuading kids to serve their country at a time when unemployment is at a 30-year low, college aid is plentiful, and dot-com dreams are flashing up on gigantic video screens outside his window. It's no easy task, he concedes.

But reinforcements are on the way. Stung by missed recruiting targets and an apathetic public, the U.S. military has launched a full-scale assault on its own image. It is marshaling money, technology, and celebrity marketing to reclaim its lost prestige. The primary target: a group of young people almost as large as the baby boomers—Generation Y.

Good luck. As members of Generation Y—those born after 1978—come of age, the military isn't even on their radar screens. They have more alternatives than any generation since the draft. They've lived without the threat of war. And they've grown up in a decade of military downsizing and scandals over gay-bashing and sexual harassment. "Join the army? You've got to be kidding, right?" says Terence Jones, 18, loitering near the Times Square station, the military's busiest, with about 10,000 visitors a year. Jones and his friend, Mark Walters, laugh when confronted with new ads that show enlistees at play. "That's like the one minute of fun you're gonna get," Walter snorts.

That attitude is creating a king-size problem for the armed services. Even though the military is about 30% smaller than it was a decade ago, recruiters are having a hard time making their numbers. The Army fell 6,300 recruits short of its 1999 target of 74,500 last year. The Air Force missed its goal by more than 5%. Offers of pay raises and corporate-style signing bonuses aren't doing the trick. Even in poor and minority communities, where the military has traditionally been strong, economic expansion has created new civilian jobs, making it harder to find soldiers. **SLICK ADS.** Now, the military is fighting back, using the same tactics that any corporation with a marketing problem would employ: high-powered advertising. Spending by the four branches is up by a third over last year, to $286 million. Slick new ads show recruits at leisure time around the world. A commercial for the Navy includes a group of young men jamming with guitars atop an aircraft carrier. Marine Corps ads dispense with live action and instead place a young man in a video-game setting, doing virtual battle with a fire-breathing dragon. "We have to show that it's not what you see in Forrest Gump," says Air Force Recruiting's chief of advertising, Tim Talbert. "You don't brush the floor with toothbrushes."

To bring that point to life, the Air Force will begin a national tour of the "Air Force Experience" this month. The carnival-style road show features videos, flight simulators, and an F-16 jet. It will make stops at shopping-mall parking lots and schools in communities across the country.

Meanwhile, Defense Secretary William S. Cohen is on a mission to enlist Hollywood and sports celebrities to his recruiting drive. In January, he went to Los Angeles, meeting with about a dozen celebrities, including Steven Spielberg, hoping to persuade them to join the marketing blitz. He's negotiating with Fox TV's NFL Sunday to have the commentators broadcast from an aircraft carrier later this year.

There are some early signs that the beefed-up marketing may make this younger generation take notice. In 1998, the Navy had an advertising budget of $63.4 million and fell nearly 7,000 short of its enlistment target—getting 48,429 recruits when it wanted 55,321. Last year, it hired movie director Spike Lee to create realistic spots and managed to make its target of 52,524.

But an improved sales pitch can't make up for the fact that today's teens lack the military role models of previous generations, says Albert J. Martin, a military-marketing consultant. They've grown up in an age of volunteer service, so fewer of them have close relatives who served in the military. Up until now, "there's no national leader who is supporting the role of the military and holding it up as having a special place in society," he says. With high-profile veterans such as Senator John McCain (R-Ariz.) coming on the scene, that may change, Martin says, but advertising alone won't make the difference.

Nor are ads stronger than the force of the economic expansion. It's not just that 18-year-olds can get good jobs in today's economy. Their parents can afford to send them to college in greater numbers, taking a big chunk of middle-class kids out of the traditional recruiting pool.

That's even the case for military parents. Air Force recruiter Sutton has encouraged his 18-year-old son to try college first. "I'd like him to join, but he has other interests," Sutton says sheepishly. Most of his son's peers do, too.

By Diane Brady in New York

Marketers put a price on your life
Years of buying matters most

By Greg Farrell
USA TODAY

NEW YORK—The next time you order a Coke, don't think of it as costing $1.25; think of it as a small down payment on the $6,000 you might be worth to Coca-Cola over your lifetime.

Or when you're at a Chevrolet dealer, don't think of that Cavalier as a $15,000 car — think of it as the first installment on the $276,000 you might be worth to General Motors as a lifetime customer.

Even if you prefer not to think of these purchases as down payments on sizable lifetime investments, be forewarned: Marketers across the USA are looking at them exactly that way.

Marketers are focusing on the lifetime value of a loyal customer, not just this quarter's sales.

"It's the new real advance in marketing," says Peter Sealey, an adjunct professor of marketing at the University of California at Berkeley. Sealey, former head of marketing at Coca-Cola, uses the Coke and GM examples in presentations to would-be marketers. "There can't be a marketer who's not brain dead who's not doing this now."

"You don't have to think about all the customers," says Martha Rogers of Peppers & Rogers marketing consultants. "You just have to think about the right customers. If I'm Coke, I really want to know which 6% of customers in the U.K. drink 60% of the colas. I want to get as big a share of those customers as possible. I want them to be Coca-Cola loyalists, not just cola loyalists."

Several developments have pushed marketers toward the lifetime value approach:

▲ Consumers have less time. Marketers know consumers don't want to spend time on brand decisions; most will stick with the tried-and-true.

▲ It costs a lot more to capture a new customer than to care for one you have.

▲ The Internet is giving marketers a better idea of who their regular customers are. More important, marketers can figure out exactly how much it costs to acquire customers on the Web, so they are compelled to figure out how much each of those customers is worth.

"Computers are driving this way of marketing," says Rogers. "If I can build a dialogue with customers, I can get you to tell me something. I can know something about you that my competitors don't know, which makes it possible for me to do something for you that competitors can't do."

The concept of the lifetime value of a customer isn't altogether new. Alfred Sloan assembled General Motors around the principle of a "value ladder," meaning that GM should have a specific line of cars to sell to customers at each stage of their lives.

That principle remains in place today. "We value loyalty at General Motors," says Martin Walsh, general director of marketing for Cadillac. "And we recognize the value of moving customers from one division to another."

What is new is the ability to use the Internet as a tool to deepen ties with heretofore anonymous buyers.

"We're focused on the lifetime value of the customer," says Gateway Computer CEO Ted Waitt.

KEEPING THE CUSTOMER HAPPY — FOR A LIFETIME

The loyal customer is worth more than the sum of her purchases. A faithful General Motors customer can be worth $276,000 over her lifetime, including the 11 or more vehicles bought, plus a word-of-mouth endorsement making friends and relatives more likely to consider GM products.

Estimated lifetime value of a customer for **General Motors:** $276,000

Procter & Gamble (two or more brands) $10,000

Gateway Computer $25,000

Safeway/Albertson's (upper income family, with children) $4,800 per year

"There's a lot more in that relationship than just the box." Gateway is using the Internet to build loyalty. It offers a year's Internet service with the purchase of a new computer.

Executives at rival Dell also are thinking long term. "Hopefully, customers don't view us as one transaction," says Bob Langer, director of Dell.com. "The approach we take is all about building long-term relationships with customers. The end of the transaction is the beginning of the relationship."

Although neither company would give numbers, Aaron Goldberg of Ziff-Davis estimates the lifetime value of a sophisticated computer user — one who buys a new machine and software about every two years — to be about $45,000. A non-technical user who puts off computer purchases as long as possible has a lifetime value closer to $25,000, he says.

For old-line marketers selling several brands, the idea of looking at the consumer's total value doesn't come easily. Procter & Gamble CEO Durk Jager estimated at a recent press conference that the lifetime value of a customer for just one P&G brand could be several thousand dollars, but he didn't know how much that customer was worth across all the company's product lines.

"It hasn't happened in consumer packaged goods," says Sealey. "The Internet is going to permit us to do it far better than ever before. On line, we can order, get customer service, have a dialogue. The Web's going to be an enormous facilitator of this."

Don't snicker at long-time purveyors of toothpaste and soaps. A lot of on-line marketers are even more clueless about the lifetime value of their customers.

"Most Internet firms are fighting for one transaction at a time, and that's an expensive way to do it," says Kathy Biro, CEO of the Strategic Interactive Group.

Hewlett-Packard is trying to make a business of helping Web sites develop customer loyalty programs. It sells "quality of service" software for e-commerce sites.

"If you go to the grocery store, people will wait three minutes in line before getting antsy," says Ann Livermore, CEO of enterprise computing at H-P. "On the Web, people are not willing to look at that hourglass for 30 seconds.

"We allow you to assign a priority to certain transactions and customers. So if the Web gets busy, and it impacts quality of service, your site gives priority of service to certain customers."

"Most of the recipes that made for good business before the Web still make for good business on the Web," Livermore says. "The company that figures out how to have the best customer loyalty on the Web will have the advantage because of how quickly people can jump from place to place on line."

Finding Target Market Opportunities

NOW, COKE IS NO LONGER 'IT'

New CEO Daft promises a fundamental shift of focus as consumers flock to bottled water, juice, and tea

Jill Friedman, a 21-year-old college student in Atlanta, says she used to sip Diet Cokes all day long but now prefers bottled water. "As I've gotten older, I've realized that drinking five Diet Cokes a day isn't good for you," she says. Walking away from caffeine and aspartame may have been a smart choice for Friedman, but it's bad news for Coca-Cola Co.

Coke's problem is the countless number of people out there who, like Friedman, have cut way back on their soda consumption. For years, consumers have been moving in droves toward juice, bottled water, tea, and other noncarbonated beverages. Now, after decades of focusing almost exclusively on selling the world a Coke, the company has a new chief executive, Douglas N. Daft, who is gearing up to take on the nonsoda market in a big way.

Coke has a lot of catching up to do. Competitors such as The Perrier Group and Quaker Oats Co., maker of Gatorade, have already made big strides in noncarbonated drinks, weakening Coke's soda sales. After nearly two decades of 7% annual gains in unit volume sales, Coke's global volume grew just 1% last year, while its operating profits plunged 20%, to $3.98 billion. Says Tom Pirko, president of New York consultant Bevmark: "If Coke wants to succeed, [it has] now got to embrace other beverages."

Given Coke's long tradition of focusing most of its marketing clout on its cola brands, that's a tall order. Over the years, Coke has tended to treat its noncarbonated offerings as second-class beverages, giving them far less aggressive marketing than the flagship product. Indeed, one Coke insider acknowledges that in noncarbonated categories, the company has been content to produce what he terms "me-too" or "second-in-the-market" products that have produced small-but-easy profits. "I don't think we've gone at [alternative categories] with our heart and soul," says the executive.

BRIBERY. Making matters worse has been Coke's long-term strategy of subsidizing its noncarbonated beverages to keep competitors off store shelves. In return for cash payments that run into thousands of dollars per store, many stores agree to hand over shelf space to Coca-Cola products, including less popular drinks, such as juice-flavored Fruitopia. Invariably, the practice has left little room on store shelves for rivals such as New Age SoBe and Veryfine juices.

But that strategy may soon wear out its welcome. Some retailers have begun to revolt, scaling back on Coke subsidies in favor of stocking more popular brands. Now, on the shelves of many 7-Eleven Stores, Coke's Nestea, for instance, has had to make more room not just for the better-selling Pepsi brand Lipton but also for Snapple and Arizona Iced Tea. Other Coke products, including its newly launched Dasani bottled water and its Powerade sports drink, are getting squeezed by more popular brands, such as Poland Springs water and Gatorade. Says Jim Jackson, beverage manager for 7-Eleven: "In stores where they're competing on a level playing field, consumers usually choose competitors' products."

That's going to change if Daft has anything to say about it. Departing from years of Coke-centric tradition, Daft says he's ready to give beverage drinkers the variety of products they crave. His goal is to remake Coke into "a leader of the beverage sector, as opposed to a soft-drink company."

Daft and his team agree with analysts that to get back to those halcyon days of 7% annual growth in volume and 15%-or-better annual increases in profits, Coke will have to generate as much as 30% of its future growth from noncarbonated categories. "For us to achieve the growth rate that people are expecting, we have to become more diversified," says Steve Jones, Coke's new chief marketing officer. "We have to move beyond Coke and the carbs."

To that end, Daft, Jones, and other top Coca-Cola executives are pushing hard to shake up the company's culture. In the less than three months since Daft has been in the top job, he has shuffled his management team to promote executives with a track record in noncarbonated products. What's more, Daft hopes that his bombshell move on Jan. 26 to lay off roughly 20% of Coke's workforce will help reduce bureaucracy and allow more new ideas to bubble up from the field.

Next on Daft's agenda is laying out basic guidelines for new products, packaging, and marketing. Then he intends to cut his local managers loose to develop products tailored to local tastes. While Coca-Cola already sells some 300 diverse beverage products around the globe, Daft envisions a day when Coke will offer 2,000 or more, many of which will be new juices, teas, and hybrid products, such as carbonated tea. "We will be trend-setting," he vows.

That would surely mark a dramatic shift from Coke's predicament today. And Daft

> ### Will the Coke name mean anything to buyers of mango juice or rice milk?

has a fighting chance. For starters, Coke's vast global network of independent bottlers, valued by some analysts at $100 billion, gives it a reach that no other beverage company can match. Even so, analysts believe that those bottlers, many of which are financially stretched from costly expansions of the past two decades, may be reluctant to plunge into the nonsoda market. Generating the volume needed "to provide profits . . . is going to be a challenge," says Scott Wilkins, an analyst at Deutsche Banc Alex. Brown Inc.

Even if Coke persuades bottlers to carry its new drinks, some question whether the company will enjoy the same brand equity in, say, mango juice in Latin America or rice-based drinks for Asia as it does with Coke. "Without the Coke name, they're just another brand on the shelf," says Brown Brothers Harriman & Co. analyst Roy D. Burry.

Still, beverage experts say Daft is on the right track. With consumers voting convincingly for new noncarbonated beverages, it would be suicide to cling to cola alone, they say. Just ask Jill Friedman and the many others like her. They're not drinking as much Diet Coke, but they are drinking something. And whether it's juice, tea, or water, Doug Daft is determined that they'll soon start buying it from Coca-Cola Co.

By Dean Foust, with Deborah Rubin in Atlanta

Men Are on the Minds of Hair-Dye Makers

BY JIM CARLTON
Staff Reporter of THE WALL STREET JOURNAL

Gray is increasingly passe in men's hair fashions, and dye purveyors have launched an advertising push to get the word out.

Television and print ads aimed at getting men to dye the gray out of their hair have tripled over the past decade, in line with an explosion in sales of hair-coloring products for men. Those sales soared to $129.3 million last year from $39.6 million in 1989, according to estimates by market researchers A.C. Nielsen.

And while dyed males are still outnumbered about 10-1 by their female counterparts, they are narrowing the gap. According to pollster Roper Starch Worldwide, 36% of men recently questioned indicated they had either tried coloring their hair or were open to it.

Not so long ago, gray hair on men was considered distinguished. That's apparently changing with the business world's increased obsession on youth. "Business is moving so fast it is no longer the gray-haired guy who gets the deference and respect," says Roger Selbert, publisher of Growth Strategies, a trend letter based in Santa Monica, Calif. "Now it's how sharp are you, and are you up on the newest software."

Indeed, many job recruiters are advising middle-aged male clients to dye their hair. "I don't think I would even have gotten in the door if I hadn't changed my hair color," says Dan Lambert, a 45-year-old restaurant manager who followed the advice when he sought a new job recently.

There is also the question of sex appeal. Nearly two-thirds of women responding to a recent online poll by the dating service Datelynx rated as unattractive men whose photos showed them with natural gray hair. But after the same men hit a bottle of dye, the women rated them handsome.

Of course, hair dye isn't for everyone. Actor Richard Gere was named People magazine's sexiest man alive in 1999, despite his silver mane, while TV funnyman Jay Leno frolics with his gray pompadour to no apparent career detriment. Even in youth-obsessed Silicon Valley, many tech companies boast of keeping a few "gray hairs" around, referring to over-40 types hired on to impart wisdom that only experience can offer. "That's mostly because the investors want to see 'em," says Guy Kawasaki, a longtime valley entrepreneur.

And the coloring doesn't always achieve the desired results. "Men will tell me the dye makes them look younger, but it doesn't always," says Anthony Palermo, a colorist at Manhattan's Oribe Salon. "And it can wash out to a strange color. Sometimes you see men walking in fluorescent lights and their head looks purple or red."

Men's hair coloring has been around since 1961, when **Combe** Inc. introduced its Grecian Formula product. But early technology forced customers to spend more time applying the dye with less certain results than today. A combination of technological changes and social advances changed that. Combe, White Plains, N.Y., introduced its Just for Men coloring product in 1987, which touted the fact it required just five minutes to apply.

Meanwhile, the rise of the fast-paced computer industry put younger executives into the work force, heightening society's worship of youth.

"There's a whole new generation right behind us that's pushing real hard, so men want to stay on top of their game," says Dominic DeMain, senior vice president of U.S. marketing for Combe.

Just for Men accounted for $72.4 million in U.S. sales during the 52-week period ended Dec. 5, dominating the men's hair coloring category, according to Information Resources, a market-research firm in Chicago. Meanwhile, traditional women's oriented beauty companies have been attracted to the market. **Bristol-Myers Squibb** Co.'s Clairol unit, for instance, has launched a Men's Choice haircoloring brand that attained $12.3 million in sales last year, according to Information Resources. French cosmetics giant **L'Oreal** SA is also pursuing the market.

As a result, men's sales have become the hottest segment in the U.S.'s $1.3 billion-a-year hair-coloring industry. According to officials of one national drug retailer, which asked that their company's name not be used, the store space they devote to men's hair dyes has grown to six 3-foot shelves from two over the past decade. Stoking the interest is a barrage of product advertising, which grew to $32 million last year from $10 million a decade ago, according to Competitive Media Reporting.

"Guys will see me do this, and then they will do it," says Rollie Fingers, the retired Oakland Athletics pitcher and a Just for Men pitchman. Another pitchman, former Chicago Bears great Dick Butkus, says dyeing one's hair used to seem unmanly. "Ten years ago, I'd slap the guy who suggested putting color in my hair," says the 57-year-old Mr. Butkus, who recently darkened his salt-and-pepper flattop. "But now, your appearance means so much."

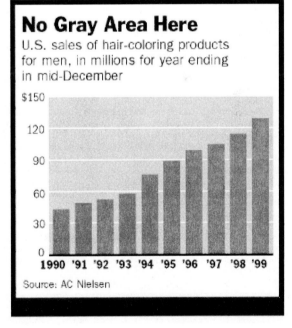

No Gray Area Here

U.S. sales of hair-coloring products for men, in millions for year ending in mid-December

Source: AC Nielsen

TOYOTA: CHASING BOOMERS' BABIES

With its buyers well into middle age, it needs a Gen-Y edge

When Marie Stevenson, 30, went car shopping recently, she thought about a Toyota. After all, she works for an auto insurer, so she knows all about Toyota's reputation for quality. The impulse, however, passed quickly. Stevenson says the new ECHO subcompact "looks kind of goofy." Eventually, she bought a white Nissan Xterra SUV, the perfect stablemate for her husband Brian's dark green Volkswagen Jetta.

That's hitting Toyota Motor Corp. where it hurts. The Japanese auto maker built its fortunes in the U.S. catering to the tastes of baby boomers, starting back when they were buying their first cars. But so far it's been unable to build a similar connection with the next generation. With a median age of 46, according to researcher AutoPacific Inc, in Tustin, Calif., Toyota buyers tend to be older than those of any other Japanese car company. Even though Toyota's sales will be up a healthy 10% this year, the company is worried about what happens when its core customers hit retirement.

Now, Toyota has set a goal of lowering its customers' age by a decade. A year ago, it gathered eight twenty- and thirtysomethings from around the company into a new, ethnically diverse marketing group called "genesis." Their first assignment was to launch three cars meant to pull in younger buyers: the entry-level ECHO subcompact, a sporty new two-door Celica, and the MR2 Spyder, a racy convertible roadster. Under Mark Del Rosso, then a 34-year-old Lexus field manager, genesis began by coming up with a marketing campaign for the ECHO that would speak to people like Stevenson.

FIRST-TIME DRIVERS. The group has an estimated $30 million to spend to get the three cars off the ground. Ads from the new campaign hit TV screens in September, just ahead of the October arrival of the ECHO and the Celica in showrooms. (The Spyder isn't due until spring.) Toyota executives say they're pleased with the results so far. Both the ECHO, a replacement for the Tercel, and the Celica, now in its seventh generation, zipped past their sales targets. More important, the median age of buyers dropped, from 42 to 33 for Celica and to 38 for the ECHO, down from 43 for the Tercel. "We're beginning to see single, young, adult, first-time drivers in our stores," says Steven P. Sturm, marketing vice-president for the Toyota brand. "It's a younger buyer that we haven't seen for a while."

But Toyota is still a long way from its goal. It wants nothing less than a reprise of the strategy that proved so successful with boomers. When that generation was young, Toyota pulled first-time car buyers in with low-priced models such as the Corolla, then moved them into bigger, more expensive models as they aged.

To do the same with the children of the boomers, Toyota needs a car that draws raves from Generation Y. But critics say the ECHO, with its stubby, quirky looks, is the wrong car. Toyota will sell a lot of the model, says George Peterson, president of AutoPacific, "but to older, less-affluent people rather than to younger ones."

To be sure, the built-in-Japan car was designed before the U.S. unit decided to make it the centerpiece of its effort to reach young consumers. Short from back to front but with a high roof, the ECHO isn't winning much applause for its styling. Toyota's advertising, in fact, tacitly acknowledges the shortcomings, using language such as "designed from the inside out" and "funky." Says Peterson: "It's a funny-looking car. That's definitely a problem."

It's not as if Toyota's in trouble yet. Unlike other powerful boomer brands, such as Levi's and Nike, which woke up one day to discover that "relaxed fit" jeans weren't phat, or that teenagers would rather "just do it" in hiking boots than athletic shoes, Toyota is on a roll. The company will sell about 1.5 million vehicles this year, almost 9% of the U.S. market. The Camry family sedan will be the country's best-selling passenger car for the third year in a row. The luxury Lexus brand roared past Cadillac and Lincoln this year and outsold market leader Mercedes until last month. But the competition does better with young buyers. The median age of customers for the Corolla is 45, compared with 38 for the Honda Civic and a mere 31 for the Jetta.

That's where Del Rosso's group comes in. Toyota gave the team its own space in a building across the parking lot from the company's Torrance, Calif., headquarters. To visitors, it could almost be the digs of a dot.com startup, with its wide-open feel and big computer screens. "They gave me the latitude to organize and structure the group the way I wanted it," Del Rosso says, "with the idea of differentiating the Toyota brand and making it relevant to the post-baby-boom consumer."

Right now, Volkswagen is the company to beat when it comes to appealing to younger buyers. "We use advertising to go after the emotional side of the target, with humor, real

AGING APPEAL	Toyota's problem: How to attract younger buyers					
MEDIAN BUYER'S AGE FOR THE 1999 MODEL YEAR						
VOLKSWAGEN	**HONDA**	**NISSAN**	**SATURN**	**TOYOTA**	**CHEVROLET**	**FORD**
36	37	43	43	46	47	47

DATA: AUTOPACIFIC INC.

(Cont.)

people in real-life vignettes, and innovative music," says Elisabeth K. Vanzura, director of marketing for Volkswagen of America Inc. in Auburn Hills, Mich. "We let them discover the rational side of the brand—styling, engineering, product, and features—on their own."

Toyota's attempt to replicate Volkswagen's formula was launched on Sept. 22 with a 45-second spot called "Revolution" that's a virtual remake of the legendary "1984" spot that introduced the Apple Macintosh computer. A casually-dressed youth races against the flow of somber-suited business types and hurls the jack of his boom box cable into the building's sound system. Glass shatters, and the three new cars appear on pedestals. Del Rosso professes not to have gotten the Apple connection until he read it in reviews later. The more recent spots for the Celica employ the all-too-familiar metaphor of sports car as jet plane, photographed on a stark desert road. Only ads for the ECHO are closer to the mark, centered on lifestyle and fun rather than features and specifications.

> **Right now Volkswagen is the company to beat in appealing to younger buyers**

PRICE IS RIGHT. If the ad campaigns are still a work in progress, however, Toyota has gotten the pricing right. The ECHO starts at $10,000, the least-expensive Japanese subcompact on the market and a full $2,200 less than the new Focus, Ford Motor Co.'s similar attempt to lure post-boomers to an aging franchise. The new Celica, at $17,000, is slightly smaller and edgier—and $4,700 cheaper—than its predecessor. And, with the launch of next spring's Spyder, Toyota hopes to recreate the success of its 1984-model MR2, a two-seater sports car. The Spyder will go for around $25,000, well beneath such other premium roadsters as the BMW Z3 and Porsche Boxster.

Genesis has turned Toyota's traditional media buys upside down. Instead of network TV, most of the ads appear on such cable TV venues as MTV, VH1, and Comedy Central. When Take My Picture, the new music video of the band Filter, premiered on MTV on Oct. 15, Toyota's "Revolution" was right behind it. Spliced to the commercial was a 15-second plug for the hot group's first Web-cast— exclusively on Toyota's Web site.

Toyota's new Web site, that is. The genesis bunch pulled out all the stops to create a flashy no-text site full of 360-degree video, edgy music, and what boomers would call "irritating noise." And, in a gentle poke at the corporate higher-ups, they gave it an irresistible address: www.isthistoyota.com. Even the suits across the parking lot are hoping that the answer will someday be "yes."

By Larry Armstrong in Torrance, Calif.

Aiming to please women

Business travel industry introduces more services for female customers

By Salina Khan
USA TODAY

Businesswoman Patty Kincaid didn't think much of Wyndham Hotels & Resorts' plan for attracting female business travelers.

Giving away five-minute phone cards wouldn't work, she told executives at a meeting of the chain's Advisory Board of Women Business Travelers last month. But a more efficient check-in system that reduced waiting might, she said.

Wyndham is taking Kincaid's advice, in the end improving something that will help all of its customers. The episode illustrates two trends changing the travel industry:

▲ Travel businesses are paying more attention than ever to the wants and needs of female business travelers, whose numbers are growing. Women are expected to account for half of all business travelers in 2002 compared with only 1% in 1970.

▲ When travel businesses get women's point of view on how to improve, men often benefit, too. The additional office equipment in guestrooms, business lounges with meeting space and better security that all hotel guests enjoy were prompted by suggestions from female travelers. Male guests find makeup mirrors now in hotel rooms are better for shaving.

"It's not about men vs. women," says Kincaid, who heads a media consulting firm in Scottsdale, Ariz., and is one of 18 businesswomen on Wyndham's advisory board. "It's about women voicing their opinions and asking for friendly service, good accommodations and quality amenities."

Companies say they're courting female travelers harder these days not just because their numbers are increasing, but also because their allegiances are still forming. In a 1998 survey, Total Research found 81% of 217 female business travelers said they would be more loyal to companies that address their special needs.

"We tend to be more demand-ing but more rewarding," says Melissa Biggs Bradley, editor of Town & Country magazine. "Maybe we're used to orchestrating what's convenient for us at home and want to do it on the road. It comes second nature to us to ask for what we want."

Hotels and airlines seeking women's opinions are finding they have to deliver faster, friendlier, more personalized services to gain women's business. That may not sound very different from what many men want. What is different is that women value those services more.

For example, express check-in and check-out were considered extremely or very desirable by 87% of female business travelers but by only 77% of men, according to the 1999 Business Travel Monitor by Yesawich Pepperdine & Brown and Yankelovich Partners. A higher percentage of women also want complimentary shuttle service to and from the airport, ticketless travel and delivery of bags to the hotel for an extra fee.

"Women are better able to articulate what they want," says Cary Broussard of Wyndham. "And it's usually what men want, anyway."

Wyndham began four years ago researching what

Business travel by gender		
	Women	Men
Domestic business trips per year	6	14
International business trips per year	1	3
Usually bring spouse/friend	32%	12%
Extend stay to enjoy leisure activities	12%	6%
Least favorite city	Miami, Los Angeles	New York

Source: 1998 Crowne Plaza Hotels Travel Index

female travelers want. Today it is in the forefront of the hospitality industry's effort to win over female business travelers. Its Women On Their Way program includes the all-female advisory council, a partnership with the National Association of Women Business Owners and special amenities such as loofah mitts and skirt hangers in hotel rooms. Its Web site for female business travelers, www.womenbusinesstravelers.com, gets 14,000 hits a month.

Other examples of services targeted to women:

▲ Guests can hire a jogging partner at the Omni Hotel in Detroit as well as at all Loews hotels. Running escort services at the Luxury Collection Hotel in Houston are complimentary and include chilled bottled water, fresh fruit and a plush towel upon return.

▲ Loews Hotels and the Wyndham Hotel in Itasca, Ill., are among those that set aside networking tables in their restaurants for solo travelers who prefer to eat with others. Anyone can dine at the tables, but it was the women's advisory board members who suggested them.

▲ Pebble Beach Resorts in California offers golf lessons just for businesswomen because "as many deals are sealed on the golf course as they are in the boardroom," says golf academy director Beth Ramos. In addition to understanding the strategies and techniques of golf, women learn how to network while playing the sport and hear lectures from people who have successfully used golf for business.

▲ Wyndham started giving guests a ring five minutes before room service delivery upon the suggestion of its advisory council. "They don't want to be in the shower or have to rush to get dressed for someone to come into the room," Broussard says. Hotel workers also liked the policy because it saved return trips, says Wyndham President Les Bentley. The call is now mandatory at all 100 Wyndham hotels.

RETRAINING EMPLOYEES

Women also say they want to be given the same respect and level of service accorded to men. About half of the women surveyed by Total Research say they feel slighted by flight attendants and get passed over when upgrades to the first-class cabin are made to frequent fliers.

Erin Eckert, an associate professor at Tulane University, says she was infuriated when a flight attendant on a full flight to South Africa asked her if she would move to the economy cabin.

"She picked me out because I was the only woman in first class and she thought I would agree," Eckert says. "But I didn't."

Such criticism has not gone unheard in the air-

Travel on line before the trip
Internet sites for female business travelers

▲ **www.hermail.net**   An international directory of female business travelers where women can connect by e-mail to share experiences and tips.

▲ **www.delta-air.com/womenexecs**   Executive Woman's Travel Network provides discounts on Delta airfares, hotel rooms and clothing. Two cities are profiled every month.

▲ **www.womenswire.com/biztravel**   Runs stories on everything from how to get upgrades to business protocol to fashion advice.

▲ **www.womenbusinesstravelers.com**   Provides a forum for discussions about business travel, reviews of travel-related books and tips on being on the road.

▲ **www.journeywoman.com**   Lists articles on making solo dining fun, travel tales about wearing saris in India and "gal-friendly" city sites.

▲ **www.christinecolumbus.com**   Catalog of travel gear "well-suited for the woman traveler," as well as tips and links to other sites.

By Salina Khan

---

lines' executive suites. Trans World Airlines is sending 10,000 frontline employees — flight attendants and airport workers — to two days of training this fall that will stress the importance of treating female business travelers respectfully. Employees will be taught how to address their top concerns: safety, receiving help with luggage and the perception that men receive preferential treatment.

In February, all Wyndham employees who interact with guests received their first special training on how to accord female business travelers the same respect as men. One tip: Don't assume that a woman traveling with a group of men is not the boss. They were encouraged to make helpful suggestions, such as pointing out light meals on the room service menu.

DESIGN TRENDS

Dark woods, dark marble interiors and club-like lounges are no longer standard hotel decor. Women often prefer lighter colors, lots of windows and stylish furnishings, and that's what many of the new hotels are giving them.

Starwood's new W hotels, with huge windows and chaise lounges in the lobbies, were designed with the

(Cont.)

female road warrior in mind, says Brian Windle, vice president of marketing.

"Women business travelers are very attuned to style and design and like the comforts of home," Windle says.

The sleek guestrooms of London's contemporary One Aldwych are outfitted with alpaca beige and lettuce green carpet, fret linens and stainless steel chairs. Fresh fruit, bottled water and flowers are delivered to the rooms daily.

The push to draw female customers affects marketing strategies, too. Crowne Plaza Hotels and Resorts hired a new ad agency last year when targeting female business travelers became a priority. Jennifer Ploszay and other women in the hotel chain's marketing department work closely with the agency to include women in ads and brochures. A recent TV ad showed a female business traveler telling her child a bedtime story over the phone.

> **"Women are better able to articulate what they want. And it's usually what men want, anyway."**
> —*Cary Broussard of Wyndham Hotels & Resorts*

Delta Air Lines has been building a network of fliers for three years with its on-line Executive Woman's Network. The airline works with American Express to attract female frequent fliers through discounts on airfares, hotel stays and apparel purchases. Members must fill out a survey upon entry and Delta uses direct-mail promotions to stay in touch with them.

Making a good impression on women can mean many happy returns.

Lalia Rach, associate dean of the Center for Hospitality, Tourism and Travel Administration at New York University, says she'll never forget when she misread the flight departure time and missed her plane. The attendant at the United Airlines desk "did everything to make sure I got on the next flight," Rach says.

Now she flies United.

'Mom, the Airlines Don't Like Me!'

BY WENDY BOUNDS AND LAUREN LIPTON
Staff Reporters of THE WALL STREET JOURNAL
Most businesses are wooing kids like crazy — but not airlines. Some are dropping everything from preboarding rights to youth fares. It's even hard to find those little toy wings. Wendy Bounds and Lauren Lipton report.

On a recent United flight to San Francisco, Carol Ann Band brought along her two-year-old son Adam and discovered just how unfriendly the skies can be.

For starters, she wasn't allowed to board ahead of anyone else. Then the family was denied roomier bulkhead seats in favor of passengers with special needs — one of whom turned out to be an able-bodied college student. That left Ms. Band and her husband holding up an aisle of impatient passengers while they struggled to install Adam's child-restraint chair. With the plane so crowded, several passengers knocked young Adam in the head with their suitcases.

Says Ms. Band of her boarding experience: "There was nothing good about it."

What is good about flying with children these days? Today, businesses from Baby Gap to luxury hotels are doing cartwheels to attract kids. But when was the last time you found a youth fare for air travel or saw an airline offering any special assistance to a mother with an infant? And what about saving a few roomier upfront seats for families? These once-popular measures are fading as fast as legroom. And, with the skies only getting more crowded, some airlines are now starting to cut privileges parents have relied on for decades.

Last year, United and Delta Air Lines eliminated preboarding announcements for families with small children; both carriers say it isn't "efficient." Other airlines raised the fees they charge for unaccompanied minors. Even free travel for infants riding on parents' laps — long an industry tradition — may soon vanish completely with an impending government ruling that would mandate child-restraint chairs on airplanes.

All of which means that most kids traveling today are lucky if they get those little pilot wings. And for the parents, the treatment is only more upsetting when compared with the perks the industry keeps lavishing, for example, on business fliers. "The world understands the importance of children," says Keith Waldon with Virtuoso, a Texas-based network of 244 travel agencies. "Airlines are just behind schedule on this."

It's not that airlines are out to get kids; adult leisure fliers usually get the same level of pared-down service. The truth is, much of the change is about economics — and the realities of modern jet service. With 71% load factors, planes haven't been this packed since

the 1940s, which only makes it harder for carriers to offer families any special attention or better seats. Airlines also argue that most families these days care more about price than amenities. "Don't get the idea that we don't welcome kids," says Joe Hopkins, a spokesman for United. "The world has changed. It is mass transportation in the sky. We're trying to provide the highest level of service."

Indeed, the bottom line is that kids, who don't typically fly in first or business class, aren't big money-makers. Nearly two-thirds of airlines' revenue is derived from business travelers who take up only about one-third of seats, estimates Sam Buttrick, an airline analyst with PaineWebber. By contrast, child passengers account for as little as 5% to 6% of an airline's revenue. "Airline executives don't sit around thinking about how to improve the travel experience of the average adolescent," Mr. Buttrick says. "And I'm not sure they should."

Still, many travel experts says the airlines may be missing an opportunity here, applying the wrong strategy to a group that's becoming more important to the industry. While still a small portion of overall air voyagers, more kids are becoming seasoned travelers as time-crunched parents increasingly make business trips into family affairs. Children under 18 accompanied adults on more than 26 million air trips in 1998, according to the Travel Industry Association of America, up 30% from just two years earlier. And let's not forget that many of those prized business travelers are parents themselves.

Can't Win

Airlines can't win "by doing bad things to children," says Michael Allen, head of the aviation-information business Back Associates Inc. A parent of two young children, he says any airline that entertained his kids more would "have my business in a second." Indeed, many foreign carriers have noticed this; British Airways has a toy chest in its economy sections, while El Al offers both an in-seat TV channel for kids and a special family-seating section onboard. "It's nice because kids can be together — and drive flight attendants crazy together," says an El Al spokeswoman.

Of course, international carriers typically have more time in-flight to devote to children and bigger planes to hold more amenities. "Young travelers are the future business travelers, and I don't know any company that wouldn't bend over backward to make sure they have a good experience," says Dean Breest with Air France, which operates "Planete Bleue" airport lounges with games and toys. Forced to compete, many U.S. carriers also offer more family perks on overseas flights.

To this day, many parents can still recall the days before airline deregulation when airlines could afford to lavish attention on children. As recently as the late '70s and early '80s, flight attendants would pin metal wings

on kids' lapels and invite them to the cockpit. Steep discounts for youth were common, as were onboard diapers and even the occasional sit-down video games. Thom Nulty, president of Navigant International, a large travel agency, still recalls when airlines routinely offered scores of comics and coloring books. "I can't remember the last time I saw those things," he says.

Indeed, in-flight entertainment for children is just one area that's become a sore spot for parents. Of the 36 magazines offered right now on Continental Airlines flights, including Latin Finance and Luxury Golf Homes, none are specifically for children. Several airlines do offer activity books and audio channels for children on certain flights, but the options pale in comparison to, say, the 25 personal video titles available in many American Airlines first-class cabins this month. On United, three of the four movies offered on its domestic flights in February, while edited for airline use, contain either violence, sexual situations or adult themes, according to its company magazine.

That leaves parents on their own during long flights, forced to cart their own assortment of toys, books, video games — anything — to keep antsy children busy in a cramped space. And just trying to bring on the load can be tricky, given the industry's new crackdown on carry-ons. "I've learned not to expect anything from airlines," says Juliett Giordano, who describes the travails of keeping her three-year-old son in check for a four-hour flight to New Orleans. Her tools: Play-Doh, Hot Wheels, crayons and other toys, all in a backpack the family had to lug aboard along with all their other carry-ons.

Happy Meals

A limited selection of airline meals for kids, meanwhile, has forced parents to include kiddie chow in their carry-ons too. United offers 10 meals for passengers with special medical diets; three vegetarian selections; three religious meals and five additional options, including a seafood meal and Obento Japanese. Kids get one choice: a McDonald's Happy Meal, which must be ordered 24 hours in advance. Unhappy with all the junk food options on most airlines, Elizabeth Schimel says she has to lug along juice boxes and carrots on trips with her two young sons. She also complains most domestic airlines make no effort to feed children first, something many foreign carriers do. "Their stomachs are not on the schedule of airlines' feeding plans," says the New York-based executive of Wit Capital.

Another beef: seating. Most airlines now reserve the front of the plane for their top-tier frequent fliers — including the roomy bulkhead seats so coveted by families. On her Thanksgiving trip, Mrs. Giordano says she twice requested bulkhead seats for her family — and still ended up being assigned five rows from the back. Another parent, Renee Berliner Rush, says she inevitably finds herself separated from her nine-year-old son, Wylie, on

(Cont.)

most flights. "We are always having to call upon the kindness of strangers" to switch seats, she says.

In response, airlines insist they do try to leave some good seats open until the day of departure for families. "You may have a full-fare business traveler who isn't happy with his seat, but we may also rearrange seats to keep families together," says USAirways spokesman David Castelveter.

Teddy Bear Teas

Other parts of travel industry, meanwhile, are going gangbusters for kids, including Amtrak, which offers 50% fare discounts for children up to 15 years old. (On most domestic airlines, children pay adult fares at age two.) In San Diego, parents at Loews Coronado Bay Resort can reach into the "Kids Kloset" to borrow games, car seats, strollers and bedtime books. The Boca Raton Resort & Club in Florida has developed a baby-food menu, while several Ritz-Carlton properties now hold "Teddy Bear Teas."

Compare that to the way some airlines handle the sticky issue of diapers. The last time Holly Hunnicutt flew with her son James, now nine months old, she resorted to laying him on the toilet-seat rim for changing. The reason: Despite having added 25% more leg room to a typical business-class seats in the last few years, many airlines still don't provide changing facilities onboard. Never mind germs, gripes the Langhorne, Pa., mom: "I was afraid he was going to fall in." It's not that planes don't have room. Continental says it offers facilities on every flight, while Northwest and United have refurbished many of their planes to include them.

Right now, the outlook for youth fliers and their parents seems to be getting more turbulent. During the last 18 months, several major airlines raised the fees they charge unaccompanied minors — in some cases doubling the charge to $30 a flight segment and charging extra for connections. And a few, including Northwest and Continental, raised the age for which minors can travel alone without charge to 15 from 12. Divorced parents whose kids fly frequently back and forth are "not happy, obviously," says Seattle travel analyst Steve Danishek. "They thought there were certain costs that disappeared as the kid gets older."

At the same time, as airlines crack down on on-time departure, preboarding for families is disappearing. Delta cut out the practice after finding they typically got a "mass of people at the door claiming to need extra assistance," says spokesman John Kennedy. He notes that the airline will try to preboard anyone who requests it, "time permitting." Same for United, says Lindsey Peterik, who works with the airline's airport-service planning, adding that the new policy "streamlines boarding."

That's little consolation to Kathy Bernstein, mother of two, who always needs the extra time to install a car-seat for her children. With everyone boarding simultaneously, "you're hitting first-class passengers in the head," complains Ms. Bernstein of Studio City, Calif. "I've never had a flight attendant help me. It's a nightmare." What's more, while domestic airlines recommend safety seats, they don't provide them, which means she must carry her own. By contrast, most car-rental agencies rent such seats for $5 a day.

The mayhem may worsen with an impending Federal Aviation Administration proposal that would make child-seats mandatory; the agency is still debating who should supply them. Worse yet, for some parents and their wallets, is that the ruling could end free travel for so-called "lap babies." Major airlines now charge 50% of the accompanying adult's ticketed fare for kids under two riding in safety seats.

"Margins in the industry are thin enough," says Northwest spokesman, Jon Austin, explaining that in a 100-seat plane, one or two full-paying passengers make the difference between a "profitable and unprofitable flight." American Airlines, which was the first to institute the 50% fare, states: "American is a business like any other. We feel our 50% infant fare makes economic sense — both for parents and the airline — and is an affordable way to safely keep infants in their seats."

Yet with all the focus on boarding efficiency and seat revenue, some parents wonder if airlines aren't growing just a bit too uptight. On his last Christmas trip from Jackson, Miss., to Houston, Kevin Schultz was stunned when a Southwest flight attendant chastised him for being one item over the carry-on limit. She counted his baby, who didn't have a seat of her own, as a piece of luggage. Southwest says this isn't standard policy, but Mr. Schultz was soured by the experience.

"Who would consider a child carry-on luggage?" says the father. He's already mulling an alternative route for their next holiday trip: 13 hours, by car.

Different Strokes

Amazon, EToys Make Big, Opposing Bets; Which One Is Right?

It's an Old Debate, Niche Vs. Mass Market, but Now With an Internet Twist

Plenty of Betty Spaghettys

BY GEORGE ANDERS
Staff Reporter of THE WALL STREET JOURNAL

Toby Lenk, founder of eToys Inc., is sure he knows the secret behind e-commerce: Build a single-focus Internet site, laser in on one swath of the marketplace, and don't let customers get confused by clutter from other goods or services.

Jeff Bezos, founder of Amazon.com Inc., is just as confident about his strategy: Build the world's biggest online department store, then offer everything from Milton to modems, so shoppers can get whatever they want with one click on their Web browsers.

Messrs. Lenk and Bezos are true pioneers, Internet innovators with astonishing net worths. So if they're both so shrewd, how could they take such widely disparate gambles?

That question, in one form or another, is on the minds of executives everywhere. In businesses ranging from aerospace to telecommunications, CEOs are making big strategic bets, trying to position their companies to take advantage of productivity and technology trends that they are only beginning to understand. And very often, major players are making completely divergent bets within the same industry.

It makes for exciting, if uncertain, times — particularly at a powerhouse like Amazon, which now offers about 18 million items on its site. Asked what his company's brand message is, book chief Carl Gish says: "That's a great question. I don't know the central message. If it were easy to come up with a slogan, we'd already have done it."

The contrast between Amazon and eToys is, in some ways, as old as retailing itself. In the traditional economy, mass merchandisers like Sears, Roebuck & Co. held the upper hand for decades. Then, in the 1980s, highly specialized "category killers" like Circuit

City Stores Inc. and Toys "R" Us Inc. came on strong. Then the balance of power switched again, as Wal-Mart Stores Inc. became the nation's No. 1 seller of music, toys and other items previously considered best handled by specialists.

But the speed and slickness of the Internet are redefining this tussle in striking ways. Suddenly, all-purpose stores can offer enormous variety without building huge showrooms that rack up costs and alienate many shoppers. Being really big doesn't seem to have the old drawbacks. Instead, it could become a savvy way to build a household-name brand, spread many one-time costs over a wider customer base and pitch an ever-greater selection of goods at frequent visitors.

That vast ambition isn't cheap. Last week, Amazon reported a $197 million loss for the third quarter and warned of even more red ink ahead, mostly because of spending in its newest product categories. Amazon told analysts that its U.S. book business is on the brink of profitability but will be used to subsidize losses in areas such as toys. That wasn't what investors wanted to hear; since that disclosure, Amazon's shares have slumped more than 10%.

Even so, Amazon keeps spreading its reach wider. In September, Amazon invited thousands of small merchants to do business in a new section on its Web site, called zShops. There, vendors have begun selling items ranging from honey-glazed pecans to concert tickets. Many of these are "small markets that deserve to be small," Mr. Bezos says. But together, he says, they can be big business — and a revenue source for Amazon, which gets a small cut of each vendor's sales.

That philosophy is anathema for hundreds of rivals, from eToys on down. Specialists such as Garden.com Inc., CDNow Inc. and Blockbuster Inc.'s Reel.com are focusing on a single category, hoping to attract loyal customers with some combination of lower prices, better display or nimbler customer service. "We could add music, and we might succeed at it," says David Rochlin, chief operating officer of Reel.com, an online movie

Jeffrey Bezos

store. "But it's unlikely we'll go that way. We don't want to lose our core audience."

Some niche stores are responding by pursuing exclusive selling arrangements for certain goods — especially those made by high-end manufacturers that don't want their products displayed next to cut-rate rivals. They also are banding together in various "online shopping malls" run by the likes of Yahoo! Inc. and America Online Inc. Just as in the physical world, the malls make it easier for customers to wander from one merchant to another.

Most of all, specialty merchants are trying to pack their stores with twists that defy easy imitation by superstores. Computer retailer OnSale Inc. has a 50-person customer-service department, including one expert who handles nothing but memory-chip questions. "There's nothing quite like that at Amazon," says OnSale's chief executive, Jerry Kaplan.

At eToys, based in Santa Monica, Calif., everything has been adjusted to fit families' needs and desires. "We don't sell Playboy videos," Mr. Lenk says. "We don't sell Tupac Shakur rap music. We're child-sensitive, and we get all the special details of that market right."

That focus extends down to the smallest details. The company has removed its name from the return addresses on boxes, so kids won't be tempted to open them prematurely. EToys can gift-wrap several items from an order separately, then send them in one big shipment with appropriate "To/From" tags attached. General merchandisers aren't likely to imitate that cumbersome, costly service, Mr. Lenk contends, because it's of little value for nontoy orders.

Whether such nifty details give specialists enough ammunition to ward off mass merchandisers is unclear. Amazon has indicated it will spend as much as $260 million on advertising, fulfilling customers' orders and other sales and marketing costs this quarter. That's the biggest such budget among online retailers, and far exceeds the estimated $40 million that eToys will spend.

Toby Lenk

COME INTO MY WEB

Amazon.com and eToys typify two radically different approaches to electronic commerce. Amazon is big and varied; eToys is tightly focused on one category: children's goods.

amazon.com		eToys.com
$356 million	Revenue Sept. 30 quarter	$13.3 million
$197 million	Net loss Sept. 30 quarter	$44.9 million
13.1 million	Customer accounts	611,000
One-line listings for 18 items including Oscar Peterson's "Night Train" CD, Burt Lancaster's film "The Train," and "Thomas the Tank Engine" toys	Search for "train" and you will find	The Train Station, a Web page with five pictures and information about toy trains sold under the Brio, Playmobil and Thomas brands
"We have recommendations for you in books, music and video"	Home page welcome	"Need a last minute gift? Gift certificates to the rescue."

Estimates are that less than 10% of Amazon's revenue now comes from its newest product categories, toys and electronics, combined. But even that sliver can be a big amount. A recent survey by PC Data Inc., a Reston, Va., research firm, estimated that Amazon led all online merchants with 1.1 million customers in September. EToys ranked 19th, with an estimated 70,000 customers.

Says Mr. Bezos: "It's very natural for a customer to wonder: 'Can you really be the best place to buy music, books and electronics?' In the physical world, the answer is almost always: 'No.'" But on the Internet, "all the physical constraints go away." Indeed, a world where shelf space is infinite "forces you to rethink all your intuitions about how a store should work," he says.

Lisa McNeill has seen both ways of doing business. For eight years, she worked as a buyer for Dayton Hudson Corp.'s Target unit, filling more than 800 all-purpose discount stores with children's playthings. Shelf space was scarce, so she concentrated on Barbie dolls, Tonka trucks and other obvious best-sellers. Shoppers wanting something out of the ordinary needed to patronize a pure toy store.

Now Ms. McNeill is a senior buyer at Amazon. "One of my favorite things about this job is that I get to say yes to vendors a lot more," she says. Take Betty Spaghetty wire dolls, which have detachable body parts and bendable limbs. At Amazon, she decided to stock all 13 models, though the most eccentric versions may attract just 100 orders this Christmas season. At Target, she wouldn't

have dared to offer more than three selections.

For a single-category specialist like eToys, it's still possible to stay a half-step ahead of Amazon in variety — but the gap between specialist and mass merchandiser is a lot narrower than it would be in the physical world. Lego Systems Inc., for example, sells only its top 60 or 70 best-sellers at land-based mass merchandisers. Amazon has 110 Lego selections already and is adding more, while eToys has all 200 of Lego's offerings.

As online niche stores look for an edge over their bigger all-purpose rivals, their best hope may be in trying to get exclusive rights to some upscale goods. Brio Corp. of Germantown, Wis., for example, sells its wooden train sets and other toys through eToys but has shied from Amazon. That's because a specialty store like eToys can better showcase Brio's carefully crafted toys, says Peter Reynolds, Brio's president.

At a mass merchandiser, Mr. Reynolds worries, his wares might be stuck next to cheaper alternatives. Brio's profusion of gates, bridges and other add-ons could be pared back to a bare-bones selection if sales didn't meet targets — a prospect that he regards as a cruel injustice to both his company and its young enthusiasts.

Amazon insists those concerns are overblown. "We wouldn't compare his products to cheaper alternatives," says Mr. Bezos. "We'd contrast them and show what's special about Brio." Still, the two companies have yet to strike a distribution deal.

As Amazon keeps expanding, its breakneck pace has contributed to management

turnover, with three vice presidents leaving in the past six months. But Mr. Bezos, who owns more than 30% of the company's stock, has been able to recruit new talent from some of America's biggest companies. He says he would be "disappointed" if Amazon next year couldn't expand its retailing offerings at least as much as it has this year.

Meanwhile, specialty-store operators sometimes wonder if they should widen their scope. EToys recently flirted with the idea of buying Bluemountainarts.com Inc., the leading online greeting-card company. But the company backed away, in part because of concern that many Bluemountainarts customers wouldn't relate to the children's market. Instead, Excite At Home Corp. agreed to buy the card company for as much as $1 billion.

As the Christmas season approaches, online stores of all varieties are scrambling to assemble deep inventories of hot-selling products — or strong ties to wholesalers that can get the goods. It is, after all, much harder to ship goods reliably than to build a good-looking Web site.

Some of the Internet's mass merchandisers have stumbled as they try to deliver everything. AltaVista Co.'s Shopping.com unit shrunk its superstore earlier this year, dropping out of the market for baby products and home-improvement gear when it had trouble finding wholesalers to reliably stock those items. AltaVista still sells computer equipment, books and videos directly, but it steers customers to other merchants if they want out-of-the-way goods.

The clearest way for online merchants to

(Cont.)

avoid inventory and shipping snags is to take command of those processes themselves and build giant warehouses. Both Amazon and eToys have embarked on that route. How that expensive strategy will work is anyone's guess. EToys says it is happy with its delivery initiatives; Amazon acknowledges some "speed bumps" in getting its warehouses up to speed, but says it expects to offer greater reliability as it goes along.

In courting customers, superstores hope to get the upper hand by using the Internet for cross-category merchandising. Last month, Amazon's toy section included a Halloween shopping list that urged visitors to try everything from a "Nightmare on Elm Street" video to a Halloween cookbook and e-mail Halloween greeting cards. Such tie-ins can be created and dismantled within hours on the Internet, at a very low cost. Something similar might take months of planning and hundreds of employee hours at a traditional chain.

Still, tie-ins alone can't boost traffic in a lackluster department, any more than a television network can attract viewers to a dull show by constantly promoting it in the midst of a hit.

A case in point is Amazon's online auction site, launched in April. People selling treasures such as Ernest Hemingway's typewriter can have their items mentioned, free of charge, on Amazon's purchase pages for Hemingway novels. Even with that feature, a recent survey by Prudential Securities found that Amazon had less than one-tenth the auction volume of eBay Inc., the industry leader — a single-specialty company that does only auctions.

Online superstores should have one undeniable edge: the ability to spread fixed costs over a larger customer base. At Amazon, software written to help organize auction listings is now being used by the toy-selling team to rearrange their catalog by price, age group and

other variables. That "cost us almost nothing," says Mr. Miller, the toy-store manager.

Superstores may have a harder time projecting an appealing image to customers across all categories. Amazon built its book, music and video businesses on a reputation for convenience and big selection, without trying to win every price war. While that has worked well so far, it may be the wrong strategy for electronics, where more than 40 online stores are in the midst of kamikaze battles for market share.

Competitors aren't about to help Amazon resolve its quandary. As Jerry Kaplan, the CEO of computer retailer OnSale, says, "If your brand stands for everything, it stands for nothing."

Republished with permission of Dow Jones, Inc. from *The Wall Street Journal,* November 2, 1999; permission conveyed through Copyright Clearance Center, Inc.

Pillsbury Presses Flour Power in India

By Miriam Jordan

Staff Reporter of The Wall Street Journal

BOMBAY, India — The Pillsbury Dough-boy has landed in India to pitch a product that he had just about abandoned in America: plain old flour.

Pillsbury, the Diageo PLC unit behind the pudgy character, has a raft of higher-margin products such as microwave pizzas in other parts of the world but discovered that in this tradition-bound market, it needs to push the basics.

Even so, selling packaged flour in India is almost revolutionary, because most Indian housewives still buy raw wheat in bulk, clean it by hand, store it in huge metal hampers and, every week, carry some to a neighbor-hood mill, or chakki, where it is ground be-tween two stones.

To help reach those housewives, the Doughboy himself has gotten a makeover. In TV spots, he presses his palms together and bows in the traditional Indian greeting. He speaks six regional languages.

Pillsbury is onto a potentially huge busi-ness. India consumes about 69 million tons of wheat a year, second only to China. (The U.S. consumes about 26 million tons.) Much of India's wheat ends up as roti, a flat bread prepared on a griddle that accompanies al-most every meal. In a nation where people traditionally eat with their hands, roti is the spoon. But less than 1% of all whole-wheat flour, or atta, is sold prepackaged. India's cli-matic extremes and deplorable roads make it difficult to maintain freshness from mill to warehouse, let alone on store shelves.

Then there are the standards of the Indian housewife, who is determined to serve only the softest, freshest roti to her family. "Pack-aged flour sticks to your stomach and is bad for the intestines," says Poonam Jain, a New Delhi housewife.

Pillsbury knows that ultimately it won't make fistfuls of dough from packaged flour. Its aim is to establish its flour business and then introduce new products to carry its cus-tomers up to more lucrative products.

That payoff may take a decade or two. "As a food company, we have to be where the mouths are," says Robert Hancock, market-ing director for Europe and Eurasia. "We'll get our rewards later."

Starting a flour operation meant turning back the clock for Pillsbury. Though it was born as a U.S. flour-milling company 130 years ago, the Diageo unit all but exited from that business in the early 1990s to focus on products such as frozen baked goods and ice cream. The food giant thought of introducing

high-value products when it first explored India. But it quickly learned that most Indians don't have enough disposable income for such fare. Many lack refrigerators and ovens, too.

Pillsbury is betting that flour will generate sales volumes to compensate for the razor-thin profit margins. "We wanted a product with huge and widespread mainstream ap-peal," Mr. Hancock says.

Pitching packaged flour meant overcom-ing thousands of years of tradition. "I'd never met women so intimately involved with the food they prepare," recalls Bill Barrier, who led a Pillsbury team that spent 18 months try-ing to decode Indian wheat and consumers.

Marketing managers climbed into the at-tics where housewives store their wheat and accompanied them to their tiny neighbor-hood flour mills. "Anywhere else, flour is flour," says Samir Behl, vice president of marketing for Pillsbury International. "In India, the color, aroma, feel between the fin-gers, and mouth feel are all crucial."

Pillsbury had hoped to establish contracts with existing mills, but inspectors found hy-giene and safety at some to be appalling. Pillsbury scouts visited 40 plants, where they encountered mice, rotting wheat and treach-erous machinery. They often left coated in fine flour dust, whose presence is a severe fire hazard. In fact, when the electricity went out during a visit to one mill, Pillsbury exec-utives were dumbfounded to see one worker light a match in the dark.

Pillsbury eventually found two mills capa-ble of the required standards. But even then, their rollout was delayed by several months be-cause the company rejected 40% of the wheat delivered to the mills after the 1998 harvest.

Many focus groups and lab tests later, Pillsbury came up with its packaged wheat blend, Pillsbury Chakki Fresh Atta. Godrej-Pillsbury Ltd., its joint venture here, launched the flour in southern and western India last year. The blue package, which features the Doughboy hoisting a roti, has become the market leader in Bombay, India's largest city, eclipsing the more established Kissan Anna-purna brand from the Anglo-Dutch company **Unilever** PLC.

"People said [prepackaged flour] would-n't taste the same, but my husband and I don't find any difference," says Shivani Za-veri, a Bombay housewife who was intro-duced to Pillsbury by a friend who works and so has less time to cook.

Responding to consumers' biggest con-cern, Pillsbury pitches the flour with a promise that rotis made from it will stay soft "for six hours." Jigna Shah of Bombay, who makes 60 rotis a day and has tried rival pack-aged brands, is sold. She uses Pillsbury Chakki Fresh Atta to make rotis for her hus-band's lunch box "that don't dry up around the edges or get rigid."

The company declines to say what ingredi-ents keep the flour tasting fresh, though it says there are no artificial preservatives. The pack-aging is made of a robust plastic laminate that

Doughboy *does New Delhi, hoisting a roti*

costs about two and a half times as much as the paper wrappers typical in the U.S.

It's too early to declare the Doughboy's foray into India a success. The market is still minuscule, and gains will depend largely on how quickly Indian housewives embrace convenience. Several local companies famil-iar with Indian tastes have launched branded flour in recent years, only to flounder.

The value of the packaged-flour market in India is $7.14 million. It has expanded by about 45% a year since 1997, according to industry estimates, even though flour made the traditional way costs about 30% less.

To undermine its U.S. rival, Unilever has offered freebies to consumers, such as a free one-kilogram packet of flour with every five-kilogram packet, and a free sample of Surf detergent with every flour pack. Pillsbury has fought back with such promotions as a free sample of sunflower oil with every five-kilogram package of flour. It has also been paying grocers to display a standing card-board Doughboy with its product in a visible spot in shops. That's a novelty in this market, where most people buy their staples at small, crammed grocers, which have no room for promotional displays.

Unilever, which went nationwide in Janu-ary 1998, predicts that its sales by volume will double this year to about 100,000 tons. Pillsbury anticipates production of about 50,000 tons in 1999. That's only a drop in the bucket, given that 30 million tons of wheat are consumed as rotis each year.

AN EAGLE EYE ON CUSTOMERS

When Mary Aehlich gave up her career as a weapons controller in an Air Force AWACS spy plane to become casino administrator at The Venetian resort in Las Vegas, she joked that she went from "combat boots and flight suits to sequins and high heels." But now the stay-at-home mom of two babies is again on the front lines, of sorts. As an occasional at-home Web site tester, she's part of an early warning system for e-tailers—helping them figure out what works and what doesn't in the uncharted world of Web commerce.

Take Aehlich's December sortie onto the jewelry site Miadora.com. Following a script prepared by the market research software company Vividence Corp., she shopped for a xen bracelet, a Jordan Schlanger necklace, and a round diamond. Although she enjoyed the site, it was difficult to locate some items. She said as much in an online critique she typed as she worked her way through the exercise. Feedback like hers from 200 testers was priceless for David A. Lamond, Miadora.com's vice-president for business development. Within two days of getting Vividence's report, he ordered changes to make the site easier to navigate. "This is as close as you can get to reading the mind of your customer," he says.

Vividence's product is just one example of a vast array of new software products that are designed to help companies read customers' minds and win them over—whether in cyberspace or on Main Street. The latest advances in software technology make it possible for companies to amass detailed profiles of customers, offer them just the things they're likely to buy, reward them for loyalty, and quell their frustrations. And, thanks to the Web, companies can keep all of their information about customers in a single electronic storehouse, easily accessible through Web browsers for executives at headquarters, salespeople on the road, and service reps in remote call centers. It's all about delivering TLC—Internet style. "Everybody is scrambling to grab the customer and not let them go," says David Caruso, a vice-president at market researcher AMR Research.

It's a mad dash that's creating a vast new software category: call it customer management software. Included is the Old World of so-called customer relationship management software—giant packages such as Siebel Systems Inc.'s program that lets corporate sales forces track their customers and analyze markets. That's now merging with new programs for the Web that manage everything

from online sales to customer service. The whole shebang is expected to grow from $4.45 billion last year to $21.8 billion in 2003, according to AMR—a growth rate nearly five times that of the overall software market.

WANTED WIDGETS. Why are companies opening their wallets so fast? The technology promises to transform the way they do business. Gone are the days when they could afford to build products without knowing for sure if customers would snap them up. Now they can learn precisely what their customers want before they design a single widget. Manufacturers can even let buyers specify the key features they would like before a product is assembled. And by using technology to track their every encounter with a customer, companies can easily separate out the best from the bad—and focus their marketing muscle on customers who are likely to buy often and pay their bills on time.

The new software already is delivering cash rewards to its early adopters. For starters, it cuts costs: A self-service package tracking system for customers that IBM built for United Parcel Service Inc. saves the shipping company $450,000 a day in customer service expenses. And this stuff boosts revenues, too: Thanks to call-center software

A GUIDE TO CUSTOMER MANAGEMENT SOFTWARE

SALES-FORCE AUTOMATION
Field sales representatives can track accounts and prospects—plus check goals and inventories—from the office PC or a notebook computer on the road. At the same time, their bosses can keep tabs on their performance. New Net-only versions allow individuals and small teams to handle accounts from Web sites for $50 a month or less.

CALL-CENTER AUTOMATION
Creates customer profiles and provides scripts to help service representatives solve customers' problems or suggest new purchases. The latest versions allow companies to coordinate phone calls and messages on Web sites—plus reps can carry on phone conversations with customers while seeing the Web pages the customers are looking at.

MARKETING AUTOMATION
Helps marketers analyze customer purchasing histories and demographics and design targeted marketing campaigns—then measures results.

WEB SALES AND PERSONALIZATION
Basic e-commerce software manages product catalogs, shopping carts, and credit-card purchases. New features allow repeat customers to keep shopping lists on the Web and quickly resubmit orders. Web shops can create special, on-the-fly prices for specific customers.

WEB CONFIGURATOR
Walks consumers through the process of ordering complex custom-assembled products like computers, and, in the future,

cars. It's even more important for business-to-business transactions. A retailer that brands refrigerators or stoves made by others can specify the features they want.

WEB SERVICE
Self-service packages and e-mail limit the need for live customer service representatives. New artificial intelligence features suggest solutions for problems to customers or service reps.

WEB ANALYSIS AND MARKETING
Warehouses of digital data allow Web sites to track the online activities of individual shoppers and offer them merchandise they're likely to buy based on past behavior. It also enables targeted marketing of individuals via e-mail.

*The Davids and Goliaths of Customer
Software Square Off*

The Goliaths

SIEBEL SYSTEMS INC.

MARKET CAP: $19.4 billion.

REVENUES IN THE MOST RECENT QUARTER: $268 million, up 109%.

NET INCOME: $45 million, up 127%.

WHAT THEY SELL: Software for managing field sales; telesales and marketing departments in large corporations.

STRATEGY: To beef up offerings for Web site sales and service and to provide companies with a single view of their customers on computer screens no matter how they buy—on the Web, or off.

COMPETITIVE POSITION: The leader in the traditional corporate customer relationship management market, it's becoming a force to reckon with in e-business, too.

ORACLE CORP.

MARKET CAP: $170.3 billion.

REVENUES IN THE MOST RECENT QUARTER: $2.32 billion, up 13%. Customer relationship software sales totaled $49 million, up 300%.

NET INCOME: $384 million, up 40%.

WHAT THEY SELL: Products for customer relationship management and e-commerce are relatively recent add-ons for a company whose core products are databases.

STRATEGY: To offer large organizations one-stop-shopping for their key pieces of software that can be integrated with one another.

COMPETITIVE POSITION: Oracle's databases power the top 10 consumer e-commerce sites, so it's in a strong spot to hawk software for Web sales and online service.

NORTEL NETWORKS CORP.

MARKET CAP: $161.6 billion.

REVENUES IN THE MOST RECENT QUARTER: $6.99 billion, up 21%.

NET INCOME: $755 million, up 53%.

WHAT THEY SELL: Telecommunications gear, and, because of a pending $2.1 billion acquisition of Clarify, a suite of customer management software. Clarify revenues were $71.6 last quarter.

STRATEGY: To combine the Clarify products with its software for call-center routing.

COMPETITIVE POSITION: Clarify is the strongest of Siebel's traditional competitors. If the potential synergies with Nortel pay off, it could dominate the call-center software business—and be a strong contender in other markets.

(continued)

competitors in this new land grab: software giants SAP and Oracle Corp. Even Nortel Networks Corp., the maker of telecom gear, wants in on the action. It's about to close a $2.1 billion acquisition of Clarify, the call-center software maker.

While the giants duke it out, hundreds of small fry are cooking up new products for everything from personalizing online sales pitches to customer service software for the Web. Some have solid traction, such as Vignette Corp. and BroadVision Inc., which are each logging more than $40 million in revenues per quarter for Web site sales software. Many are minuscule—such as Salesforce.com in San Francisco, which just launched its Web-only sales-management site. But even some of the little guys already loom large on Wall Street. Kana Communications Inc., a seller of e-mail systems for customer support, has watched its stock soar from $45 a share at its initial public offering last September to about $240 today—giving it a market cap of $6.9 billion.

Ultimately, expect only a handful of players to claim the lion's share of this market. Siebel and Oracle look like big winners. They already have relationships with thousands of large customers and offer a broad array of software packages. Up-and-comers such as Vignette, BroadVision, and Kana stand a good chance of succeeding, too. They lead in their segments and are rapidly broadening their product portfolios.

With hundreds of others vying for this new software prize, consolidation is a sure bet. Those that survive are apt to be the players that put together the most compelling soup-to-nuts packages. They'll either develop products themselves or buy up smaller competitors—often with stock. It's already happening. On Feb. 7, Kana announced a $4.2 billion purchase of Silknet Software Inc., a maker of self-help software for Web sites. "The companies with the biggest market caps will be the winners," predicts Kevin Harvey, a partner at Silicon Valley venture-capital firm Benchmark Capital.

Some large corporations are already demanding one-stop shopping for customer management software. Honeywell International, for instance, aims to revamp totally the way it does business. Rather than making products and then finding out later if customers will buy them, it's using a software package from Siebel Systems to anticipate more accurately what its customers will want. Honeywell's $5.2 billion air-transport business, which makes jet engines and avionics gear, uses Siebel to track all of its interactions with customers and publishes monthly analyses so executives can quickly spot problems and opportunities. One early result: It noticed that airlines were frustrated with managing parts inventories, so it's rolling out new services that will spare them that headache. "Our focus used to be from the inside out. Now it's the reverse," says division General Manager Lynn Brubaker.

from Clarify Inc., Automatic Data Processing Inc. handed 8,000 customer service reps detailed information about its 80,000 payroll clients—improving the customer retention rate by 5% and upping revenues by $100 million last year. Based on its surveys of six industries, Andersen Consulting estimates that with just a modest 10% improvement in customer management operations, a $1 billion business can reap $40 million to $50 million

a year in pretax profits.

With customers lining up to do business, hundreds of software companies are busy staking claims. Some are well-established players in the customer software arena, such as Siebel, with revenues of $790 million and a 19% market share of the $3.7 billion market for corporate sales and marketing software. But as big as it is in its own market, Siebel has to watch out for even brawnier

(Cont.)

The software giants have taken the lead in assembling packages capable of handling huge jobs such as Honeywell's. Siebel has spent the past two years adding call-center and Web commerce components to its sales-force management software. The newest pieces delivered last year include a package for setting up Web shops and an e-mail marketing product. The empire-building effort is paying off big time: Siebel just landed a deal worth tens of millions of dollars to supply IBM with practically its entire suite of products for 55,000 IBM sales and marketing employees to use internally.

Oracle and SAP are going further. They're packaging customer software with their suites for managing finances, employees, logistics, and manufacturing. Their pitch: While companies must attach Siebel's suite to the rest of their computing systems manually, Oracle's and SAP's pieces come ready-mixed.

It's not just established companies that want the kind of end-to-end package that Oracle and SAP offer. Many Web upstarts have similar needs. Consider Streamline.com in Westwood, Mass., which sells groceries and household items online and delivers them in Boston and Chicago. "We're really a logistics organization. We've got warehouses and trucks. We're focused on operations," says John Cagno, vice-president for information technology. That's why he bought a suite of software from SAP that includes customer, finance, and logistics software all linked together. When the new system rolls out in March, Streamline.com's customers will be able to chose from its actual inventory, so there's no risk of their picking out-of-stock items and being disappointed with substitutions. The goal: improve customer loyalty and cut down on service calls.

Now, companies want a way to view all customer information in one place. Often companies keep multiple databases for each business and each way of reaching customers—and those repositories aren't easily synced up. This new generation of software offers a way to gather information collected by companies' Web sites, direct-mail operations, customer service, retail stores, and field sales. H&R Block Inc., for instance, is using software from Clarify to combine and coordinate the customer records at its tax offices, discount brokerage, Web site, and customer-service center. Armed with that central storehouse of information, sales people in the stock-trading business, for instance, can look at detailed descriptions of tax customers and size up which of them would be good prospects.

Not every company wants software that will handle the whole enchilada of customer needs. Many—especially dot-coms—shop for single pieces of software that solve problems or boost revenues in a matter of weeks. They shun complex packages that can take months or even years to install. Vignette, for instance, has grown fast because its software allows Web sites to generate pages on the fly that are custom-made for individuals. Web site operators can analyze customers' online behavior and pitch them products that are likely to pique their interest. And the software is relatively easy to get going. Thanks in part to Vignette, Iwon.com, the four-month-old Web sweepstakes portal, was able to launch in just 4 1/2 months.

The more narrowly focused the software, the easier it is for companies to see results. Using Silknet's new virtual sales assistant, for instance, online computer retailer cozone.com created "Jill—the Notebook Advisor." It's a piece of software that walks customers through a series of questions about their lifestyles and what they're looking for in a computer—then makes recommendations. Cozone.com gathers a vast amount of data from cybershoppers and can use it later to target them with e-mail promotions. But mostly, "Jill" is about making customers feel good about their experience so they come back for more.

Often, customers want software to bridge the Web and other businesses. Williams-Sonoma Inc. for instance, uses e-mail soft-

HOW MARRIOTT NEVER FORGETS A GUEST

When retiree Ben B. Ussery Jr. goes on vacation, he typically spends hours beforehand nailing down golf dates, scouting shops for his wife, and making restaurant reservations. But last year, when the Usserys and another Richmond (Va.) couple chose to spend a week at Marriott's Desert Springs resort in Palm Desert, Calif., he let the hotel do the legwork. Weeks in advance, Marriott planning coordinator Jennifer Rodas called Ussery to ask what he wanted to do. When all was set, she faxed him an itinerary. She had even ordered flowers for his wife. "Marriott made it a real smooth experience," says Ussery. "I'm ready to go back."

What makes such velvet-glove treatment possible is Marriott International Inc.'s use of customer management software from Siebel Systems Inc. The hotel chain, based in Bethesda, Md., is counting on such technology to gain an edge with guests, event planners, and hotel owners. The software lets Marriott pull together information about its customers from different departments, so that its reps can anticipate and respond more quickly to their needs. It starts with reservations. Says Chairman J. W. Marriott Jr.: "It's a big competitive advantage to be able to greet a customer with: 'Mr. Jones, welcome back to Marriott. We know you like a king-size bed. We know you need a rental car.'"

Mariott, America's No. 1 hotel chain, is the industry leader in using technology to pamper customers. The company, which manages 1,850 hotels and resorts worldwide, began installing Siebel software in late 1998 and is spending just under $10 million for the initial pieces. A few other hotel chains are dabbling in customer-info systems, but Marriott is ahead of the pack, says analyst Bryan A. Mayer of Credit Lyonnais Securities. "It's a huge advantage," he says.

The biggest boost from the Siebel software is in the hotel chain's sales operations. Marriott is transforming its sales teams from order-takers for specific hotels to aggressive marketers of all Marriot properties. A sales person in Dallas—who understands both the needs of his local customers and the chain's world inventory of hotel rooms and other facilities—can now pitch and book orders for hotels in Hawaii or China.

NO HASSLES. Early results are promising. In 1998, the sales-force software helped Marriott generate an additional $55 million in cross-chain sales. Anecdotal evidence also suggests there has been a jump in bookings from event planners, who find it easier to give business to Marriott, which has their needs on file, than put it out for bid.

Eliminating hassles for guests is the appeal of Marriott's free personal-planning service, too. It's now available at seven resorts, but Marriott aims to extend it to all 32 resorts by 2001. The software tracks guest preferences, so personal planners can anticipate amenities that repeat guests may want. "Our spa is very popular," says Doug Mings, personal planning supervisor at Marriott's deluxe Camelback Inn in Scottsdale, Ariz. "If you don't plan ahead, sometimes you don't get in."

The service also gives Marriott reps an opening to pitch hot-air balloon rides and other fee-generating activities. Happy customers, fatter sales: With that kind of advantage, no wonder other hotel chains, such as Hilton Hotels Corp., are starting to follow Marriott's technology lead.

By Amy Borrus in Washington

ware from Kana to cross-promote its Web site, mail-order businesses, and Williams-Sonoma and Pottery Barn retail stores. Patrick Connolly, general manager of the company's direct-marketing businesses, says he wants to avoid simply transferring sales from stores to the Web site. He can use e-mail addresses collected at stores and on Web sites to send targeted promotions. He recently sent e-mail to shoppers at the company's outlet stores inviting them to come back for 15% discounts. The response rate was 12%—far above the typical 1% response to e-mail solicitations.

BIGGER FASTER. In spite of victories like these, the upstarts can see the writing on the wall. They've got to broaden their portfolios of products if they hope to cement relationships with customers—and compete with the bigs. Even before the Silknet deal, Kana began taking advantage of its outsized market cap by buying NetDialog, for Web self-service software; Business Evolution Inc., for real-time e-mail and chat; and Connectify Inc., for e-mail marketing. "We have to get big fast so when Siebel does come, we're ready for them," says Kana CEO Michael McCloskey.

What could derail the industry giants? The Net is a wild card. All of the major players have converted their applications so they can be accessed via Web browsers. But the newer software companies that built their products from the ground up with Web delivery in mind can offer faster service over the Internet. That could become crucial if corporations and dot-coms opt for the convenience of having applications delivered over the Net by hosting companies. Siebel Systems Chairman Thomas Siebel is convinced that will be only a small part of the market. "None of my customers are asking for it," because they want to control their own technology, he says dismissively.

He better not get too smug. The competitive landscape could change radically in the next couple of years. Siebel charges premium prices for its software—often hundreds of thousands of dollars per sale. Already, competitors such as SalesLogix Corp., a five-year-old company in Phoenix, offer many of the same capabilities for much less. Del Webb Corp., the Phoenix housing developer, bought SalesLogix software to coordinate the activities of 700 salespeople and paid just $600 for each user, vs. the $2,000 that Siebel would have charged. "The big companies haven't rebelled yet, but I believe they will," says SalesLogix CEO Patrick Sullivan.

Siebel and the other high-priced big shots won't have a lock on the ability to give corporations a comprehensive view of their customers, either. The California State Auto Assn. is doing that with a comparatively cheap $1 million purchase from E.piphany Inc., a maker of market-analysis software in San Mateo, Calif. CSAA uses the upstart's software to extract customer information from separate databases controlled by its travel agency, emergency roadside service, insurance business, and Web site. That gives it the capacity to size up customers and give each one a "lifetime value score"—singling out the best customers for special treatment. "It's been a revelation," says Alexandra Morehouse, the association's corporate marketing officer.

Make that an epiphany. If more people have stirring experiences like Morehouse, there could be a revolution in the works for the customer-management software business.

By Steve Hamm in New York, with Robert D. Hof in San Mateo, Calif.

(Cont.)

SALESFORCE.COM: AN ANT AT THE PICNIC

There was a time when Marc K. Benioff could call Thomas M. Siebel and set up lunch. After all, the pair cut their teeth together during the early go-go days at software giant Oracle Corp. These days, though, Siebel won't return Benioff's calls. It may have something to do with the mission of Benioff's San Francisco startup, Salesforce.com Inc., which was officially launched on Feb. 7. "Our objective is to put Siebel Systems out of business," Benioff says flatly.

Never mind that Benioff, 35, was an initial backer of Siebel Systems Inc., the king of software for making salespeople more productive, and that he has pocketed more than $20 million from that 1993 investment. He revels in the thought that Salesforce.com can use the Web to undermine the classic business model that generated $790 million in sales for Siebel last year. Benioff, chairman of Salesforce.com, expects the Internet to change the way salespeople track customers. Right now, his Web site does only a fraction of what Siebel's software can do. But in the future, he believes, instead of buying expensive packages of software, even large companies will pay monthly fees to get what they need from Web sites like his.

With Salesforce.com, Benioff has made a first stab at fulfilling that vision. It's a handy tool for individual salespeople or small groups. For just $50 a month, users click on tabs to move quickly from their contact list to account information to sales leads.

The Web site's simplicity is appealing to customers such as Robert G. Muscat. As head of business development for W.L. Gore & Associates' Industrial Dry Filtration unit, Muscat initially considered Siebel software to link his 15 sales reps. But it would have cost him close to $60,000 to buy and install. "You're talking some big bucks here," Muscat says.

At this point, Salesforce.com is nothing more than an ant at Siebel's picnic. With 150 customers to Siebel's 1,000, it can hardly be considered a threat yet. "Web applications are a compelling story for small startups. But for big companies like General Motors and Microsoft—no way," says David Schmaier, Siebel's senior vice-president for products. To be sure, Salesforce.com isn't for big corporate customers that want all of Siebel's market-analysis features.

SHARED NICHE. Even for small sales operations, Salesforce.com has its shortcomings. Its greatest advantage—being a Web site—could also be its greatest drawback. For sales reps who travel, finding Web connections can be even more difficult than finding a good cup of coffee. "It's not an acceptable solution," Forrester Research Inc. analyst Bob Chatham says of Salesforce.com. He thinks this technology makes sense mainly for small stationary sales forces.

Salesforce.com doesn't have this niche to itself, either. Upshot.com Inc. and SalesLogix Corp. have developed sales-management Web sites. And Siebel is getting into the action too—recently spinning off its Sales.com Web site, which offers some of the features of its core sales-management software.

But Salesforce.com's backers don't seem worried. The company is about to close another round of financing that will bring its total funding to $52 million and value it at $350 million. And Benioff expects to go public this year. If that happens, his $20 million Siebel windfall could seem like pocket change.

By Jay Greene in San Francisco

Evaluating Opportunities
in the Changing Marketing
Environment

Inside Sony, a Clash Over Web Music

Japanese Giant Faced Discord Between Its Record Label And Its Electronics Group

By ROBERT A. GUTH

Staff Reporter of THE WALL STREET JOURNAL

TOKYO — In the global race to market music on the Web, Sony Corp. has had an unusual rival: Sony.

As both an electronics company and a top record label, Sony wants to capitalize on any musical revolution online, making the latest in listening gadgets for it — just as it has done before, with everything from the Walkman to compact disks.

But the Japanese giant has also had to referee a potential conflict with its own music label — whose artists include Fiona Apple, Celine Dion and Savage Garden — which fears losing out to illegal copying.

For more than a year, it's been a management challenge to push a single strategy through a music house divided. The differences erupted publicly as the two sides argued at industry meetings — even after one of the sons of Sony founder Akio Morita was called in to smooth out organizational differences.

But Sony's campaign to balance their sometimes conflicting interests is beginning to pay off: Sony Music Entertainment (Japan) Inc. last month started selling songs online. Called "bitmusic," the Japanese service will be followed in coming months by a similar service from its sister company in the U.S.

It is Sony's first fully orchestrated effort to cash in on all aspects of the burgeoning Internet music business, from the music itself, to the copyright technologies protecting it, to the devices for playing it. Sony, whose divisions have excelled through autonomy, is the only major company trying to do it all.

To get here, Sony executives have invested in more than a dozen music-related Internet companies, signed technology agreements with Microsoft Corp. and Web-music pioneers such as Liquid Audio and Real-Networks Inc., and rolled out copyright-protection technologies for online music.

For years, Sony and competing labels had been cooking up online music-distribution

schemes in-house. But most were caught off guard by the rapid rise last year of music piracy on the Web. Now they're rapidly laying the necessary technology foundation so that over the next year they can expand their services selling tunes directly over the Internet. Adding to the urgency: America Online Inc.'s plans to merge with Time Warner Inc., which this week unveiled plans to build a music giant by hooking up with EMI Group PLC. Other music companies are hurtling toward selling tunes online, as well.

Sony's race to the Internet started at the foot of Japan's Mt. Fuji in September 1998. At an annual world-wide management retreat there, top Sony officials held their first serious debate over what role digital networks like the Internet would play in Sony's future.

Sony's labs were already brimming with technology and devices for downloading digital music and playing it back. The company's hardware side, the spiritual progeny of the late Sony founder Mr. Morita, was eager for a chance to unveil their work.

But the hardware loyalists learned a lesson from the company's attempt in 1991 to market a high-end digital tape recorder. Record companies feared it would be used by music pirates — and they banded together to quash the product.

"That is embedded in everybody's heart here," says one Sony official. "We didn't want to repeat that mistake."

Sony's own record companies in Japan and the U.S. had been planning trials of online music, but thought sales of music over the Internet to portable devices was still some ways off. One crucial voice was Mr. Morita's second son Masao, who was at the retreat. A 45-year-old who spends his days escorting Sony acts such as Aerosmith and Mariah Carey around Tokyo, Mr. Morita is head of Sony Music Entertainment Japan's interna-

tional business. Having spent most of his career on the electronics side, he saw the long-term potential of the Internet but argued at the retreat that it could smash Sony's music business if mishandled.

The reason: music downloaded from the

Sony just began selling tunes online in Japan. Next stop: the U.S.

Internet is easy to pirate and hard to charge for. Record labels needed more time, he and other Sony music officials at the retreat explained, to figure out how to charge for music online and prevent illegal copies from swamping the market. In the end, everyone agreed that a trial with other major record labels the following year would be a safe first step. "People didn't want to go too fast," says Mr. Morita. "It could have had a lot of repercussions."

Within months, however, the listening habits of American teens were changing fast, making Sony's cautious approach perilous. In the U.S., college dormitories and high schoolers' bedrooms had become hotbeds for a technology revolution called MP3, a type of computer software that made downloading music from the Internet easy. The format offered no copyright protection and rapidly became a standard for music pirates posting tunes on the Net for free.

The format also sparked a new market for portable players that store MP3 tunes on memory chips so they can be listened to on the go — just like prototypes Sony had in its labs. Led by Diamond Multimedia, an army of little-known hardware companies from the U.S. and South Korea seized the opportunity and rolled out the MP3 players starting in late 1998.

Rattled, the Recording Industry Association of America, an industry group for major record labels including Sony, moved to halt shipments of Diamond's MP3 player through a court order.

When that failed in late 1998, Tommy Mottola, the chairman of Sony Music Entertainment in the U.S., joined in on an announcement in New York of an industry initiative to settle the piracy problem. The RIAA-led group invited hardware and software makers to propose a single specification for protecting music downloads from illegal copying. It vowed to complete the work in time for that year's Christmas buying season.

Sony's race to the Net was on. Starting in January, Sony's hardware specialists fanned out around the world to make sure their soft-

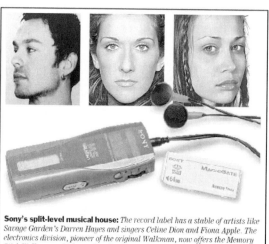

Sony's split-level musical house: *The record label has a stable of artists like Savage Garden's Darren Hayes and singers Celine Dion and Fiona Apple. The electronics division, pioneer of the original Walkman, now offers the Memory Stick Walkman, which can download music from the Web.*

(Cont.)

ware and devices were compatible with an array of programs that protect and allow for the downloading of music.

In February, Mr. Morita was sitting in his office in the piano-shaped Sony Music building in Tokyo when he got a call from company president Nobuyuki Idei. Mr. Idei wanted him to represent the music business on a company-wide committee he was setting up to hash out the issues online music was raising throughout Sony. Mr. Morita then started regular trips to Sony Music Entertainment in New York to help coordinate efforts between the U.S. and Japan.

Meanwhile, Sony's music and electronics divisions publicly faced off at regular meetings of the RIAA forum. In March, at a meeting near Washington, the portable-device makers, including Sony, argued for adding functions like digital recording to their players. But the record companies, including Sony, argued that such features would only enable piracy.

In April, at the launch of a high-end CD player that Mr. Idei himself had started into development eight years earlier, the Sony chief underscored just how willing he was to spotlight Sony's future on the Internet. At the Blue Note jazz club in Tokyo, after a half-hour of live music by Tito Puente and his Latin All Stars, Mr. Idei unveiled the Super Audio CD.

But as he drew to a close, instead of highlighting the shining CD player, he surprised Sony officials when he pulled out a tiny, purple device that could store music from the Internet. "With this we want to introduce . . . what you might want to call a Netman," he hinted to the crowd.

By November, Sony would showcase the device, formally called the Memory Stick Walkman, at a major computer industry show in Las Vegas. There, Sony also announced another portable player, the Vaio Music Clip,

---

Last March, at an industry forum, Sony's music and electronics divisions squared off on whether to include digital recording functions in players

---

and a string of agreements with technology companies so that Sony devices could work with a range of software for protecting and managing music online.

But as the crucial Christmas season approached, it was clear many pieces weren't in place. The RIAA initiative, for one, was bogged down by infighting over a copyright

technology. The issue wasn't settled until November, by which time most major record companies — including Sony Music in the U.S. — had decided to delay the launch of full-blown music download services.

In the U.S., Sony officials say they didn't want to start online music sales until portable music devices with built-in piracy protections came out. Al Smith, senior vice president of Sony Music Entertainment, says these digital players are scheduled to begin appearing on the market here in a few months, with a device from Sony Electronics due out this month or next.

Back in Japan, Mr. Morita didn't want to wait. He wanted his product ready in Japan for the holiday season. Days after the copyright-technology fight was settled, he dispatched one of his staff to Boston carrying a hard-drive loaded with 44 songs. There, Aris Technology installed the protection into each track. By Christmas, Sony Music Japan was selling music on the Internet for 350 yen ($3.30) a tune.

Martin Peers contributed to this article.

Net effects

Why e-commerce makes UPS a complete package, but not FDX.

Will FDX and UPS deliver the goods to your portfolio? Wall Street thinks so and has been pushing both stocks as backdoor Internet plays. Buy one of the shipping giants and get a piece of the e-commerce boom without astronomical prices or the risks of an untested start-up. As good as gold—or fool's gold? Shares of UPS, priced at $50 when the company went public in November, quickly soared to $74 and have held most of their first-day gain. FDX is a different story. After reaching a 52-week high of 61⅛ last May, the Federal Express parent plunged to 34¾ when investors decided UPS was better equipped to rule online shipping. More than $10 billion abandoned FDX—much of it heading to Big Brown.

But now things look overdone. UPS is trading at 44 times earnings, unprecedented for a shipping stock. And FDX, at 22 times looks like a remnant from Filene's Basement. "Anyone who says there can be only one winner is an idiot," says Jeffrey Kauffman, an analyst at Merrill Lynch. There's no question that both UPS and FDX will be busier because of online retail and business-to-business deliveries. UPS already handles 55% of the merchandise sold online, while FDX is repositioning itself to increase its 10% share. A year ago Barron's called FDX the "cheapest Internet stock"; today it isn't just cheap, it's unwanted. Meanwhile, UPS is trading above the most bullish expectations. Should UPS, which doesn't have a record for dealing with shareholders, really be priced like a dot-com? Should FDX, until recently the most innovative shipping company, be left on the loading dock?

Even without the dot-com bonus, UPS is a powerhouse. It earned about $2.3 billion last year on estimated sales of $27.2 billion. It has billions in cash to pay for acquisitions that could deepen its reach into Europe and Asia, where analysts see potential gains that dwarf those of e-commerce back home. Profits are expected to grow 13% this year, to $2.6 billion. FDX is no cream puff either. It earned $631 million last year on $17.5 billion in sales. Despite a 6% decline in profits last quarter because of higher jet fuel prices, FDX has a strong outlook, particularly with trade barriers falling in Asia and a recent fuel surcharge providing a buffer from higher prices. Profits are expected to be $659 million this year, on sales of $18 billion.

Based on market and financial leadership, analysts say UPS should trade at a 30% to 40% premium to FDX. The fact that the premium is 100% has spooked some. Rich Crable at Loomis Sayles bought UPS at the offering, then sold when it sprinted up like a no-name dot-com. He had earlier sold FDX near its high because it, too, was overpriced. Says Crable of UPS: "At $50 a share, UPS would have a substantial premium over FDX."

Even in a wired world, transporters can't escape the economy. Unlike dot-com stocks that soar in a universe disconnected from traditional valuation methods, the fortunes of FDX and UPS still turn on such old-economy events as rising fuel prices, interest rates, and business sentiment. E-commerce may give the shippers a broader base of customers, but those customers won't be placing as many orders if Federal Reserve rate hikes slow the economy.

The bottom line: If you're an investor with a five-year horizon, UPS on a 10% pullback would look ripe. It is fast becoming a must-own blue chip. If trading is your thing, battered FDX oozes opportunity. One or two quarters that top estimates could help it win back fans who left for Big Brown. Just don't expect that to happen by 10 A.M. tomorrow.

—David Rynecki

---

that ship lots of packages have learned they can profit from widespread public misconceptions that FedEx is quicker and more reliable than UPS. Although both companies charge shippers similar prices for similar services, many consumers willingly pay a few dollars more to get something via FedEx. "We love it when customers ask us to ship on Federal Express," says an executive at one New Jersey company. "We can charge more, even though our cost is about the same." His company, naturally, pockets the difference.

FedEx deliberately pursues that tony image, says Tompkins. "It sponsors golf tournaments and even had the Orange Bowl renamed the FedEx Orange Bowl. You wouldn't see UPS do that in a million years. There's far less pizzazz in UPS's marketing." The different histories of the two companies help explain why. FedEx was founded by Smith, a Yale graduate with a background in economics. At UPS, on the other hand, virtually every executive—including CEO Kelly—began by driving a truck. "The UPS guys get ahead by scrambling all the time," says Tompkins. "They get promoted and hustle like mad and yell at the drivers to make their section profitable and get their

bonus. They don't care about image. They're tough. Their attitude is, 'Whaddaya mean, I can't drive through that brick wall?'"

Even as the two companies invade each other's turf, they have different visions of where the package delivery business is going and where they want to be. United Parcel is eager to capture the traffic to homes that the Internet will generate. Federal Express thinks the Internet will drive demand for high-end shipping services for corporations; it is intent on capturing that so-called supply-chain management.

Although both companies claim to be capable of matching any service the other provides, United Parcel clearly has a leg up on FedEx in delivering to homes. According to Forrester Research, a Cambridge, Mass., consulting firm, UPS delivered 55% of the items ordered over the Web and shipped to homes during Christmas a year ago; it estimates UPS handled at least that proportion during Christmas 1999. The U.S. Postal Service made about 30% of e-tail deliveries. FedEx, with its less-developed ground-based system, handled about 10%. "United Parcel is much more focused on the movement of goods from busi-

ness to consumer," says Stacie McCullough, a Forrester analyst. "That's not a big part of their overall business now [about 80% of UPS's deliveries are business to business]. But deliveries to consumers are expected to grow exponentially in the next few years."

The value of goods ordered over the Net and shipped to homes was a fairly modest $20 billion in 1999, about 1% of traditional retail sales, says McCullough. That is expected to rise to $180 billion by 2004. During the same time, McCullough predicts, the volume of homeward-bound parcels should rise from three million to eight million a day.

Delivering to homes is less profitable than delivering to businesses because homes are more scattered. (UPS charges an extra dollar for residential delivery to help cover the additional cost.) But margins should rise as the Internet boosts the flow of boxes to apartments and suburbs. "Business-to-residential adds to profit," says Michael Eskew, UPS's senior vice president for planning. "It fills in the network. The delivery person can do air express in the early morning, business deliveries in the late morning, and residential in the afternoon. Density and scale are a big part of this."

> ### Number of employees
> ### UPS: 326,000 vs. FedEx: 141,000

The looming rival to UPS in the home-delivery business is more likely to be the U.S. Postal Service than Federal Express. The merry mailmen are not much of a threat now, because the post office lacks the sophisticated computer systems that would enable it and its customers to track packages. Customers of both UPS and FedEx can check the status of shipments themselves on the Internet to learn exactly when a package was received and who signed for it. The post office has hired Lockheed Martin to devise just such a tracking system, which should be ready in about two years. Tompkins, who has seen it, says he is impressed: "It will be as good or better than what UPS and FedEx have now."

Because the post office already delivers letters to virtually every address in the country, the added cost of packages will be low. FedEx and UPS executives rail at the intrusion of the post office, noting that it can subsidize its package delivery operations with money from its monopoly on mail and that the post office doesn't even pay taxes. Most galling, federal law requires FedEx and UPS to set their package list prices twice as high as those of the post office. Tompkins predicts that the post office's share of Internet-driven package deliveries to homes will rise from about 30% now to 50% in a few years.

Over the long term, FedEx is placing its biggest bets on the build-to-order revolution under way in manufacturing, epitomized by Dell Computer. Dell doesn't build a zillion identical computers, flood them out to retailers, and hope you like what you see. It waits until it has your custom order (and your money), then orders components from suppliers and assembles the parts. Some components, like the monitor or speakers, may be sent directly from the supplier to your home (never passing through Dell) and arrive on your doorstep at the same time as everything else.

That may sound like old news. "Just in time" inventory and delivery systems were popularized by the Japanese in the 1970s and adopted by Western corporations in the 1980s. But they required private data networks that were expensive and difficult to use. Even the automakers got only about 20% of their suppliers to connect to their systems. The Internet, vastly cheaper and easier to use, promises to make it possible for a small widget maker in Sri Lanka to receive an order and ship parts to an assembly plant in San Jose or even directly to a customer. Because transportation and warehousing account for about 10% of the price of all goods, cutting costs with sophisticated Internet-based logistics and supply-chain management tools has become a minor obsession for many corporations.

Both FedEx and UPS have seen the opportunities here. Both are working to tie their tracking systems to warehouse and inventory software from the likes of Oracle, SAP, and People-Soft. Both do sophisticated warehousing for hundreds of big and small companies; UPS boxes and ships sneakers for Nike, while FedEx does the same with computer peripherals for Hewlett-Packard. FedEx, however, seems hungrier. When Cisco Systems wanted a more precisely timed way of delivering routers to customers, it approached both FedEx and UPS. UPS's response was rather ho-hum, says one Cisco executive. "It was: 'Cisco has an itch. Give us a few million and we'll scratch it for you.'" FedEx, by contrast, jumped: "They pulled out their wallets and said they'd do whatever it takes."

The problem for Cisco was that a big client might order 100 routers at a time. (Routers control the flow of information on computer networks.) Some might be shipped from San Jose, others from Mexico, the rest from Asia. Unfortunately for Cisco, customers want all the routers to arrive at the same time. FedEx can easily coordinate shipments when Cisco's factories are running smoothly. But suppose Cisco discovers that a bunch of routers at the San Jose plant have a problem and will be delayed for two days? Meanwhile, the routers made in Asia and Mexico are already on their way to the customer. How does Cisco keep them from arriving ahead of the California routers?

It's not a trivial matter. Items arriving in dribs and drabs cause all sorts of frustration. If the routers from Mexico get to the customer before the ones from California, the guy who signs for them on the receiving dock may think the order is botched. He won't know whether to send along what he's gotten to the tech center or hold everything in storage until the entire order arrives. Maybe the customer has hired a group of technicians to install the routers, but now they're standing around doing nothing because the full shipment isn't in.

In the old days, the way to guarantee coordinated shipments was to keep plenty of routers in a warehouse and put them all on one truck. But Cisco wants to avoid the cost of keeping millions of dollars' worth of routers in inventory. FedEx agreed to install systems for Cisco that would enable the company to accelerate or retard parts of an order on short notice, thus ensuring coordinated deliveries.

One shipping expert familiar with the deal says Cisco was impressed with FedEx's enthusiasm for the proposal: "FedEx told Cisco, 'The way you're looking at this is very much the way we see the world going, and we'd like to develop this product for you.'" He estimates that Fed-Ex will spend $100 million on the project. "It means system changes and ripping up the physical plant and changing how drivers do things," he explains.

All this is just beginning, but if it works, it will make a big difference for Cisco: "It will blow away warehouses. The cost of doing this with warehouses looks like it would be twice the cost of doing it the new way. And it will give Cisco so much flexibility about where it puts its factories around the world."

Whether FedEx will benefit from the improvements as much as Cisco remains to be seen. Certainly FedEx will have many admirers if it can become the brains and brawn of a

> ### 1999 Air express growth rate*
> ### UPS: 9.3% vs. FedEx: 3.6%
>
> *First three quarters

global, Internet-based system that moves and tracks goods around the world with the precision of a master chess player—and that wipes out trillions of dollars in costly inventories. But will this new system pay? Paul Schlesinger, a securities analyst for Donaldson Lufkin Jenrette, has covered FedEx for nearly 20 years. He worries that the company is infatuated with technology at the expense of earnings. "At some point you begin to question if it's such a great company," says Schlesinger. "It's got great morale, great service, and all that. But how great a company can it be when its returns are so poor? FedEx has a tendency to over-engineer. In the basic operations where FedEx does something that UPS doesn't, it's not clear that FedEx makes money."

FedEx officials say they aren't concerned. United Parcel may have taken the early lead in capturing what the Internet has to offer, observes Dennis Jones, the chief information officer at FedEx, "but that's like Russia bragging that it launched Sputnik. Russia didn't put a man on the moon."

You get the sense, though, that UPS isn't chasing the moon right now. It seems content with its wheels on the ground and 12 million boxes a day passing through its trucks. The battle between Big Brown on the ground and FedEx in the air seems certain to get more heated. And it won't be over anytime soon.

20

The Producers:

Extension Cords

Electric utilities, spurred by deregulation, are trying to get into all sorts of new businesses

By J.C. CONKLIN

Ms. Conklin is a Staff Reporter in THE WALL STREET JOURNAL'S *Dallas bureau.*

Electric utilities are zapping new life into their once-staid business.

Having seen telephone and cable-television companies merge into huge monoliths capable of offering multiple services to consumers, power companies are trying their own brand of convergence. Electric utilities are beginning to spread more tentacles into homes — most notably by offering natural-gas service. But they are also experimenting with telephone service and even plumbing, heating and air-conditioning repair.

Since deregulation of utilities began less than four years ago, there has been a frenzy of takeovers of natural-gas companies by electricity outfits. Three years ago, Dallas-based Texas Utilities Co., now renamed **TXU** Corp., bought Enserch Corp., and Houston Industries Inc., now **Reliant Energy** Inc. in Houston, acquired NorAm Energy Corp. In the past few months, **Dominion Resources** Inc., a Richmond, Va., electricity company, said it will buy Pittsburgh-based **Consolidated Natural Gas** Co., and **Scana** Corp., a Columbus, S.C., utility, agreed to acquire **Public Service Co. of North Carolina,** a Gastonia, N.C., natural-gas concern.

Since 1995, there have been 22 acquisitions of natural-gas companies by electric utilities, some pending, with a total value of about $30 billion.

Smoother Ride

For electric utilities, providing natural-gas service helps smooth out the seasonal earnings cycle. Electric companies see earnings rise in the summer with the use of air conditioners and fans, while natural-gas companies see sales surge in the winter with home heating. What's more, the use of natural gas as a power-plant fuel is increasing, giving electric companies more interest in gas providers. Natural gas is projected to make up 33% of all electricity generation by 2020, up from just 15% in 1998, according to the U.S. Energy Information Administration.

For customers, the expansion of services is likely to result in improved service, analysts say. Instead of paying four separate bills each month, a customer may soon be able to write only one check for several services. Though analysts and power companies say merged utilities don't yet offer one-bill bundling, some say they will be able to next year. Also, if something goes wrong with phone service or heating service, there would be one number to call.

With competition likely to increase at the local level, utilities see natural-gas cousins as a way to become more intertwined with consumers, who eventually may find themselves purchasing a host of services from the once-boring electric company.

As deregulation spreads, electric utilities have grown eager to gain toeholds in new territory where they will someday be able to sell electricity. Buying natural-gas companies gives them a foot in the door in unfamiliar areas, making their names known to consumers in advance of deregulation. And it becomes a springboard to offering other services over a wider area.

Scana, in particular, has been aggressively branching out. In Georgia, which deregulated natural gas in October, Scana is expanding its natural-gas offerings, marketing to consumers through retail kiosks and storefronts and offering cash rebates to new gas customers. By mid-April, about 21% of households statewide had switched to Scana from the established gas provider, Atlanta-based **AGL Resources** Inc.'s Atlanta Gas Light Co., according to Scana and Georgia Natural Gas, an affiliate of Atlanta Gas.

And by year end, Scana says it expects to be selling home-security systems, appliance warranties and cellular-phone service at most of its retail outlets.

Vital Services

Conectiv, a Wilmington, Del., company formed through last year's merger of Delmarva Power & Light Co. and Atlantic City Electric Co., started offering heating, air-conditioning and plumbing services in addition to its electricity and natural gas. It has since added phone services and intends to eventually offer customers repair contracts on home heating, air conditioning and plumbing.

"We want to be a vital-services provider," says Howard Cosgrove, Conectiv's chairman and chief executive. "It's an easy jump from electricity to heating to telecommunications."

Conectiv's telephone service, which started a little more than a year ago, has garnered about 60,000 phone lines with 25,000 customers, Mr. Cosgrove says. The telecom unit isn't yet contributing to earnings, but Conectiv expects it will by the end of this year. The power utility projects that telecommunications will contribute as much as 25% of overall earnings in about five years, reaching 500,000 customers.

Conectiv says it offers local service at a price about 10% less than the dominant provider in the area, **Bell Atlantic** Corp.

Ells Edwards, a spokesman for Bell Atlantic, says, "I think it all depends on the package you're looking at. I would say generally some of Conectiv's prices are lower than Bell Atlantic's, but consumers don't choose on price alone." He does say that Conectiv's goal of 500,000 customers is achievable: "Conectiv's very aggressive."

Analysts agree. "Getting that many phone customers is within the realm of possibility," says Ronald S. Tanner, an analyst at Legg Mason Wood Walker in Baltimore.

Utilities say profit margins are higher in services than in their traditional power business. While electricity typically garners margins of 2% to 3%, plumbing delivers 8% to 10% profit margins, and telecommunications ranges from 20% to 40%.

"Electric companies looked at phone companies with all the options they can offer — voice mail, call waiting — to make more

---

'We want to be a vital-services provider,' says one electricity CEO. 'It's an easy jump from electricity to heating to telecommunications.'

---

money, and started to drool," says David M. Schanzer, an analyst at Janney Montgomery Scott Inc. in Philadelphia. "Now, they have their turn."

Unused Cable Lines

Telecommunications is a natural fit, utilities say, because they own more than 40,000 miles of fiber-optic cable, much of it unused up to now, that links power plants with substations and other energy-control points. By renting space on a local telephone company's fiber-optic cables that go directly into the home, utilities can quickly assemble telecommunications networks and provide retail phone service.

Montana Power Co. in Butte, Mont.; TXU; Boston-based **BEC Energy** Co.; and **Potomac Electric Power** Co., the electric utility based in Washington, D.C., are all aggressively pursuing telecommunications businesses.

To be sure, it can be difficult to attract consumers to the raft of services many utilities are trying to float. **UtiliCorp United** Inc., Kansas City, Mo., formed a joint venture in 1997 with **Peco Energy** Co. of Philadelphia and offered a package of services including electricity, natural gas, home-security services and discount long-distance telephone connections to AT&T Corp. in seven Midwestern states.

The idea was to offer customers the convenience of one provider, and eventually one bill to pay, for many services. And once hoped-for national deregulation was completed, the venture would be able to expand into more states and achieve economies of

(Cont.)

scale, which would allow the program to offer significant cost savings to consumers.

But the campaign, known as EnergyOne, was junked last year.

Peco and Utilicorp say the national marketplace wasn't developing as rapidly as the companies had hoped. Al Butkus, vice president of corporate communications for UtiliCorp, says national deregulation still looks to be years away. "In light of that," Mr. Butkus says, "EnergyOne wasn't useful," because it couldn't expand into enough states to make it lucrative for the utilities and cheap for consumers.

"Customers won't switch unless utilities offer significant cost savings," says Mr. Tan-ner of Legg Mason. "UtiliCorp's plan didn't offer a lot of savings."

21

How Big Mac Kept From Becoming a Serb Archenemy

By Robert Block

Staff Reporter of The Wall Street Journal

A tray liner *used when McDonald's restaurants in Yugoslavia reopened on April 17—also the date of the Belgrade marathon. The Cyrillic lettering at the top left reads: "Mac is the biggest natural source of energy." McDonald's also began putting a sajkaca, a traditional Serbian cap, atop its coveted golden arches to evoke Serbian identity and pride.*

BELGRADE, Yugoslavia — During most of the 78-day air war against Yugoslavia, while NATO kept the bombs dropping, McDonald's kept the burgers flipping.

Vandalized at the outset by angry mobs, McDonald's Corp. was forced to temporarily close its 15 restaurants in Yugoslavia. But when local managers flung the doors open again, they accomplished an extraordinary comeback using an unusual marketing strategy: They put McDonald's U.S. citizenship on the back burner.

To help overcome animosity toward a quintessential American trademark, the local restaurants promoted the McCountry, a domestic pork burger with paprika garnish. As a national flourish to evoke Serbian identity and pride, they produced posters and lapel buttons showing the golden arches topped with a traditional Serbian cap called the sajkaca (pronounced shy-KACH-a). They also handed out free cheeseburgers at anti-NATO rallies. The basement of one restaurant in the Serbian capital even served as a bomb shelter.

Now that the war is over, the company is basking in its success. Cash registers are ringing at prewar levels. In spite of falling wages, rising prices and lingering anger at the U.S., McDonald's restaurants around the country are thronged with Serbs hungry for Big Macs and fries. And why not, asks 16-year-old Jovan Stojanovic, munching on a burger. "I don't associate McDonald's with America," he says. "Mac is ours."

This is music to Dragoljub Jakic's ears. The 47-year-old managing director of McDonald's in Yugoslavia was the mastermind behind the campaign to "Serbify," at least during the war, an American icon. "We managed to save our brand," the six-and-a-half-foot-tall Mr. Jakic says with a grin.

That was no easy task. As the fast-food industry's superpower, McDonald's is a global symbol of Western pop culture, Yankee know-how and American corporate cunning. But prominence on the world stage can be a lightning rod for trouble, and the company is often exposed to outbursts of anti-American sentiment and a myriad of political grievances. Last month, a McDonald's restaurant in Belgium was burned down, and animal-rights activists are the suspected arsonists.

The sacking of McDonald's in Yugoslavia came after only one night of air strikes. Whipped to patriotic fervor by the state-controlled media attacks on the "NATO criminals and aggressors," mobs of youths — many wearing Nike shoes and Levi's jeans — targeted three McDonald's branches in Belgrade and restaurants in the cities of Jagodina, Cacak and Zrenjanin, smashing windows and scribbling insults on doors and walls.

The incidents shocked Mr. Jakic, who was more worried at the time about stray NATO bombs than the rage of his fellow citizens. "We have been in Yugoslavia for years, during which time we sponsored schools, sports clubs and children's hospitals," he says. "We're part of the community. We never thought anyone would do something bad to us."

McDonald's, in fact, was once the pride of Belgrade, opening in the capital on March 24, 1988 — exactly 11 years to the day before the North Atlantic Treaty Organization began bombing. It was the first branch in Central Europe and quickly became a source of local pride. At soccer matches in the old Yugoslavia, when teams from Belgrade met opponents from Zagreb, the Croatian capital, Belgrade fans would taunt their rivals with chants of "We have McDonald's and you don't!"

In 1996, the company began expanding, opening restaurants in seven other Serbian cities. But on March 26, the day after the mob attacks, Mr. Jakic closed all his restaurants. He then called his top managers to Belgrade for brainstorming sessions to devise a survival strategy.

Within a week, they had launched a campaign to identify the plight of ordinary Serbs with the big burger joint. "McDonald's is sharing the destiny of all people here," read a sign at one branch. "This restaurant is a target, as we all are. If it has to be destroyed, let it be done by NATO."

A key aspect of the campaign was to present McDonald's as a Yugoslav company. Though they are registered as local businesses, every restaurant in Yugoslavia in fact is 100% owned and operated by McDonald's. Mr. Jakic says McDonald's needed to get Serbs to view the company as their own.

It was in this vein that he and his team decided to redesign the logo with the Serbian cap, cocked at a haughty angle over one arch. Traditional national emblems, like the sajkaca, have undergone a revival in recent years with the rise of Serbian nationalism.

Mr. Jakic says the choice of the cap had nothing to do with politics. "The sajkaca is a strong, unique Serbian symbol. By adding this symbol of our cultural heritage, we hoped to denote our pride in being a local company," he says.

The company also brought back the McCountry pork burger, first released throughout Central Europe in early March, and lowered its price. The economy of preindustrial Yugoslavia was based on the pig trade, and pork is considered the most Serbian of meats. Mr. Jakic says his relaunch wasn't an attempt to pander to local sentiments, but to give people a break during hard times.

There was no time for premarket trials of his plans. "We just jumped in," Mr. Jakic says. In less than a week, McDonald's had printed new banners, tray liners, lapel buttons and posters of the redesigned arches set against the blue, white and red colors of the Serbian flag. On April 17, Belgrade restaurants were reopened and more than 3,000 free burgers were delivered to the participants of the Belgrade marathon, which was dominated by an anti-NATO theme. At the same time, the company announced that for every burger sold it would donate one dinar (about a nickel) to the Yugoslav Red Cross to help victims of NATO's airstrikes.

At McDonald's corporate headquarters in Oak Brook, Ill., spokesman Chuck Ebeling says the Yugoslav campaign was a product of local management and was in no way directed or encouraged by the head office. Mr. Jakic "was functioning as a hamburger guy and not as a politician," Mr Ebeling says. "He was doing what he felt he should do, and needed to do, to be locally accepted and to maintain the support of local government and of his employees. He demonstrated how adaptive he could be under the circumstances."

Mr. Jakic says he was praised by his superiors at a meeting at McDonald's regional headquarters in Vienna. And while he says he

(Cont.)

is happy his campaign helped McDonald's to prosper during exceptional circumstances, he was also quick to return to business as usual. As soon as the war ended, on June 10, the arches reappeared, without the green cap. "We simply believed that our message was received and there was no reason to continue," Mr. Jakic says.

Asked if the cocky sajkaca had been ditched forever, Mr. Jakic smiles. "We will make an investigation to see how it worked, and then maybe we'll fine-tune it," he says. "We've not abandoned it completely."

The campaign certainly made an impression here. At one McDonald's, a green book for customer comments records the delight of Belgraders when the restaurant reopened and unveiled its new approach. "We are so happy to see the campaign to help people hurt by the war. It's very humane and the only way to justify the business of an American restaurant in Yugoslavia," wrote Andjela, Aleksandra and Dragan, on April 18. The same day, Isidora wrote: "McDonald's is the only American who wished to become a Serb."

—*Richard Gibson*
contributed to this article.

Republished with permission of Dow Jones, Inc. from *The Wall Street Journal,* September 3, 1999; permission conveyed through Copyright Clearance Center, Inc.

22

CYBER CRIME

First Yahoo! Then eBay. The Net's vulnerability threatens e-commerce—and you

The scenario that no one in the computer security field likes to talk about has come to pass: The biggest e-commerce sites on the Net have been falling like dominoes. First it was Yahoo! Inc. On Feb. 6, the portal giant was shut down for three hours. Then retailer Buy.com Inc. was hit the next day, hours after going public. By that evening, eBay, Amazon.com, and CNN had gone dark. And in the morning, the mayhem continued with online broker E*Trade and others having traffic to their sites virtually choked off.

The work of some super hacker? For now, law enforcement officials don't know, or won't say. But what worries experts more than the identity of this particular culprit or outlaw group is how easily these attacks have been orchestrated and executed. Seemingly, someone could be sitting in the warmth of their home and, with a few keystrokes, disrupting electronic commerce around the globe.

DEAD HALT. Experts say it's so easy, it's creepy: The software to do this damage is simple to use and readily available at underground hacker sites throughout the Internet. A tiny program can be downloaded and then planted in computers all over the world. Then, with the push of a button, those PCs are alerted to go into action, sending a simple request for access to a site, again and again and again—indeed, scores or hundreds of times a second. Gridlock. For all the sophisticated work on firewalls, intrusion-detection systems, encryption and computer security, e-businesses are at risk from a relatively simple technique that's akin to dialing a telephone number repeatedly so that everyone else trying to get through will hear a busy signal. "We have not seen anything of this magnitude before—not only at eBay, but across so many sites," says Margaret C. Whitman, CEO of eBay.

No information on a Web site was snatched, no data corrupted, no credit-card numbers stolen—at least so far. Yet it's a deceptively diabolical trick that has temporarily halted commerce on some of the biggest Web sites, raising the question: How soft is the underbelly of the Internet? Could tricks like these jeopardize the explosive growth of the Web, where consumers and businesses are expected to transact nearly $450 billion in business this year? "It's been war out there for some time, but it's been hidden," says James Adams, co-founder of iDEFENSE, an Alexandria, Va., company that specializes in cyber threats. "Now, for the first time, there is a general awareness of our vulnerabilities and the nature of what we have wrought by running helter-skelter down the speed race of the Information Highway."

To be sure, not even the most hardened cyber sleuths are suggesting the Net is going to wither overnight from the misdeeds of these wrongdoers. But the events of recent days are delivering a shrill wake-up call to businesses that they need to spend as much time protecting their Web sites and networks as they do linking them with customers, suppliers, contractors—and you. Consider just a quick smattering of recent events: In December, 300,000 credit-card numbers were snatched from online music retailer CD Universe. In March, the Melissa virus caused an estimated $80 million in damage when it swept around the world, paralyzing e-mail systems. That same month, hackers-for-hire pleaded guilty to breaking into phone giants AT&T, GTE, and Sprint, among others, for calling card numbers that eventually made their way to organized crime gangs in Italy. According to the FBI, the phone companies were hit for an estimated $2 million.

Cyber crime is becoming one of the Net's growth businesses. The recent spate of attacks that gummed up Web sites for hours—known as "denial of service"—is only one type. Today, criminals are doing everything from stealing intellectual property and committing fraud to unleashing viruses and committing acts of cyber terrorism in which political groups or unfriendly governments nab crucial information. Indeed, the tactic used to create mayhem in the past few days is actually one of the more innocuous ones. Cyber thieves have at their fingertips a dozen dangerous tools, from "scans" that ferret out weaknesses in Web site software programs to "sniffers" that snatch passwords. All told, the FBI estimates computer losses at up to $10 billion a year.

As grim as the security picture may appear today, it could actually get worse as broadband connections catch on. Then the Web will go from being the occasional dial-up service to being "always on," much as the phone is. That concept may be nirvana to e-tailers, but could pose a real danger to consumers if cyber crooks can come and go into their computer systems at will. Says Bruce Schneier, chief technical officer at Counterpane Internet Security Inc. in San Jose, Calif.: "They'll keep knocking on doors until they find computers that aren't protected."

Sadly, the biggest threat is from within. Law enforcement officials estimate that up to

---

Storming the Fortress

THE WEAPONS:

DENIAL OF SERVICE This is becoming a common networking prank. By hammering a Web site's equipment with too many requests for information, an attacker can effectively clog the system, slowing performance or even crashing the site. This method of overloading computers is sometimes used to cover up an attack.

SCANS Widespread probes of the Internet to determine types of computers, services, and connections. That way the bad guys can take advantage of weaknesses in a particular make of computer or software program.

SNIFFER Programs that covertly search individual packets of data as they pass through the Internet, capturing passwords or the entire contents.

SPOOFING Faking an e-mail address or Web page to trick users into passing along critical information like passwords or credit-card numbers.

TROJAN HORSE A program that, unknown to the user, contains instructions that exploit a known vulnerability in some software.

BACK DOORS In case the original entry point has been detected, having a few hidden ways back makes reentry easy—and difficult to detect.

MALICIOUS APPLETS Tiny programs, sometimes written in the popular Java computer language, that misuse your computer's resources, modify files on the hard disk, send fake e-mail, or steal passwords.

WAR DIALING Programs that automatically dial thousands of telephone numbers in search of a way in through a modem connection.

LOGIC BOMBS An instruction in a computer program that triggers a malicious act.

BUFFER OVERFLOW A technique for crashing or gaining control of a computer by sending too much data to the buffer in a computer's memory.

PASSWORD CRACKERS Software that can guess passwords.

SOCIAL ENGINEERING A tactic used to gain access to computer systems by talking unsuspecting company employees out of valuable information such as passwords.

DUMPSTER DIVING Sifting through a company's garbage to find information to help break into their computers. Sometimes the information is used to make a stab at social engineering more credible.

THE PLAYERS:

WHITE-HAT HACKERS They're the good guys who get turned on by the intellectual challenge of tearing apart computer systems to improve computer security.

BLACK-HAT HACKERS Joyriders on the Net. They get a kick out of crashing systems, stealing passwords, and generally wreaking as much havoc as possible.

CRACKERS Hackers for hire who break into computer systems to steal valuable information for their own financial gain.

SCRIPT BUNNIES Wannabe hackers with little technical savvy who download programs—scripts—that automate the job of breaking into computers.

INSIDERS Employees, disgruntled or otherwise, working solo or in concert with outsiders to compromise corporate systems.

60% of break-ins are from employees. Take the experience of William C. Boni, a digital detective for PricewaterhouseCoopers in Los Angeles. Last year, he was called in by an entertainment company that was suspicious about an employee. The employee, it turns out, was under some financial pressure and had installed a program called Back Orifice on three of the company's servers. The program, which is widely available on the Internet, allowed him to take over those machines, gaining passwords and all the company's financial data. The employee was terminated before any damage could be done.

The dirty little secret is that computer networks offer ready points of access for disgruntled employees, spies, thieves, sociopaths, and bored teens. Once they're in a corporate network, they can lift intellectual property, destroy data, sabotage operations, even subvert a particular deal or career. "Any business on the Internet is a target as far as I'm concerned," says Paul Field, a reformed hacker who is now a security consultant.

It's point and click, then stick 'em up. Interested in a little mayhem? Security experts estimate that there are 1,900 Web sites that offer the digital tools—for free—that will let people snoop, crash computers, hijack control of a machine, or retrieve a copy of every keystroke. Steve O'Brien, vice-president for information operation assessments at Info-Ops.com, an Annapolis (Md.)-based company that provides intrusion detection services and security solutions, says the number of ways to hack into computers is rising fast. He tracks potential threats both from hacker groups and from the proliferation of programs. Once a rare find, he now discovers at least three new nasty software programs or vulnerabilities every day. And those tools aren't just for the intellectually curious. "Anyone can get them off the Internet—just point and click away," says Robert N. Weaver, a Secret Service agent in charge of the New York Area Electronic Crimes Task Force.

UNLOCKED DOORS. It's an issue that has crimefighters up in arms. At a hastily called press conference in Washington, D.C., on Feb. 9, Attorney General Janet Reno pledged to battle cyber crime. "We are committed to tracking down those responsible and bringing them to justice" and ensuring "that the Internet remains a secure place to do business," she said. But Ron Dick, chief of the Computer Investigations & Operations Section of the National Infrastructure Protection Center, pointed out that Internet security can't be assured by the government alone. Companies need to vigilantly monitor their computers to ensure that hackers don't surreptitiously install programs from which to launch attacks. "For the Internet to be a safe place, it is incumbent on everyone to remove these tools," he says. Using them, "a 15-year-old could launch an attack."

Make that an 8-year-old, once the Internet is always on via fat broadband connections. There are currently 1.35 million homes in America with fast cable modems, according to market researcher International Data Corp. By 2003, the number will grow to 9 million, and there will be an equal or larger number of digital subscriber line (DSL) connections.

That gives hackers a broad base from which to stage an attack. When a PC is connected to a conventional phone modem, it receives a new Internet address each time the user dials onto the Net. That presents a kind of barrier to hackers hoping to break in and hijack the PC for the kind of assault that crippled eBay, Yahoo, and others. In contrast, cable and DSL modems are a welcome mat to hackers. Because these modems are always connected to the Net, they usually have fixed addresses, which can be read from e-mail messages and newsgroup postings. Home security systems known as personal firewalls are widely available for cable and DSL subscribers. But until they reach nearly 100% penetration, they won't prevent intrusions.

In the coming age of information appliances, the situation could get worse. According to many analysts, the U.S. will soon be awash in Web-browsing televisions, networked game consoles, and smart refrigerators and Web phones that download software from the Net. "These devices all have powerful processors, which could be used in an attack, and they're all connected to the Net," Schneier says.

True, broadband customers can switch off their Net connections. But as cool applications come onstream, nobody will want to do that. "There will be streaming music and video, 24-hour news, and all kinds of broadband Web collaboration," says John Corcoran, an Internet analyst with CIBC World Markets. "To take advantage of that, the door will be open 24 hours a day."

Corporations are no better off. There, security is becoming an expensive necessity. "At least 80% of a corporation's intellectual property is in digital form," says Boni. Last year, Corporate America spent $4.4 billion on sales of Internet security software, including firewalls, intrusion-detection programs, digital certificates, and authentication and authorization software, according to International Data. By 2003, those expenditures could hit $8.3 billion.

And still computer crime keeps spreading. When the FBI and the Computer Security Institute did their third annual survey of 520 companies and institutions, more than 60% reported unauthorized use of computer systems over the past 12 months, up from 50% in 1997. And 57% of all break-ins involved the Internet, up from 45% two years ago.

As big as those numbers sound, no one really knows how pervasive cyber crime is. Almost all attacks go undetected—as many as 60%, according to security experts. What's more, of the attacks that are exposed, maybe 15% are reported to law enforcement agencies. Companies don't want the press. When Russian organized crime used hackers to break into Citibank to steal $10 million—all but $400,000 was recovered—competitors used the news in marketing campaigns against the bank.

That makes the job even tougher for law enforcement. Most companies that have been electronically attacked won't talk to the press. A big concern is loss of public trust and image—not to mention the fear of encouraging copycat hackers. Following the attacks on Feb. 8 and Feb. 9, there was a telling public silence from normally garrulous Internet executives from E*Trade to priceline.com. Those that had not been attacked yet were reluctant to speak for fear of painting a target on their site, while others wanted no more attention.

And even when the data are recovered, companies are sometimes reluctant to claim their property. Secret Service agent Bob Weaver waves a CD-ROM confiscated in a recent investigation. The disk contains intellectual property—software belonging to a large Japanese company. Weaver says he called the company, but got no response.

Thieves and hackers don't even need a computer. In many cases, the physical world is where the bad guys get the information they need for digital break-ins. Dallas FBI agent Mike Morris estimates that in at least a third of the cases he's investigated in his five years tracking computer crime, an individual has been talked out of a critical computer password. In hackerland, that's called "social engineering." Or, the attackers simply go through the garbage—dumpster diving—for important pieces of information that can help crack the computers or convince someone at the company to giving them more access.

"PAGEJACKING." One problem for law enforcement is that hackers seem to be everywhere. In some cases, they're even working for so-called computer security firms. One official recalls sitting in on the selection process for the firm that would do the Web site security software for the White House. As the company's employees set up to make their pitch, one person walked into the room and abruptly walked out. It turns out one of the people in the audience was with law enforcement, and had busted that person for hacking.

It's not just on U.S. shores that law enforcement has to battle cyber criminals. Attacks from overseas, particularly eastern European countries, are on the rise. Indeed, the problem was so bad for America Online Inc. that it cut its connection to Russia in 1996. Nabbing bad guys overseas is a particularly thorny issue. Take Aye.Net, a small Jeffersonville (Ind.)-based Internet service provider. In 1998 intruders broke into the ISP and knocked them off the Net for four days. Steve Hardin, director of systems engineering for the ISP, discovered the hackers and found messages in Russian. He reported it to the FBI, but no one has been able to track down the hackers.

As if worrying about hackers weren't enough, online fraud is also on the rise. The Federal Trade Commission, which responds to consumer complaints about bogus get-rich schemes or auction goods never delivered, says it filed 61 suits last year. How many did it have back in 1994, when the Net was in its infancy? One. So far, the actions have resulted in the collection of more than $20 million in payments to consumers and the end of schemes with annual estimated sales of over $250 million.

The FTC doesn't want to stop there. On Feb. 9, commissioners testified before a Senate panel, seeking an increase in the commission's budget in part, to fund new Internet-related policies and fight cyberfraud. The money is needed to go after ever more creative schemes. In September, for example, the FTC filed a case against individuals in Portugal and Australia who engaged in "pagejacking" and "mousetrapping" when they captured unauthorized copies of U.S.-based Web sites (including those of PaineWebber Inc. and The Harvard Law Review) and produced lookalike versions that were indexed by major search engines. The defendants diverted unsuspecting consumers to a sequence of porno sites that they couldn't exit. The FTC obtained a court order stopping the scheme and suspending the defendants' Web-site registrations.

All of this is not to suggest it's hopeless. Experts say the first step for companies is to secure their systems by searching for hacker programs that might be used in such attacks. They also suggest formal security policies that can be distributed to employees letting them know how often to change passwords or what to do in case of an attack. An added help: Constantly updating software with the latest versions and security patches. Down the road, techniques that can filter and trace malicious software sent over the Web may make it harder to knock businesses off the Net. Says Novell Inc. CEO Eric Schmidt: "Security is a race between the lock makers and the lock pickers." Regulators say that cybercrime thrives because people accord the Internet far more credibility than it deserves. "You can get a lot of good information from the Internet—95% of what you do there is bona fide," says G. Philip Rutledge, deputy chief counsel of the Pennsylvania Securities Commission. "Unfortunately, that creates openings for fraud."

And other forms of mayhem. That's evident from the attacks that took down some of the biggest companies on the Net. If blackouts and other types of cyber crime are to be avoided, then Net security must be the next growth business.

By Ira Sager in New York, with Steve Hamm and Neil Gross in New York, John Carey in Washington, D.C., and Robert D. Hof in San Mateo, Calif.

23

A CRACKDOWN ON E-DRUGGISTS

Online pill-pushers are in U.S. regulators' sights

On Nov. 22, a 15-year-old boy in Michigan got on the Internet and visited the Web site of ConfiMed, the self-described "original online source" for Viagra and other medication. He filled out an order for Xenical, a weight-loss drug with side effects including bloating, cramps, and diarrhea. The next day, he got a puzzled e-mail from ConfiMed: "At 5 foot 9, 130 pounds, there would be a question as to why you might need Xenical," it wondered. "Please send further explanation."

Oops, the teenager replied, his weight was really 180. Five days later, on Nov. 29, the pills arrived in the mail, complete with a prescription written by ConfiMed's founder, Seattle's Dr. Howard J. Levine. Unfortunately for Levine, the purchase was a sting set up by the Michigan attorney general's office. In December, the attorney general charged ConfiMed and nine other online companies with selling prescription drugs without adequate medical consultation and proper licenses. Levine denies breaking any laws.

The Michigan crackdown is just one piece of a broad new legal attack on Internet drug-sellers. There have always been doctors and merchants who dispensed prescription drugs out the backdoor. But now the Internet is giving them global reach. Law enforcers estimate that there are now more than 400 online drug peddlers, tapping into the more than $110 billion spent on retail prescriptions in the U.S. each year.

A few sites, such as PlanetRx.com and HealthCentral.com, sell drugs only to those with a valid prescription. But others are freely dispensing everything from Viagra and hair-loss preventer Propecia to steroids and amphetamines with only a perfunctory questionnaire. Indeed, regulators point to the case of a 52-year-old Illinois man who was able to buy Viagra online, despite having chest pains and a family history of heart disease, and who died during sex. Online drug peddling "poses enormous health and safety issues," says Michigan Attorney General Jennifer M. Granholm. "It's the wild, wild West out there."

Now, the sheriffs are arriving—in force (table). Last year, Illinois, Kansas, and Missouri also took action against Web drug merchants, and the National Association of Attorneys General is now establishing a working group to plot a wider assault involving dozens of states. Meanwhile, the Clinton Administration in December announced a new plan to give the FDA $10 million per year to use in tackling online drug peddlers, as well as new authority to impose fines.

ELUSIVE. But even though law enforcers are on the attack, it's not clear they'll ever completely succeed in taming the cyberfrontier. As has already been discovered with online gambling and securities fraud, the Web is much harder to police than the brick-and-mortar world. Many of the worst drug sites, for example, operate outside of U.S. control in loosely regulated foreign havens such as Thailand and the Caribbean. "The foreign sites are...very active, very illegal, and very dangerous," says Carmen Catizone, executive director of the National Association of Boards of Pharmacy (NABP).

Because their companies are built of electrons, the cyber drug merchants are also proving to be very evasive—even when they're based in the U.S. "One of the most difficult challenges has been finding the companies and people responsible," explains Kansas Attorney General Carla J. Stovall. Her staff has had to pierce through a variety of evasive tactics, including multiple-shell corporations and addresses that turned out to be mail drops. In Texas, meanwhile, investigators have found that the sites pay close attention to who visits—and frequently manage to stay one step ahead of the law. "When we go in and look at a site, it logs us in," says Cynthia T. Culmo, director of the Division of Drugs & Medical Devices at the Texas Health Dept. "The next time we try to access it, it's shut down."

AD NAUSEAM. In spite of the difficulties, enforcers say the fight has only just begun. Government gumshoes estimate that sales at the online prescribers are in the tens of millions of dollars and growing. And some of the sites are all but daring authorities to shut them down. The opening Web page for KwikMed, for example, brazenly proclaims: "No prescription? No problem...." KwikMed lawyer James W. Hill says that is just the "grabber"—and that the site goes on to explain "ad nauseam" how buyers must fill out an online questionnaire, evaluated by a doctor, to get Viagra, Propecia, and other drugs. But regulators say such online consultations are woefully inadequate. Indeed, the questionnaires on many sites—including KwikMed's—already have the correct answers filled in.

The FDA is currently investigating 100 sites and plans up to 50 actions later this year. But recognizing the limitations of traditional law enforcement, the agency also plans to attack the problem in other ways. For example, it supports a certification program developed by the NABP that gives a seal of approval to totally legit sites: Four have won approval so far, with 12 more expected soon—and 60 applications are pending. "The certification makes consumers realize there are good and bad guys," says FDA policy chief William K. Hubbard.

Of course, many online drug merchants think the crackdown is unnecessary and unfair. The typical drugs sold by the sites—Viagra and Xenical, among others—are so "benign" that just having "consultations"

(Cont.)

with cyberdoctors is more than adequate to protect the public's health, argues ConfiMed's Levine. "Unless someone grossly lies, the worst that could happen is that the drug won't help them very much," he says.

Online defenders note that a man with a heart condition can get Viagra just as easily by telling a lie to a doctor in person. So why shut down Web sites in a futile attempt to protect people from themselves? Moreover, the Web shields people's privacy—a big concern for many Viagra users, who are embarrassed by the necessity of visiting local doctors and drugstores. "If there wasn't a need for this [type of site], it wouldn't exist," says William A. Stallknecht, owner of The Pill Box Pharmacy, a Houston chain whose online site has been fined by Missouri. (Stallknecht insists that he's trying to comply with the state's laws.)

Nonetheless, the NABP, state attorneys general, and the FDA have drawn a firm line: Prescriptions must come from face-to-face visits with a doctor, or from a consultation with a patient's regular doctor. "Prescription drugs are dangerous drugs," explains Culmo. Online pharmacies "are going outside the lines of safety that were put in place," she says.

That may be the case. But the sites are certainly not lacking for customers. And unless that changes, this problem will continue to plague the regulators.

By John Carey in Washington

DRUGMAKERS: COULD A MOUSE CLICK DRAG THEM INTO COURT?

How's this for a drug company's legal nightmare? A man buys Viagra from an illicit online drug peddler, then dies during sex. An autopsy discovers that he had a heart condition—and should never have been allowed to use the medication. Lawyers scent blood. Knowing it's not worth suiing the tiny e-drug merchant, they go after deep-pocketed manufacturer Pfizer Inc. for not keeping the drug from being sold through dubious channels.

PROWLING. Is this hypothetical scenario far-fetched? Not necessarily. "Industry is concerned that, if companies had knowledge that these drugs were being misused . . . they could be deemed negligent," explains Washington food and drug lawyer Marc J. Scheineson.

That's why companies aren't sitting idly by. Pfizer declined to comment on its potential liability for drugs illegally sold online. But the company has been prowling the Web to find sites that offer Viagra. "Once we learned of them, we contacted the medicine or pharmacy board in those states," says spokesman Andrew B. McCormick. That's a smart move. Given the liability threat, "diligent companies should be monitoring the Internet and at least appearing to do something," says drug industry consultant Steven M. Weisman.

Regulators wish that the drug industry would cut off distributors that sell to shady sites. Cynthia T. Culmo, of the Texas Health Dept., believes one reason they don't do so is the fear of losing extra revenue. As this issue continues to generate controversy, the drug industry is likely to feel at least some of the growing heat.

By John Carey

24

Going against the flow
Consumers yearn for the power of old toilets

By Dru Sefton
USA TODAY

Dave Hitt misses his good old toilet, the one that slurped down everything in the bowl in just one flush, every time.

"My wife and twin daughters long for the days when you could flush a toilet and walk away, confident that it would do its job," says Hitt, 44, a computer engineer in upstate Round Lake, N.Y.

The family's water-closet woes began in 1994 when a remodeling contractor installed two ultra-low-flush (ULF) toilets in their house.

Those toilets use 1.6 gallons of water per flush; older toilets use anywhere from 3.5 to 7 gallons.

A week after the remodeling, Hitt's 12-year-old daughter flushed one of the new toilets. The bowl didn't clear, so she flushed again.

The toilet promptly overflowed. The water seeped to the first floor, staining the new kitchen ceiling. That was just the beginning.

"The thing clogs regularly and overflows from time to time," Hitt says.

He wishes he could have installed a larger-capacity toilet in '94, "but by then Congress had decided it should make the choice for me."

Congress did that in 1992, with the Energy Policy and Conservation Act. An amendment requires contractors to install ULF toilets in all remodeling and new-home jobs.

Now, of the 225 million toilets in the USA, nearly 50 million are ULF, according to the Plumbing Manufacturers Institute. More are installed every day.

The ULF toilet is great for saving water, even with occasional double flushes, its proponents say. They cite statistics such as a 1998 study showing that water consumption from toilet flushes decreases from an average of 19.3 gallons per person per day with an old toilet to 9.3 gallons with a ULF toilet.

But the problem with the ULF toilet, critics say, is that it's lousy for getting rid of solid waste.

Manufacturers are busy rethinking toilet designs and now offer options such as power-assisted flushing. They insist that ULF toilets are getting better all the time.

But all the homeowners hovering over toilets, plunger in hand, are growing impatient. They're griping to plumbers: Why won't this gunk go down like it used to? Plumbers are complaining to contractors: Why can't you install toilets that work? Contractors are calling manufacturers: Why don't you make toilets that work better?

And everyone is blaming Congress for plunging America into this swirl of controversy in the first place.

But disgruntled flushers could be getting some satisfaction soon. Rep. Joe Knollenberg, R-Mich., has pledged to see that the issue receives attention in the current congressional session.

After discussing the issue on a radio talk show in early 1997, Knollenberg says, he received "thousands and thousands of complaints from people around the country," prompting him to introduce a bill to repeal the 1.6-gallon requirement.

A hearing on that bill took place in July; Knollenberg's office predicts a vote on the bill this session.

ONE SIZE DOESN'T FIT ALL

The ULF toilets present a double whammy for irritated consumers.

"When they discover that they can't go back to the old-style product, their frustration doubles," Knollenberg says. "So it's a combination of unhappiness over performance and lack of choice."

In June and July, more than 1,400 homeowners and builders logged on to the Web site of the National Association of Home Builders Research Center to respond to a questionnaire about ULF toilets. The nonprofit group, based in Upper Marlboro, Md., reported that 594 of 757 builders in the unscientific survey complained of problems with ULF toilets; 511 of 681 homeowners had problems.

As Knollenberg says: "This particular mandate, frankly, insists that one size fits all. And it doesn't."

The fount of all the trouble is the water spot — what you see when you raise the toilet lid.

Americans like their water spot big. Very big. That causes a problem for manufacturers. The more water in the water spot, the less in the back of the toilet to flush stuff down.

"Cleanliness in the bowl and odor control are factors important to U.S. consumers," and both necessitate a large water spot, says Mike Chandler, associate product manager for toilets, urinals and bidets for the Kohler Co. in Kohler, Wis.

Many countries have a "very small or nonexistent" water spot in their toilets, Chandler says. It's just

(Cont.)

Americans who demand a big water spot.

So Kohler is one of many manufacturers getting creative. The company offers a Power Lite option, with a 0.2-horsepower electric pump inside the tank. " A very powerful but quiet flush," Chandler says.

Or there is the "dual flush actuator": One side of the button flushes 1.1 gallons for liquid waste; the other side flushes 1.6 gallons for solid waste.

Those options are available on Kohler's high-end toilets, which sell for up to $800. Chandler says consumer response has been "overwhelming."

If you're talking about flushing, Tom Kenney is the expert. As director of laboratory services for the National Association of Home Builders Research Center, he determines a toilet's flushability. A good part of his time is spent tossing little round sponges and wadded-up brown paper into toilets, flushing and counting how many pop back up.

Kenney is on the American Society of Mechanical Engineers committee that sets the voluntary industry "hydraulic performance requirements for water closets and urinals." In other words, how toilets should flush.

"There's been concern for several years now about the standard not being as robust as it needs to be," Kenney says.

The committee meets in October to begin revising the recommended standards. After flushing thousands of sponges and paper wads down dozens of toilets hundreds of times, "our data has shown a distinction between water closets. Some do better at flushing than others," Kenney says. That's why performance-testing standards are important.

The ULF toilets pose a tough issue politically.

"Houses with water-conserving fixtures, vs. older fixtures, use less water, there's no doubt about that,"

Kenney says. "Even with two or three flushes, we're still seeing net savings on water consumption.

"But what we're not seeing in studies is the product satisfaction with the user."

GOING NORTH FOR RELIEF

Dissatisfied toilet users are looking for alternatives.

Canadian retailer Tony Pasqua is happy to oblige. He owns The Master Bath in Sault Ste. Marie, Ontario, and gets about six calls a week from Americans wanting to buy the old-style toilets. On average, he sells three or four a week to Americans.

Some drive up to The Master Bath to pick up their toilets, loading them into pickup trucks or vans; others pay up to $100 for shipping.

Pasqua has sold toilets to homeowners in 42 states.

He has advertised 3.5-gallon toilets for 18 months and says he has been getting calls "since Day 1. It's amazing."

And it is not illegal for a U.S. homeowner to buy a toilet in Canada for use in the USA. Rumors of a "black market" in Canadian toilets have been circulating for years.

The only illegal purchase of a larger-capacity Canadian toilet would be if a contractor brought one back across the border for resale or installation. Such a contractor could face fines of up to $2,500.

So, no, there are no residential "toilet smugglers," says Cherise Miles, a U.S. Customs Service public affairs officer in Chicago.

"All you have to do is declare the toilet, and you're on your way."

25

Here's the Turnoff

In the Market for Guns, The Customers Aren't Coming Back for More

With Hunting on the Wane And Stigma on the Rise, The Pool Is Shrinking

'You Feel Like a Smoker'

By Vanessa O'Connell
and Paul M. Barrett
Staff Reporters of The Wall Street Journal

Michael Maul doesn't have anything against guns; he owns six. But the Houston radio-station engineer hasn't hunted for eight years, and he doubts that he will ever buy another gun. When he wants to shoot animals these days, Mr. Maul, 40 years old, uses a camera.

"It's a lot easier in the city to go to a nature trail or an arboretum," he says.

The gun business is losing customers. Hunters and target shooters — the industry's core market — are gradually walking away from those sports. Subdivisions have encroached on land once used for hunting. Bicycling, kayaking and other hobbies are luring people away from firing ranges.

Most ominously, gun companies' efforts to cultivate new buyers among women and teenagers have failed to stem the erosion. And gun manufacturers face a dramatic shakeout, as recent high-visibility killings have made guns less socially acceptable in many people's eyes.

"Our future is rather tenuous," says Paul Jannuzzo, vice president of the U.S. unit of Austrian handgun maker Glock GmbH.

Mr. Jannuzzo's industry has attracted public attention lately as it attempts to fend off a legal assault by 28 cities and counties across the country. But however that courtroom fight ends, gun companies face the peril of a shrinking consumer market. U.S. gun production and imports have fallen more than 20% since the late 1970s, and despite an unusual buying surge this year, industry analysts predict little to no overall growth in the decade ahead.

Retail giants such as Wal-Mart Stores Inc. and Kmart Corp. recently have reduced their gun and ammunition displays in favor of other sporting goods. The ranks of gun wholesalers — the middlemen between the factory and the store — have thinned by 16%, to about 160, since 1996.

A consolidation wave among manufacturers is already under way. Colt's Manufacturing Co. just this month eliminated its less expensive civilian-handgun lines and is negotiating a possible merger with rival Heckler & Koch Inc. Three small California makers of inexpensive handguns have either shut down or sought bankruptcy-court protection this year. Smith & Wesson Corp., the largest U.S. handgun manufacturer, is diversifying into everything from police bikes to car parts to clothing.

With more than 200 million guns already in civilian hands, industry officials worry that the market is nearing saturation. Just 10 million people own roughly half the national stock, which translates into about 10 guns per owner.

In the 1980s, the proportion of men who said they personally owned a gun held steady at 52%, but by 1998, the figure dropped to 38%, according to regular surveys by the National Opinion Research Center at the University of Chicago. Female ownership has hovered around 11% since 1980.

The lurid massacres of the past two years are statistically an aberration; violent crime has dropped nationally for seven straight years. But round-the-clock reports of gun killings have created a "much broader negative perspective, a tainting" of firearms, says Douglas Painter, executive director of the National Shooting Sports Foundation, the main industry trade group. In the wake of the Littleton bloodshed, his group dropped its first-ever mainstream-magazine advertising campaign, what would have been a $3 million effort to create a wholesome image for shooting sports.

Shooting traditionally has relied on family relationships and word-of-mouth promotion to attract neophytes. But fear of social disapproval is muffling veteran participants, Mr. Painter says. "Does that have a negative impact? You bet it does."

Lory Ambriz bought a new gun every year for more than four decades, displaying his favorites, including an assault rifle, above the fireplace in his La Mirada, Calif., home. But following this year's school shootings, his grandchildren and other house guests questioned why he kept such a potentially dangerous arsenal.

"I began to think I don't need them anymore," says the 68-year-old retired truck driver, who hadn't fired a gun for years. He says he has moved his more than 40 weapons to a neighbor's safe and plans to sell them soon.

To be sure, there are tens of millions of loyal gun users who still raise their children to hunt or target shoot. Mark Anderson, an insurance agent in Columbia, Mo., for example, was taught to shoot by his father and today owns more than 20 guns. A recent purchase was a .22-caliber rifle for his 12-year-old son, who is interested in target shooting. His next purchase is likely to be a quail-hunting shotgun for the boy, Mr. Anderson says.

But in many gun-owning families, these traditions aren't being passed to the next generation. Mr. Maul of Houston learned to hunt with his older male relatives, but they are back in rural Illinois, where he grew up, and as an adult, he hasn't found new hunting buddies. He doesn't plan to encourage his own son, now three years old, to take up the sport. "I expect he'll develop other interests, as I have," Mr. Maul says.

The upshot is that each of the industry's key markets is eroding. Hunting, which accounts for about 60% of consumer gun sales, has declined steadily for decades. The number of adults who hunt tumbled 17% from 1990 to 1998, according to Mediamark Research Inc., a market-research firm. The number of hunting licenses issued annually by states fell 11%, to 14.9 million, from 1982 to 1997, the most recent year for which statistics are available from the U.S. Fish & Wildlife Service.

Target shooting, which accounts for 25%

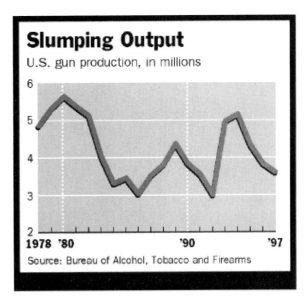

Slumping Output
U.S. gun production, in millions

Source: Bureau of Alcohol, Tobacco and Firearms

(Cont.)

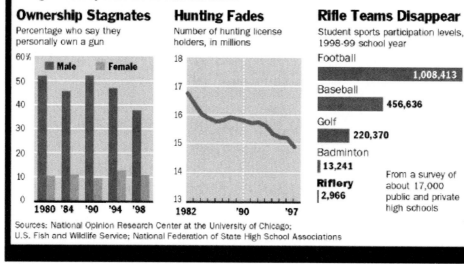

Losing Customers

The gun industry watches its markets shrink

Ownership Stagnates

Percentage who say they personally own a gun

Male   Female

60%
50
40
30
20
10
0

1980 '84 '90 '94 '98

Hunting Fades

Number of hunting license holders, in millions

18
17
16
15
14
13

1982   '90   '97

Rifle Teams Disappear

Student sports participation levels, 1998-99 school year

Football **1,008,413**

Baseball **456,636**

Golf **220,370**

Badminton **13,241**

Riflery **2,966**

From a survey of about 17,000 public and private high schools

Sources: National Opinion Research Center at the University of Chicago; U.S. Fish and Wildlife Service; National Federation of State High School Associations

of sales, is slowly fading, too. From 1993 to 1997, participation fell 5%, to 18.5 million people, according to a survey by the National Sporting Goods Association.

As their ranks thin, hunters and shooters are graying. At last month's New Jersey State Outdoor Pistol Championship, in the town of South River, 66 mostly grandfatherly types fired at paper bull's-eyes. Competitor James Phillips, 72 years old and clad in surgical stockings and orthopedic shoes, describes his fellow shooters as "a bunch of old men." Lone spectator Bill Nolan recalls that in the 1950s and 1960s, the parking lot overflowed with the recreational vehicles of 200 young and middle-age shooters and their families. "Boy, have times changed," says Mr. Nolan, 58.

People who buy firearms for self-protection, mostly handguns, make up the remaining 15% of the market. In an anomaly, sales in this area increased this year, partly because of the threat of stiffer gun-control measures and fear of social breakdown related to year-2000 computer problems. But the larger trend, as crime rates have fallen, is a drop in demand for self-protection guns. In any event, this isn't particularly fertile ground for gun makers because consumers buying only for protection tend to tuck a handgun away in a closet and not return to the gun store for more purchases.

Attitudes toward guns vary from region to region. They are more popular in the South, less in the Northeast. But there is growing anecdotal evidence from around the country that some gun enthusiasts are viewed — and view themselves — as pariahs with an unseemly habit, akin to cigarette smoking. Indeed, the danger for the industry would be

that gun ownership could become as unfashionable and frowned upon as chain-smoking, a habit that as recently as a decade ago wouldn't have raised eyebrows.

Fred Cunnings, a gun owner in Holiday, Fla., felt like such "an outsider" that he sold the pistol he had kept for years in a closet. "You almost feel like a smoker in a restaurant," says the 48-year-old landlord.

Most gun makers seem resigned to the erosion of their core customer base and are focusing on finding new faces. "The No. 1 challenge facing the gun industry is finding nontraditional consumers — women, young people, and suburbanites — to make up for the gradual decrease in traditional male hunting customers," says Ronald Stewart, who was chief executive of Colt's from 1996 through late last year.

Neither Colt's nor the industry at large is succeeding.

Since the late 1980s, handgun makers such as Colt's, Smith & Wesson and Italy's Beretta SpA have tried to convince women that they need to protect themselves and their families. Smith & Wesson, for example, pitched its LadySmith revolver, with pearl handles, as a "personal security plan" for women. But as crime rates eased in the late 1990s, the portion of women who personally own a gun dropped to 10.7% in 1998 from its recent high of 13.8% in 1993, according to the National Opinion Research Center.

Paxton Quigley, a handgun advocate who endorses Smith & Wesson products, recalls a "frenzy of interest" in her all-women handgun self-defense classes following the Los Angeles riots in 1992. Held at gun ranges nationwide, the classes now typically draw only

15 students, down from 35 in the early 1990s, she says.

For years, Dawn Brachmann, a homemaker in Holiday, Fla., kept her husband's .25-caliber Sterling pistol loaded and in a bread box on top of her refrigerator. But she asked him to get rid of it last month after a church sermon on gun violence at schools caused her to worry that her three-year-old son might stand on a chair and get at it. "I don't want to own any more guns," she says, "but I wouldn't mind finding something else to use in my self-defense."

In addition to problems recruiting women, gun makers acknowledge that they are failing to win over enough young people to replace aging shooters and hunters.

In recent years, the gun industry has aggressively courted kids, getting nearly three million a year to participate in rifle programs sponsored by the NRA and groups such as the farming-oriented 4-H clubs and the U.S. Junior Chamber of Commerce. Some manufacturers have tried to capitalize on this activity. H&R 1871 Inc., Gardner, Mass., says that by lending firearms to these programs, among other promotions, it has doubled annual sales of youth guns since 1995, to more than 50,000.

But aside from such small pockets of success, overall efforts to recruit younger customers aren't working, gun executives say. People between the ages of 18 and 24 made up only 8% of all hunters in 1995, down from 17% in 1986, according to the National Shooting Sports Foundation. In one major hunting state, Pennsylvania, sales of junior hunting licenses have dropped 40% during the past three decades, to roughly 98,000.

At a time when participation in scholastic sports is at an all-time high, riflery drew just 2,966 participants in the 1998-99 school year, 47% fewer than in 1974-75, according to a survey of 17,000 schools by the National Federation of State High School Associations. More than four times as many students played on badminton teams.

Robert Soldivera, who coaches shooting teams at three private high schools in Staten Island, N.Y., says that at first, many children "want to learn to shoot because it is the forbidden fruit." But that curiosity tends to wear off quickly, as students conclude that "making holes in paper targets gets boring really fast," Mr. Soldivera says. He estimates that

(Cont.)

fewer than 20% of his students remain active through their senior year; most quit after just a few months.

Like schools, many summer camps are phasing out shooting programs. Kent Meyer, who oversees Camp Chief Ouray in the Colorado Rockies, suspended its 92-year-old rifle program in response to this spring's school shootings in Littleton and Conyers, Ga. Scott Brody, who owns Camps Kenwood and Evergreen in Potter Place, N.H., dropped rifle programs in June and added more woodworking and dance. "They don't have the dangers of the riflery program," says Mr. Brody.

Worried about a stagnant gun market, some major manufacturers are putting more emphasis on military and law-enforcement sales or diversifying into other products altogether. Sturm, Ruger & Co., Southport,

Conn., the largest U.S. gun manufacturer, makes golf equipment. Ed Shultz, Smith & Wesson's chief executive, says he is steering his 147-year-old company, which once made only firearms, toward a 50-50 balance of gun and nongun products.

Other companies are trying more exotic niche-marketing strategies. Smith & Wesson, Springfield, Mass., Colt's, based in West Hartford, Conn., and Mossberg & Sons Inc., North Haven, Conn., are scrambling to be the first to offer a "smart gun" to women and people generally who otherwise wouldn't buy a firearm because of safety concerns. Smart-gun prototypes rely on microchip technology to allow only authorized users to pull the trigger. But the cost and reliability of smart guns are very much in doubt.

Savage Arms Inc., Westfield, Mass., aims

to boost sales among aging diehards by designing new guns for older, arthritic hands. Savage reduced the weight of some of its rifles to 5 1/2 pounds from eight pounds by using plastic parts rather than wood and added devices to reduce the sometimes-painful recoil that comes with firing a gun.

Both modifications appear to be hits with Savage's maturing customer base, says company President Ronald Coburn. But the problem, he adds, is that "as our audience matures, the younger generation isn't coming up behind them."

Republished with permission of Dow Jones, Inc. from The Wall Street Journal, October 26, 1999; permission conveyed through Copyright Clearance Center, Inc.

Buyer Behavior

Politics & Society: On the Move

People are migrating at record numbers, as the gap between the haves and the have-nots grows. The big question: Can it continue?

By Bernard Wysocki Jr.
Staff Reporter of The Wall Street Journal

Human wandering is as old as humankind, but the world has never seen so much of it.

Yet we will see even more.

The flow of migrants across borders is large and accelerating, approaching four million people a year. Globally, some 125 million people today live outside their country of birth.

But why? And how will mass migration shape the future?

In crassly economic terms, migration involves the poor flowing to the rich. In modern times, that means people go from the sending nations of South Asia, Africa and Latin America to the receiving nations of Europe and North America.

There's little doubt why migration has reached an all-time high. Income inequality between the richest and poorest nations has been rising for well over a century, at least.

The World Bank notes the ratio in average incomes between the richest and poorest countries was about 11 to 1 in 1870, 38 to 1 in 1960, 52 to 1 in 1985, and 49 to 1 in 1998.

"Migration is a result of differences — in demographic growth, in resources and jobs, and in security and human rights," says Philip Martin, chairman of the University of California's immigration and integration program. "And these differences are widening."

Stark Contrasts

At the dawn of the new millennium, these contrasts grow even starker: The richest countries are recording 3% to 5% increases in gross domestic product, while some of the poorest actually slide lower — victims of famine, war, social disintegration, inept leadership, and the flight of their best and brightest.

With ethnic and religious conflict raging in the former Yugoslavia, the Caucasus, Indonesia, sub-Saharan Africa, the Middle East and elsewhere, refugees increase the flow.

WHERE WILL ALL THE BABIES GO?

A powerful demographic fact leaps from the gulf between the haves and the have-nots of the global economy: The have-nots are having the vast majority of the babies.

Birth rates have stagnated or even declined in many developed countries, from Italy to Japan. By contrast, birth rates have exploded in Africa and in South Asia.

The obvious question: Who is going to employ all those working-age people? And just as significantly, perhaps more so, in the long run: Where will the less-fertile nations find the labor necessary to sustain growth?

Consider these numbers from United Nations studies: In 1950, the developed world had 524 million people in the prime working years of 18 to 65. By 1995, the number had risen to 780 million. But the U.N. projects that in the year 2030, this number will actually decline slightly, to 762 million.

By contrast, looking back to 1950, the developing world had 999 million in the 18-to-65 age group. That jumped to 2.76 billion by 1995.

The projections to the year 2030 are staggering: almost another doubling, to 4.9 billion people. In Africa, the number of working-age people will more than double, to 1.01 billion; in Asia, it will rise more than 50% to 3.46 billion; and in Latin America it will almost double to 490 million.

Assuming that home countries can't absorb these kinds of population increases, where will they go? Certainly, the U.S. is projected to absorb many immigrants, from Asia and especially from Latin American, above all Mexico. By the year 2050, the U.S. is expected to have a population of 393 million, of which 24% will be Hispanic (up from 11% today) and 8% will be Asian (up from 4% today). The U.S. has usually been quick to raise or lower borders depending on its work-force requirements, and the influx of immigration could be a godsend in a country full of retirees.

Japan, by contrast, will have to deal with potentially devastating labor shortages amid cultural taboos against immigration. Socially and racially, Japan is virtually homogeneous, with fewer than 1% of its population foreign-born. Even among businesspeople today, opposition to an increase in foreign labor runs at about 80%. The only alternative is a significant pickup in childbirth by today's Japanese women. The average Japanese woman today has 1.39 children during her lifetime.

Demographers predict that if current immigration and birth-rate patterns prevail, Japan's current population of 120 million will shrink to 100 million by 2050 and to 67 million by 2100. By the middle of the 21st century, one-third of Japanese will be over 65, placing a crushing financial burden on a shrinking working-age population.

—Bernard Wysocki Jr.

Nowadays the world counts some 15 million refugees a year, up more than fivefold in just 25 years.

Adding to this strife is separatism, which is spreading fast in this turbulent world. The number of nations has jumped to about 200 today from 75 at the end of World War II, and some futurists think this is only the beginning. Futurist John Naisbitt has predicted that there will be 1,000 nation-states by the year 2150. A fivefold increase in the census of nations would surely intensify migration pressures.

But no one knows for sure whether present trends are going to continue. Will separatist movements really go that far, spilling record numbers of displaced persons into the arms of strangers? Will rich nations, or once-rich nations in decline, turn protectionist, closing their doors on would-be immigrants?

Four Scenarios

Where we don't have certainty, we have scenarios. Consider these four possibilities — drawn from the Millennium Project, a panel organized by the United Nations University — to describe alternative futures for the world between now and 2050.

No. 1: Cybertopia

Technology creates a better world. China and India become software powerhouses. The gap between rich and poor widens, but telemedicine, tele-education and telebusiness partnerships spur developing countries' economies. World Trade Organization-sponsored global social safety nets discourage masses of poor from migrating.

Migration level: **Low.**

No. 2: The Rich Get Richer

Population growth slows everywhere, but remains higher in Africa and South Asia. The sharp disparity in personal income between richest and poorest nations widens, from 50 to 1 today to 80 to 1 by 2025. Migration rises, creating tension. By 2025, global corporations step in to develop more skilled workers, offer venture capital, etc.

Migration level: **High.**

No. 3: Passive, Mean World

The problem is jobs. Population growth outstrips jobs growth in much of the world. In the rich countries, living standards stagnate. Small "virtual" companies succeed with transient work forces migrating from country to country. "Drifting and dancing" becomes a way of life. By 2025, trade wars envelope the regional economic blocs. Protectionism spreads in many forms, including nontariff barriers and restrictive immigration policies.

Migration level: **High, but resisted strongly.**

> *"Migration is a result of differences— in demographic growth, in resources and jobs, and in security and human rights," says one expert. "And these differences are widening."*

No. 4: Trading Places

The once-booming economies of East and Southeast Asia recover and grow, challenging the U.S., the European Union and Japan. The North-South economic gap disappears, a quaint notion from the 19th and 20th centuries. Regions equalize in wealth.

Migration level: **Low.**

Lasting Trends

It is worth asking amid all this uncertainty whether some trends appear so durable that they're likely to persist as far as the years 2500 or 3000. The answer is: probably. Whatever the future levels of immigration, it's pretty much clear that immigration works for the immigrants themselves, and often for both receiving and sending countries. That's why it has persisted and is likely to continue.

"A permanent migration is successful about 90% of the time," says Richard Meier, professor emeritus of environmental design at the University of California at Berkeley. It has a ripple effect, he says, and this "affects the poorest people" — people whom "public policy is rarely able to target successfully."

Prof. Meier speaks anecdotally of a Guatemalan emigrant who exemplifies a global phenomenon. She arrived in the San Francisco Bay area at age 19 to escape civil strife. She married there and has given birth to two daughters. She sends 40% of her earnings back home, providing a brother and other kin a chance to escape the grinding poverty of her Guatemalan village. Prof. Meier himself has visited this village, and he concludes that her success "pulled about 10 people after her into a brighter world."

Both within and between countries, another seemingly unstoppable trend is urbanization, making the continuing surge of the city, and megacity, look all but unstoppable. The problems will mount, of course. The byprod-

ucts of urbanization include deforestation, depletion of water supplies and toxic levels of air pollution. These already threaten Mexico City and other metropolitan areas. Long term, given that so many cities have been built near seacoasts, the prospects of global warming could cause great migrations inland as coastal hordes flee rising waters.

Either way, few authorities expect the share of urban dwellers to do anything but continue rising.

It will be as if much of the developing world does in the next half-century what South Korea has done in the past 50 years. In the 1950s, Korea was largely rural, and one of the poorest countries in Asia. By the 1970s, it was rapidly modernizing. Seoul grew to a metropolis of 10 million, representing 25% of the population. Yet, as late as 1982, as many as 200,000 Koreans a year left to work in another country. They moved for jobs, mainly to the Middle East.

By the mid-1990s, South Korea had joined the industrialized world. It was prospering and importing labor, and well-educated Koreans who had moved to the U.S. were torn. Kyong Yu, a software manager in Dallas, who came to the U.S. as a student in the 1980s, sat in a restaurant over lunch in 1997, and weighed his decision. His brother had returned to South Korea to be a teacher. He decided to stay. He longed for his homeland and for the camaraderie of after-hours drinking and socializing so common in Seoul. But his economic opportunity, especially at this juncture, lay in the U.S.

CHARTING MIGRATION

Sending and Receiving

Migration by region from 1990 to 1995

REGION	NET MIGRANTS (in thousands)
■ **Sending Regions**	
Africa	**−63**
Eastern	−128
Central	+4
Northern	+69
Southern	+2
Western	+10
Asia	**−1,366**
Eastern	−171
South-Central	−664
Southeastern	−485
Western	−46
Latin America	**−392**
Caribbean	−99
Central America	−202
South America	−91
■ **Receiving Regions**	
Europe	**+739**
Eastern	−109
Northern	+47
Southern	−20
Western	+821
North America	**+971**
Oceania	**+111**
Australia-New Zealand	+122
Other Oceania	−11

Sources: United Nations; World Population Prospects

Staying Home

Not everyone thinks the pressure or the impulse to emigrate will remain so strong. "People have an attachment" to their homelands, says Graham Molitor, vice president of the World Future Society. He thinks money itself will "be of less interest to people" as

(Cont.)

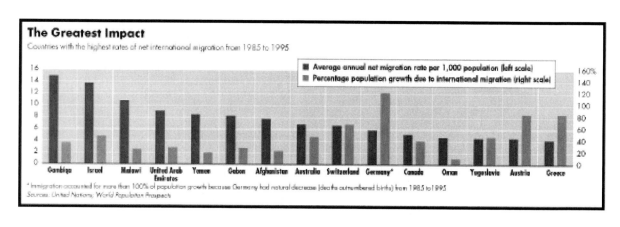

The Greatest Impact

Countries with the highest rates of net international migration from 1985 to 1995

■ Average annual net migration rate per 1,000 population (left scale)
■ Percentage population growth due to international migration (right scale)

Gambia, Israel, Malawi, United Arab Emirates, Yemen, Gabon, Afghanistan, Australia, Switzerland, Germany, Canada, Oman, Yugoslavia, Austria, Greece*

* Immigration accounted for more than 100% of population growth because Germany had natural decrease (deaths outnumbered births) from 1985 to 1995

Sources: United Nations; World Population Prospects

wealth becomes more pervasive in the world. A preposterous view? Here's how he sees the next thousand years playing out:

By 2015, the leisure-time era dominates, with recreation, tourism, adventure, the arts, media and socializing (on the Internet and elsewhere) consuming more of people's time in the developed world. Working hours drop, vacation time rises.

The developing world becomes economically enfranchised in the next phase — the life-sciences era, which takes hold in 2100. Developments in agriculture are stunning. Bioengineered crops thrive in hostile environments. Genetic technology produces crop yields far beyond the "green revolution" of the 20th century. With rising wealth, the residents of developing countries are more likely to remain in their homelands.

Then, between 2100 and 2500, a new age of nuclear power provides substitutes for dwindling supplies of oil, natural gas and coal. "Thermonuclear technologies will dominate the economy when obstacles to controlling fusion are overcome," Mr. Molitor believes. The concept of resource deprivation becomes obsolete.

And finally, a new space age emerges in the years 2500 to 3000. Extraterrestrial enterprise becomes an important feature of the world economy, creating, in Mr. Molitor's view, a great new wave of human migration: to long-term residency in space.

It may sound far-fetched to imagine large-scale business operations beyond Earth. On the other hand, imagine how far-fetched the 20th century's technologies would have sounded to someone living in the 10th century.

27

Net company Terra aims for Hispanic connection

By David J. Lynch
USA TODAY

MADRID, Spain – If Juan Perea is right, the next new thing to hit the Internet won't come from a garage in Silicon Valley. It'll spring from a turquoise-accented, faux Greek temple in an office park outside Spain's capital.

This is the home of Terra Networks, Europe's answer to Internet fever and the continent's largest Net company in terms of market capitalization.

With only 9% of Spaniards online, Spain is about the last place you'd look for an Internet powerhouse. After all, this is a country known for Picassos, not portals.

But when Terra went public in November, brokers dubbed the resulting uproar the terramoto, or earthquake. The tiny company, whose Nasdaq shares have more than quadrupled in value since, is valued at more than $27 billion. Pretty good for a 14-month-old outfit that won't see its first dollar of profit for at least three years.

What are investors thinking? Just that Terra could be the play on bringing the Internet to folks who speak something other than English. The company, a spinoff from Spanish and Latin American telecommunications giant Telefonica, is targeting the 550 million Spanish speakers worldwide – including an estimated 31 million in the USA.

"The big players have not addressed in a big way the U.S. Hispanic segment," says Terra CEO Perea, who was in New York on Wednesday to officially launch the U.S. network. "We feel there's still room for us to attack."

Over the next decade, Hispanics are expected to be the fastest-growing slice of the American pie. By 2010, they will be nearly 44 million strong, a 39% gain from today. The Spanish-speaking Internet audience is "where the English-language Net was three or four years ago. It's going to develop fast," Yankee Group analyst Beate Groeger says.

Perea, 36, an investment banker by training, had never used the Internet when he left Bankers Trust at the end of 1996 for a job with Telefonica, which established Terra Networks as a subsidiary at the end of 1998.

But he's learned fast. Through swift acquisitions, Terra has become the No. 1 Internet service provider in Spain, Chile, Peru and Guatemala and is No. 2 in pivotal Brazil and Mexico. In the USA, Terra will sell access through IDT, a long-distance telecommunications company based in Hackensack, N.J.

Thanks to its Telefonica links, the company starts with access to 54 million customers in the Hispanic world. Terra also makes money from advertising and e-commerce on the Spanish- and Portuguese-language portals it operates in those countries.

HUNT FOR MARKETS IS ON

True, the numbers – a worldwide customer base of 1.1 million and about $17 million in annual revenue – are Lilliputian by America Online standards. But as Internet penetration in the Web-saturated USA flattens, companies seeking rapid growth must turn to less-developed markets. That's why AOL has expanded into Europe and Latin America. That's why Terra is going after Spanish speakers wherever they reside.

The growth potential is enormous. In Mexico, today's 1 million Net users (1% of the total) are expected to reach almost 5 million in three years, according to Jupiter Communications. Argentina is likely to see a similar mushrooming. Brazil's online cohort should more than double to 7.5 million over the same period.

Still, Latin America isn't North America. Many homes don't have phones, let alone computers and modems. Transportation networks can be problematic, rendering speedy deliveries difficult or impossible.

So Terra is deliberately eschewing a mass-market approach in favor of a precision appeal to the most

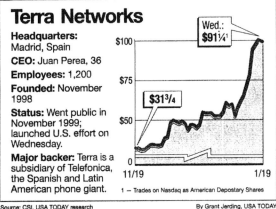

Terra Networks

Headquarters: Madrid, Spain

CEO: Juan Perea, 36

Employees: 1,200

Founded: November 1998

Status: Went public in November 1999; launched U.S. effort on Wednesday.

Major backer: Terra is a subsidiary of Telefonica, the Spanish and Latin American phone giant.

Wed.: $91¼[1]

$100

$75

$31¾

$50

0

11/19   1/19

1 – Trades on Nasdaq as American Depositary Shares

Source: CSI, USA TODAY research

By Grant Jerding, USA TODAY

prosperous one-fifth of Hispanics. These urbanites are people with Third World addresses but first world lifestyles.

"Remember, the Internet is all about focusing," says Gary Arlen, a Bethesda, Md.-based consultant.

To date, the Net's pronounced Anglo tilt – an estimated 96% of the Web is in English – may have discouraged Spanish speakers from logging on. About half of all U.S. households are online, but among Hispanics, the proportion is somewhere between one-fifth and one-third.

> **"There's no reason not to believe that one of the largest Internet companies in the world will be one serving the Spanish- and Portuguese-speaking market."**
>
> *—Juan Perea,*
> *Terra Networks CEO*

Terra aims to combat that disparity with a "global-local" solution providing targeted Spanish- and Portuguese-language content for audiences in eight countries, including the USA. AOL offers the masses Motley Fool investment tips and chats with Rosie O'Donnell. Terra will give U.S. Hispanics immigration forms and Jennifer Lopez.

DEALING WITH DIFFERENCES

But with Hispanic populations split among five different words for "straw," it's not as easy as translating existing English-language material into Español, says Terra content chief Rafael Bonnelly. The former Spanish-language newspaper editor says what works in Chile won't necessarily appeal to Argentines, Mexicans or American Latinos.

"Our Brazilian product doesn't have anything to do with our Mexican product, other than it's under the same brand," he says. "Our U.S. product is not targeted to Latin America. It's targeted to the U.S."

Last week, drawing on its alliance with content providers such as The Miami Herald, Terra's U.S. portal had extensive coverage of the story of Elian Gonzalez, the 6-year-old Cuban boy at the center of a dispute between Washington and Havana. Terra's Spanish and Chilean sites were more interested in the extradition saga of former Chilean dictator Augusto Pinochet.

Perea has a clear strategy, but he concedes success is far from guaranteed. Terra must unite newly acquired Latin American Web sites under its own multicolored brand. Plus, it faces competition from, among others, StarMedia, Quepasa.com, Yupi.com, Prodigy and AOL, which recently launched service in Brazil.

Almost two-thirds of U.S. Hispanics are of Mexican origin. But with sizable groups from each of the countries Terra is targeting, the USA represents an important test.

"The U.S. is a keystone area for us," says Enrique Rodriquez, who oversees Terra's Internet access business. "There are almost as many Spanish-speaking people in the U.S. as in Spain."

QUESTIONS LOOM

Still, there are questions about what proportion of U.S. Hispanics want their Net with a Spanish accent. About two-thirds of third-generation Hispanics speak English exclusively, according to Pepperdine University's Gregory Rodriquez.

It'll also be an additional three months at least before Perea has assembled a Spanish-speaking team of Americans to honcho Terra's U.S. operations. Hiring was slowed by his inability to offer stock options until Terra's IPO in November.

Terra also is under pressure to make an acquisition in the USA to match the Internet companies (and their customer rosters) that it has purchased in Latin America. The company confirms it is actively considering possible U.S. purchases.

So will Perea prove to be a Quixote or a conquistador? He thinks he knows the answer: "There's no reason not to believe that one of the largest Internet companies in the world will be one serving the Spanish- and Portuguese-speaking market."

28

GENERATION Y

Today's teens—the biggest bulge since the boomers—may force marketers to toss their old tricks

At malls across America, a new generation is voting with its feet.

At Towson Town Center, a mall outside of Baltimore, Laura Schaefer, a clerk at the Wavedancer surf-and-skateboard shop, is handling post-Christmas returns. Coming back: clothes that fit snugly and shoes unsuitable for skateboarding. Schaefer, 19, understands. "They say 'My mom and dad got me these'," she says.

At the Steve Madden store in Roosevelt Mall on Long Island, N.Y., parents, clad in loafers and Nikes, are sitting quietly amid the pulsating music while their teenage daughters slip their feet into massive Steve Madden platform shoes. Many of the baby boomer-age parents accompanying these teens look confused. And why not? Things are different in this crowd.

Asked what brands are cool, these teens rattle off a list their parents blank on. Mudd. Paris Blues. In Vitro. Cement. What's over? Now, the names are familiar: Levi's. Converse. Nike. "They just went out of style," shrugs Lori Silverman, 13, of Oyster Bay, N.Y.

Ouch. Some of the biggest brands on the market are meeting with a shrug of indifference from Lori and her cohorts. A host of labels that have prospered by predicting—and shaping—popular tastes since the baby boomers were young simply aren't kindling the same excitement with today's kids. Already, the list includes some major names: PepsiCo Inc. has struggled to build loyalty among teens. Nike Inc.'s sneaker sales are tumbling as the brand sinks in teen popularity polls. Levi Strauss & Co., no longer the hippest jeanmaker on the shelf, is battling market share erosion. Meanwhile, newcomers in entertainment, sports equipment, and fashion have become hot names.

What's the problem? These kids aren't baby boomers. They're part of a generation that rivals the baby boom in size—and will soon rival it in buying clout. These are the sons and daughters of boomers.

Born during a baby bulge that demographers locate between 1979 and 1994, they are as young as five and as old as 20, with the largest slice still a decade away from adolescence. And at 60 million strong, more than three times the size of Generation X, they're the biggest thing to hit the American scene since the 72 million baby boomers. Still too young to have forged a name for themselves, they go by a host of taglines: Generation Y,

Echo Boomers, or Millennium Generation.

Marketers haven't been dealt an opportunity like this since the baby boom hit. Yet for a lot of entrenched brands, Gen Y poses mammoth risks. Boomer brands flopped in their attempts to reach Generation X, but with a mere 17 million in its ranks, that miss was tolerable. The boomer brands won't get off so lightly with Gen Y. This is the first generation to come along that's big enough to hurt a boomer brand simply by giving it the cold shoulder—and big enough to launch rival brands with enough heft to threaten the status quo. As the leading edge of this huge new group elbows its way into the marketplace, its members are making it clear that companies hoping to win their hearts and wallets will have to learn to think like they do—and not like the boomers who preceded them.

Indeed, though the echo boom rivals its parent's generation in size, in almost every other way, it is very different. This generation is more racially diverse: One in three is not Caucasian. One in four lives in a single-parent household. Three in four have working mothers. While boomers are still mastering Microsoft Windows 98, their kids are tapping away at computers in nursery school.

With the oldest Gen Yers barely out of high school, it's no surprise that the brands that have felt their disdain so far have been concentrated in fashion, entertainment, and toys. But there's a lot more going on here than fickle teens jumping on the latest trend. While some of Gen Y's choices have been driven by faddishness and rebellion, marketing experts say those explanations are too simplistic. "Most marketers perceive them as kids. When you do that, you fail to take in what they are telling you about the consumers they're becoming," says J. Walker Smith, a managing partner at Yankelovich Partners Inc. who

Some of the biggest, most successfully marketed brands of the past decade are facing shrugs of indifference from these buyers

specializes in generational marketing. "This is not about teenage marketing. It's about the coming of age of a generation."

Smith and others believe that behind the shift in Gen Y labels lies a shift in values on the part of Gen Y consumers. Having grown up in an even more media-saturated, brand-conscious world than their parents, they respond to ads differently, and they prefer to encounter those ads in different places. The marketers that capture Gen Y's attention do so by bringing their messages to the places these kids congregate, whether it's the Internet, a snowboarding tournament, or cable TV. The ads may be funny or disarmingly direct. What they don't do is suggest that the advertiser knows Gen Y better than these savvy consumers know themselves.

Soon a lot of other companies are going to have to learn the nuances of Gen Y marketing. In just a few years, today's teens will be out of college and shopping for their first cars, their first homes, and their first mutual funds. The distinctive buying habits they display today will likely follow them as they enter the high-spending years of young adulthood. Companies unable to click with Gen Y will lose out on a vast new market—and could find the doors thrown open to new competitors. "Think of them as this quiet little group about to change everything," says Edward Winter of The U30 Group, a

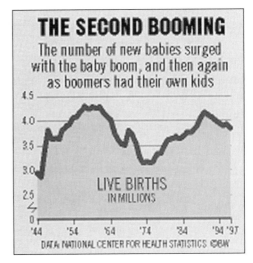

THE SECOND BOOMING

The number of new babies surged with the baby boom, and then again as boomers had their own kids

LIVE BIRTHS IN MILLIONS

DATA: NATIONAL CENTER FOR HEALTH STATISTICS. ©BW

(Cont.)

COOL STUFF

According to Boomers	According to Generation Y
LEXUS LS400 What to drive when you have your own parking spot. It says you've arrived without the ostentation of a Beemer.	**JEEP WRANGLER** Who cares about gas mileage? It looks great in the high school parking lot.
MAJOR LEAGUE BASEBALL Mark McGwire and the New York Yankees have made the game hot again.	**SKATEBOARD TRIPLE CROWN** Stars compete for glory instead of multiyear contracts.
GAP Those chinos and jeans still look cool. Really.	**DELIA'S** Definitely not your mother's dress catalog.
ER A worthy successor to Marcus Welby, MD.	**DAWSON'S CREEK** High school drama with sizzle.
SUPERBOWL ADS Usually they're more entertaining than the game.	**LILITH FAIR SPONSORSHIP** Supporting the sound of new voices.
HARRISON FORD Tough and fiftysomething. Plus, his action figure is a hot collectible.	**LEONARDO DICAPRIO** Dashing, sensitive, and irresistible to 12-year-olds.
ESTEE LAUDER For the way we ought to look.	**HARD CANDY** For the way we really look.
L.L. BEAN A favorite for decades, but does anyone actually go duck-hunting in those boots?	**THE NORTH FACE** Does anyone actually go mountain climbing in that stuff?
PALM PILOT A Rolodex for your pocket, with a high-tech edge.	**MOTOROLA FLEX PAGERS** Stay in touch anytime, anyplace.
NICK AT NITE All our favorite reruns in one convenient place.	**WB NETWORK** Creating new favorites and a new look for prime time television.
POLITICAL ACTIVISM Make yourself heard.	**VOLUNTEERISM** Make yourself useful.
THE BEATLES Rock 'n' roll as the signal artistic achievement of a generation.	**SPICE GIRLS** Rock 'n' roll packaged and marketed to children.
COKE Water + sugar + caffeine. Besides, it's the real thing.	**MOUNTAIN DEW** Water + sugar + more caffeine. Besides, it's an extreme thing.
DAVID LETTERMAN Late-night TV, slightly mellowed with age. Still among the Top Ten reasons to stay awake.	**JENNY McCARTHY** Think Carol Burnett with a bad attitude.
NIKES From Michael to Tiger, no shortage of sports celebs saying Just Do It.	**VANS** No sports celebs allowed. And they're the coolest shoes on skateboards.

Knoxville (Tenn.) consulting firm.

Nike has found out the hard way that Gen Y is different. Although still hugely popular among teens, the brand has lost its grip on the market in recent years, according to Teenage Research Unlimited, a Northbrook (Ill.) market researcher. Nike's slick national ad campaigns, with their emphasis on image and celebrity, helped build the brand among boomers, but they have backfired with Gen Y. "It doesn't matter to me that Michael Jordan has endorsed Nikes," says Ben Dukes, 13, of LaGrange Park, Ill.

Missteps such as Nike's disastrous attempt to sponsor Olympic snowboarders two years ago and allegations of inhumane overseas labor practices added to Gen Y's scorn. As Nike is discovering, success with this generation requires a new kind of advertising as well as a new kind of product. The huge image-building campaigns that led to boomer crazes in everything from designer vodka to sport-utility vehicles are less effective with Gen Y. "The old-style advertising that works very well with boomers, ads that push a slogan and an image and a feeling, the younger consumer is not going to go for," says James

R. Palczynski, retail analyst for Ladenburg Thalmann & Co. and author of YouthQuake, a study of youth consumer trends.

Instead, Gen Yers respond to humor, irony, and the (apparently) unvarnished truth. Sprite has scored with ads that parody celebrity endorsers and carry the tagline "Image is nothing. Obey your thirst." J.C. Penney & Co.'s hugely successful Arizona Jeans brand has a new campaign showing teens mocking ads that attempt to speak their language. The tagline? "Just show me the jeans."

NET EFFECT. Which isn't to say echo boomers aren't brand-conscious. Bombarded by ad messages since birth, how could they not be? But marketing experts say they form a less homogeneous market than their parents did. One factor is their racial and ethnic diversity. Another is the fracturing of media, with network TV having given way to a spectrum of cable channels and magazine goliaths such as *Sports Illustrated* and *Seventeen* now joined by dozens of niche competitors. Most important, though, is the rise of the Internet, which has sped up the fashion life cycle by letting kids everywhere find out about even the most obscure trends as they emerge. It is the Gen Y

medium of choice, just as network TV was for boomers. "Television drives homogeneity," says Mary Slayton, global director for consumer insights for Nike. "The Internet drives diversity."

Nowhere is that Net-driven diversity more clear than in the music business. On the Web, fans of even the smallest groups can meet one another and exchange information, reviews, even sound clips. Vicki Starr, a partner in Girlie Action, a New York-based music promoter, last year booked No Doubt, a band with a teen following, into a small Manhattan venue. She says that on opening night the house was packed with teenage girls dressed just like the lead singer. "How do they know this? How do they keep up with what she's wearing? It's not from network television," says Starr. "It's online."

The Internet's power to reach young consumers has not been lost on marketers. These days, a well-designed Web site is crucial for any company hoping to reach under-18 consumers. "I find out about things I want to buy from my friends or from information on the Internet," says Michael Eliason, 17, of Cherry Hill, N.J. Even popular teen TV shows,

(Cont.)

such as Warner Bros. Television Network's Buffy the Vampire Slayer and Dawson's Creek, have their own Web sites.

Other companies are keeping in touch by E-mail. American Airlines Inc. recently launched a college version of its popular Net-Saver program, which offers discounted fares to subscribers by E-mail. "They all have E-mail addresses," says John R. Samuel, director of interactive marketing for American. "If a company can't communicate via E-mail," he says, "the attitude is 'What's wrong with you?'"

This torrent of high-speed information has made Gen Y fashions more varied and faster-changing. Young consumers have shown that they'll switch their loyalty in an instant to marketers that can get ahead of the style curve. No brand has done a better job of that than Tommy Hilfiger. When Hilfiger's distinctive logo-laden shirts and jackets starting showing up on urban rappers in the early '90s, the company started sending researchers into music clubs to see how this influential group wore the styles. It bolstered its tradi-tional mass-media ads with unusual promo-tions, from giving free clothing to stars on VH1 and MTV to a recent deal with Miramax Film Corp., in which teen film actors will appear in Hilfiger ads. Knowing its customers' passion for computer games, it sponsored a Nintendo competition and installed Nintendo terminals in its stores. Gen Y consumers have rewarded that attentiveness by making Hilfiger jeans their No. 1 brand in a recent American Express Co. survey.

Compare that record with Levi's, one of the world's most recognized brands and an icon of boomer youth. It got a harsh wake-up call in 1997, when its market share slid, and research revealed that the brand was losing popularity among teens. With its core boomer customers hitting middle age, both Levi's advertising and its decades-old five-pocket jeans were growing stale. "We all got older, and as a consequence, we lost touch with teenagers," says David Spangler, director of market research for the Levi's brand. Now, Levi's is fighting back with new ads, new styles, a revamped Web site, and ongo-ing teen panels to keep tabs on emerging trends. "We never put much muscle into this sort of thing before, but now, we are dead serious about it," says Spangler. "This is a generation that must be reckoned with. They are going to overtake the country."

Marketers who don't bother to learn the interests and obsessions of Gen Y are apt to run up against a brick wall of distrust and cynicism. Years of intense marketing efforts aimed directly their way have taught this group to assume the worst about companies trying to coax them into buying something. Ads meant to look youthful and fun may come off as merely opportunistic to a Gen Y consumer. That's what happened to PepsiCo in its attempts to earn Gen Y loyalty with its Generation Next campaign, says William Strauss, co-author of the 1991 book Generations: The History of America's Future. The TV ads, in which kids showed off branded trinkets, from jackets to gym bags, fell flat. "They were annoying," says Philip Powell, 14, of Houston. "It was just one long 'Please, please, buy me.'"

'WE ARE GOING TO OWN THIS GENERATION'

The morning after the Delia's catalog arrives, the halls of Paxton High School in Jacksonville, Fla., are buzzing. That's when all the girls bring in their copies from home and compare notes. "Everyone loves Delia's," says Emily Garfinkle, 15. "It's the big excitement."

If you've never heard of Delia's, chances are you don't know a girl between 12 and 17. The five-year-old direct mailer has become one of the hottest names in Gen Y retailing by selling downtown fashion to girls everywhere. Already, the New York cataloger, which racked up sales of $98 million over the past three quarters, has a database of 4 million names, and its fastest growth may still lie ahead: Gen Y's teen population won't peak for five or six years.

TIGHT FOCUS. A lot of thriving Gen Y companies fell into the market by accident. Not Delia's. Founders Stephen Kahn, a 33-year-old ex-Wall Streeter, and Christopher Edgar, his ex-roommate at Yale University, realized that few retailers had taken the trouble to learn this market. So they carefully honed the Delia's concept: cutting-edge styles and mail-order distribution with a Gen Y twist.

Delia's trendy apparel is definitely not designed with mom and dad in mind. "I think the clothes are too revealing," says Emily's mother, Judy. "I tell her I'll buy her anything she wants at the Gap." But Emily dismisses the Gap as "too preppy," preferring Delia's long, straight skirts and tops with bra-exposing spaghetti straps. Delia's order form even includes tips on how to order pants so they conform to the parentally despised fashion of drooping

> **KAHN:** The Delia's catalog offers tips on how to order pants so they droop well below the hips

well below the hips, with hems dragging. In keeping with Gen Y preferences, the catalog illustrates these fashions with models who look like regular teen-agers, not superglam androgynes.

Delia's youthful image isn't just a facade. Most of the company's 1,500 employees are well under 30. And its phone reps—mostly high school and college students—do more than take orders: They offer tips and fashion advice. "Delia's speaks the language of its consumers," says Wendy Liebmann, president of consultant WSL Marketing.

Instead of mass-market advertising, Delia's gets the word out in the ways Gen Y prefers: with local campaigns such as catalog drops in schools and with hot Web sites. In 1997, the company bought gURL.com, a popular fashion, chat, and game site for girls. It also launched its own Web site, with news and entertainment stories, catalog-request forms, E-mail, and online shopping. That effort helped buy some buzz for Delia's stock, which has gyrated between $4 and $32 a share over the past year. In December, buoyed by news of an online shopping venture, the stock shot up more than 50%, to a recent 15.

So far, the company has sold mostly clothing, but it has recently branched out into home furnishings, such as bean bag chairs and throw rugs. "Girls like to do their rooms," says Kahn, who defines his business by its customers rather than by a product category. He foresees a day when Delia's will get these girls their first credit card, first car loan, and first mortgage. "We'll follow them and broaden our offerings," says Kahn.

Next up: boys. The company recently bought TSI Soccer Corp., a sportswear catalog and launched Droog, a catalog for boys. "We are going to own this generation," Kahn says. Or at least a sizable portion of its members' wallets.

By Ellen Neuborne in New York

(Cont.)

> Just as network TV has given way to cable, *Sports Illustrated* and *Seventeen* face an explosion of niche magazines.

Ironically, Pepsi already has one of the biggest teen soda hits with Mountain Dew, but the drink's success has little to do with advertising. Instead, kids found out about Dew from their most trusted endorsers—each other. "[Kids] believe—true or not—that they're the ones who figured out and spread the word that the drink has tons of caffeine," says Marian Salzman, head of the brand futures group at Young & Rubicam Inc. "The caffeine thing was not in any of Mountain Dew's television ads. This drink is hot by word of mouth."

Along with cynicism, Gen Y is marked by a distinctly practical world view, say marketing experts. Raised in dual-income and single-parent families, they've already been given considerable financial responsibility. Surveys show they are deeply involved in family purchases, be they groceries or a new car. One in nine high school students has a credit card co-signed by a parent, and many will take on extensive debt to finance college. Most expect to have careers and are already thinking about home ownership, according to a 1998 survey of college freshman for Northwestern Mutual Life Insurance Co. "This is a very pragmatic group. At 18 years old, they have five-year plans. They are already looking at how they will be balancing their work/family commitments," says Deanna Tillisch, who directed the survey.

GRASSROOTS. That means marketers who want to reach worldly wise Gen Yers need to craft products and pitches that are more realistic. To rejuvenate its Gen X hit House of Style, for example, MTV switched the emphasis on the weekly fashion show from celebrity lifestyles to practical information, with segments on decorating your bedroom and buying a prom dress. "We adapted the show to be more of what they wanted to see," said Todd Cunningham, director of brand research for MTV.

To break through Gen Y's distrust, marketers are also trying to make their campaigns more subtle and more local. A growing number, including Universal Studios, Coca-Cola, and McDonald's, use "street teams." Made up of young people, the teams hang out in clubs, parks, and malls talking to teens about every-

thing from fashion to finance, trying to pinpoint trends as they emerge. Other marketers are trying to build grassroots support for their brands. Following the lead of underground rock bands, mass marketers have taken to "wild postings," that is, tacking up ad posters on street corners and construction sites. Others sponsor community events or hand out coupons and T-shirts at concerts and ball games. Golden Books Publishing Co. distributed sample chapters from a new teen book series at movie theaters. The idea is to let kids stumble onto the brand in unexpected places.

Last year, when Lee Apparel introduced Pipes, a line of oversize, multipocketed pants aimed at 10- to 14-year-old boys, it spent its marketing dollars on the Internet, outdoor posters, and skateboard magazines. "As a brand, you need to go where they are, not just pick a fashion statement, put it on TV, and wait for them to come to you," says Terry Lay, president of the Lee brand. Even Coke, a master of slick advertising, looks for more personal ways to reach Gen Y. Last summer, it courted teens with discount cards good for movies and fast food. To build credibility, it mailed them directly to high school sports stars and other leaders first before handing out more at stores.

Of course, plenty of marketers continue to reach for this group with national TV campaigns. The ones that work are funny, unpretentious, and often confusing to older consumers. Consider Volkswagen of America Inc. Although VW doesn't market direct-

> The biggest change is the Net. Fashion trends that used to spread slowly now hit everywhere instantly.

ly to teens, both its Golf and Passat models show up on surveys as Gen Y faves. Part of the credit goes to the carmaker's quirky TV commercials, which are about as far from the traditional image-building ads Detroit churns out as possible. "We're a little edgier, a little more risk-tolerant, and not so mainstream," says VW marketing director Liz Vanzura. While other marketers fled the airwaves when Ellen DeGeneres came out of the closet on her show last spring, VW used the groundbreaking episode to introduce a new commercial showing two guys in a car who pick up a discarded chair. The ad, funny and oblique, became a favorite among young adults and teens.

With the oldest Gen Yers turning 20 this year, a lot of other companies will soon find themselves grappling with this new generation. Toyota Motor Corp., noting that 4 million

new drivers will come of age each year until 2010, unveiled the Echo at this year's Detroit auto show. With low emissions and a price well below the Corolla, the new subcompact is aimed squarely at boomers' kids who are buying their first cars. General Motors Corp. is putting together a task force to figure out how to appeal to Gen Y. The auto maker brings teens and children as young as sixth-graders into car clinics, where researchers probe their opinions of current models and prototypes of future cars. Michael C. DiGiovanni, GM's head of market research and forecasting, says Gen Y kids have an entirely different aesthetic from their parents. Their sense of how a product should look and feel has been shaped by the hours they spend at the keyboard. "One of the trends that will manifest itself is computers," says DiGiovanni. "The design of products will be influenced by the way a computer screen looks."

Meanwhile, computers and other high-tech products are starting to look less industrial and more sleek in an effort to attract younger buyers. By using bright colors and cool designs, Motorola Inc. helped transform the pager from a lowly tool for on-call workers to a must-have gizmo for teens. Apple Computer Inc. appeals directly to the same group with products such as its rounded, space-age-looking iMac computer. "For this generation, the computer is like a hot rod," says Allen Olivo, Apple's senior director for worldwide marketing, who says kids are constantly comparing features and styling with their friends' systems.

Apple's stylish iMac may or may not become the computer of choice for this new generation. But Apple and other marketers that attempt to chart the Gen Y psyche now could have an advantage as this generation moves into adulthood. After all, some of the biggest brands on the market today got their start by bonding with boomers early and following them from youth into middle age. Will the labels that grew up with baby boomers reinvent themselves for Generation Y? Or will the big brands of the new millennium bear names most of us have not yet heard of?

29

Big Footprints

Hey, Baby Boomers Need Their Space, OK? Look at All Their Stuff

They Like Gourmet Kitchens And High Ceilings, Too, So Homes Get Pricier

'Not That Anybody Cooks'

BY CARLOS TEJADA
AND PATRICK BARTA
Staff Reporters of THE WALL STREET JOURNAL

SOUTHLAKE, Texas – The nation's average price for a new home now exceeds $200,000, the Commerce Department reported yesterday. To see why, take a peek inside Rich and Diane Bean's double-decker walk-in closet. It's under the staircase, just down the hall from their two-oven kitchen and steps from the master bathroom, with its vaulted ceiling.

Even though the Beans culled their wardrobes before moving to this Dallas suburb in September they hang some of their more seldom-worn apparel on racks more than 10 feet above the floor. Mrs. Bean, who is 48 years old and of average height, can barely touch the hems. "If you're 10 feet tall, they're great," she says as she reaches up to tug on a skirt.

In the heavily windowed family room of the Bean's new $360,000 home, a Carpenters song on the radio fills the expanse beneath a 20-foot-high ceiling. Mr. Bean, 50, a construction-company president, concedes that the big windows and the house's generous size – 3,800 square feet – may make it less energy efficient than it could be. But, he says, "We just wanted that, whatever the price may be."

More Amenities

Like the American waistline, the new American home is getting larger. Empty nesters, baby boomers at the tops of their careers and the young and options-rich all are buying homes with more bedrooms, more bathrooms and more flourishes than ever before. And it shows: The average new-home price was $209,700 in November, up 4.2%

from an upwardly revised $201,300 in October and up 17% from a year earlier. The increase reflects both the demand for more amenities and the higher costs of land, building materials and labor.

Even luxury builders are amazed at the depth and breadth of the demand. "Does anybody need all this? No," says Robert Toll, chief executive officer of Toll Brothers Inc., the nation's largest high-end homebuilder. His company builds some of its homes with recesses designed to display statues or outdoor features such as pillared driveway entrances. "We sell what nobody needs," he says.

In fact, need is hardly a consideration these days. Thanks to low unemployment, relatively low mortgage rates and a long run of stock-market profits, more and more home buyers feel like they can buy what they want, and that, it turns out, is quite a lot.

Though about half of today's new homes sell for $167,400 or less, the average size is 2,230 square feet, about 10% more than a decade ago. Most have at least three bedrooms, and more than half have two stories and at least 2 1/2 baths, roughly one for each member of the average household. "People want incredible amounts of space now," says Leslie Barry Davidson, a Houston architect. They "don't come in and say they want good materials, good labor, good craftsmanship. They come in and say, 'I want space for all my stuff, for my clothes, my skis, my junk.'"

'Showing Off'

To Houston architect William Stern, who builds just two or three large homes a year, the trend is appalling. The bigger-is-better trend is about "showing off to neighbors," he says. "People are saying, 'I can be a 1920s tycoon like anybody else.'"

Perhaps that's why the high end of the market is particularly frothy. In northern New Jersey, builders are putting up as many as 25 speculative homes each month with price tags between $500,000 and $1 million each. Most of the homes are targeted at executives relocating to the New York area, but a handful are designed specifically for Wall Street types with incomes fattened by year-end bonuses.

Whether the buyers will actually be there when the homes are finished isn't clear. "The relocation market makes sense; the magic money market is a little harder to predict," says Patrick O'Keefe, chief executive of New Jersey's builders association.

Though some expect higher interest rates to put the brakes on the current housing boom, the trend toward bigger homes reflects a demographic shift and a general feeling that homes aren't just housing, but an investment. A couple of decades ago, first-time homebuyers were almost forced to turn to the suburbs because that was where they could find cheap land and affordable tract homes. Now, while some new homes are "tear downs" in established urban neighborhoods, the vast majority are in suburban developments often aimed at repeat home buyers

who want a bigger piece of land and an escape from the pressures of city life.

With housing prices climbing just about everywhere the last few years, buyers also seem to have forgotten the crashes that devastated home values a decade ago in California, New York and Texas. "Generally, people believe the stock market is more volatile" than the housing market, says Nicolas P. Retsinas, director of the Joint Center for Housing Studies of Harvard University in Cambridge, Mass.

The Beans, for instance, wanted a big, comfortable home to come home to after moving 13 times since the early 1980s while Mr. Bean was climbing the corporate ladder. The upstairs TV room, outfitted with University of Nebraska football souvenirs, has room for a pool table. The oversized bedroom houses exercise equipment. The half-acre lot will get a dog. "We're going to be here long enough, so we made it the way we wanted," Mr. Bean says.

The couple also studied the nation's surging housing market and concluded that a big house would have better resale potential than a smaller one. "Perhaps we got more house than we needed because of that," Mr. Bean says.

The big home isn't a new idea. In the 1890s, economist Alfred Marshall noted that as people progressed economically, they wanted better food, better clothes and larger houses – both for comfort and social standing. In the first two decades of the century, says Houston architectural historian Stephen Fox, home buyers preferred spacious houses with lots of windows, large rooms, and ceilings that exceeded nine feet and often reached 12 feet.

By the 1930s, however, the Depression and changing tastes drove builders to construct smaller homes with smaller rooms and fewer windows. Ceiling heights dropped to what became a standard eight feet. Homes grew again after World War II, but the average new home actually shrank slightly during each recession of the past three decades, according to National Association of Home Builders.

Today, Americans again are feeling confident about buying big. More than 10% of U.S. households had incomes of more than $100,000 in 1998, up from 7.5% in 1992. Then, there's the long run-up in the stock market. Michael Levine, a 43-year-old garment executive, funded the extra amenities in his new home by selling shares of Microsoft Corp. His 5,000-square-foot, $640,000 home, currently being built on an acre lot in the Philadelphia suburb of New Hope, Pa., will include a conservatory with a view of the mountains, as well as a spacious, well-appointed kitchen. "Not that anybody cooks, but it looks impressive," says the New York garment-industry executive.

About two days a week, Mr. Levine commutes more than an hour each way to New York. When he comes home to his new house, his garage will easily accommodate his two sport-utility vehicles. He is also looking forward to the special warming drawer that will keep his supper warm when he works late. Next, Mr. Levine wants to put a piano in his living room, though the room otherwise won't see much use. "Do I need one? I don't need one," he says.

For the same appearance reasons, maple cabinets made up 23% of the wood-cabinet market in 1998, up from 15% four years before, while use of more affordable oak has declined. And Broan-NuTone Group Inc., which sells home accessories, has seen a 50% increase in orders since 1998 for a line of Italian-crafted range hoods selling for $900 to $35,000. "They want a trophy kitchen. They know they're not going to use it, but they want the look," says Karen Collins, a Broan spokeswoman.

Toll Brothers, based in Huntingdon Valley, Pa., has been in business for years, but its high-end market began to soar in the 1990s. For the fiscal year ended Oct. 31, it sold 3,555 homes at an average price of more than $400,000, up from 1,324 homes at an average price below $300,000 in 1993. In recent years, it has piled on the amenities, such as double ovens or twin dishwashers. Master bathrooms often have two sinks and two toilets. It gives the first residents in a new neighborhood landscaping bonuses so subsequent customers will be encouraged to upgrade as well.

Executives lately are studying options for a new line of empty-nester homes that, while smaller, can be just as lavishly accessorized, if not more so. "Will they pay for this?" Edward D. Weber, a vice president, asks one

morning as he points to an optional bay window in one design. "Seniors throw money at them. No problem," says Jed Gibson, the company's director of architecture.

Toll Brothers decks out its model homes with its glitziest options in hopes that one will clinch a sale. It might be a 20-foot-tall closet or a circular driveway edging up to the front step. A favorite of Mr. Weber's: a second-floor master bedroom that opens into a walk-in closet with mirrored walls. At the other end of the closet is the bathroom, with a large bathtub below a window. The span from bedroom to tub is 72 feet, or about the length of the typical mobile home.

The builder has been able to make rooms bigger because stronger trusses have eliminated the need of most walls to act as supports. Though ceilings have crept up past nine feet, better insulated walls and tighter windows have made heating and cooling the big spaces less costly.

In part to get around a chronic shortage of skilled labor, Toll Brothers makes the walls and ceilings in a factory and assembles them on site. It builds its developments with the houses at varying distances from the street to avoid a symmetrical, cookie-cutter look. The company plants fatter, three-year-old trees along its streets so they look more impressive than the saplings planted in other builders' neighborhoods.

In a 4,600-square-foot house here in Southlake, Antoine Jenkins is delighted that Toll Brothers keeps raising its prices, which he hopes will add value to the $380,000, five-bedroom home he and wife Karen bought this

past fall. He believes the house, with its two staircases, big double doors and embedded alcoves for plants or statues, will do better at resale than his previous home, a smaller one in Manassas, Va. But before investment value, Mr. Jenkins, 36, a human-resources executive at computer-services concern Sabre Holdings Corp., demanded comfort. He enjoys the fact that, because of the space and acoustics, he can't hear his three daughters running the water or flushing the toilet in another room. He loves the bathtub big enough for his stocky frame. Most of all, he loves the den, which has the wall-size bookcase he ordered and a big window overlooking the backyard. "The study is where I'll put my humidor and cigars, with the bottle of port on the side. There'll be a music system. When I come home, that's where Daddy goes," he says.

For the down payment, he rustled up $40,000 from the sale of his shares in Nextel Communications Inc. and American Express Co., as well as shares of Microsoft he received when he worked for the software giant. But he realizes it might not all last. A thus-far successful investor, Mr. Jenkins nevertheless lost money last year while playing stock options. But he isn't worrying. "If it happens, it happens. I'm here today, who knows where I'll be tomorrow?" he says. "If you look for the downturn, you miss the good times. I'll get it now and I'll have no regrets later."

Extreme Nesting

Knock knock: Who's there? Your haircutter, the car-repair guy, even the doctor. June Fletcher finds overstressed families staying home and bringing the world to their door.

By June Fletcher

Staff Reporter of The Wall Street Journal

Michael Kempner is buying time.

Two years ago, Mr. Kempner ran himself ragged most weekends, driving around town doing errands. "I was totally on the run," he says. "I always felt stressed." But these days, he hangs around the house most weekends, doing puzzles with his three kids or watching sports on television. The difference? He now pays extra to have everyone from dry cleaners to car washers come to his house. "Life has become so compressed," he says, "that I decided my time with my family is worth more than money."

Now that we've journeyed all the way into the new millennium, a lot of us just want to stay home. Many families have become so overscheduled and overloaded that they're rebelling – by not going anywhere. Exhausted from hectic work schedules, long commutes and family demands, people are increasingly reluctant to go out again, for almost any reason, once they get home. The hunker-down mentality is fueled by the fact that, thanks to the booming economy, many people now have the affluence to fund their stay-at-home fantasies.

As a result, more consumers are shelling out extra cash to have goods and services delivered, or paying other people to run their errands. Feeling that they have more money than time, some Americans are willing to pay a premium for the privilege of being a couch potato.

Mr. Kempner, owner of a public-relations firm, has found all kinds of businesses will come to his Cresskill, N.J., home – for a price. His personal trainer, his car detailer, his wife's masseuse and his children's piano teacher all make regular visits. He bought his wife's birthday present from a jeweler willing to send a selection of watches for him to review in his living room. And last Friday, while others were out celebrating New Year's Eve, he had the party come to him: flowers, sushi, chips and salsa were delivered to his house.

"A year or two ago, I don't think all of these businesses would have been willing to come to my home," says Mr. Kempner, who says the convenience usually adds at least 5% to the price. "But now they're beginning to realize that busy people like me won't buy from someone who won't deliver."

Indeed, plenty of businesses, big and small, are capitalizing on the yearnings of stressed-out consumers to give up on gridlock and let the world beat a path to their doors. Making house calls can be lucrative, even for small entrepreneurs. Stephen Newman, who runs a come-to-your-house brake-repair service, charges up to $200 – more than twice the rates the big chains offer. A car buff and former stockbroker from Fairfax, Va., Mr. Newman says his business has grown more than 25% during the past five years, so much that lately he's been turning new customers away.

Even the doctor's house call, pretty much a thing of the past, is starting to show signs of life: The American Academy of Home Care Physicians says its membership has doubled, to 700 members, during the past two years.

Certainly, the very rich have always enjoyed the convenience of having their tai-chi instructors or dog groomers come to their homes. But now, a whole new group of people can afford – and are willing – to pay for such pampering. Priscilla La Barbera, an assistant professor of marketing at New York University, regularly has an $80 hourlong massage in the privacy of her one-bedroom apartment. At first, she felt it was "self-indulgent." But after a few sessions, she realized how much more she enjoyed home massages than those done in spas, and stopped feeling guilty about the expense. "Afterwards, it's so relaxing not to have to get dressed and go back out into the elements," says Ms. La Barbera, who often drifts off to sleep on the portable table the masseuse sets up in her living room.

In recent years, there's been a "societal shift" in the way people view the worth of their free time, says Ms. La Barbera, and the market has responded. "So many things can be ordered through one toll-free call," she says. "And people are beginning to realize that their time has real value."

The strong stay-at-home sentiment has been a perfect fit for the Internet. Online shopping and Web-based delivery companies play right into the batten-down-the-hatches mentality, which has fueled their growth. According to Jupiter Communications, an Internet research firm in New York, online grocery purchases increased more than 50% since 1998, to $233 million, and should continue to rise rapidly, reaching a whopping $7.5 billion in 2003. While it remains to be seen how many of the new Web-based delivery services will actually survive, it's clear they've tapped into a well of pent-up feelings.

Streamline.com, a Westwood, Mass., delivery service that went public in June, thinks there's money to be made in doing "necessity-based, menial shopping," says Chief Executive Timothy De Mello. For a flat charge of $30 a month, the company delivers groceries, as well as dry-cleaning, repaired shoes, rental videos, fresh flowers, stamps, processed film, bottled water and prepared meals (home-office supplies and liquor soon will be added). In the past four years, the company's customer base has grown to 4,000 households from 200; its revenue for the quarter ended Oct. 2 more than doubled, to $3.62 million, from the same period a year earlier – although, like most Web companies, it has yet to show a profit. "We're banking on the idea that people want to offload a lot of boring activities," Mr. De Mello says.

Time With the Kids

The idea of paying someone else to do the routine stuff is especially appealing to two-career couples. "My day is completely scheduled, every single day," says Valerie Andrews, a Boston attorney, who has two preschoolers. She and her husband, also a lawyer, commute an hour each way to work, putting them under "real time constraints," she says. "I want more time to be with my kids, or work in the office."

Mrs. Andrews, a Streamline customer since 1997, says the system isn't without flaws – occasionally an item has been left out of her grocery order, and the selection isn't as big as it would be in a supermarket. But on the whole, she thinks online shopping has made her more "systematic and efficient." And though she doesn't think the company's food prices are bargains – she describes them as on par with upscale local markets – she's noticed that her grocery bill has actually gone down during the past two years: "When you're buying food online, you can't be tempted with how something smells or looks, so you're less likely to buy it on impulse."

No task seems too special to hire out. At Your Service, a Burke, Va., company, says that during the holidays, several time-pressed customers paid the company to buy, address and mail stacks of Christmas cards – complete with fake "personal" greetings and signatures. "It works well because most people don't know what their friends' handwriting looks like," says co-owner Stacey Both. For rates of $15 to $30 an hour, the company does all sorts of errands for customers, from taking the family dog to the vet to getting a car registration renewed.

Buying more free time is money well spent, some consumers say, even if they don't do much with it. Debra Thomas, a Houston public-relations consultant, pays a personal assistant $75 to run errands and do small tasks four hours each week, ranging from watering the plants to changing the cat litter. Handing off the petty chores gives her guilt-free time to relax, Ms. Thomas says, though she often spends it doing nothing more than lounging in bed and drinking a glass of red wine. "Before, I always had a sinking feeling each weekend that I should be doing this or that," she says. "Now, I just put it on the list for my assistant."

FROM REENGINEERING TO E-ENGINEERING

Companies large and small are racing to revamp operations for the Internet Age

Men and women who have spiced up their sex lives with Viagra can thank the Web for its quick arrival on the market. Here's why: Pfizer Inc. now dashes off electronic versions of its drug applications to Washington for Food & Drug Administration approval. In the old days, it had to truck tons of paper to regulators and thumb through copies of all those pages manually whenever the feds had a question. By managing documents on the Web, Pfizer sliced the old one-year approval timetable nearly in half and sped Viagra into the world's boudoirs.

Post-Viagra, Pfizer's drugs will move through the pipeline even faster. The company's wired researchers now use the Web to mine libraries of technical data and collaborate on new drug development. "We've reengineered our business–digitally," says Vice-President for Research James Milson.

Reengineering. It was all the rage in the mid-'90s. But the vast and speedy Internet is ushering in an even bigger wave of business transformation. Call it E-engineering. Companies realize it's not enough to put up simple Web sites for customers, employees, and partners. To take full advantage of the Net, they've got to reinvent the way they do business–changing how they distribute goods, collaborate inside the company, and deal with suppliers.

This isn't just about saving time and money. The Web gets creative juices flowing, too. Employees who formerly spent their days faxing and phoning basic information to customers and suppliers are freed by the Net's magic to do more valuable work.

NEW BELIEVERS. Technology companies like Intel, Dell, and Cisco Systems were among the first to seize on the Net to overhaul their operations. At Intel Corp., for example, Web-based automation has liberated 200 salesclerks from tediously entering orders. Now, they concentrate instead on analyzing sales trends and pampering customers. Cisco Systems Inc., for its part, handles 75% of sales online. And 45% of its online orders for networking gear never touch employees' hands. They go directly from customers to the company's software system and on to manufacturing partners. That helped Cisco hike productivity by 20% over the past two years. But what grabs attention is sales: The

troika is doing a booming $70 million in online business each day.

With numbers like that, it's no wonder the tech jocks are being joined by a second wave of believers, ranging from Rust Belt manufacturing giants like Ford Motor Co. to foreign companies like Mexican cement seller Cemex. Even Corporate America's walking wounded are joining in. Just last month, troubled silicone supplier Dow Corning Corp. appointed an E-commerce czar. "Every businessperson I call on today is filled with greed or fear when it comes to the Internet," says James L. Barksdale, CEO of Netscape Communications Corp. "They're asking, 'How do I do it to them before they do it to me?'"

Doing it is no simple matter. Reengineering projects can be hugely complicated, with technology, business, and organizational upheavals all rocking the corporate foundations at once. There are harrowing risks. Casualties will include some companies that were too bold–but even more that were too timid.

Ford plans to be neither. It's taking on the E-engineering challenge holistically. One executive, Bernard Mathaisel, is both chief information officer and leader of its reengineering efforts. His plan is to fundamentally retool the way Ford operates with the help of the Web, cementing lifelong relationships with customers and slashing costs. "We're bringing new practices into every aspect of the company," says Mathaisel.

Already, E-business has begun to spread through the organization from front to back. Rather than relying on dealers to handle all customer contacts, Ford has put up a Web site that lets tire-kickers pick and price cars–then refers them to dealers. Ford then routes the customer feedback from the Web site to its marketers and designers to help them plan new products.

In the design process, the Web brings 4,500 Ford engineers from labs in the U.S., Germany, and England together in cyberspace to collaborate on projects. The idea is to break down the barriers between regional operations so basic auto components are designed once and used everywhere. When design plans conflict, the software automatically sends out E-mail alerts. Next, Ford's going to roll out a system for ordering parts from suppliers. When all of these pieces are in place, the com-

pany hopes to transform the way it produces cars–building them to order rather than to forecasts.

Other companies need to get wired to defend themselves. In the PC industry, the threat comes from Dell Computer Corp., which has deftly translated its hugely successful direct sales model to the Internet. Other PC companies have to match Dell's efficiencies–or die. Enter Ingram Micro Inc., the PC industry's largest distributor, which has teamed up with Solectron Corp., a giant contract manufacturer of high-tech gear.

TEAM EFFORT. In April, they plan to launch a brand-new way to build custom-made PCs inexpensively for companies like Hewlett-Packard Co. and Compaq Computer Corp. Instead of the PC companies handling orders and manufacturing, Ingram and Solectron will do it for them using a Web-based system that will hasten communications and slash assembly times. The PC companies are still in the driver's seat. They continue to build the value of their brands, designing and marketing their products and handling quality assurance. But now it's a team effort. "Customers are doing business with a virtual company," says Ingram President Jeffrey R. Rodek.

Figuring out what you do best is a crucial piece of Web reengineering. Few companies have pursued that philosophy as aggressively as Provident American Corp. in Norristown, Pa. In December, it took a radical step. It sold off nearly all of its life-insurance business and reinvented itself as HealthAxis.com, an online service that sells insurance products from other companies. CEO Michael Ashker decided the company was best at selling simple, high-volume insurance policies to consumers and taking a commission–rather than managing risk and independent agents.

There are some real shockers in this process. Like: Not all your customers are equal, or worthy. Weyerhaeuser Co. Inc., the forest-products company uses the Web to help it mine information from its suppliers, price products, and measure demand. More down-to-the-minute knowledge paid off: The plant boosted production by 60% to 800,000 doors last year. Weyerhaeuser can also offer more accurate bids to builders. In some cases, it can charge $40 less for certain doors–and still make a profit. That spells entré into some new

(Cont.)

These days, most PCs for business customers are made by PC companies based on sales forecasts and shipped through distributors. The PC company, distributors, and the resellers who deal with customers all keep inventories and often have to reconfigure computers to a customer's specifications. Ingram Micro, a distributor and assembler, and Solectron, a contract manufacturer, have come up with a system that will build computers to order and cut costs substantially. The amount of time a PC sits in inventory is expected to be reduced from months to hours.

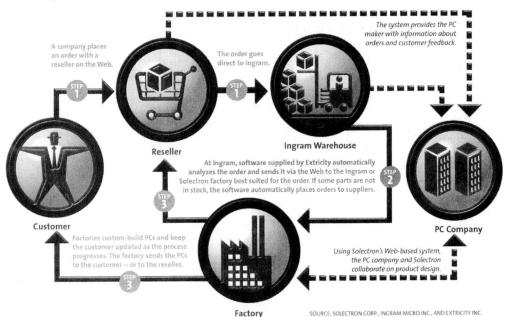

A company places an order with a reseller on the Web.
STEP 1

The order goes direct to Ingram.
STEP 1

The system provides the PC maker with information about orders and customer feedback.

Reseller

Ingram Warehouse

At Ingram, software supplied by Extricity automatically analyzes the order and sends it via the Web to the Ingram or Solectron factory best suited for the order. If some parts are not in stock, the software automatically places orders to suppliers.
STEP 2

STEP 3

Customer

Factories custom-build PCs and keep the customer updated as the process progresses. The factory sends the PCs to the customer -- or to the reseller.
STEP 3

PC Company

Using Solectron's Web-based system, the PC company and Solectron collaborate on product design.

Factory

SOURCE: SOLECTRON CORP., INGRAM MICRO INC., AND EXTRICITY INC.

markets. What's more, it now knows which customers bring in the big revenues and which don't. It can shed the ones that eat up too much time and order little.

That's painful for some customers. But E-engineering, badly executed, is even tougher on organizations. Just ask the engineers at NASA's Ames Research Center in Moffett Field, Calif. They spent $100 million building a Web-based collaborative engineering system to help accelerate development of the space station. Turned out they didn't have the technology plumbing in place to handle the job and lost some valuable data. Among the missing information: the plans for the Saturn V rocket.

Technology isn't always the hangup. In some cases, it's a stodgy corporate culture. "For many older executives, converting to E-business is like changing their religion," says John Thorp, vice-president of DMR Consulting Group Inc. And sometimes resistance comes from a pencil pusher down in purchasing. At Canadian Imperial Bank of Commerce in Toronto, purchasing agents missed the point of a new Web-based system for or-

dering supplies. They tried squeezing suppliers for price cuts when in fact the point was for everyone to buy from an electronic catalog–to land volume discounts. The bank set them straight with tailored incentive bonuses.

Perhaps the greatest danger is that business units will act independently, and the results will be piecemeal. The last thing you want is "tack-on" technology. To work, this effort must be coordinated at a high level–and changes should be fundamental, says analyst Bobby Cameron of Forrester Research Inc.

CHANGE FATIGUE. Citigroup gets it. As an executive vice-president in charge of advanced technologies, Edward D. Horowitz defines his job this way: to get the company's top 200 executives marching to the same drumbeat when it comes to the Internet. Horowitz's first salvo was to send them all copies of Clayton M. Christensen's best-selling book *The Innovator's Dilemma: When New Technologies Cause Great Firms to Fail*, about managing the dislocating effects of technology. Then he gave them a homework assignment: start banking online. At the

time, only a handful were doing it. "The message was you've got to use the product you're selling," says Horowitz.

That's a lot to ask of busy executives who are scrambling to complete the $80 billion merger of Citicorp and Travelers Group. But these days, change is relentless. Many corporate executives are just now finishing up major retooling of their financial and manufacturing processes. Plus, there's the Y2K problem. After a while, change fatigue sets in. "Companies are exhausted," says Michael Hammer, author of the 1993 book *Reengineering the Corporation: A Manifesto for Business Revolution*. His advice: "Suck it up. You have to face it again." In the era of E-engineering, risking burnout is better than getting fried.

*By Steve Hamm and Marcia Stepanek.
Contributing: Andy Reinhardt*

32

AT FORD, E-COMMERCE IS JOB 1

No other manufacturer is pushing so boldly onto the Web

The Rust Belt is approaching Net-speed. It was just last June, when a Ford Motor Co. task force made a presentation to Chief Executive Jacques A. Nasser and his top managers. Originally assigned to study how the Internet could improve manufacturing, the team had gone all out, showing Nasser a computer simulation of the auto company of the future. The vision was breathtaking: factories that built cars to order, dealerships that reported problems instantly so that plants could make adjustments, and suppliers that controlled inventories at Ford factories—much the way retailer Wal-Mart Stores Inc. does when it gives vendors responsibility for stocking its store shelves. "We were mesmerized," says Alice Miles, a veteran Ford purchasing manager. Nasser gave it an instant thumb's-up. "This is nothing short of reinventing the auto industry," he says.

Since then, the old-line Ford has been latching on to the Net like some new dotcom. In January, Ford showed off futuristic "24/7" concept vehicles packed with cybergoodies such as Internet connections and e-mail. Miles now heads auto-xchange, a newly created online trading mart for Ford's 30,000 suppliers that began taking orders in February. And in an effort to wire up its far-flung workforce of 350,000 people, Ford announced on Feb. 3 that it would offer each of them a home computer, a printer, and Internet access for $5 a month.

Some 90 years after Ford led the world into the era of mass manufacturing, the No. 2 auto maker wants to reprise its trailblazing role—and cash in the way it did decades ago. By using the Net to bust up bureaucracy and unleash radically new ways of planning, making, and selling cars, Ford could become a model of efficiency in the Internet Age. Streamlining suppliers and distribution using the Web could amount to savings equal to 25% of the retail price of a car, says analyst Jonathan Lawrence of Dain Rauscher. The auto-xchange mart could generate $3 billion in transaction fees within five years—of which Ford would get a hefty cut. And that doesn't take into account the monthly service fees of $20 to $25 that Ford could collect if drivers should want to hop on to the Net while roaring down the highway. Says David Bovet, an e-commerce expert at Mercer Management

> Ford's sweeping system, called CustomerConnect, will link buyers and factories with financiers, parts suppliers, and designers

Consulting Inc.: "Detroit will be where the rubber hits the road on the Information Highway, a real acid test for the potential of e-business."

Nasser's vision is a sweeping one. He pictures the day when a buyer hits a button to order a custom-configured Ford Mustang online, transmitting a slew of information directly to the dealer who will deliver it, the finance and insurance units who will underwrite it, the factory that will build it, the suppliers that provide its components, and the Ford designers brainstorming future models. To buyers, it will mean getting just what they ordered delivered right to their doorstep in days.

OUT IN FRONT. Plenty of old-line manufacturers are moving into cyberspace, but none so boldly or so broadly as Ford. And, with the exception of archrival General Motors Corp., none on such a huge scale. This past summer, GM launched e-GM, an initiative to link its suppliers and dealers and to forge Net ties with consumers at their PCs and in their cars. GM, however, has not yet announced plans to wire up its entire workforce. Still, the two are miles ahead of the rest of auto-dom, says David Cole, director of the University of Michigan's Office for the Study of Automotive Transportation. "They're just scaring the liver out of everyone else," he says.

Or are they? DaimlerChrysler and Toyota Motor Corp. are pursuing online ventures and experiments, but on a much smaller scale. Jurgen Hubbert, a member of Daimler-Chrysler's management board, says he's not worried about rushing into grand Internet deals: "Why jump into this sort of business when nobody makes money?" he asks.

So far, Wall Street isn't impressed, either. Despite its bold moves, Ford's stock is down 7.5%, to 46, since its sweeping plan was unveiled on Sept. 15. Analysts wonder if Nasser has bitten off more than he can chew. While tantalized by the potential of e-business, they worry that all the cyberdazzle will distract Ford from its bread-and-butter task of designing and building cars and trucks.

Certainly, there are plenty of risks. Skeptics wonder if consumers really want vehicles loaded with costly gadgetry that may be prone to technical problems and obsolescence. "People want to bring their portable communications devices with them," says DaimlerChrysler Chairman Robert Eaton. "Are we going to embed all those devices in every car? No." And some suppliers fret that the big cost savings Ford says will result from its online bazaar auto-xchange could instead squeeze vendors to the breaking point.

And for all its potential, e-commerce may find itself up against the biggest roadblock of all: a century-old industry with an infrastructure that impedes change. Slick new online ways to sell cars directly to buyers collide with an entrenched dealer base protected by tough state franchise laws. And systems that are capable of building custom cars actually clash with the economics of the high fixed costs that prod plant managers to run factories at full tilt.

It's not just ignorance that has made the Rust Belt slow to imitate such tech idols as Dell Computer Corp. Detroit is saddled with a much more complex manufacturing task than that faced by any computer outfit. Starting from scratch allowed Dell to create a state-of-the-art, direct-sales model. Over a 16-year period it has been able to tune its ordering and manufacturing processes—and update them for the Web. That's how it was able to custom assemble more than 25,000 different computer configurations for buyers last year. The company deals with hundreds of suppliers, but about 90% of its parts and components come from two dozen companies. And it works closely with them to make sure the parts are designed for snap-in assembly and for just-in-time delivery to its factories.

But even Dell's level of complexity is mere child's play compared with the challenges in the build-to-order auto business. Cars can contain 10,000 parts and, across Ford's entire line, some 1 million possible variations. Ford's F-150 full-size pickup truck, alone, is offered in well over 1,000 possible combinations of engine, transmission, body style, and color—without counting the truck's optional features.

(Cont.)

FORD'S NET STRATEGY: WHERE THE RUBBER MEETS THE INFORMATION HIGHWAY

Ford has launched an e-business strategy to rewire the auto maker. The ultimate vision: To use the Net to do everything from ordering a car to linking 30,000 suppliers. Here is the game plan:

What	How	Goal
RETAILING	Set up BuyerConnection Web site and joined MSN CarPoint site, where consumers can order custom-assembled cars, track their progress, and apply for financing.	Reduce working capital by shrinking excess inventories and wipe out costly rebates needed to move unwanted cars off dealer lots, thus saving up to $650 per car.
CUSTOMER SERVICE	OwnerConnection Web site lets owners get online help, manage their warranty service, and check on financing.	Improve service with 24-hour access. Gather better data on customer problems. And cut costs with automated help.
SUPPLIERS	Launched auto-exchange Web site for online purchasing and swapping of information between 30,000 suppliers and 6,900 dealers.	Save up to $8.9 billion a year in discounts and reduced transaction costs on parts, raw materials, and supplies. Speed data exchange with partners while collecting up to $3 billion a year in exchange fees.
MARKETING	Teaming up with Yahoo!, TeleTech, CarPoint, iVillage, and bolt.com to monitor the interests and buying patterns of Web-surfing customers.	Improve factory efficiency by anticipating customer demand. Funnel data on customer preferences to car designers.
DIGITAL DASHBOARD	Equip new cars with Web access, satellite phone services, and e-mail capabilities.	Make Ford the carmaker for an Internet generation. Collect millions of dollars in fee-based services.
FINANCING	Shift more of the activities of Ford Credit to the Net for online financing and collections.	Cut service costs by 15% to 20%, while boosting revenues by reaching new customers.
WIRED WORKERS	Offering all 350,000 employees a computer, printer, and Net access for $5 a month.	Makes the workforce Web-savvy so it will quickly adopt the Internet initiatives, while enabling the CEO to send weekly e-mail to employees.

To pull off the monumental task, Nasser has created a business group called ConsumerConnect that is driving the e-business efforts across company lines. He also went outside the company to find the team he wanted to lead it. Brian P. Kelley, 39, a former General Electric Co. appliance sales boss who was known there for championing customer communications and launching a GE Web site, was named to head ConsumerConnect last September. Since then, the boyish Kelley has recruited dozens of other Net whizzes from the likes of Whirlpool, Booz, Allen & Hamilton, and Procter & Gamble. Says Michelle Guswiler, director of corporate initiatives: "We see ourselves as a kind of Alpha squad, here to lead change and help make the cultural difference required to bring Ford into the 21st century."

One of ConsumerConnect's most promising efforts is auto-xchange, an online trading site where its 30,000 suppliers can be linked to Ford for quicker communication, better prices, and faster delivery. Analysts say auto-xchange could save Ford $8 billion in procurement prices, and nearly $1 billion more from reduced overhead, paperwork, and other transaction efficiencies each year. Ford owns a majority of auto-xchange, with Silicon Valley giants Oracle Corp. and Cisco Systems Inc. each having a stake.

The troika's plans for auto-xchange are much dreamier yet. They hope it will become so popular that everyone in the auto industry will use it to barter for parts and office supplies. Indeed, Wall Street is expecting that Ford will take auto-xchange public by 2001, when it would have estimated revenues of more than $500 million.

BIRD'S-EYE VIEW. To make Ford's e-commerce ventures robust, there's a lot that must go on under the hood. Oracle is doing the heavy lifting on the software and databases needed to swap information and conduct transactions seamlessly. Cisco, which signed on as a partner on Feb. 9, will provide much-needed networking expertise. And Microsoft Corp.'s CarPoint, an auto sales and information Web site, will help Ford develop a build-to-order service. Internet service provider UUNet, PC maker Hewlett-Packard, and middleman PeoplePC signed on to put Ford's sprawling workforce online, starting in April.

Other tech partners are helping Ford get closer to its customers. Online powerhouses Yahoo! and Priceline.com, along with Denver-based call-center wizard TeleTech, will design systems that deliver highly personalized warranty, loan, repair, and customized services based on more detailed knowledge of driver lifestyles and buying habits. "It could give us a bird's-eye view of what consumers want out of a car before we build it," says Ford design chief J Mays.

Meanwhile, ConsumerConnect and Ford's Visteon auto-parts unit are teaming up to wire future Fords for e-mail and news, voice-recognition systems, and satellite phone

FEAR AND LOATHING IN THE SHOWROOM

Fort Worth auto dealer Cliff Johnson says he's pretty sure that the Internet won't put him out of business anytime soon, but he's wary of e-commerce anyway. Johnson, like many car dealers across the country, doesn't want auto makers and dot-coms getting in between him and his customers. "The Net is making everyone fight for what they perceive as a customer," Johnson says. "And that's a problem."

And not just for Johnson. As auto makers push forward with plans to use the Net to sell more cars, build them more cheaply, and deliver them faster to consumers, traditional dealerships are feeling the heat. Auto makers' motivation to put the squeeze on them is strong: Dealer overhead adds up to $2,000 to a car's price—after it leaves the factory—and adds weeks to order-to-delivery times.

STEALING. Costly, 80-day inventories of cars on dealer lots is also what General Motors Corp. CEO Jack Smith calls "a huge amount of waste...and the Internet can help us cut that." Smith and others also want their companies to use the Net to get closer to customers rather than remaining one step removed, as they are now.

For now, though, getting rid of costly middlemen isn't an option. So far, state franchise laws and political clout in statehouses across the nation protected dealers from any head-on digital encroachments. The fiercely protective Texas Auto Dealers Assn., for example, was able to win passage of state laws last fall, thwarting efforts by Ford and GM to sell late-model used cars to customers directly, via the Internet.

But auto makers are finding other ways to get cozier with customers. New dealer-rating systems are being rolled out to reward only those dealers who become more Net-friendly. Daimler-Chrysler Corp.'s Five Star dealership program, for example, only funnels sales leads from the company's Web site to those dealers who meet toughened new standards for service, facilities, and Internet savvy—about half of the company's 4,400 dealers. General Motors sends leads from its GM BuyPower Web site to only 75% of its dealers, including those that answer Net queries from customers within 24 hours.

Failure to comply carries a high sticker price: Slick new e-biz partnerships with Internet service providers give auto manufacturers a way to bypass dealers who refuse. "The manufacturer could steal the lead and steal the customer and give it to whoever they want," say Philadelphia car dealer Geno Barbera.

That's why savvy auto dealers are warming up to the Web. Today, 65% of the nation's 22,600 auto dealerships have at least one dedicated Internet salesperson, 61% have a Web site, and 40% participate in online buying servcies, according to Forrester Research Inc. "There are some dealers who see opportunity in the Net and some who just want it to go away," says Maryann Keller, president of Net company Priceline.com's auto division. The latter, she says, "will go away."

Cliff Johnson, for one, will keep working the Net so that nobody comes between him and his customers.

By David Welch in Detroit

services that will, says Kelley, "turn the family car into a Web portal on four wheels." The payoff: a whole array of new services in a marketplace where basic car prices are declining. Better yet, Web services and phones can be sold on a subscription basis, generating monthly fees that keep cash flowing into Ford's coffers for the life of the car.

Given the risks, why does Nasser chance it–especially since Ford is already the most profitable player in the global auto industry? The Net offers a chance to reinvent manufacturing. Forget marginal efficiency improvements. At stake here is the holy grail of carbuilding: Changing from the century-old "push" model to a streamlined "pull" system would save auto makers billions of dollars. Traditionally, an auto plant cranks at full capacity–building a predetermined mix of cars–and ships them to dealers who then rely

on strong-arm tactics or fat rebates to move the ones customers don't want.

PINPOINT TAILORING. In a pull model, customers decide what they want built. That could shorten the current 64-day average time from customer order to delivery, freeing a good chunk of the $60 billion now tied up in U.S. completed-vehicle inventories, say Ernst & Young auto consultant Lee A. Sage.

To do this, carmakers would need to deliver those cars swiftly. And they would need to tailor vehicles and pricing with pinpoint accuracy, or high-overhead factories would sit idle. Kelley says Ford hopes to deliver its first high-volume built-to-order vehicles within two years. The company would probably first offer certain popular combinations for quick delivery, taking more time for unusual configurations. Ford hopes to see the results in its bottom line within five years. By

then, Kelley says, Ford's Net initiatives could save the company billions in waste.

Reinventing manufacturing while juggling high-tech alliances may be a Herculean task, but Nasser figures he has no choice. Still, Nasser is determined to forge ahead. "We're going to turn the old ways on their ears," he says. "It might not happen right away, but change is inevitable." Judging by Ford's progress since last June, Nasser intends to make sure the company wastes no time making it happen.

By Kathleen Kerwin in Detroit and Marcia Stepanek in New York, with David Welch in Detroit

33

The Users:
Supply Side

New software can streamline the often onerous task of procurement

By David A. Patton

Staff Reporter of The Wall Street Journal

When Hewlett-Packard Co. began a cost-cutting effort a year ago, it fell to Greg Spray to figure out how the computer giant could save money on everything from paper clips to computer servers.

Mr. Spray is H-P's director of operations procurement – a job that covers purchases of the equipment employees need to do their jobs, excluding material purchased to manufacture products or provide services. It's a job that's often focused on office supplies, computers and the like, but also includes maintenance and services, such as travel arrangements.

Mr. Spray found one glaring problem: The way H-P made those purchases wasn't particularly efficient. H-P's 104 divisions relied on "a handful of locally grown procurement systems trying to offer access to employees, but we didn't really work together across sites," Mr. Spray says. Instead, he says, each group within H-P would negotiate individual contracts and rely on different software applications to send orders to suppliers and track billing. It was a practice that left the company with a patchwork of deals struck with more than 70,000 suppliers – and with ample opportunity to save money.

Enter **Ariba** Inc. The Sunnyvale, Calif., software firm is one of a handful of companies trying to streamline the onerous task of procurement by letting companies connect with suppliers over the Internet.

The idea: Companies buy special software to connect to Ariba's online catalog of office supplies. The companies then get their suppliers to join Ariba's network and have their prices posted in the catalog. Buyers can then have their whole company order from one supplier, using one standard form, cutting down on equipment and personnel costs – and giving the company leverage to negotiate better deals with suppliers. Meanwhile, in theory, suppliers also get a benefit by joining the network – any of Ariba's clients can see the suppliers' prices posted in the online catalog. So, if their prices are competitive, suppliers could attract new business online.

Matching Visions

In late 1998, H-P decided to put Ariba to the test, and Mr. Spray was asked to head a group that would roll out the latest version of Ariba's Operating Resource Management System software, or ORMS, to some 400 users at two sites that best represented the needs of H-P's overall work force.

"We looked at almost everybody," Mr. Spray says, referring to the growing number of firms offering systems for managing operations procurement. "Our vision matched Ariba's."

Ariba installed software on H-P's servers that lets employees go to a Web site on the company's internal network – or intranet – and review the supply catalog. The list covers all the usual office items – paper clips, pens, paper – all the way up to computers, software, chairs, desks and travel services. (Some clients, Ariba says, even list company cars in the catalog.)

Ariba's software is browser-based, using either Netscape Navigator or Internet Explorer, meaning it can be set up on computer systems from PCs to workstations. Employees are led step-by-step through the buying process by a user interface that allows orders to be tracked as they are approved by managers, received by suppliers and shipped. If an approval is needed, it is e-mailed to the appropriate person; if that person fails to take action within a set period, the approval notice is automatically forwarded to the next person up the corporate ladder.

The orders are then routed to Ariba via the Internet, and passed along to suppliers. Bills are sent to buyers electronically.

Because the catalog is located on a central server, Mr. Spray's group can add or subtract items, change prices or add new suppliers with a few mouse clicks. If employees want an item not in the catalog, or are seeking more information about a product, Ariba's software will route them to a supplier's Web site.

Mr. Spray notes that Ariba is easy to use not only for system administrators but also for end users. "The trick of this is to create a compelling catalog site that gives the casual user a way to find what they want," he says.

The savings promise to be considerable. Mr. Spray estimates that implementing Ariba will wind up costing between $12 million and $25 million, a figure that includes the cost of the intranet H-P, of Palo Alto, Calif., has built over the past few years. Gregson Siu, the manager of H-P's operations-procurement solutions center, estimates that by using Ariba, H-P will be able to wring savings of 3% to 5% a year out of its operations-procurement

spending. That spending totaled roughly $2 billion a year – indicating annual savings of $60 million to $100 million – before H-P's planned spinoff of Agilent Technologies Inc., its measurement-equipment unit. Mr. Siu says he can't yet estimate the impact of the Agilent spinoff on H-P's procurement spending.

Mr. Siu, who joined the effort to implement Ariba after "evaluating the architecture and technology of Ariba's business model" while at H-P Labs, says the cost of the software and the people needed to manage it are minimal.

"Whatever we're investing today in the systems will be less than what we are spending on our existing operations-procurement systems," Mr. Siu says. "But we will be getting more."

Ariba isn't alone in offering such software – its competitors include **CommerceOne** Inc., **Trilogy** Inc. and **Sterling Commerce** Inc., as well as traditional enterprise-resource-planning firms, such as **Oracle** Corp., **PeopleSoft** Inc. and **SAP** AG. But Ariba was the first to offer an Internet-based operations-procurement system, and has attracted several major clients, including **Merck** & Co., **General Motors** Corp. and **Lucent Technologies** Inc.

Getting Together

Ariba dates back to October 1996, when three groups of Web entrepreneurs working on e-commerce strategies aimed at business buyers crossed paths at Benchmark Capital, a Silicon Valley venture-capital firm. The three teams joined their efforts, formed Ariba and raised $6 million in venture funding.

In July 1997, Ariba shipped the first version of its ORMS. The company is now up to the sixth version, has more than 50 large corporate buyers and has signed up thousands of suppliers.

Mr. Siu expects Ariba to be available to 40,000 of H-P's workers in North America by the end of the company's fiscal first quarter in January 2000. He says old procurement processes will be phased out as Ariba reaches most of Hewlett-Packard's 80,000 workers world-wide by the end of next year. Mr. Siu has 25 people devoted to the deployment, but he expects the staffing needs for administration and help-desk support for the Ariba software will be minimal.

"Nobody has to be trained to use a Web site," says Ariba's Mr. Rome.

Suppliers have been strong supporters of the system. Mr. Siu says some suppliers offered to cut their prices as much as 20% to be in it – and thereby get access to the other buyers in the network. He adds, "The suppliers are our biggest cheerleaders because they

> *'Nobody has to be trained to use a Web site,' says one software provider*

will save money" through standardizing the order process.

Slow Start

That will take time, however, as H-P supplier Terry Kallen attests. Ms. Kallen, manager of emerging technologies for **Boise Cascade Office Products** Corp., Boise, Idaho, says the cost savings will be minimal at the outset because suppliers must still deal with the variety of systems that buyers use to place orders.

"It's not really a significant cost savings, but systems like Ariba do offer a savings in that all of one customer's orders are coming in through one format," she says. "To see major savings, all of our customers would have to move to one system, and that isn't likely to happen."

Still, H-P's managers have welcomed Ariba. Mr. Spray says managers have been skeptical until they see the benefits it offers for cutting costs and tracking spending.

"There has been tremendous sponsorship from executives," Mr. Siu says. "Many have said this is a no-brainer because the payback is there."

Mr. Patton is an editor for The Wall Street Journal Interactive Edition in New York.

Getting Information for Marketing Decisions

34

SAFE AT ANY SPEED?

Online testing: Package-goods companies embrace the Internet despite the dangers

by Jack Neff

Procter & Gamble Co. executives were stunned last month to discover private concept images for its Crest brand posted anonymously on the Yahoo! Finance message board. It took 11 days for the images, which had been used in online focus groups, to be removed.

No doubt about it: Online testing can be highly risky. But even conservative package-goods companies are embracing such methods in record numbers as the breakneck race to market becomes ever more intense.

LOW-COST ALTERNATIVE

Used as a faster, less expensive alternative to traditional tests, the Internet has opened up a new forum for everything from focus groups to real-world market simulation.

"There's a lot of pressure to move as fast as you can with the best possible information," said Ellen Gottlich, associate director of consumer understanding for Unilever's Home & Personal Care unit. That's a leap for an industry where P&G, for example, tested Febreze, Dryel and Fit Fruit & Vegetable Wash for more than five years before launching them nationally. Compare that to the same company's Crest MultiCare Flex & Clean, which rolled out this fall, less than a year after online tests.

But while the advantage of speed is clear—Ms. Gottlich said online focus groups can shrink testing time from the usual two to three weeks to one—it comes with added uncertainty.

"Certainly we are concerned about a brand new product concept ending up in the hands of a competitor" said Bill Reynolds, director of marketing services at Unilever Home & Personal Care. "We have weighed in with that concern [to our vendors], and I'm sure we're not alone in that area."

In the case of the Crest fiasco, Charles Hamlin, president of InsightExpress—an NFO Worldwide unit that shares an Internet server with the NFO//net.discussion service from which the P&G concepts were leaked—said someone hacked into the server to find and post links to the images. He added that NFO, which conducted the P&G tests, is investigating.

'AN ISOLATED INCIDENT'

"This is really a one-time, isolated incident, and steps have been made to ensure it doesn't happen again," said Bryan McCleary, supervisor-oral care, public relations, at P&G. "We strongly believe that Internet testing is a wonderful advance and a powerful new way of getting to know our consumers and that the benefits strongly outweigh the risks."

Research industry observers have long seen risks in sending sensitive concept images to the computer screens of consumers, but the usual fear isn't hackers. "You just honestly can't [provide complete security] on the Web," said Dan Coates, VP-consumer intelligence of online marketing feedback site Planetfeedback.com, and a founder of two interactive market research units. "For every technology we would try to deploy to protect the concepts, there was another technology that could surpass it."

But other testing forms, such as mail, pose risks as great, Mr. Hamlin said. And he doesn't believe security concerns will thwart rapid growth of online testing, which he expects to account for 25% of consumer market research by 2002, up from less than 1% currently.

Lower costs also could be a factor in that rise. Offline testing can cost anywhere from $2,000 for a focus group to more than $25,000 for a concept test run in a shopping mall, Mr. Coates said. When marketers test dozens or hundreds of concepts a year, it adds up.

Marketers, however, are wrestling with the issue of determining how well Internet users represent consumers generally, and whether online tests deliver results as reliable as offline forms.

"We know from years of validation that mall-intercept testing or consumer panel testing correlates with real-world purchase data," said Doug Hall, founder and president of new-products consultancy Richard Saunders International. "But we know that online [test results] don't correlate with mall intercept and there's no evidence that they correlate with consumer purchases."

COMPLETING 'VALIDATIONS'

Aware of such concerns, Unilever is "in the process

of completing a number of validations [of online consumer testing] and the results look fairly good," Ms. Gottlich said.

She acknowledged that Web users score new concepts lower for uniqueness than do consumers tested offline, and that distribution of data is different. But in the end, she said, Unilever executives appear to be making the same decisions using online tests that they would if they used offline testing.

WEB-SAVVY

Even with the growth of the online population, it's too soon to conclude that Web users accurately reflect consumers generally, research executives believe. Online researchers are trying various ways around the problem, including Inter-Survey, a Palo Alto, Calif., company that's putting free WebTV Internet access into a representative sample of households that agree to take surveys regularly.

But people who agree to take Web surveys tend to be more Web-savvy than others online, one research executive said, meaning that online researchers are getting a relatively sophisticated segment of the online population.

Even the same consumers tend to score concepts differently online than off, according to research from Burke Marketing. That research found consumers grade concepts closer to the middle range online and more at the high or low ends in verbally directed surveys.

Those middle-range responses are probably closer to how consumers really feel, said Jeff Miller, exec VP of Burke. But they can present new challenges in calibrating tests for accurate decision-making and in comparing online results with offline databases, Mr. Coates said.

On the positive side, Burke also found Web participants enjoy taking more surveys, finish faster and are more likely to repeat the process than are offline participants, Mr. Miller said.

MERWYN

As a solution to concerns about Internet testing—as well as to increase speed and lower costs—former P&G executive Mr. Hall has developed Merwyn, software that forecasts consumer acceptance of new products and services using a database of 4,000 concepts that has been tested over the past two years by such companies as AC-Nielsen Corp.'s Bases, NPD Group and AcuPOLL International.

Merwyn analyzes consumer purchase intent for concepts based on how well they measure up to what past consumer tests showed to be "the laws of marketing physics," Mr. Hall said.

Those laws state that the most successful concepts are those that convey overt benefits, real reasons to believe in those benefits and dramatic differences from existing products or services. The software also suggests ways marketers can improve a concept's scores.

Like online market researchers, Mr. Hall bills his product more as a way to screen preliminary concepts than test final ones. But he claims that running hundreds of concepts through Merwyn to find the handful that merit further development can whittle to as little as a day a process that Andersen Consulting estimates now takes 17 weeks.

> *"There's no evidence that [online test results] correlate with consumer purchases."*

Using simulation of a different sort, Information Resources Inc. last year launched IntroCast, which can trim time off test markets by forecasting a new product's volume based on past products' results.

IRI clients are using IntroCast to monitor whether a new product's trial and repeat purchase numbers are on pace to meet long-term goals and gauge how various levels of advertising and promotion will affect volume. Using IntroCast can trim the $1 million cost of a traditional in-market test by about 25% and, in some cases, up to 50%.

"With most new products, we can [use IntroCast to] do a decent job of forecasting year-one [national sales] potential after 12 to 16 weeks [in a test market]," Mr. Findley said, a quarter of the time required for a traditional test.

Such speed translates into lower cost and less risk of competitors discovering test markets in time to monitor or disrupt them, he said. IntroCast "also lets you play with alternative marketing plans," Mr. Findley said, without having to use simultaneous tests in multiple cities.

IRI client P&G, which in the past often ran tests in two or more cities to try different marketing support levels, is using just one BehaviorScan market each for such products as Impress plastic wrap and Bounty napkins, though Mr. Findley didn't comment on whether these moves are linked to IntroCast.

UNIVERSAL SIMULATION?

Not every product is ripe for simulation, however, Mr. Findley acknowledged. Repeat purchase rates are dif-

(Cont.)

ficult to project for products in new categories, such as P&G's Dryel and Swiffer, so marketers generally either have to test longer or supplement their testing with consumer surveys. (While P&G's rival S.C. Johnson & Son didn't test its Swiffer follow-up, Pledge Grab-It, it can be argued that the company had the benefit of monitoring P&G's test results for Swiffer).

IntroCast will likely mean shorter test markets in fewer cities, but the software is still no replacement for in-market testing, Mr. Findley said, adding: "Test market-

ing is alive and well."

Unilever's Mr. Reynolds however, believes marketers will keep looking for ways around test marketing.

"If it's a high-risk, high-return idea in one of your key strategic categories, that would argue for deeper testing," Mr. Reynolds said. "But because of the cost and time and visibility to the competition, there will be a general trend to do less in-market testing."

35

New ways to get into our heads

Marketers ditch old focus groups for video cameras, beepers, chats over coffee

By Melanie Wells
USA TODAY

GLENCOE, Ill. – Something odd is happening in Mary Flimin's kitchen.

As she chops onions for risotto late one afternoon, a pair of video cameras and two market researchers stationed in a corner are recording her every move. Meg Armstrong and Joel Johnson, who represent a cookware company, want to see how a gourmet like Flimin cooks and what she likes.

"It's my best friend, this pan," Flimin tells them, somewhat awkwardly.

Hours later, Armstrong and Johnson review their observations. Even though Flimin said she often makes cakes and bakes with fresh fruit, Armstrong notes that "her baking dishes are stashed in the boondocks, so she doesn't bake much."

That insight may not revolutionize cookware, but the way it was gained illustrates how market research is adapting to an ad-weary, marketing-savvy public. Sterile conference rooms with one-way mirrors – the traditional focus group setting – are no longer marketers' favorite window on real people. Instead, companies are cozying up to consumers in their homes, schools, offices and after-work hangouts. They're eavesdropping on conversations, peering into bedroom closets and poking around in bathroom cabinets. They're hiring anthropologists and psychiatrists to plumb willing consumers' product choices, verbal responses and even body language for deeper meanings.

Catherine DeThorne, ad agency Leo Burnett's director of planning, calls these techniques "getting in under the radar."

"Finding real insights about people is getting harder," she says. "A lot of marketers still think focus groups are fine, but it's not where we get great insights. We groomed a generation of professional respondents. Everyone has been in a focus group."

"Focus groups generate less than the entire truth," says anthropologist Ilsa Schumacher of Cultural Dynamics, which has worked for Amtrak and Porsche, among others. "There is an image to maintain; a public persona; a need to identify with the other members of the group. In a one-on-one discussion with an anthropologist in your home, there is no competition, no need to impress, no chance to strike a false note."

Not everyone is cheering for the modern methods.

"It's kind of pathetic that people are willing to be subjects in order to help marketers get inside a certain group's head and sell, sell, sell," says Michael Jacobson of the Center for Science in the Public Interest. "If anything, this type of research will become more pervasive and more sophisticated."

Some of it is already quite sophisticated. E-Lab, the market research and design company where Armstrong and Johnson work, uses professional recruitment firms to find subjects and typically pays consumers at least $100 to participate in a study.

"Often, we end up describing to clients the relationship people have with their stuff. A lot of times we hear from the company, 'Oh, I should have known that,' " says Rick Robinson, E-Lab principal. "I'm surprised at the range of clients we've had and the things we've been asked to study and develop."

His strangest project: A toothbrush maker asked him to find out what motivates people to brush their teeth or use mouthwash. It wanted to develop products that would give people a just-brushed fresh mouth.

Some research is done on the cheap. Motorola product designers solicited opinions on cell phone designs from Captain Kirk wannabes and Spock fans at a Star Trek convention.

LATEST MARKETING TOOL: BEEPER STUDIES

Marketers also have found ways to track consumers' tastes without actually trailing them around. Instead, they do "beeper" studies, in which participants are instructed to write down what they're doing when they are paged.

Thomson Electronics hired E-Lab to perform such a study to learn how consumers mix listening to music with their daily activities. When participants were paged, they recorded where they were; what music, if any, was playing; who picked it; and their mood. Researchers also tailed people around their homes, noting where they kept their stereo and how their music collection was organized.

"We wanted to know how often people sit down to enjoy a CD as opposed to using it for background music," says Lou Lenzi, vice president of new media at

Thomson, which wanted information for new products coming out next year.

Where traditional focus groups were meetings among strangers, marketers today often infiltrate groups of friends, perhaps joining them for cocktails after work.

Ad agency Leo Burnett arranged such a meeting one night recently in Chicago. Six professional female friends in their late 30s and 40s gathered over wine and crudites at a coffee house called Urban Blend. At one point, the women discussed a Wells Fargo ad that touts its investment in women-owned businesses.

"I'd put my money there if there were a Wells Fargo around here," says Nancy Arnold, 37, as her friends nod approvingly.

But in another session, some younger women later think the ad is pandering to them. Both sets of opinions are interesting to Leo Burnett, which handles advertising for the New York Stock Exchange and Morgan Stanley Dean Witter. Burnett will consider those views when it creates ads that target either group.

Watching what people do when they're in the privacy of their homes intrigues some marketers most. They're hiring companies to videotape people – like Flimin – behind closed doors. Sometimes, they also ask people to tape themselves. They say they get more insights from experts who are trained observers.

Other companies still favor focus groups, but they use unusual techniques to get people to open up.

Before a Miramax movie opens in theaters, the previews are usually screened for groups of movie-goers around the country by psychiatrist Russ Ferstandig. As people watch the previews and answer Ferstandig's questions, he watches their body language. Based on what he hears and sees, he may recommend that the Disney unit change previews to make them more compelling to audiences.

"I might recommend something as subtle as a second-and-a-half pause that will let people catch up with a message, or, as in the case of the upcoming *An Ideal Husband*, I might suggest changing wording in the trailer," he says. "Trailers aren't about being true to the movie; they're about generating ticket sales."

The trailer for a movie version of Oscar Wilde's *An Ideal Husband* initially touted the film as "a new comedy from Miramax." Ferstandig urged the studio to scrap the word "comedy."

"I thought we should let people interpret the movie as they wanted to," he says. "They have a much greater chance of finding something they like about the movie if they can decide what genre it is – comedy or drama – rather than sitting there thinking 'an Oscar Wilde comedy?' "

ANTHROPOLOGIST AS VAMPIRE

Robert Deutsch, a cognitive neuroscientist and cultural anthropologist hired recently by ad agency DDB Needham, says it's important to use people who are trained observers in focus group settings.

"If someone isn't trained to listen, he or she will miss a lot," he says.

Deutsch, who likens himself to a vampire – "I suck information out of people, and they love it" – spent part of his training studying chimpanzees with zoologist Jane Goodall. Now he applies what he learned in the field to watching and listening to people in groups of 10.

The MacManus Group uses a TV talk show format called Just Ask a Woman to encourage research participants to speak up.

In a recent project for Continental Airlines, 19 female business travelers gathered in a Manhattan loft set up like a talk show set. Cameras rolled, and two women with microphones encouraged the participants to stand up and share frustrations they encounter on the road – from bad airplane food to inefficient rental car service.

It was as if Sally Jessy Raphael were on the set. As soon as the lights and cameras came on, the participants seemed to vie for the microphone.

"People are drawn to the opportunity to become the focus of undivided attention, to be asked their opinion, to reveal their feelings, to describe how they resolved a problem," Schumacher says. "Talk is therapy. Talk constitutes fame."

Sometimes a company wants to use information it gets through this type of research to change its image. Other times, companies are primarily interested in insights that will help them develop new products. Backpack maker Eastpak is trying to do both.

At Norman Thomas High School in Manhattan, Inez Cintron, 14, chats exuberantly with her girlfriends between classes. The topics: singer Lauryn Hill, Old Navy clothes and the NBC hit Friends.

Tru Pettigrew, a 30-year-old researcher for a company called Triple Dot, leans close. The trend hunter has dropped by the public high school to glean intelligence for Eastpak. He listens to the girls mix Spanish phrases into their English chatter – something new to Pettigrew that may result in Eastpak ads with "Spanglish."

Pettigrew also is interested to hear that the teens, who preferred rival Jansport's packs, buy as many as eight backpacks to mix with their wardrobes.

"That's a key piece of information," he says later.

36

Attention Shoppers:

This Man Is Watching You

Do you breeze by store displays? Avoid narrow aisles? Paco Underhill knows you do, and his methods are changing retail behavior. ■ *by Kenneth Labich*

Retailers are in the throes of a crisis. There are too many retail outlets and too few consumers–experts estimate 20% to 30% excess retail capacity–and the competition for eyes, ears, and dollars is downright savage. It doesn't help that shoppers are behaving weirdly. They have become less loyal to brand names and less predictable in other ways as well; more than half the purchases people make at grocery stores these days are unplanned. Consumers can't even be trusted. In exit interviews and focus groups, says Karen Hyatt, category-development manager at Hewlett-Packard, "people tend to be overly polite and tell you what they think you want to hear."

Enter a tall (6-foot-4), balding New Yorker named Paco Underhill. He doesn't have to trust what people say, because he sees what they do. For more than 20 years, Underhill, 47, has been using hidden cameras and other means to track 50,000 to 70,000 shoppers annually, in an effort to determine why we buy what we buy. Demand for his peculiar brand of research–Underhill calls himself a "retail anthropologist"–has taken off. His company in New York City, Envirosell Inc., now boasts a client roster that includes dozens of top retailers such as Sears, Walgreens, and the Gap; consumer-products giants like Coca-Cola, General Mills, and Johnson & Johnson; and big food-service players like McDonald's, Burger King, and Starbucks. He's even written a hot new book about his work (*Why We Buy: The Science of Shopping,* Simon & Schuster, $25). Jim Lucas, an Envirosell client and director of research and planning at Frankel & Co., the promotion agency for McDonald's and other big retailers, is an ardent fan of Underhill's work. "It's sort of the difference between knowing what people say they do–and what they really do," says Lucas.

Such plaudits are especially sweet for Underhill, who struggled for years to get his methods accepted and his business off the ground. After graduating from Vassar, he took a job with a New York City outfit called People for Public Spaces, which sends out researchers to follow and film urban pedestrians in the hope of improving the design of public facilities. Underhill played urban geographer for a couple of years, filming people as they waited at stoplights or settled down on park benches. There was, however, one problem. Underhill is seriously afraid of heights, and much of the group's work involves videotaping from the top of tall buildings. One windy day in Seattle, as he perched uneasily on a swaying rooftop, Underhill underwent an epiphany: He had to find a ground-level job or go nuts.

An escape route presented itself a few months later. A friend who helped manage Lincoln Center, the Manhattan arts complex, asked Underhill if his videotaping techniques might help in the design of a customer-friendly souvenir shop. Underhill set up his cameras and made several suggestions that led to the shop's success. More important, the experience sparked the notion that he might make a living indoors using his pedestrian-tracking techniques.

Underhill got his big break in the mid-1980s, when AT&T hired him to help design its chain of retail phone stores. More jobs followed, and as Envirosell staffers studied hours of tapes and analyzed field reports, they found consistent and surprising patterns of customer behavior. After watching countless shoppers breeze past elaborate displays at store entrances, they dubbed the first 30 feet or so of floor space the "decompression zone." They

advised retailers that any attempt to snare buyers before they get their bearings is pointless. Underhill and his employees were also baffled by the fact that nearly all shoppers turn right after entering a store. Was it because most people are right-handed? After working a few jobs in Britain and Australia, they discovered that shoppers in those countries veer left after entering a store. We shop, it seems, as we drive.

Another baffler: After viewing thousands of hours of tapes, Envirosell staffers concluded that most shoppers, especially women, are extremely reluctant to enter a narrow aisle; goods in those aisles generally went unsold. After many interviews, Underhill's troops came to the conclusion that people really hate being jostled from behind and will go to great lengths to avoid it. At Envirosell they call this the "butt-brush factor."

Perhaps the biggest surprise of all was just how often stores were making unpardonable errors that turn off customers and eat into profitability. Says Underhill: "A lot of people in retailing and consumer goods talk about strategy, but not many talk about tactics. And tactics are often about not doing stuff that's stupid." Classic blunders: junk food on high shelves out of the reach of kids; hearing-aid batteries on bottom shelves where the elderly have to bend over to get at them; a drugstore chain marketing hair products for blonds in a Washington, D.C., neighborhood that is 95% African American.

Spying on the American consumer over the years has given Underhill some specific insights that he preaches to nearly all his clients, and you can see the impact everywhere. He advises all manner of storekeepers to keep stacks of shopping baskets around their premises. The results are dramatic: About 75% of the shoppers who pick up a basket buy

(Cont.)

SHOPPING GLOSSARY

Here are some of the terms Paco Underhill 's firm, Envirosell Inc., uses to describe shopping behavior:

◆ **DECOMPRESSION ZONE**   The first 30 feet or so inside a store entrance, which shoppers breeze through before getting their bearings.

◆ **BUTT-BRUSH FACTOR**   The reason shoppers, hoping to avoid being jostled from behind, tend to avoid narrow aisles.

◆ **CONVERSION RATE**   The percentage of shoppers who actually buy something after entering a store.

◆ **BOOMERANG FACTOR**   The practice of grocery shoppers who go part of the way down an aisle to grab a product and return the way they came.

some items–usually more than they would have otherwise. Of those who don't pick up a basket, only 34% will buy something.

Underhill is also a strong advocate of the chair. Women who shop with other women spend about twice as much time in a store as when they are with a man, presumably because he's being a pain in the posterior about being dragged along. The solution, Underhill argues, is to make sure that there's plenty of available seating so men can park themselves while the women make their tour. But placement of that seating can be crucial. Underhill cites the folly of the Florida clothing store that placed chairs near a display for Wonderbras. The seats were often occupied by elderly gentlemen who loudly debated the physical merits of women grazing the bra display. Sales plummeted.

Now Underhill is trying to make sense of what seems to him the most crucial retailing innovation of the era, the Internet. He's convinced that Web gazing does not spell the end of actual shopping trips. "We're still a tribal animal," he says. "Movie theaters haven't died because of cable TV." At the same time, Underhill is working with various cyber-age clients to develop more effective Websites. Says Joel Granoff, Internet marketing manager at Compaq, an Envirosell customer: "He puts a new focus on the Internet by looking not just at what technology will do but at what consumers will do." For the moment, Underhill's approach revolves around having staffers test-shop at various sites and report the pluses and minuses of graphics, architecture, and the like. He's soon to begin a program of bringing civilians into his offices, then taping and interviewing them about their likes and dislikes as they surf the Web for specific products and services. There's one big question that's still to be resolved, though: What's the Web equivalent of the "butt-brush factor"?

37

Looking for Patterns

Data mining enables companies to better manage the reams of statistics they collect. The goal: spot the unexpected

BY LISA BRANSTEN

Staff Reporter of THE WALL STREET JOURNAL

A few years ago, owning a hot Porsche or a zippy Corvette almost guaranteed you would pay more for car insurance. After all, both conventional wisdom and decades of data collected by insurers suggest that drivers of high-performance sports cars are more likely to have accidents than are other motorists.

But upon a closer look at such statistics, insurer **Farmers Group** Inc. discovered something interesting: As long as the sports car wasn't the only vehicle in a household, the accident rate actually wasn't much greater than that of a regular car.

Based on that information, Farmers changed its policy that had excluded sports cars from its lowest-priced insurance rates. By eliminating that rule, "we figured out that we could almost double our sports-car market," says Melissa McBratney, vice president of personal lines at the Los Angeles insurer. Farmers estimates that just letting Corvettes and Porsches into its "preferred premium" plan could bring in an additional $4.5 million in premium revenue over the next two years, without a significant rise in claims.

The pattern Farmers discovered isn't intuitive – it had eluded even most insurance veterans. But that's the beauty of software tools that dig through such data: They can find patterns that people wouldn't dream of hunting for.

Data Filter

"We used to develop a hypothesis and then get the data to prove us right or wrong," says Ms. McBratney. But with this new software, "we put all of our data into a very large database and had it spit out" patterns that it saw.

Much of this new software is based on a technology called data mining, which enables computers to apply sophisticated mathematical formulas to ferret out patterns in data. And companies are finding that it not only allows them to better manage the reams of statistics their systems have been amassing for years, but also helps monitor consumer behavior, catch trends and, as in the case of Farmers, spot the unexpected.

Today, only a small number of businesses use software that incorporates this technology, but analysts expect that to change: According to Forrester Research Inc., Cambridge, Mass., a recent survey of 50 executives from large companies found that only 28% were actively mining their databases, but all planned to do so by 2001.

Based on those figures, Forrester analyst Frank Gillett estimates that spending on database software to accommodate data mining will more than double to $3.56 billion in 2001 from $1.56 billion last year. "It's one of the few remaining places to get a tangible competitive advantage," he says.

Many Web-based businesses are also seeking to capitalize on information about customer behavior with specialized software tools. In many cases, however, they are finding that the potential reach remains far ahead of their actual grasp. The businesses must be wary of Web users' privacy concerns, but there are more basic problems: Effective data mining demands time and resources that many Web-based start-ups simply can't afford to divert to it.

"It's a huge deluge of data, but you really need to have something to help you drill down and analyze it," says Nick Mehta, vice president of marketing at **chipshot.com**, a Sunnyvale, Calif., online seller of custom-made golf clubs.

Companies have been using a variety of technologies to amass and store huge quantities of data from any number of sources for years. But the increasing appeal of data mining now reflects its ability to manipulate information in a new way, unlocking details previously left to rot in "data jails" because processing, organizing and analyzing it has been too difficult.

Consider how some information systems are set up. In many databases, statistics often aren't kept in uniform formats – a customer may be listed as "John Smith" in a retailer's order-entry system's database, but as "Smith, John" in the customer-support database. In cases such as this, it is hard for the computer to know the two entries are the same customer.

Moreover, many databases have been designed as one-trick ponies that let companies very quickly look at specific types of information, such as whether an order has been shipped. That makes aggregating data about customer behavior that lurk in several different databases slow and awkward.

Time and Money

In order to make its discovery about sports cars and accident rates, for example, Farmers first had to combine information from five different databases into an organized central repository. It was a task so complicated it took three times as long as Farmers had expected, according to Ms. McBratney. (Luckily for Farmers, it benefited from an early contact: Because the insurer had agreed to test a program developed by a team from **International Business Machines** Corp.'s business-intelligence unit, it got the software at a substantially reduced rate.)

Another barrier to data mining's use has been that, until recently, the computer hardware needed to store and process so much data was prohibitively expensive for most companies.

Catalog retailer Fingerhut Cos., for example, needed a database that could store nine terabytes of data in order to use a software program it developed to help cut mailing costs. That's no small undertaking: Ten terabytes is equivalent to the entire printed collection of the Library of Congress.

"Two or three years ago...you would have

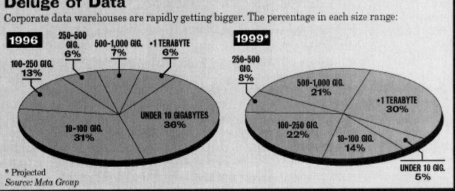

Deluge of Data

Corporate data warehouses are rapidly getting bigger. The percentage in each size range:

1996
- 250–500 GIG. 6%
- 500–1,000 GIG. 7%
- +1 TERABYTE 6%
- 100–250 GIG. 13%
- 10–100 GIG. 31%
- UNDER 10 GIGABYTES 36%

1999*
- 250–500 GIG. 8%
- 500–1,000 GIG. 21%
- +1 TERABYTE 30%
- 100–250 GIG. 22%
- 10–100 GIG. 14%
- UNDER 10 GIG. 5%

* Projected
Source: Meta Group

(Cont.)

had to have had NASA at your disposal to do something like that," says Will Lansing, chief executive officer of Fingerhut, a unit of **Federated Department Stores** Inc. "The hardware is making things happen faster and better."

Mr. Lansing says Fingerhut's investment in data mining – which he declines to quantify – is already paying off.

The software developed with IBM keeps track of the hundreds of items each Fingerhut customer purchases. Since Fingerhut has some products that are featured in all of its catalogs, the company figured it could save money by reducing the number of catalogs sent to its regular customers. Mr. Lansing says that in areas where Fingerhut tested the technology last year, mailing expenses dropped 8% while revenue declined by 1.5%, suggesting that the mail savings can contribute to the company's bottom line over time.

Specialized Software

Other variations of data-mining software gaining popularity help traditional retailers determine how their customers shop by letting them dig even deeper into data culled from cash registers and bar-code scanners. Such products are called "market-basket analysis" tools because they help the retailer peer into a customer's shopping basket and determine what products are typically purchased together.

"Typically in the past, merchandisers could track on a weekly or monthly basis what was sold, but they had to guess at who was buying what," says Lynne Harvey, a

senior consultant at Patricia Seybold Group in Boston, a high-tech advisory firm.

Wal-Mart Stores Inc. is generally hailed as a data-mining pioneer, with nearly a decade of experience and a database that trails only the U.S. government's in size. The Bentonville, Ark., retailer uses data mining to supply answers for any number of questions, such as what commonly purchased items should be placed together on shelves and what soft drinks sell best in different areas of the U.S.

And where Wal-Mart has led, other retailers are looking to follow – sometimes too closely for the giant's tastes. Last fall, Wal-Mart sued Internet giant **Amazon.com** Inc. in state court in Benton County, Ark., charging that Amazon stole trade secrets by recruiting Wal-Mart employees and business partners in order to duplicate the discounter's massive computer systems. (To settle the suit, Amazon agreed to, among other things, require all former Wal-Mart employees to return any Wal-Mart property they possessed.)

Meanwhile, **Walgreen** Co. is using data-mining software developed by **Knowledge Discovery One** Inc. of Austin, Texas, to tinker with its own store displays and to measure the success of promotional offers such as 2-for-1 sales, says David Arrington, manager of consumer research at the Deerfield, Ill., drugstore chain.

In the past, the success of such a promotion was judged largely on the product's sales and, by inference, how much traffic it brought into the store. Using the KD1 tool, Walgreen can see what's selling with its

promotional items and tune its programs so that it puts things on sale that people tend to buy in tandem with high-margin items.

Web retailers, meanwhile, can theoretically take gathering customer information a step further because they have so much information about not only what their customers buy, but also how they travel around a site. By placing "beacons" on pages within a site, San Francisco-based **Personify** Inc. can help companies match information about where customers travel within the site with information about what they purchase. The company then mines the data for usage patterns that can help Web commerce companies improve their business.

That feature was especially helpful to chipshot.com. One of the hardest decisions for a start-up like chipshot.com to make is where to focus resources; Personify helped the company set priorities, says Mr. Mehta, the marketing vice president.

Chipshot.com discovered that people who added comments to the site's guestbook seldom bought clubs, but people who bought clubs almost always clicked on the customer-service area before buying. Armed with that knowledge, chipshot limited the resources earmarked for developing the guestbook and put more effort into the site's customer-service area.

(Cont.)

How do you harness the hurricane of information on the Net and elsewhere to get ahead of your rivals? Ask the gurus. Others sure are. From separate offices in Stamford, Conn., and Bowling Green, Ohio, Don Peppers and Martha Rogers are shepherding Net upstarts, as well as traditional companies, into a brave new world of E-commerce. They've written a series of hot-selling books—*The One to One Future, Enterprise One to One,* and this year's *The One to One Fieldbook*—with a simple message: The big winners will be those companies, like American Airlines Inc. and Dell Computer Corp., that best use the data they collect on constantly shifting customer tastes. "It's a learning relationship that involves interacting with the customer, customizing, and then doing it all over again, says

Peppers. That message is striking a chord: The pair do more than 400 annual seminars, workshops and speaking engagements in places as far-flung as Turkey. Peppers and Rogers pinpoint two key advantages to cozying up to customers. First, by tailoring products and services to a buyer's every fancy, clients will become loyal, shunning the competition. Even better, as customers tell the company more about themselves, sellers can create new products that have built-in buyers. "It's not just using the information I know about a customer to figure out better-targeted harassment," says Rogers. "It's about figuring out what this customer needs next from us, when, in what form, at what price, and how." Now that's not just getting ahead of rivals, but customers, too.

people out there with shotguns," says Jason Catlett, a privacy advocate and consultant on writing privacy policies.

If they can overcome those concerns, says marketing consultant Don Peppers, companies may finally provide the kind of frictionless commerce that both they and consumers have always sought. The ideal, he says: "You already know what I want–I don't even have to tell you." For better or worse, customers may soon find that no one–not even Mom, hubby, or their faithful dog Spot–knows them better than their friendly merchant in cyberspace.

By Heather Green
Contributing: Linda Himelstein and Robert D. Hof in San Mateo, Calif., with Irene M. Kunii in Tokyo

PRIVACY: OUTRAGE ON THE WEB

A lawsuit against DoubleClick may be just the start of a backlash

For DoubleClick Inc., a hot Internet advertising company, things have suddenly gotten a little too warm. On Jan. 27, Harriet Judnick, a Marin County (Calif.) administrative assistant, filed a lawsuit against the company alleging violation of privacy rights and deceptive business practices. It's a case of the mouse that roared, and it signals how ordinary consumers are getting wise to the intricate workings of online marketers and the lack of privacy on the Web.

DoubleClick is the top ad-server company on the Web. Its computers insert banner ads and other promotional messages on about 1,500 Web sites. Those messages can be precisely aimed at the most likely customers, thanks to little text files called cookies, which allow DoubleClick to track what people are looking at and build detailed profiles of them—about 100 million profiles to date. These profiles show how Web surfers—who are identified only by their cookies—move around among sites, what books and CDs they buy, what places they spend the most time in.

What prompted Judnick to call a lawyer was DoubleClick's latest marketing tour de force: It quietly reversed an earlier policy of providing only anonymous data about Web surfers to marketers and last fall began combining its online profiles with information from direct mailers and others that help determine the actual identity of the Web surfer. In November, DoubleClick paid $1.7 billion for Abacus Direct Corp., a data-warehouse company that has records of consumers' catalog purchases, including name and address data. It has also begun pulling in similar personal data from Web partners. The result: DoubleClick not only knows where you go online and what you do there but also who you are, where you live, and your phone number. This is nirvana for direct marketers, but it gives Judnick the creeps. She says she got a stream of unsolicited e-mails from insurers, loan companies, and other firms after she recently looked up medical-insurance information online.

WHAT POLICY? Privacy advocates say the allegations in the DoubleClick suit are just one sign of how the Internet's data-grabbers routinely go too far. The advocates concede that consumers willingly give up information about themselves when they register at a site but they insist that most surfers have not understood how a little bit of data can turn into a big invasion of privacy. Another issue: Even when sites have strong privacy policies, they are often overlooked. The Health Privacy Project at Georgetown University released a study on Feb. 1 showing that many online health sites don't follow their own privacy policies–and in some cases share health information about visitors with their business partners.

Internet companies have every incentive to gather as much customer data as they can–and few reasons to stop. Indeed, integral to the business plans of many Web companies is the notion that they can reach clearly identified individuals rather than an "audience." Advertising agencies say they are willing to pay a premium of 10% to 20% for such targeted advertising. "The Internet is the first medium that offers advertisers the ability to speak to your customers," says Susan Nathan, senior vice-president at ad agency McCann-Erickson Worldwide Inc., whose clients include Microsoft Corp. and HotJobs.com Ltd. "The more you know, the easier and more fruitful it is to do that."

A suit filed against Yahoo! Inc. gives a peek at how vital private data is to Web businesses. Universal Image Inc., which makes educational videos, sued the portal in December, seeking damages of up to $4 billion for allegedly not living up to a contract to provide data, including customer e-mail information, that Yahoo culled from surfers who downloaded video from its Web site. The contract had been signed between Universal Image Inc. and Broadcast.com Inc. before Broadcast.com was acquired by Yahoo. Yahoo declines comment on the case.

DISSECTING ONLINE PRIVACY POLICIES

WHAT THEY SAY . . .	*. . . AND WHAT THAT CAN MEAN*
➤ We could exchange your name with another company whose products and services interest you	➤ The site could be selling your information to anyone—other sites, online advertisers, or direct marketers
➤ We may use the information you give or we collect about your online behavior to enhance your experience	➤ The site could be sharing or selling that information with all kinds of marketers
➤ The seal on this site means we are part of a self-regulating privacy organization	➤ Membership may no longer be current, and there is no enforcement of the rules
➤ We automatically track information based on your behavior on our site	➤ The site may record what you looked at, what you purchased, and where you live or work
➤ We use the information internally	➤ You may never get to see the data or correct errors

Online marketers say the data-gathering is nonthreatening–that it is merely a way of fine-tuning marketing for the convenience of consumers as well as marketers. But with cybercitizens up in arms, Capitol Hill is listening to the complaints. Online-privacy legislation is expected to be a major bipartisan issue in Congress this year, with at least five legislators preparing to introduce bills that require companies to better inform consumers about their practices, let Web surfers know exactly what they're agreeing to, and provide enforcement if companies drop the ball. Several states are also taking legislative and enforcement initiatives. "This issue has gone off the Richter scale in terms of public sensitivity," says Senator Ron Wyden (D-Ore.)

Judnick is representative of the breed of Netizens who just want to be left alone. Her suit contends that DoubleClick, with the new Abacus data, is using personal information without the knowing consent of Internet users. "I didn't feel like my information should be sold," Judnick says. DoubleClick says its policy has always been to inform online users and give them the option to opt out. "If we have personally identifiable information, it must be true that you have been given notice, and you have chosen not to opt out," says Jonathan Shapiro, DoubleClick's vice-president for business development.

But privacy policies can be deceptive, says privacy advocate Richard M. Smith, who has been documenting online privacy breaches. He has charged Amazon.com Inc. with gathering more personal information about customers than consumers would expect if they read its privacy policy. "The more experience we all have with the inadequacy of these policies, the more sense there will be to enact some protections," says David Sobel, general counsel at the Electronic Privacy Information Center in Washington.

LITTLE WARNING. Net companies insist that they are capable of regulating themselves and that it would be self-defeating to abuse customer privacy: It's in their best interest to keep customers happy and surfing. And so far, regulators have taken a hands-off approach. While the Federal Trade Commission has watched online privacy closely and issued rules governing the online privacy of children in October, it has so far declined to establish any rules regarding adults. In November, the FTC concluded a privacy workshop with promises from the 10 leading adservices companies to come up with voluntary guidelines. Since then, the companies have not put anything forward.

Privacy advocates maintain that consumers are not adequately warned about how the information they volunteer, or that they allow a specific site access to, will be used. In her suit, Judnick is asking the court to force DoubleClick to request permission before it tracks consumers' online behavior. She is also asking that the company be forced to destroy all data it acquired without users' consent.

As the privacy issue gets more attention, momentum is building for government action. States including New York and Hawaii have pending legislation, and California, Maryland, and Virginia are expected to follow. In a case that could be a taste of things to come, the New York State Attorney General reached settlements with Chase Manhattan Bank and Sony Music Entertainment Inc.'s online service InfoBeat to curtail information-sharing practices with outside partners. The office says Chase was violating its own privacy policy, though the bank contends it didn't.

In this election year, many federal legislators are taking a range of initiatives. Oregon's Wyden and Senator Conrad Burns (R-Mont.) are co-sponsoring a bill that gives consumers the chance to block the collection of information and the right to access any data that has been gathered. A bill from Senator Patrick J. Leahy (D-Vt.) bolsters the ability of consumers to opt out and tackles government intrusion into personal privacy. This year's campaign slogan could be: It's online privacy, stupid.

By Heather Green in New York, with Norm Alster in Boston and Amy Borrus and Catherine Yang in Washington

THE PRIVACY WAR OF RICHARD SMITH

Richard M. Smith knows the data snatchers are out there. From the third-floor aerie of his rambling Victorian-style house in the tony Boston suburb of Brookline, Mass., this virtual sleuth spends untold hours, surrounded by his toy robot collection, tapping on his trusty laptop. His mission: to track the efforts of software companies and online services to collect information about what individual Web surfers are doing.

Smith's avocation as a digital bloodhound started last year, when he heard that Intel Corp. was encoding a unique serial number into every new Pentium III microprocessor. He wondered whether other hardware identifying numbers were being copied onto documents created with Microsoft Word. A veteran programmer and co-founder of Phar Lap Software Inc., which makes "tools" for software writers, Smith used a "hex dumper"—a program that shows the actual bytes of information in a computer file—to inspect a Word file.

He discovered that the word processing program also contained an electronic marker that was "stamped" onto every document he created. That made it possible for somebody to unlock the code—a company eager to uncover a whistle-blower, for instance— to identify the source of any Word document. Microsoft has since changed its system. Among other online privacy violations, Smith also discovered that RealNetworks Inc. collected computer ID numbers from Web surfers who downloaded ite RealJukebox software to hear CDs.

Last fall, Smith quit his job at Phar Lap to take a sabbatical and devote himself full-time to privacy issues. He says he's alarmed by the steady erosion of personal privacy online and wants to raise consumer awareness of the threat. "People don't understand that every little move they make can be monitored," he says. "My role is to shine a light on [privacy abuses], and then we can have a converstaion about what to do about it."

NAILING AMAZON. Smith, 46, has become a well-regarded expert in the field. Federal regulators ask for briefings on Web bugs and other online monitoring gizmos. Reporters and others call or e-mail regularly with tips on alleged cyber-snooping. And e-commerce companies shudder as he exposes the methods they use to track unsuspecting consumers.

In December, for example, he charged that Internet-monitoring software created by an Amazon.com Inc. subsidiary gathered personal information about customers without their knowledge.

Says David Medine, an associate director at the Federal Trade Commission: "The publicity sends a message: 'You don't want to be next on Richard Smith's list.' Everyone takes him seriously."

Even Microsoft programmers praise his technical savvy. "He eats and breathes bits and bytes of data," says Richard Purcell, Microsoft's director of corporate privacy. "We respect the work he does." So much so that last June, Microsoft brought Smith to its campus in Redmond, Wash., to discuss the use of software user ID numbers.

Smith's latest finding: On a tip from a Seattle software developer, he determined that Sprint cell phones that offer wireless Web connections transmit a user's phone number to whatever sites they access. "It's a marketer's dream," says Smith. "Once Web sites realize this, they'll have salespeople call you up on your cellphone." The company defends the feature, saying it's for the user's convenience—allowing callers to quickly reconnect to a site if they are disconnected—and notes that Sprint's service agreements mention the feature. Besides, insists John Yuzdepski, a Sprint vice-president, Sprint's Web service providers are "very secure sites that know how to deal with the privacy issue." Maybe so. But with Smith on the case, they better be.

By Amy Borrus in Brookline, Mass.

Product

Hefty's Plastic Zipper Bag Is Rapping Rivals

BY DEAN STARKMAN

Staff Reporter of THE WALL STREET JOURNAL

A little zipper has touched off a tempest in a plastic bag.

In four years, Hefty OneZip bags, which are sealed with a sliding tab, have zipped from zero to fourth place in the market for sandwich, freezer and food-storage bags, which totals $900 million in sales annually.

The better mousetrap, made by **Tenneco** Inc., has been followed by at least one rival zipper bag, which sparked a federal patent lawsuit. And with legions of lunches and leftovers at stake, OneZip is about to launch an advertising and promotional blitz.

Beyond being a hit with brown-baggers, the zipper innovation has spread to packages for vegetables, bubble gum, even diaper wipes. And with Tenneco in talks to sell its easy-closing zipper bags to makers of everything from laundry detergent and medical waste to cigars and potato chips, consumer-products giants **S.C. Johnson & Son** Inc. and **Clorox** Co. are circling with their own bags.

The Hefty zipper could "revolutionize" consumer packaging the way screw tops did orange-juice cartons, says Robert M. McMath, a new-products consultant in Ithaca, N.Y. "This is the kind of thing that is very subtle but helps products move."

The zipper innovation is one of those rare plot points in the plodding history of everyday household products. The forerunner of the newfangled wrappers, humble waxed paper, was in vogue in the 1940s. **Mobil** Corp. launched the plastic Baggie in the mid-1960s and later added a tuck-in flap. In 1970, **Dow Chemical** Co. weighed in with Ziploc, the original pinch-and-slide bag.

Today's OneZip, known technically as the "rolling-action zipper profile and slipper," was developed during the early 1990s by a Mobil team working in strict secrecy. Mobil went through numerous zipper designs before settling on the boxcar-shaped version. It snaps over dual plastic tracks and slides like a gondola on a cable.

Mobil had invested $25 million to $50 million in OneZip and demanded a premium for it when Tenneco bought Mobil's plastics business four years ago for $1.27 billion.

"We knew this was a product that had some legs," says Richard Wambold, a Tenneco executive vice president.

Indeed, OneZip racked up $130 million in sales last year, up 9.4% from 1997. And it's gaining on Ziploc, which still dominates the category with $314 million in sales last year, after a gain of only 3.5%. Meanwhile, Glad-Lock, the bags with the blue and yellow strips along the top that turn green when

pressed together, reported flat sales of $149 million, according to Information Resources Inc., a Chicago market-research firm. Tenneco says OneZip, which competes only with larger bags, has done even better when sandwich sizes are subtracted from the category.

The reason OneZip is thriving is transparent: Americans pay up for convenience. In Ypsilanti, Mich., Faith M. Paull, who has nerve damage in her fingers, used to carry her pills in the pinch-and-slide bags. But she switched to OneZips last year as soon as she spotted them in her local grocery store. Even if the bags cost more, she says, "I'm willing to pay."

A 40-count box of quart-size bags costs about $3.19, roughly 15% more than the tongue-in-groove style. A few years ago, the premium was about 30%, but improvements in assembly-line technology have narrowed the gap.

Now competition is heating up. In the past two years, two marketing powerhouses have jumped into the plastic-bag market. S.C. Johnson took control of category leader Ziploc early last year, when it bought Dow Chemical Co.'s consumer-products unit for $1.13 billion. The closely held company, based in Racine, Wis., has made household names of Windex, Pledge, Raid and other products. And since acquiring Ziploc last year, the company says, it has raised ad spending 30%. Says a spokeswoman, "We know a winner when we see one."

In January, Clorox took control of Glad bags when it bought First Brands Corp. for $1.6 billion plus debt. Clorox has built a reputation for buying and turning around languishing brands, including cleaners Armorall, Pine-Sol and S.O.S.

Based in Oakland, Calif., Clorox has already conducted 50 focus groups on Glad this year and plans to boost advertising spending "by an order of magnitude," says Glenn R. Savage, a Clorox vice president and general manager of Glad products. Clorox will also push its more expensive GladWare disposable containers, which are also finding many nonfood uses.

Mr. Savage says the company plans to repackage the products and use its leverage with retailers to create a "sea of Glad" in grocery-store aisles.

Clorox and S.C. Johnson are formidable rivals for Tenneco, a consumer-products neophyte that churns out mufflers, shocks, egg cartons and protective packages for other manufacturers.

But it's game for the battle. Tenneco, based in Greenwich, Conn., plans to boost this year's OneZip ad budget fourfold over 1998 and is considering switching ad firms. (That's news to the agency that currently has

the account, DDB Needham Chicago, says a spokeswoman.) Tenneco is even pondering a joint venture with a consumer-products company to help market OneZip.

"We know we're in the big leagues now," says Dana G. Mead, Tenneco's chairman and chief executive. To compete this spring and summer, Tenneco officers say, they expect to unleash a blizzard of plastic-bag ads, coupons and bonus bags in boxes.

Tenneco has already challenged the competition in court. Last year, S.C. Johnson launched Slide-Loc, a Ziploc freezer bag with serrated edges that make a *zzzz* sound when zipped. After seeing Slide-Loc, Tenneco filed suit last May in federal court in Chicago, alleging that S.C. Johnson and its manufacturer infringed on Tenneco's patent for OneZip. The suit seeks to enjoin S.C. Johnson from making the Slide-Loc. Says an S.C. Johnson spokeswoman, "We stand behind our products 100%, and we will vigorously defend them against any challenge."

Meantime, Tenneco is peddling the zipper well beyond food bags. In July, **Kimberly-Clark** Corp., of Irving, Texas, bought the zippered package for its Huggies Supreme Care baby wipes. It puts Hefty's name on its package. The feature helped boost the brand's market share two to three percentage points to 37.5% as of March 13, says Philip C. Rundle, Kimberly-Clark's marketing director for its Wet Wipes sector. "That's enormous," he says.

Bolthouse Farms Inc., a closely held carrot packer in Bakersfield, Calif., put the zipper on its new three-pound size of baby carrots two months ago. Sales have climbed despite a hefty 12.5-cents-per-bag added cost Bolthouse passes on to retailers. "No one's complaining," says Andre Radandt, a Bolthouse executive vice president. "It's a way-better mousetrap."

And people continue to find inventive uses. Anglers use the bags to hold nightcrawlers. Rachel Shaw, a 55-year-old insurance-claims inspector in Charlottesville, Va., enlists them to organize memorabilia she collects on vacations. Her 27-year-old son recently used them as ice packs after he had his wisdom teeth pulled.

In Taylor Mill, Ky., 16-year-old Kristen Moore used them when she bought goldfish recently. The pet store put the fish in one bag, but she has two aquariums. At home, she separated the fish into two OneZip bags and dropped them into the tanks so the fish could acclimate and so they wouldn't be shocked by different water temperatures. "You have to float the fish for about an hour," she says.

> '*This is the kind of thing that is very subtle but helps products move,*' says consultant Robert McMath.

You've Got Mail (With Cash !)

PayPal Sees Torrid Growth With a Service That Sends Money Across the Internet

By Jathon Sapsford

Staff Reporter of The Wall Street Journal

If your acquaintances are even slightly tech-savvy, it may not be long before somebody beams money into your e-mail in-box.

Don't delete it. The money's good.

It's all part of a new online payment system called PayPal.com, and it's growing by 9,000 new users a day just three months after its official launch. The system responds to many of the needs that led to the creation of virtual currencies with names like "beenz" and "Bippy dollars." But PayPal uses real dollars. And now, instead of just techno-nerds, the service is attracting mainstream users.

Driving PayPal's torrid growth is a simple joining of two proven technologies: e-mail and the credit-card network. Registered users can send a payment to anybody with an e-mail address just by writing a dollar amount into an online form. When the e-mail is sent, the payment is charged to the sender's credit card or bank account. Registration takes five minutes.

If the person on the other end isn't a registered PayPal user, that's OK. The receiver just fills out the form attached to the e-payment to tap the money, which is already waiting in a PayPal.com account in the receiver's name.

Completing the form also registers the receiver as a user. "This is what people in technology call a viral product," says Peter Thiel, the chief executive of PayPal.com. "It's easier than catching a cold. And it is spreading as fast as a virus."

Taking the money out of the system isn't as quick. PayPal will cut a check and send it to you through the regular mail, credit it to your credit card or transfer it into your bank account – all of which can take up to a week. But the big fans of the system keep the money in their accounts to use again.

That last option is the key to how PayPal, based in Palo Alto, Calif., hopes to thrive. The PayPal account doesn't provide interest, so PayPal can invest any money left there until the user wants to spend it. If PayPal keeps growing at its current rate, the company hopes it will soon manage enough customer money to both make a profit and absorb all the fees involved in credit-card transactions. For now, the PayPal service is free, and Mr. Thiel says the company has no intention of ever charging its customers.

Among PayPal's most common uses is the cybersettling of accounts between family and friends. Andrew Brenner, for example, a 31-year-old tech-industry employee, recently threw a big barbecue party with friends. Afterward, he e-mailed $83 to pay his buddy for his share of the burgers and beer.

A few weeks later, another friend was short the cash for his share of a fish dinner at a Palo Alto, Calif., restaurant. Mr. Brenner knew that his buddy did have a hand-held computer with e-mail capacity. So right there in the restaurant, over the remains of prawns and swordfish, Mr. Brenner asked his friend to send him an e-mail for $20.

As the friend sent the e-payment over the red-checkered tablecloth, Mr. Brenner paid the bill knowing his friend's share would be in his account at PayPal. "PayPal is replacing currency," says Mr. Brenner flatly. "This is becoming the payment service of the Internet."

Some heavy hitters in venture capital agree. Wall Street's **Goldman Sachs Group** Inc., together with a fund tied to the West Coast Web incubator **idealab!,** recently invested $23 million in PayPal.com during its second round of venture financing. Its first round came from **Nokia** Corp., the Finnish mobile phone giant, and **Deutsche Bank** AG of Germany. Before that, the company was working with seed money from individuals and a hedge fund run by the current chief executive, Mr. Thiel.

Mr. Thiel, a blond 32-year-old who says "awesome" a lot, graduated from Stanford Law School in 1992 and soon joined the Wall Street law firm of Sullivan & Cromwell. A year later he joined CS First Boston, where he traded currencies for a few years. By 1996 he had moved back out to his native California to start up his own hedge fund. In 1998, he met PayPal's chief technology officer, Max Levchin, who wanted to launch a venture that provided encryption technology.

Mr. Thiel's hedge fund bought into the idea, and Mr. Thiel joined the new venture himself as CEO. Launched in December 1998 under the name Confiniti, the company focused on providing financial institutions with the technology to make online and mobile transactions secure. But the start-up soon saw the huge demand for secure payment systems on the Web.

When the new company hit on combining the credit-card network with e-mail and launched the PayPal service, more investors started to take note. Now, Confiniti is in the process of changing its corporate name to

PayPal, and Mr. Thiel is giving a lot of the company's money away.

That's because PayPal provides a virtual $10 coupon to any user who signs up a friend – and gives the friend a $10 coupon as well. In other words, it costs PayPal $20 for each new user, or $2 million for 100,000. Mr. Thiel says the approach is much more effective – and a lot cheaper – than buying a 30-second ad during the Super Bowl.

Other companies have also deployed or are working on online payment, including **eBay** Inc. and **CheckFree Holdings** Inc.

Since PayPal's launch, 190,000 users have signed up. Some investors value Web-based financial-services companies at $1,000 to $10,000 a customer. Using the middle of that range, PayPal's franchise would now be valued at around $500 million.

The product is a particular boon for online auction denizens because it cuts out the risks of being paid by check through the mail. Lisette McConnell, a 33-year-old graphic designer, sells custom-designed neckties on eBay. She has trusted buyers before, sending goods before checks cleared, only to find out the check wasn't any good. Other merchants spend thousands of dollars and per-transaction fees to be able to accept credit cards. But

---

PAY A FRIEND ONLINE

How to use e-mail and a credit card to send money over the Net.

1 Log onto PayPal.com. First-time users must register, supplying name, street address, e-mail address and passwords.

2 Fill in credit-card number, friend's e-mail address and transaction amount, and send.

3 Friend gets e-mail saying, 'You've got cash.'

4 Friend clicks e-mail link to PayPal.com and registers.

5 Friend asks PayPal.com to transfer payment into bank account, mail a check or leave the money at PayPal.com to use for future e-payments.

(Cont.)

PayPal makes all that unnecessary. "It's like air money," Ms. McConnell says.

There are limitations on bigger transactions, in order to combat fraud and hackers. Cathy Rowekamp, 48 years old, of Winnsboro, S.C., sells antiques online. Once shipping charges are thrown in, her prices are in the thousands of dollars. Buyers of her chests, dressers and rockers must get a form from PayPal through the mail confirming their street address to conduct transactions larger than $200.

That's supposed to take only a matter of days, but the turbocharged growth at the company has caused delays, all of which Ms. Rowekamp is finding frustrating. "I want it to work so bad," she says.

One user, Jim Bruene, had his payments frozen when he tried to get around the limit. The publisher of a financial newsletter called Online Banking Report, he sent a freelance

PayPal has sought to keep its system secure by hiring a panel of encryption advisers.

reporter several e-payments that totaled more than $200. But the PayPal fraud alarms kicked off, and Mr. Bruene's money was tied up for weeks. "If you're a consumer and a couple thousand dollars disappeared for two weeks, you probably wouldn't want to use" the service again, Mr. Bruene says.

"Sometimes I worry that we're too obsessed with security," concedes Mr. Thiel. Other online payment systems have received bad press over lax security. But long before last week's hacking attacks, PayPal sought to keep its system secure by hiring a board of

advisers staffed with heavyweights in encryption technology. One is Stanford University Prof. Martin Hellman, one of the brains behind the most commonly used form of encryption on the Internet. Another is Stanford Prof. Dan Boneh, who leads a team of researchers who specialize in code breaking.

To fire off payments for anything more than $200, a consumer must wait for PayPal to send through the mail an address confirmation, which has a coded approval number. Only after keying in that number can consumers make larger payments online. "Fraud protection is a trade-off," says Mr. Thiel. "If you make it totally airtight, it becomes less user-friendly."

42

BRANDED BLOOMS FIND FERTILE MARKET

Taking root: $15 bil segment draws big-name competitors

by Laura Petrecca

A rose by any other name may smell as sweet, but will budding Romeos care about its brand name?

Hallmark Cards and Martha Stewart Omnimedia are just two companies aiming to leverage established brands into the $15 billion floral market. Just as consumers have gotten used to stickers that now label once generic bananas "Chiquita" and oranges "Sunkist," these floral retailing newcomers hope a nationally known name will cultivate sales of labeled bouquets.

In late fall, Hallmark quietly kicked off its floral delivery service in five test markets including Albany, N.Y.; Charlotte, N.C.; and Portland, Ore., with ads from Messner Vetere Berger McNamee Schemetterer/Euro RSCG, New York. Meanwhile, Martha Stewart debuted Marthasflowers through the company's Web site and Martha by Mail catalog in time for Christmas.

Not to be outdone in the floral name game, well-known produce marketers Sunkist Growers with its Sunkist brand and Dole Food Co. with Dole have extended their names in the last year by licensing their brands for use on supermarket-distributed flowers.

GERALD STEVENS

These more widely recognized brands make their entrance as newcomer florist chain Gerald Stevens Inc., Fort Lauderdale, Fla., is buying up established local florists and using that local power along with a new Yellow Pages agency—Wahlstrom & Co., Stamford, Conn.—to establish a national presence. Gerald Stevens Chief Marketing Officer Eleanor Callison said she expects the company's 300-plus outlets—which currently operate under different names—to have a single Gerald Stevens brand identity within the next few years. Until recently, Ms. Callison was senior VP-advertising at Hallmark, now a Gerald Stevens rival.

Floral delivery is a natural outgrowth for the likes of Martha Stewart and Hallmark, which have built their companies around celebrations, gifts and hospitality.

"We're in a good position since this is an extension of the brand," said Martha Stewart Omnimedia President-Chief Operating Officer Sharon Patrick: "We can grow it slowly and steadily."

Even competitor Ms. Callison agreed: "It's brand leverage, it makes all the sense in the world," she said. "Brands matter, which is what allows a Martha or a Hallmark to get into a business that's complex and have credibility."

CALYX & COROLLA

For now, Gerald Stevens first branding efforts concentrate on its upscale floral division, Calyx & Corolla which tapped Jericho Communications, New York, earlier this month to handle advertising and public relations. Gerald Stevens also is expected to make a move into supermarkets by the end of this quarter.

These companies are edging into a market that is both fragmented and growing slowly. Retail floral sales in the U.S. were $14 billion in 1997, and increased to $14.6 billion for 1998, according to the Society of American Florists. For 1999, sales are predicted to reach $15 billion.

> **Hallmark Cards' print pitch for its flowers is themed "Everything has changed."**

The majority of those dollars, however, passed through the neighborhood flower shop. Already established national brands such as FTD/Florists' Transworld Delivery and 1-800-Flowers.com account for less than 10% of the market, according to 1999 figures from the Floral Marketing Association.

FTD and 1-800-Flowers work as brokers, taking orders and a percentage of sales sent to a local retailer. With e-commerce budding, FTD and 1-800-Flowers have begun to dabble in direct sales of their own through ftd.com and 1800flowers.com, but it's a small part of their overall operations. Other Internet sites in this arena include proflowers.com and garden.com.

Internet tracking service Forrester Research predicts

(Cont.)

the online floral industry will have sales of $354 million for 1999, up 67% from an estimated $212 million the year earlier. Forrester forecasts 2003 sales will bloom to $2.2 billion.

Floral marketers want to promote flower-giving as an any-day occurrence, not just for holidays. Martha Stewart's Martha by Mail encourages consumers to "treat yourself, or surprise someone special with fresh flowers throughout the year."

Americans increasingly are embracing a better quality of life, which includes buying flowers for themselves as well as for friends or family, said Tom Eley, director of sales and marketing at 1-800-Flowers.com.

"In Europe, flowers are much more a part of everyday life. You'll see that more and more here," he predicted.

Flower industry executives credit the booming economy for the increase in professional and personal flower purchases. But the influx of newcomers armed with marketing budgets, they hope, will fertilize the entire industry.

A SALES UPTICK?

"We've pretty much viewed sales as flat over the last few years," said Peter Moran, exec VP-CEO of the Society of American Florists. "Part of that is we really don't have a category carrier, like a Microsoft or Procter & Gamble. We know from research that consumers are predisposed to buy flowers, but they don't get enough messages reminding them to buy."

As competition heats up from better known names, Ms. Callison said she believes Gerald Stevens can hold its own in the increasingly crowded floral market.

"We don't have the brand name yet," she said, "but we do have the floral experience."

Contributing: Ann-Christine Diaz.

Chinese Officials Force Magazines To Go Without Famous Names

BY MATTHEW ROSE AND LESLIE CHANG
Staff Reporters of THE WALL STREET JOURNAL

Western publishers in China are reeling from a government clampdown that is forcing them to publish magazines without the use of their famous names and logos.

In the stringent new climate, the government has even raised the possibility that many licensing agreements forged between Western publishers and Chinese agencies may be deemed illegal.

China had been a magazine publisher's dream – a place where costs of doing business are low, the advertising market is exploding and rising income levels have produced a vast sea of educated readers. Many industry executives believe China will be the world's biggest magazine market one day.

But it has turned into a nightmare since the Chinese government began strictly enforcing regulations governing licenses that it requires of magazine publishers. Many Western publishers got access to licenses by forming joint ventures with Chinese magazine partners. Since Jan. 1, when the new enforcement took effect, Western publishers must use a direct translation of the often-obscure name that appears on their license, or use no English name at all.

Hearst Corp., for example, is leaving a big blank space on the cover of its Chinese edition of Cosmopolitan, rather than using the name on its license: "Trends Lady." Hachette Filipacchi Magazines, a unit of France's **Lagardere** SA, is doing the same for the Chinese edition of Woman's Day, faced with the equally unsexy name on its license: "Friends of Health."

"I can't believe these guys are doing this," laments George Green, president of Hearst's international magazine division, which also publishes Chinese-language editions of Esquire and Motor. "If a country takes your name off your product, you're gone."

The Chinese government contends that many companies are publishing without the proper licenses. The publishers say they're being penalized unfairly by a regime that keeps changing the rules.

Talks between publishers and Chinese officials have gone on for months. "We just want to go to the status quo ante," says Hearst's Mr. Green, "but no one's counting on it."

Under Communist rule, China cultivated magazine publishing as a propaganda machine. But as it moved toward a market economy, the state withdrew its support. Local government agencies, who had publishing licenses but no money, realized they could form symbiotic relationships with foreign publishers, who had money but no licenses.

Some curious partnerships were born. For instance, Figaro, a magazine owned by French publishing group **Socpresse,** is published in China under a licensing agreement with the Communist Youth League. The flavor is clearly pop, not political, as evidenced by supermodel Claudia Schiffer on a recent cover. Hearst publishes Cosmopolitan and Esquire in China thanks to a relationship with the National Tourism Bureau. And Hachette publishes Woman's Day in conjunction with an organization called China New Sport Magazine.

The government is arguing that foreign publishers abused their partnerships with Chinese entities by printing new magazines without approval and by putting out several magazines under a single joint-venture licensing agreement. Chinese editions of Hearst's Cosmopolitan and Esquire, for example, display the same license number. Hearst says it isn't in violation of the law.

What's behind the timing of the crackdown? Some Western publishers blame it on maneuvering by governmental factions. Inside China, many people see the government's moves as an effort to make good on its promise to clean up inefficient, formerly state-run industries.

In an effort to wipe out money-losing ventures, Beijing has ordered hundreds of magazines shut down and has cracked down on domestic firms for violations, including using book licenses to print magazines. "The regulations target all violators, no matter foreign or domestic," says Wen Bingyuan, an official at the Press and Publications Administration. "Companies that have violated the regulations are required to correct their mistakes immediately."

Figaro *magazine, as it appears in China*

The clampdown also may reflect official concern at the explosion of fashion and lifestyle magazines touched off by Western titles. The content of many Chinese editions is rather tame by Western standards. Cosmopolitan, known in the U.S. for no-holds-barred sex advice, dispenses mostly fashion and cooking tips in its Chinese-language edition. Still, the magazines' tone may be anathema to China's media mandarins, among the bureaucracy's most conservative.

The sudden change in climate has made the joint ventures unattractive to Western publishers. Under the new rules, not only must the foreign name match the one on the publishing license, it must be "significantly smaller" on the cover than the Chinese name. Publishers now also are banned from using a single license to spin out new publications. Existing foreign magazines must reapply for government approval for their ventures – in effect, putting them at risk of being declared illegal and having their publications halted.

Is China worth the hassle? After all, Cosmopolitan's circulation in China, for example, is only 200,000, compared with almost 2.9 million in the U.S.

"Given the Confucian respect for learning, it is a very viable publishing market," says Patrick McGovern, chairman of **International Data Group,** of Boston, which publishes 19 titles in China, including China Computer World, China Internet Times and Electronic Products China.

Because the Chinese postal service handles so much of the expensive side of the magazine business – sales, marketing, distribution – costs fall to around 3% of revenue, compared with more than 20% in the U.S., Mr. McGovern said, boosting margins to a hearty 40%.

In China, Western magazines are advertiser magnets. Executives estimate advertising revenues for publications linked to a Western title can be almost double those of local magazines, because of demand for ad space from foreign corporations. Magazine advertising in China totaled $860 million in 1998, up 35% from the year earlier, according to the China Advertising Association. Titles affiliated with foreign magazines hold leading spots.

Already there has been some fallout. W magazine, an upscale fashion publication owned by **Advance Publications** Inc.'s Fairchild unit, has put plans to launch a China edition on hold. Fairchild officials declined to comment.

Hoping to avoid such pitfalls, other publishers have been reluctant to invest a lot of time and money in China. **Time Warner** Inc.'s Time Inc. magazine publishing unit sells only two magazines, Fortune and a digest of articles from Time, in China. Time publishes them in Hong Kong using their English-language names and mails them to subscribers in mainland China.

Wal-Mart Stores Go Private (Label)

Power 'house': Top U.S. retailer takes on the world with own store brands

by Jack Neff

As Sears, Roebuck & Co. built such store brands as Kenmore, Craftsman and DieHard, a little-known Arkansas retailer pursued a different idea.

Sam Walton was creating a discount powerhouse out of cheap small-town real estate, ruthless efficiency and low prices on brand-name goods. Today, with Wal-Mart's sales quadruple those of Sears, Mr. Walton's way has proved superior.

Even so, the victor is borrowing a tactic from its long-vanquished foe in creating its own brands. In the past year, Wal-Mart has rolled out such brands as White Cloud paper products, Spring Valley nutritional supplements, Sam's American Choice detergent and, just last month, EverActive alkaline batteries.

Ol' Roy, named after Mr. Walton's Irish setter, has become the best-selling dog food brand in America. And although those are unadvertised, Wal-Mart's EverStart car batteries have become as ubiquitous on TV sports programming as Sears' DieHard ads once were.

Unfortunately for brand marketers, Wal-Mart's new-found devotion to store brands is where its resemblance to the darker side of Sears' past ends. Wal-Mart's private-label push is steadily stoking up—creating a fearsome rival—even as the chain's overall sales growth remains on fire. Long the nation's biggest mass-merchandiser, Wal-Mart is on pace to become the biggest food-store chain this year.

Brand marketers should be afraid, says consultant Christopher Hoyt, as Wal-Mart transforms itself from their biggest customer to their biggest competitor. The retailer will become even more of a threat as Wal-Mart nears 60% household penetration, making network TV advertising cost-effective, Mr. Holt says.

"They're going to become the marketers of their own brands," he notes. "In five years, the consumer isn't going to be able to tell the difference between a Wal-Mart brand and a national brand."

In some cases, they already can't. Besides Ol' Roy, Wal-Mart's garden fertilizer also has become the best-

selling brand in the U.S. in its category. In vitamins, Wal-Mart's Spring Valley line, launched earlier this year, may soon reach best-seller standing, too, maintains Burt Flickinger, a consultant with Reach Marketing.

PRIVATE LABEL'S PROMISE

Of course, private label is nothing new to Wal-Mart—or to retailing. Neither are dire predictions of its ascendance.

During the recession of the early 1990s, some pundits predicted private-label shares in the U.S. would reach 35% to 50% by 2000, pushing the country down the European path to private-label hell for brand manufacturers. Nothing of the kind happened. In the second quarter of 1999, private-label dollar shares in package-goods categories of food, drug and mass merchandise reached 14.3%, up only marginally from 13% in 1994.

One reason private-label brands didn't grow faster is that the 1990s saw the explosive growth of Wal-Mart, which emphasized private labels far less than its supermarket rivals. While roughly 25% of Kroger Co.'s sales come from store labels, Wal-Mart's private-label sales in package goods are believed to be more in the range of 10%; they are relatively understated because of Sam Walton's commitment to branded products, which has been carried on by current management, Mr. Flickinger says.

So why is Wal-Mart suddenly turning to a bigger, better private-label program?

Besides the obvious lure of better profits, Wal-Mart's private-label push is linked to a number of marketing and strategic forces at play in its plans to expand nationally and globally. Wal-Mart's focus on rolling back prices, which puts the retailer at odds with manufacturers, is one factor.

Record economic expansion or no, Wal-Mart's customer base remains the 60% of consumers in this country who still have not realized any real dollar gain in income since 1970, Mr. Hoyt says. To serve those consumers, Wal-Mart claims to have rolled back 25,000 prices in the second half of 1999 alone, saving them $8 billion, Mr. Flickinger says. In the past three years, the price rollback program has helped increase weekly customer counts from 80 million to a brisk 100 million, he adds.

HAGGLING

But the whistling, happy-face price rollback character that has become Wal-Mart's icon has a more sinister countenance for product marketers.

Manufacturers always had incentives to give Wal-Mart the best price to get merchandising support and shelf space, says Paul Kelly, president of Silvermine Consulting. Now, however, Wal-Mart is increasingly haggling even beyond the best offer.

"They've been turning more to manufacturers than in the past for margin growth," he says.

Manufacturers, meanwhile, have generally gotten more aggressive on pricing in the past year to fatten sales amid years of sluggish growth, Mr. Flickinger notes.

Enter private labels, particularly premium-price private labels, which are slightly less expensive than premium brands but look like the exclusive premium products.

"I think the key is that it is premium," says Andrew Shore, analyst with PaineWebber. "I think premium is there to almost forever limit the ability of manufacturers to raise prices. It's really a price cap."

Most consultants see building store brands as a fairly expensive means for Wal-Mart to control prices, even though growing excess capacity is putting more manufacturers into the private-label business. Store brands also play into other Wal-Mart strategies.

"They're going global," says Ken Harris, a partner with Cannondale Associates. "They believe the brands they sell can mean more to international consumers than national brands in the U.S., and they're probably right."

The higher private-label shares and lower disposable incomes in many overseas markets also are likely influencing Wal-Mart's growing interest in private label as it, like many of its suppliers, looks to manage its brand globally.

"Even if [Wal-Mart store] brands weren't successful in the U.S., the potential for them being successful overseas is much greater," Mr. Harris says.

Store brands also provide Wal-Mart with a point of difference that the growing ranks of dot-coms can't match, as it prepares a stronger entry into e-commerce next year, Mr. Flickinger says. They could even figure into Wal-Mart's efforts to expand its presence in the Northeast U.S—which, like Europe, presents such obstacles as high real-estate costs and entrenched opposition from local governments.

Not only could store brands help offset higher costs for Wal-Mart in potential new markets, but they also could help Wal-Mart compete more like a supermarket as it experiments with its smaller, lower-volume neighborhood market format.

That format could expand in a hurry if—as Mr. Hoyt believes it will—Wal-Mart buys the Food Lion grocery chain, which in turn will give it control over retail chain Hannaford Brothers and an overnight presence in New England without having to struggle with town councils over zoning and permit issues.

Regardless of the motivation, Wal-Mart store brands create major challenges for package-goods marketers.

"They've definitely served notice on the brand manufacturers that if you want to survive, you'd better have a reason to exist," says William Steele, analyst with Bank of America Securities. "Second- and third- and fourth-tier brands that don't bring consumers to the shelves are going to have a very hard time."

Mr. Hoyt, in fact, believes phase two of Wal-Mart's program will be ridding shelves of brands that no longer make sense after Wal-Mart has built successful store brands.

BRANDS' RAISON D'ETRE

In the past, manufacturers' brands could stay in Wal-Mart even if they didn't have a strong consumer following, as long as they delivered a price low enough to let Wal-Mart make a margin. But if Wal-Mart can build store brands that generate better margins than category also-rans with little consumer loyalty, Mr. Hoyt says, it will jettison those brands.

By eliminating some of the other competition, Wal-Mart store brands could even be allies of category leaders such as Procter & Gamble Co. or Kimberly-Clark Corp., says Gary Stibel, a consultant with New England Consulting.

K-C has been monitoring the impact of White Cloud diapers in weekly sales and share data, and has seen no impact on its category-leading Huggies diaper brand, says Kathi Seifert, exec VP at the company.

"Our belief is that [White Cloud] will take share from brands that are less premium, like Luvs and Drypers," she says.

Even major marketers, however, have second-tier brands in some cases. And the success of White Cloud could ultimately push P&G's Luvs off store shelves, Mr. Harris says.

The jury is still out, however, on whether Wal-Mart can move beyond building the brand on its storefronts to building brands on its shelves.

Ol' Roy one of many as Wal-Mart tackles the German market

Not content with simply conquering the U.S. market, Ol' Roy is taking on Germany, too.

Wal-Mart Deutschland is stepping up its private-label presence, preparing to boost its current offerings from 32 to a reported 1,000. Ol' Roy is among the private-label brands already sold in the retailer's 43 German outlets, along with brands such as Special Kitty cat food and Great Value orange juice, cola, iced tea and tissues.

A Wal-Mart spokeswoman in Germany said the retailer is "in the development phase" of additional private-label products but would not confirm the planned number of lines.

The current Great Value brands aren't advertised but the chain's friendly service is highlighted in its general advertising—a novel strategy in that country. The German spots are produced by GSD&M, Austin, Texas.

The mass merchandiser appears to be furthest along in Europe. Just last year, it acquired 74 hypermarkets in Germany from Spar Handels AG and purchased U.K. supermarket chain ADSA Group. Wal-Mart also is rumored to be eyeing the purchase of Casino Guichard Perrachon et Cie in France.

Outside Europe, Wal-Mart has a presence in Argentina, Brazil, Canada, China, Indonesia, Puerto Rico and Mexico—the last largely the result of buying a controlling interest in Mexican chain Cifra.

As a result of its global push, Wal-Mart's international sales for the third quarter ended Oct. 31 were up 100% from the corresponding quarter in 1998 to $5.91 billion. That's 14.6% of Wal-Mart's total $40.3 billion sales for the quarter.

—Dagmar Mussey and Jack Neff

LACK OF 'MARKETING MINDS'

In the U.S., neither Sears nor supermarket chains have seen store-brand programs deliver strong same-store sales growth. One reason, Mr. Harris says, is that retailers "don't have enough marketing minds in their building to pull it off, or they miss trends. They're suddenly relying on themselves to figure out the next big thing, and they can't."

An exception is Target Stores, which has made its private-label merchandise into fashion leaders, Mr. Harris says.

But given its more downscale clientele and down-home image, Wal-Mart doesn't have to be a fashion leader. It could succeed by being a fast follower, Mr. Harris says.

While Ol' Roy has flourished without advertising and EverStart batteries have flourished with it, Wal-Mart still hasn't shown it can build its own brands consistently. The chain abandoned its Sahara Supreme line of towels earlier this year, and its apparel and housewares labels have lagged Kmart's Martha Stewart or Target's Cherokee lines.

Moreover, in other cases such as White Cloud paper products or Faded Glory and Earth Shoe apparel, Wal-Mart has moved to mine residual equity of old brands, but hasn't proved it can build equity on its own.

ASKING FOR HELP

"[Wal-Mart is] a threat, no doubt about it," says one consultant. "But they require a lot of help in developing these brands. They aren't geared to do it. They aren't qualified to do it."

Whether the company is willing to go out and get that help remains to be seen. Though Wal-Mart solicited suggestions from its agencies for a brand name for its new detergent, it ultimately settled on extending its existing Sam's brand, using what several industry observers label as uninspired packaging.

Though he believes Sam's American Choice detergent could rack up $100 million to $150 million in sales and take share from second-tier players, Mr. Shore calls the branding effort behind it "a joke"—one that overseas consumers won't get.

Besides simply not catching on with consumers, Wal-Mart also risks damaging its highly cultivated image if something goes wrong with its private labels.

SPREADING DISTRUST

"The fire can either warm the house or burn it down," says Gordon Wade, a Cincinnati consultant and former P&G executive. "Companies like Wal-Mart don't have their own quality-control labs. They don't have their own manufacturing. And if you have a problem, one category can spread distrust within the Wal-Mart base for various Wal-Mart products."

One scare for Wal-Mart came a year ago, when the chain recalled packages of its Ol' Roy dog food in Dallas after 25 dogs died of liver damage caused by fungal toxins in food made by its supplier. Separately, Wal-Mart wrestled for years over publicity connected to charges its Kathy Lee clothing line was made by child labor overseas. Wal-Mart ended that exclusive relationship last year.

RIVALS BOOST ADS

But brand marketers aren't waiting for Wal-Mart to stumble. The company's embrace of its own premium brands has been one factor that has led some players to boost advertising in hopes of surviving the onslaught.

Such vitamin brands as Rexall Sundown and Nature Made began to get their first major media advertising in the past year, in part to stem the Wal-Mart threat, Bank of America Securities' Mr. Steele says. Likewise, K-C and Georgia-Pacific have begun advertising their Scott, Angel Soft and Sparkle brands this year as Wal-Mart prepared to roll White Cloud.

Even mid-tier brands can survive at Wal-Mart if they can develop a niche or a consumer following that Wal-Mart's own brands don't serve, says John Bess, consultant with Price Waterhouse Coopers.

"Wal-Mart people are business people first," Mr. Harris says. "They are not going to do something just to cling to the precept that ours is better. If a company is doing it better than they are, they will stay with it."

45

BRAND NEW GOODS

European firms are learning from the U.S. that cultivating a brand can generate bigger profits

By Thomas K. Grose/London

A man walks into a major department store in Paris wearing Caterpillar boots, a Jack Daniels cap, Club Med shades, a Cadillac polo shirt and Marlboro jeans. He smells ruggedly of Chevrolet aftershave. He buys a set of Le Cordon Bleu cookware for his wife and a Jeep radio-CD player for himself. To pay, he flips opens his Harrods leather wallet and whips out a Jaguar Visa card. He's branded to the hilt, and the embodiment of European consumerism for the new millennium.

U.S. corporations, from General Motors to Coca-Cola to Lockheed, have garnered huge benefits from going beyond mere export trade and licensing their brands abroad to manufacturers of high-quality consumer goods, ranging from apparel to toys to foods. Licensing's allure is obvious. It offers companies new revenues that require little if any capital outlay. It's an ideal way to protect trademarks from infringers. And it's an invaluable marketing method because it can enhance a brand's image and lead it to new markets. Corporate brand licensing has grown from practically zero in the mid-1980s to a $26 billion industry worldwide. But while most of the industry is either located in the U.S. or dominated by American brands, international competition is finally heating up–especially in Europe, according to the Licensing Industry Merchandisers' Association.

A growing number of European companies, including Club Med, Harrods, Aston Martin, Pernod-Ricard and Land Rover, have taken up the licensing game and are signing agreements at a furious pace. European companies are beginning to grasp that if they don't act quickly, U.S. brands could soon completely overrun their markets with new waves of licensed goods. Even a pioneer like Coca-Cola, which has been licensing in Europe since 1986, views the continent as wide-open territory. "We feel like we've only scratched the surface in Europe," says Coke spokeswoman Susan McDermott. Equity Management, the largest U.S. licensing agency, which handles licensing chores that include research, legal work and quality control for its client corporations, gives some measure of the new American interest in landing on European soil. Most of Equity's 100 or so clients are eyeing Continental markets or have already taken the plunge. Says GM's trademark-and-copyright counsel Ken Enborg: "Europe is on the verge of a corporate brand-licensing explosion."

A similar boom hit the U.S. in the mid-1980s. Then only one U.S. company in 10 bothered with brand-extension licensing. Now 65% of FORTUNE 500 companies have licensing agreements, says Glen Konkle, Equity Management's chairman. Back then, licensing was primarily the province of Hollywood studios that owned the rights to popular cartoon and movie characters like Bugs Bunny and

> **Corporate BRAND LICENSING has grown from practically zero in the mid-1980s into a $26 billion industry worldwide**

Luke Skywalker; professional sports teams and athletes; and a few fashion designers. But companies like GM had begun to realize that many of their brands had additional value.

Even in those days, GM was spending $2 million to $3 million a year to fight trademark-infringement cases on the periphery of its main line of business, trying to rid the market of unauthorized Chevy baseball caps and Corvette T shirts that were obviously striking a chord with consumers. That's when it hit Enborg that it would be easier–and more profitable–for the automaker to meet the obvious market demand for those goods itself by licensing its brand names to handpicked manufacturers. Today, GM has more than 1,200 licensing agreements generating annual revenues of $1.1 billion. They cover everything from clothes to colognes.

One of the high-profile tycoons looking to follow the American example is Mohamed Al Fayed, owner of Harrods, London's famous department store, who says he wants to copy the success of American licensed goods like the Jaguar Collection and Calvin Klein that are sold in his store. "The American brands really have no assets apart from their names, which they put on other products and designs," he says. "I want to follow that example." This November, Harrods' lines of premium-priced fine jewelry, watches, fragrances, leather goods, foods and linens will be available to consumers. "There is unlimited value in the name Harrods," Al Fayed says. Harrods and Club Med have hired executives with American licensing experience to oversee their efforts.

Jaguar, the British luxury automaker, is one of the godfathers of European licensing, but it is also just beginning a new wave of expansion. Jaguar began with a line of designer eyeglass frames 15 years ago. Today its licenses cover such products as clothes, fragrances and footwear. The company has just opened mall boutiques in the U.S., France and the Netherlands.

"It is a way to let others pay for all the things you'd like to do [with the brand] but your shareholders won't pay for," says John Maries, general manager of the Jaguar Collection. For even smaller but ultra-exclusive companies, like sports-car maker Aston Martin, licensed products can help boost a low profile. Aston Martin has only recently launched its licensing program. And, befitting the producer of a car made famous by James Bond, it's sticking with toys for big boys. Its two initial products are expensive model cars and a Sony video game.

Successful brand-extension licensing operations look easy, but they require foresight and thought. "It shouldn't be misconstrued by companies as a freebie," says Equity Management's Konkle. Every brand has a "core equity," which is its image–what it stands for in the minds of consumers. Is it a premium brand? Does it signal value? What image does it conjure up? "You can't just put out a doodad with a name slapped on it," insists Michael Stone, co-director of New York's Beanstalk Group, another large licensing agency. Missteps abound among those who have held that simplistic view. Take Virgin Clothes: British entrepreneur Richard Branson has successfully etched his Virgin trademark onto a host of

(Cont.)

products, from CDs to cola. But his apparel line is struggling, mainly because its initial styles were pricey and somewhat conservative, which went against the trendy and value-conscious image originally established by the airline Virgin Atlantic.

Then there are the challenges involved in homing in on your target audience. Though Europe clearly offers new licensing opportunities for its own firms and foreign ones, it still cannot be viewed as one big market of 370 million undifferentiated consumers. Cultural and language barriers are very much a factor in consumer choice. And some brand images vary from country to country. BMW cars, for instance, aren't considered to be particularly top of the line in Germany, but are considered luxury cars in much of the rest of the world. Rovers are commonplace in Britain, but they are seen as classy foreign imports in Southern Europe. There is not even pan-European agreement on what constitutes quality. A T shirt made from a cotton-polyester blend may suit a British shopper, but French and German consumers want 100% cotton T shirts only, please. Licensing executive Gianfranco Mari, head of the agency DIC 2 in Milan, underlines that "what sells in Italy may not sell in France." Then there is the tangle of various legal requirements and trademark laws in each nation, which the European Union has not exterminated. "Those laws can keep the lawyers happy for years," says Jaguar's Maries.

Perhaps the biggest hurdle to overcome in Europe is retailer reluctance. In the past, licensed goods from fellow European companies were often cheap promotional giveaways, so many retailers view licensed products as a form of advertising that doesn't belong on their shelves. That puts the onus on marketers to convince retailers that most of today's licensed products are well-made goods associated with top brands. It's a slow slog. But, says David Isaacs, Equity Management's international director, "it can be done."

Given the new onslaught of licensed goods heading their way, European retailers may have little choice but to change their view. Consumers, after all, like the stuff. As American-style retailing continues to take hold in Europe, shopkeepers are beginning to chant another U.S. mantra: the customer is always right–especially when wielding branded credit cards.

46

Online sales pack a crunch

New products are shaking up shipping plans

By Elizabeth Weise
USA TODAY

Electronic commerce is radically changing the kind of products we buy and expect to have on our doorstep a day or two later. It's not just sweaters from Sears, beef jerky from Hickory Farms, and apples from Harry and David anymore.

Instead, odd-shaped packages containing saws from Amazon's home-improvement section, shovels from Smith & Hawken and bags of specialty potato chips are bumping their way down conveyer belts at FedEx, UPS and Airborne Express.

And that is creating the need for a whole new kind of packaging.

"We're seeing items that would typically not be shipped as small parcels being shipped that way," says Chad Thompson, manager of the UPS package lab in Hodgkins, Ill.

Add a few hundred thousand steaks, pickaxes, orchids and live fish into the mix of the 300 million packages UPS expects to ship in the four weeks leading up to Christmas and the 75 million FedEx will ship "air express," and it's easy to understand why more is involved than packing tape, wadded newspapers and whatever cardboard box happens to be lying around.

Given the ever-increasing volumes they're dealing with, shippers take extraordinary measures to ensure every box arrives intact. A broken box or leaking carton is time-consuming and money-losing: Everything has to stop while a worker retrieves the item, puts it in a plastic bag and reroutes it down the "exceptions" chute, where it ends up in the rewrap area.

To that end, both FedEx and UPS offer free packaging design consultations. At FedEx's Memphis lab, the engineers show off their computer-aided box-cutting machine like kids with a new toy.

The huge Kongsberg cutter dominates the engineering section. It looks a bit like a giant air hockey table: clear plexiglass with hundreds of tiny holes. Air is sucked out, pulling the cardboard flat against the table for the cut.

Engineer Tom Wood uses Laserpoint Page Design software, which offers many basic box designs. He types in dimensions and other choices: tab-closed or telescoping, long and narrow or short and squat.

The design is saved to a floppy disk, which Wood then pops into the Kongsberg. He takes a large, flat piece of cardboard from shelves that hold sheets of every thickness.

The machine first checks to make sure there's enough cardboard for the box: a spinning knife swiftly traces its outlines, cutting out some pieces, creasing others. It takes only a minute to complete.

Wood springs forward, pulls the cardboard out and quickly pokes out the excess pieces. He's left with an ungainly, flapping length of cardboard. He folds and turns it like pizza dough until the flat sheet is transformed into a neat little box with a self-closing lid.

> **FedEx has designed special packaging for shipping laptop computers.**

Companies are invited to send FedEx prototype cartons for testing. Senior packaging design specialist Pati Person carefully cuts open the outer carton to reveal inner cartons full of such things as live plants.

Cardboard a few millimeters thick is all that stands between the timidly waving branches and a House of Horrors of testing equipment. Two giant plates compress a package to determine its crush point, and a drop tester spills all eight corners on concrete to test sturdiness.

A vibration tester creates a mini-earthquake, simulating a truck running through city streets. It then ramps up to mimic a jet plane in flight. Once the "plane" has landed, the platform goes back into truck mode, "driving" the package to its recipient.

Boxes also are tested under real-world conditions. To ensure goods survive shipping, testers routinely slip small microprocessors into boxes to record data such as vibration and temperature changes.

"We can determine from the data whether the package was dropped, thrown or mishandled," packaging lab manager Larry Rutledge says.

All of that is necessary because, if what the customer ordered doesn't show up on time and in perfect condition, a million-dollar marketing campaign is meaningless.

Online merchants "don't have a store, so when

(Cont.)

that package arrives at the customer's doorstep, it's almost the first real, tangible encounter with the company," Thompson says.

As more kinds of stores go online, the items being shipped become more complicated. One company he works with is an online hardware superstore.

"You're talking shovels and rakes, hammers and axes, saw blades," Thompson says. Long-haul freight companies have always shipped by wooden, forklift pallet, but single orders to customers are a different story.

Companies also must prevent sharp implements from flying down conveyer belts and satisfy customers who want shovels to look nice on arrival.

UPS ended up developing protective packaging to blunt sharp edges and created a plastic bag to wrap it in because the paper ones ripped right off.

A few years ago FedEx engineers learned manufacturers were seeing millions of dollars in damage when laptop PCs were shipped for repairs.

FedEx designers developed a special cardboard box with a taut plastic trampoline in the middle. The laptop lies flat between two such pieces, riding in its own plastic hammock, protected from shocks.

"This can be dropped from 3 feet, and it won't be damaged," Rutledge proudly says. "We've had $2 million savings in damage claims."

Another challenge was getting live plants to survive a bumpy, shaky, hot, cold and often very dry trip of 24 to 48 hours to their new homes. Last year FedEx won an award for a seedling package using die-cut cardboard to form four inner holders that stabilize and protect seedling trays on their way to gardeners.

Then there's food. It has to move quickly, stay cold and arrive in one piece. Take the steps involved in shipping cheesecakes, a popular New York and Chicago specialty.

First, they must be frozen solid so they don't "deform" during shipping. Packed in a plastic container to protect them from crushing, they're placed in a Styrofoam cooler box, often with "dunnage" (filler) to keep them from shifting. The entire box is pre-chilled.

Dry ice pellets or frozen gel packs are placed around the box, which goes into another box made of heavy-duty waxed cardboard. This will keep just about anything cold enough to arrive in a cool and sanitary condition within 24 hours.

Even something as simple as dry ice requires serious engineering and chemical expertise or it could kill everyone on a cargo jet. Dry ice, frozen carbon dioxide, is the coolant of choice because of its extremely low temperature – minus-109 degrees Fahrenheit.

But as it warms, the gas displaces oxygen – a serious problem in a confined space. Omaha Steaks ships 2 million filet mignons in 9 million pounds of dry ice from mid-November to late December.

"When we unload the trucks, we have to use fans to blow air into them and swap out the workers pretty often so we make sure they're getting enough oxygen," Rutledge says.

It's harder to step outside for fresh air in the cockpit of a cargo plane, which is why FAA regulations require shippers to track how much dry ice is on board and ensure that it doesn't exceed safety cutoffs. Otherwise, "you'd slowly black out and not even know it was happening," Rutledge says.

Then there's the case of the exploding bags of tortilla chips. UPS' Thompson was approached by a company that was shipping individual bags of them. Chips don't mind getting bumped around, but vibration can lead to a bag of crumbs, and compression could lead to one big, flat tortilla sandwich, not exactly what you want to serve guests at a party.

A series of cardboard dividers takes care of external damage. But there's the problem of the explosions: Bags are normally sealed in factories near sea level, meaning air inside them is at sea-level pressure. But in the small planes used to fly to remote locations, cargo areas usually aren't pressurized. So the air inside the bag is suddenly at 13,000 feet, an extreme difference.

"When it's unpressurized . . . these bags can blow up like balloons until maybe they burst their seams or even bulge the box out," Thompson says. Researchers are still working on a high-altitude chip bag.

47

Why Dow Chemical Finds Slime Sublime

From Monster Slobber to Soup, Some Gooey Stuff Named Methocel Has Many Uses

By Susan Warren

Staff Reporter of The Wall Street Journal

MIDLAND, Mich. – Don Coffey is serious about slime.

Recently, the 46-year-old Dow Chemical Co. scientist mixed up a batch of his newest variety – the kind of slippery, gooey stuff usually found in buckets at Halloween – and plopped a hockey-puck-size glob down on a plate. As it lay jiggling, Mr. Coffey plunged his face in the goo and snarfed it down.

"Have you ever eaten Jell-O without a spoon?" he asks.

For 15 years, Dr. Coffey has devoted his career to slime, convincing food companies that Dow's concoction should be an indispensable part of their recipes. From a handful of products originally, Dow has managed to slip slime into more than 400 foods, from frozen pot pies to whipped toppings, as well as pills, paints, shampoos and special effects for movies.

These days at Dow, slime rocks. Chief Executive William Stavropoulos boasts that the stuff, marketed under the name Methocel, is the premier product in its specialty chemicals and plastics portfolio.

But slime wasn't always so cool. Twice since Methocel's birth 60 years ago, Dow was ready to kill the product. Even its creation is said to have been a laboratory mistake.

In the 1930s, scientists at Dow and elsewhere were experimenting with wood to create a more durable material. By grinding wood into a pulp and then washing it with chemicals to break it down, they were able to create ethyl cellulose, a product used to make the first plastic wrap. It came in handy for things like canteen linings during World War II.

But, as Dow lore has it, someone at the plant goofed one day, tacking an extra carbon atom onto the molecule. The result: an oozing goo called methyl cellulose, an obscure substance previously discovered in Europe. While scientists were excited by the find, Dow managers dismissed the slop as a disgusting disaster. Methocel was quickly sidelined when cheaper, more versatile petrochemical-based plastics came on the scene.

The product gradually found a home as a thickener for tile putty and drywall mud. But business was lousy, and in the mid-1980s, Dow considered selling. With no takers, though, Dow resorted to trying to save it, slashing costs, raising prices and looking for ways to expand the market.

As a newly minted Ph.D. in food science, Dr. Coffey was recruited to cook up new recipes for Methocel. To the youthful scientist, what was sublime about slime was that, chemically speaking, it is "bass-ackwards." Most plastics get thinner when heated. But Methocel had a unique sticky layer that breaks free when the molecules are heated; the molecules bond together to form a gel with a consistency like cooked egg whites. As it cools, the stuff thins out again into an oozing slime.

Dr. Coffey saw immediately that the tasteless, odorless and calorie-free ingredient, already used in a few foods, could be expanded to thicken soups, sauces and gravies. Added to foods, the stuff has a smooth, buttery texture, compared with the sometimes pasty feel of starch-based thickeners. Though chemicals are used in the manufacturing process, the end product is all-natural wood cellulose.

After trying out recipes in his lab, Dr. Coffey hit the road to convince customers. But food companies were perfectly happy with the corn or potato starches they had been using for 100 years. Besides, food-grade Methocel costs $5 a pound, compared with about 50 cents a pound for starches, though only one-tenth as much Methocel will do the same job.

Dr. Coffey met with a wall of skepticism. On one winter sales call to a Midwestern food company, the customer didn't believe that Methocel would do everything he said it would. He and a salesman were hustled out so quickly, he says, "I'm surprised we didn't end up head-first in a snow bank."

Gradually, some food companies began trying the goo for items like soups and puddings. But most sales still went to industrial and construction product makers. Dow, a chemicals giant specializing in basic petrochemicals, wasn't sure what to do with its slimy throwback to the pre-plastic era.

In the early 1990s, Methocel found itself again on the chopping block. "We still debated whether it had been as successful as it could be," says Michael Parker, an executive vice president then charged with taking a hard look at Dow's less-stellar businesses.

Dr. Coffey, an energetic man with a fondness for food-themed neckties, had a plan. Methocel could be a big player in Dow's expanding specialty businesses, he figured – if only he had a team of food scientists. To win over the food industry, "you need to be able to help them figure out why the cheese sauce is lumpy," he says.

His passionate pitch made superiors worry that there wasn't enough substance to back it up. "The tendency was not to take him seriously," says Gerald Doyle, now the global business director for Methocel.

But the day before Halloween in 1993, Mr. Parker gave slime a reprieve. Dr. Coffey

immediately hired three Ph.D.s.

Today, the Methocel division employs 300 people, including 14 food scientists. It boasts double-digit sales growth and produces more than 200 different products. Methocel has been used as monster slobber in "Star Wars" movies and took the title role in the remake of "The Blob." Museums use it as a kind of mud mask to clean artwork, and pharmaceutical companies use it for time-release medicines and coated capsules.

As director of the Methocel food business, Dr. Coffey believes slime's brightest future is on the grocery shelf – though many customers aren't eager to boast about it. Some companies worry about revealing a chemical component in their food products (no matter its natural origins and safe reputation). Others companies want to keep a key ingredient secret. Though Methocel must be listed on the ingredients label, often as methylcellulose, it can also be disguised simply as "vegetable gums."

Incognito or not, Methocel makes cheese

(Cont.)

cheesier, gravy creamier and fillings fruitier, says one frozen-food manufacturer who declined to be named. Without it, says a company representative, "you'd have something that was either too soft or too hard or too mushy."

And more food uses keep coming. In his lab near Dow headquarters here, Dr. Coffey, sporting a bacon-and-egg necktie, hovers around lab manager Linda Steinke as she coats pepperoni bits with Methocel powder. Makers of frozen pizza snacks have had problems with oozing grease. As pepperoni heats up in the oven, the Methocel absorbs the grease as it gels.

In another corner of the lab, similar work is being done with pot pies for a manufacturer who wants to reduce "boilover."

The newest Methocel product, dubbed Supergel, can be a substitute for egg whites, working as a sort of food glue to bind vegetable patties together. That appeals to vegans who shun animal proteins. "This is the youngest 60-year-old product out there," Dr. Coffey insists.

It may also be one of Dow's most fun. By filling a surgical glove with Methocel, tinting it greenish-yellow and boiling the mess, lab workers can create a ghastly, gelled appendage. New recruits in the lab have been known to find one sitting in their chairs, slowly melting.

One of the favorite stops on Dow visitor tours is "Slime Time," where school kids can add a pinch of Methocel powder to water to make their own goo. And squeezing it through fingers has its own distinct charm. On some Halloweens, Dr. Coffey buries quarters in a bucket of the stuff and lets kids dig for them.

"Then you can rub it in your hair and make your hair stand up," he says gleefully.

Through it all, Dr. Coffey never stops selling. At a recent presentation to customer service employees, he made his overhead transparencies out of thin layers of Methocel. At the end of the talk, he challenged Mr. Doyle, the global business director, to eat one of the crinkly, ink-stained sheets.

Mr. Doyle politely declined. So Dr. Coffey wolfed it down himself. "You only have one chance to hammer home a few points," he says. "And one of them is that it's OK to eat this. And as a matter of fact, you're *supposed* to eat this."

48

Crunch Points

Product Development Is Always Difficult; Consider the Frito Pie

7-Eleven and Partner PepsiCo Took a Year to Concoct The Corn-Chip Casserole

The Hurdle: Bag vs. No Bag

BY EMILY NELSON
Staff Reporter of THE WALL STREET JOURNAL

DALLAS – Cigarettes and Slurpees are one thing. But 7-Eleven wants to serve dinner, too.

Jim Keyes, chief operating officer of 7-Eleven Inc., thinks America can stomach the idea. Which is why the nation's largest convenience-store chain is not only pushing soft drinks and snacks as never before, but also is challenging fast-food restaurants for the palates of the legions of people who love their cars, love to eat and love to eat in their cars – the people Mr. Keyes calls dashboard diners.

"We're on a journey from the place where you buy hot dogs," he says.

The journey began in 1997, when 7-Eleven began rolling out – literally, in some instances – a line of foods that are as much a main course as they are a munchy: a simple submarine sandwich with a plastic tray for catching crumbs; a Burger Big Bite, molded in the shape of a hot dog, for one-handed eating; the similarly tubular El Taco; a line of Bakery Stix, hollow breadsticks stuffed with meat, cheese and other fillings; and so on.

The expanding menu, managers say, will broaden the appeal of the chain's 5,200 U.S. stores beyond the core "beer and butts crowd." It can only help that at many fast-food restaurants these days, "it's a park-through, not a drive-through," Mr. Keyes says. "We're faster."

Maybe. But the effort that goes into developing hand-held meals is hardly fast. In early 1998, Mr. Keyes ordered up another course: a meal of corn chips, chili and cheese, all tumbled together into a nachos-style casserole. Only now, 14 months later, is the company's $1.99 "fresh" version available in a 25-store test market.

In the interim, managers, engineers, packaging specialists and others from 7-Eleven and its partner in the project, PepsiCo Inc. and its Frito-Lay snack-foods division, engaged in a process far more complicated than the simple result would suggest. This is the story of the birth of 7-Eleven's Frito pie.

* * *

It's spring 1998, and Jim Keyes has just been promoted to chief operating officer of 7-Eleven from chief financial officer. Several dashboard delicacies are on the market, others are in the pipeline, but 7-Eleven is in a funk. Half the goods in the average 7-Eleven store aren't selling at all each month. While the company is doing a huge business in Slurpees and Big Gulps, the average customer is spending just $3 a visit, and only one of every eight customers who buys a drink also buys a snack.

"That's why fresh food is so central to our future success," Mr. Keyes says. "It will change the way people see 7-Eleven."

But he also figures that customers need foods midway between snack and supper, much like subs and cylindrical burgers, to ease them toward accepting full-blown meals from 7-Eleven. "Even if we put out the best entree to take home, you'd hesitate about that today because we're not known for that," Mr.

Jim Keyes

Keyes says. The Frito pie "is a step as we get there." It also could form the linchpin of an entire line of chips-and-dip entrees that he and other 7-Eleven planners envision.

The Frito pie seems perfectly suited for the role. It's easy, quick and already popular. According to Frito-Lay lore, Daisy Dean Doolin, mother of Elmer Doolin, founder of the original Frito company, concocted the first Frito pie in the kitchen of her San Antonio home in 1932 – an attempt to turn leftover chili into something more. Whatever the origins, the pie had made its way to lunch counters and drive-ins by the 1950s. Now, it is popular across a wide swath of middle America, prepared by the consumer, or bought at mall food courts and the like. Some purists simply pour the fixings into a bag of Fritos and shake.

Mr. Keyes has something a little more presentable in mind when he takes his idea to Al Carey, PepsiCo's senior vice president of sales and retailer strategies. Mr. Carey is a casual friend whose company is a major supplier of 7-Eleven. Mr. Carey and other PepsiCo executives like what they hear. More-substantial 7-Eleven foods might solve a nagging riddle for PepsiCo: People who eat snacks and soda together seldom buy the two together, whether at 7-Eleven or elsewhere. Putting PepsiCo drinks and Frito-Lay-based entrees side-by-side might boost sales of both.

Within two months, 7-Eleven and Frito-Lay are ready to start work. On June 25, 1998, the Frito-Lay team drives to 7-Eleven's Dallas headquarters from Frito Lay headquarters in Plano. With the group are two chefs hired from a Springfield, Mo., food-marketing agency, Noble & Associates.

Heading up the 7-Eleven side is Sharon Powell, a 20-year company veteran who was promoted to vice president of fresh foods merchandising specifically to develop dashboard dinners. She has been deeply involved in developing smoothies and kiwi-strawberry Slurpees, among other products, and is overseeing a redesign of 7-Eleven stores to give greater prominence to the new foods.

The 10 participants swap business cards and joke about the sweltering heat outside. Then Ms. Powell starts. In the next month, she says, 7-Eleven will be packaging sandwiches with bags of Frito-Lay chips. Now, she says, she envisions a cup of chili and a package of shredded cheese, sold along with bags of Fritos. Eventually, she says, 7-Eleven stores will be stocked with racks of Frito pies, Tostitos nachos and other chips-and-dip dishes.

"We don't know what's possible, but we're ready to explore the options," she says, her formal suit and official demeanor contrasting with the more casual Frito-Lay managers, dressed in khakis and polo shirts.

The Frito-Lay managers and Noble chefs have spent the morning touring 7-Eleven's food-preparation facility in Lewisville, a Dallas suburb. Tim Petsch, a senior account supervisor from Noble who designs recipes for food manufacturers, is excited about the potential of the refried beans and other fixings he saw there – enough for Noble to use to create "a winning food brand," he says. Others chime in with their favorite chips-and-dip combos.

"Are you thinking of trying soup tureens in the stores?" asks Kathy Bassininski, a Frito-Lay senior product manager.

"We tried soup last year," Ms. Powell says, "and it was a fiasco." Among other things, it requires too much attention from store clerks.

As the discussion moves to cilantro and chipotle, Ms. Powell grows impatient. A 7-Eleven customer, she says, is "willing to put ketchup on my hot dog but not much more."

Ms. Powell assures the Frito-Lay team that 7-Eleven wants to move quickly. They break up, agreeing only to meet soon.

A month passes.

On July 29, the two teams gather below 7-Eleven headquarters in a labyrinthine basement of test kitchens. On shelves in glass-fronted cabinets sit plastic beakers of smoothies, bags of shredded cheese, jars of honey mustard. Counters are strewn with plastic cups, trays and lids in all shapes and sizes – including 7-Eleven's new Slurpee cup, clear plastic partitioned down the middle so patrons can buy two flavors at a time. In a room nearby, a group huddles around a woman in a white coat as she slices turkey. In another room, tasters sample Slurpee innovations.

The Noble people have brought a brightly labeled packet stamped "Deli Central Fresh Today" and a list of "menu concepts." Suggestions include a Southwest chicken sub – "succulent grilled chicken breast topped with aged provolone cheese, crisp bacon, shredded lettuce, grilled onions and Tostitos medium salsa on fresh baked bread." Further down appear "Frito-Lay Lunches," which will "offer the taste 7-Eleven patrons trust in a variety of menu choices." Among the entrants is a "FRITO pie with FRITOS Corn Chips."

Noble's Mr. Petsch suggests strategies for advertising and promoting fresh food – for instance, distributing punch cards that allow customers to collect a free meal after buying a certain number. Customers find that boring, the 7-Eleven people say. Joe Horres, 7-Eleven's category manager for grilled foods, pipes in that he already is looking for plastic trays to hold the chips and fixings for the Frito pie. For two hours, menus and marketing dominate. No one mentions pie.

"I want to go back to the original request to have Fritos next to a dip in a case," Ms. Powell says. "But you guys don't seem to be there. So I need to know, is this not the way to do it?"

The room falls quiet. The Frito-Lay managers look to Ms. Bassininski, their product manager. "If you put loose chips in a plastic tray with dip in a well," she says matter-of-factly, "the chips will absorb the dip." Exposed to air for mere minutes, chips lose their crunch. Doused with sauce, they turn to mush. "Today, we can't take anything open where it will share air," she says.

"I knew there was a reason you were leading away from this," Ms. Powell says. Mr. Keyes, 7-Eleven's COO, wants fresh Frito pie, not something in a bag. "This is leading away from his vision," she says.

The planners disperse into the Texas heat, unaware that they have come up against the greatest threat to success: Frito-Lay's concern for the integrity of its chips conflicts with Mr. Keyes's desire to sell foods that appear freshly made. "We are a packaged-goods company," says Harry Walsh, then head of Pepsi soft-drink sales to 7-Eleven. "The consumers are used to getting this," he says, waving a bag of Ruffles potato chips. "They're confident in the bag."

The issue was foreshadowed in 1996, when 7-Eleven began selling nachos – really just trays of Frito-Lay Tostitos and generic cheese sauce. So many chips were broken as workers dumped chips into trays that one worker was busy full-time just emptying

Harry Walsh,

PepsiCo vice president, 7-Eleven team leader:

Consumers, he says, "are confident in the bag," but he nonetheless is willing to consider letting the chips loose for the Frito pie. "This is one of those things we'll try," he says.

garbage pails of tortilla shards. 7-Eleven store managers complained that even more chips shattered during delivery. After a month, the project was halted.

Still, PepsiCo wants to please 7-Eleven, a major customer that can push Pepsi's "Star Wars" promotions and help launch new products such as Pepsi One, a diet soda. But it isn't accustomed to designing products to meet a retailer's whim. "This is so different for us," Mr. Walsh says. "We're consumer driven."

As summer of 1998 slides toward fall, the chips and how they will be packaged in the Frito pie become the central debate. Chips in separate bags? Chips loose in trays, with sealed chili cups and bags of shredded cheese? Bags of chips with sealed cups of chili and cheese combined, all sealed in a tray? Ms. Powell's frustration grows. "They don't get that it has to be out of the bag," she says.

Meanwhile, Mr. Horres, the 7-Eleven grilled-foods manager, is doing his part. A 29-year 7-Eleven veteran who opened the chain's first stores in Australia and Taiwan, he contributed early to the dashboard-dining program by helping to launch the Bacon Cheeseburger Big Bite. The original Burger Big Bite had hit stores nationwide in spring 1997; it soon became clear that the meat tended to dry out and stick to the grill,

prompting adjustments to flavoring and moisture content. Later that year, Mr. Horres was among those who handled the transition to the bacon cheeseburger variation, which sold better in test marketing.

Now, Mr. Keyes is pressuring Mr. Horres to speed the Frito pie. Hot dishes sell best in cooler weather. Worrying about the Texas summers, Mr. Horres wants a small trial run by March 1999. Moreover, the sooner 7-Eleven can finish the Frito pie, the sooner it can add other chips-and-dips.

Mr. Horres calls a meeting. In a windowless conference room at Frito-Lay headquarters in November, he tells the group that they must get a test product in Dallas stores by March 1 so "the heat will be off me." He

Sharon Powell,

7-Eleven vice president of fresh foods merchandising:

Early on, she frets that the Frito-Lay people "don't get that it has to be out of the bag." That, she feels, threatens 7-Eleven's vision of fresh foods.

adds: "Today is critical."

The 10 people sit around an oval table strewn with bags of chips, plastic trays and paper-cup mock-ups of dipping cups. They grab trays and pair them with cups in various combinations to demonstrate their ideas. Some people put bags of chips in trays; others open bags, pour in chips and consider the result.

The Frito-Lay people mention focus groups. Unnecessary and costly, Mr. Horres says. Instead, executives can sample the product, and 7-Eleven can hold tastings in its basement kitchen for janitors and other building workers. "They're the ones who eat in our stores," Mr. Horres says.

Mr. Horres has brought along an outside packaging engineer who scours the offerings of plastics manufacturers in search of containers for 7-Eleven. Holding a plastic tray full of Fritos and a cup of dip, Mr. Horres suggests 1.75 ounces of chips and 1.5 ounces

Joe Horres,

7-Eleven manager of grilled foods:

Since the Bacon Cheeseburger Bite, he feels pressured to keep rolling out dashboard dinners. "That's why my hair's gray," he says.

of dip, based on his own eyeball estimate.

"We did a lot of research on this," Ms. Bassininski interrupts. The research showed that people wanted more dip than chip.

The talk turns to seals. One option is "barrier film" between chips and dip. Another is a plastic lid. Perhaps the entire tray, chips and dip and all, could be covered with heat-sealed film. And there's always shrink-wrap. Mr. Horres suggests "a black tray with a black bottom and a heat-seal top."

Steve Callahan, a Frito-Lay manager of technology, frets that plastic wrap won't be adequate. Only a heat-sealed lid can ensure a shelf-life of 70 to 90 days, he says.

"But we just need two," Mr. Horres says, since the product is supposed to be fresh and will be dumped after two days on display.

As the meeting breaks up, Lisa Merino, a 7-Eleven marketing manager sitting in on the meeting, suggests to a few people within earshot that the Frito pie make use of the chili and cheese-sauce dispensers that 7-Eleven recently began installing in its stores. That way, customers could pump toppings on their hot dogs, and all 7-Eleven would have to do is swap its generic nachos in favor of Frito-Lay chips. No one responds. The dispensers have always been a fallback option with the group, but not a priority; most would prefer a tidier, all-in-one product.

After nearly 2 1/2 hours of talk, the group again agrees only to meet again – this time to let Frito-Lay engineers tour the facility where 7-Eleven assembles trays of no-name nachos.

The Frito pie group gathers Dec. 2 at 9 a.m. The Lewisville kitchens are tucked away off a highway access road, in a bare building that resembles a garage. Inside, the space is broken up into rooms where workers assemble food; they don't cook. For the nachos, about a dozen workers open bags of chips, stuff them into red plastic dishes, snap on clear plastic lids, fasten them with clear tape, slap on 7-Eleven stickers, a bar code and a nutrition label, and load the finished snack into plastic pallets. Workers toss breaks in garbage pails.

Team members don white coats, hair nets and masks before stepping onto the floor. Two Frito-Lay engineers pace about with hand-held humidity readers. Temperature? 48 degrees. Too cold? Customers don't complain after the nachos are in stores. Portions? Workers fill four-ounce trays, working through a two-pound bag of chips at a time. Waste? The plant is proud to lose just 19% of all chips to breaks.

But what if 7-Eleven trucks hit a few potholes? Do the chips break? 7-Eleven doesn't know.

THE MEETING continues in a conference room, where the debate over the form of the Frito pie resumes. Mr. Horres turns to the facility's manager, Craig Weidner. "Option one is very expensive. You guys get chili and cheese . . . and scoop it into a microwavable bowl," Mr. Horres says. "Option two, you do what you're best at, you just do assembly" and receive a sealed bowl of chili and a bag of shredded cheese to package with Fritos. Mr. Weidner says either is possible.

Six months have passed since the group started meeting, and the 7-Eleven Frito pie remains a vague, amorphous thing. 7-Eleven officials are nonetheless encouraged that new foods are helping the company's results. During a morning videoconference call with 7-Eleven field managers, COO Mr. Keyes says merchandise sales rose 7.6% to $5.6 billion in 1998, compared with a 1.9% increase in 1997. Sales at stores open at least a year rose an impressive 5.7%, about one-third of that increase coming from new products. In particular, the new Cafe Cooler, a copy of Starbucks' Frappuccino, produced $50 million in sales.

For Mr. Horres, the quick rollout of so many products has been draining. He put a new item in the stores each month – including a wiener-shaped turkey with cranberry sauce at Thanksgiving – but handling the logistics and the follow-up with store managers was trickier than he expected. And Mr. Keyes is pressuring him to introduce more. "That's why my hair's gray," he says.

Not all the new food is a smash. The sausage-like turkey, sold nationally from the end of October to Dec. 1, 1998, lighted no fires. "We're not doing it again this year. Sales weren't that great," Mr. Horres says. "It wasn't very appealing," he adds. "It didn't look like the turkey you pulled out of your oven at Thanksgiving."

As the new year starts, Mr. Horres is determined to get the Frito pie moving toward stores. He has tasted two types of chili – one for 55 cents a cup and one for 30 cents – and decided the cheaper one tastes just fine. The group needs only to pick a tray to hold the chips – in or out of a bag – and a sealed cup to hold the chili. In a Frito-Lay conference room on a Friday afternoon in January, Frito-Lay's Mr. Callahan and a product manager join Mr. Horres in sorting through plastic trays, cups, plastic wrap and bags of chips.

"That looks pretty hokey," Mr. Horres says of a partitioned black tray with loose chips on one side and a dip cup on the other, sealed with clear wrap. A salsa cup covered in tin foil in a tray next to a bag of chips that is stuffed in to fit "looks so grocery store."

"It's got to look pretty," Mr. Horres tells the Frito-Lay people. "You buy food with your eyes. . . . I'm just not happy with what I see here."

In February, as the packaging problem persists, Ms. Powell is already asking about expanding the menu. She wants Tostitos tortilla chips with salsa or Ruffles potato chips with ranch dressing.

Frito-Lay representatives, unsure about selling corn chips outside of a bag, have even stronger feelings about potato chips. Clear bags allow for unsightly grease smears, and potato chips can turn rancid when exposed to light. Also, potato chips are bagged by weight, not volume, because potato density varies from season to season, meaning an ounce of heavier, higher-density chips can look skimpy in a clear bag.

Ms. Powell is nonplused. With her plan for a whole line of chips-and-dip thwarted, she frets that the project has far less sales potential. "I thought we were talking about potato chips all along," she says.

Mr. Horres has doubts about Frito-Lay's commitment. "I don't know how excited they are about this, frankly," he confides. "I don't see them jumping on the table."

Frito-Lay, though, says it is making 7-Eleven more of a priority than ever – so much so that it has created a team dedicated to working only with 7-Eleven. Gone are the two separate sales groups – one for chips and snacks, the other for soft drinks – and the fluid roster of Frito-Lay people who have been working on the Frito pie. Now, one team is dedicated exclusively to 7-Eleven; it is headed by Mr. Walsh, who becomes Pepsi-Co's vice president overseeing relations with 7-Eleven.

Mr. Walsh reports directly to Mr. Carey, the PepsiCo senior vice president of sales and retailer strategies and previously Frito-Lay's chief operating officer. In the past, Mr. Carey says, "we would send over people to call and sell as much as we could. Today, we're trying to solve problems and drive business."

With new members, the next bilateral gathering turns into a rerun of meetings past.

Al Carey,
PepsiCo senior vice president of sales and retailer strategies:
Ultimately, it's his decision to let the Fritos out of the bag. "We're going to do it because we think it's a great opportunity."

Mr. Walsh is surprised that PepsiCo would go so far to tailor its products for a customer – 7-Eleven – that it would even consider letting its chips out of the bag. "This is one of those things we'll try," he says. "We still think a bag is a better way to go." His greater fear is that the Frito pie will inspire retailers to start demanding other customized PepsiCo products. "We're not about to create a 7-Eleven-shaped chip," he says.

But Mr. Walsh is quick to take the reins when he realizes the group has been stuck on the same problem for months. The conclusion: have their bosses, Mr. Keyes and Mr. Carey, decide whether to let the chips out of the bag.

No one is thrilled about going to the top without a final Frito pie to present. So at a meeting six weeks later, on May 14, they prepare a presentation scheduled for May 25 of what they have – and haven't – accomplished. Again, it comes down to the bag vs. no-bag debate. "We've got a pretty firm foot in the ground that says, going forward, everything we do will be a bag in a tray," says Julie Nelson, a PepsiCo sales manager. "I guess that's something we need to talk about."

"Jim and Al need to talk about that," Ms. Powell replies. "At the meeting on the 25th, we need to say Frito is willing to test [loose chips] in Dallas, but if we go national, our position is bags."

Without a finished product, Ms. Powell suggests presenting their early designs at the meeting. "I want to show him where we started and how ugly it was," she says. Mr. Horres adds, "We've got to get to the bags because Jim's not going to be happy with that."

They discuss preparing mock-ups and having the graphics department come up with labels. Who should lead the presentation?

"I'll lead, but you'll help me," Ms. Nelson says to Ms. Powell.

"Yes," Ms. Powell says.

In subsequent smaller gatherings, Ms. Powell, Mr. Horres and Mr. Walsh retrace their work to prepare a slew of options – from trays of loose chips packaged with cups of chili to the more-primitive unadorned chips for the customer to embellish with cheese and chili from the pumps.

Two weeks later, the group gathers in a room adjacent to Mr. Keyes's 41st-floor office. Outside spread grand views of downtown Dallas. Sipping a can of Pepsi One, Mr. Keyes listens as Ms. Nelson, Ms. Powell and the rest describe their work to date. He then tries to explain what 7-Eleven wants. Mr. Keyes sees a parallel in sushi. Five years ago, he notes, Americans ate sushi only in Japanese restaurants; today, people buy California rolls at the supermarket.

"Could we take a fresh nacho and make it available with eight pieces in a tray like a California roll?" Mr. Keyes wonders aloud. Just as the seaweed shields the rice from the fish in a sushi roll, he says, is there a "cheese seaweed" to keep chips crisp underneath chili and cheese toppings?

Not likely, the PepsiCo team responds politely.

Mr. Keyes points out that the average 7-Eleven store sells 15 trays of no-name nachos a day. Both companies think sales could double or better with the Frito-Lay name on the trays, so why not simply ditch the generic nachos and let the customers buy branded Fritos to adorn as they see fit with the existing chili and cheese dispensers? That would

MAKING THE PIE

1 At $1.99, the unadorned 7-Eleven Frito pie comprises a plastic tray containing approximately 40 Fritos Scoops, sealed to keep the chips fresh.

2 Upon purchase, the customer peels back the clear-plastic seal and adds free chili from dispensers 7-Eleven has already installed in its stores for buyers of hot dogs.

3 After the chili comes the cheese. Unlike the classic Frito pie, which uses cheese that has been grated or shredded, this version makes use of more easily dispensed cheese sauce.

4 The finished pie, to be eaten with one's hands or with plastic utensils that 7-Eleven makes available.

exploit the power of a brand name and eliminate the packaging debate that has consumed a year of work, he figures, and it could be taken to market quickly.

MR. CAREY consults with his director of research and development, and then relents. Frito-Lay will forgo the bag, but for the test only. If 7-Eleven wants to go national later, he will reconsider. "It's not something we do very well," he says, "but we're going to do it because I think it's a great opportunity."

Frito-Lay insists on packaging and delivering the chip trays itself. This time, Mr. Keyes is the one to give in.

Finally, the group has a product: One rectangular tray of large Fritos Scoops corn chips, sealed with clear plastic. Customers will add chili and cheese from 7-Eleven dispensers, the contents provided by Market-Fare Foods, an Austin, Texas, producer of foods for convenience stores and vending machines. Mr. Horres has insisted all along that the pie not sell for more than $2, and at the agreed price of $1.99, the pie will yield a margin of about 50%.

It isn't the ideal pie. The chili and cheese, runny enough to move through the pump, won't please all Frito pie aficionados. Mr. Keyes is frustrated, too, but he also can appreciate why an agreement took so long. "It seems so ridiculously simple in a way. You put chips in a tray," he shrugs. But for PepsiCo, he adds, picking up a bag of Cracker Jack, "this is their business. They see a bag as connoting freshness. We're saying you don't have to stop at the bag. Take it to a new level, a tray."

With a decision from the top, the two teams move quickly. In the next few weeks, Frito-Lay throws about 30 people at the project, including tray vendors, label vendors and staffers from sales, product supply, pur-

chasing, graphics, technology research and marketing.

Mr. Horres wants the chip tray covered with a clear film, printed with both Fritos and 7-Eleven logos. But the printing would take 12 weeks, so he settles for a sticker with both logos that, once affixed to the clear-plastic film, covers half the top. Frito-Lay engineers worry about chip grease sullying the clear cover. Solution: pack the trays sideways, sticker-side down, so that when the chips settle and bump up against the seal, the sticker hides grease spots.

Both companies are getting excited. "Normally, the pre-test is one year," Mr. Walsh says. "We've taken a year's process down to three months." That has meant forgoing, among other things, taste tests with the janitorial staff.

By July, 7-Eleven's Mr. Horres has samples in his office. Late one afternoon, more to soothe his nerves than his appetite, he grabs a tray of Fritos and goes downstairs to the 7-Eleven store in the building's basement. He squirts chili and cheese on a tray of generic corn chips and on a tray of Fritos. He sets his timer.

The Fritos alone pack 640 calories, 360 from fat, before counting the red chili and bright yellow cheese, which together could double the tally. The nutrition label says the tray contains four servings, or about 10 large chips a person. But everyone on the team figures most customers will treat the whole thing as one serving.

After two minutes, Mr. Horres digs in. Still tasty, still crunchy. He continues tasting at two-minute intervals. Both trays turn to goo after 10 minutes or so, but the Fritos "had a little more flavor. Our chips are pretty bland." For dashboard diners, he says, the concoction works. "I was just concerned this thing would turn into nacho soup," he says.

Tech Star

Cisco is famous as one of Wall Street's hottest stocks of the '90s

STOCK PRICE

If you invested **$1,000** in 1990 it would be worth **$845,000** today

MARKET VALUE (BILLIONS)

Microsoft	$576
General Electric	496
CISCO	**362**
Wal-Mart	305
Intel	274

brown bunker-like buildings that seem to extend to the horizon, differentiated only by banners proclaiming, for example, that this particular building birthed THE FIRST QUALIFIED DOCSIS-COMPLIANT HEAD-END ROUTER IN THE INDUSTRY. "It's a great place to work if you're an engineer," says one. "I can't think of why anyone else would work here."

Actually, Cisco is run by a nonengineer.

John Chambers sits amid the expanse of cubicles in an office as austere and tiny as an entry-level programmer's. His motto is, "Never ask your employees to do something you wouldn't be willing to do yourself." This culture of self-sacrifice and frugality means that Chambers and all top execs fly coach and have no reserved parking spaces. The same quest for efficiency has driven Cisco to make cutting-edge use internally of the networks it sells to other companies. Everything at Cisco–from health-insurance issues to softball schedules–is available on the Web. Already, Cisco makes 84% of its sales over the Web, accounting in 1999 for about $9.5 billion in business-to-business e-commerce. To put that in perspective, mighty Amazon sold about $1.5 billion worth of products online.

Chambers is customer obsessed, a characteristic that will serve the company well as it moves into consumer markets. He discovered the dogma of customer service as a salesman at IBM and and then saw firsthand the cost of losing customer focus when he joined minicomputer maker Wang in the late '80s. As Wang's business eroded–in part because Wang didn't listen to customers–Chambers, the top sales executive, was forced to lay off 4,000 workers. He vows never to do that again, even if it means keeping his company leaner and meaner than seems necessary. "Laying off workers in a tough job market was the worst feeling in the world," he says as he sips his fourth Diet Coke of the day. "It made me physically ill."

Even as the company has grown to become the king of the data network, it has remained, in many consumers' minds, a question mark. Ask most people what Microsoft or Intel do, and they'll tell you. But Cisco? "I don't know," says Harriet Sumner, 30, a customer-service manager for a computer-game company, "but I own the stock."

Chambers thinks it's important that people such as Sumner do know, especially now that Cisco wants to be successful in its other bold strategy: a march into the telecom business, where it will face a whole new level of well-entrenched competition. The $250 billion-a-year telephone-equipment business is where giants like AT&T's equipment-making spin-off, Lucent, and Canadian counterpart Nortel have built powerful, decades-long relationships with telephone companies and service providers. As voice and data networks converge–and data come to account for more than 90% of network traffic– Cisco has boasted that its networks, which are predominantly data or IP (Internet protocol) networks, will also become the leading voice networks.

Consumers, however, are still uneasy about IP telephone service. Do you really want your voice to be as unreliable as your Web connection? Cisco swears it has closed the gap and made its IP networks as reliable as voice networks. What would help, Cisco believes, is for consumers to come to believe in the Cisco brand to the point where they are exerting upward pressure on telephone companies and service providers to run Cisco networks. In other words, for Cisco to be able to apply a two-way squeeze from the corporate side and the consumer side so that your phone company will have no choice but to go with Cisco. "Name recognition and branding are crucial to us," says Chambers. "We want the small business, the medium-sized business and even the consumer to want Cisco-powered networks."

Cisco, in its history, has never gone after a major market and failed. Lucent and Nortel, are you ready?

Place

50

Krispy Kreme at a Krossroads

Doughnut Chain's Expansion Risks Eroding the Mystique Of Its Sought-After Product

BY JAMES R. HAGERTY

Staff Reporter of THE WALL STREET JOURNAL

When a Krispy Kreme doughnut shop opened in the Van Nuys district of Los Angeles last year, half a dozen TV stations sent crews to film the event. Newspapers and magazines printed rave reviews. "A famous deep-fried Southern sin has come West," gushed the Los Angeles Times.

Could a company ask for more? If it's **Krispy Kreme Doughnut** Corp., it doesn't have to. Shortly before a Krispy Kreme shop opened in a suburb of Phoenix last year, a public-relations aide to Sheriff Joe Arpaio of Arizona's Maricopa County asked whether the sheriff could be the first customer. Krispy Kreme gladly obliged Mr. Arpaio, who bills himself as "the toughest sheriff in America" and has become a local celebrity by requiring his prisoners to wear pink underwear. The sheriff ate his doughnut before a thicket of TV cameras. Then he uttered the perfect sound bite: "These doughnuts are so good they should be illegal."

As the 63-year-old chain spreads out from its traditional base in the Southeast, it is basking in free publicity that is sweeter than the glaze on its pillowy pastries. Krispy Kreme doughnuts have had cameo roles in the movie "Primary Colors" and on such TV shows as "Ally McBeal" and "NYPD Blue." On "The Tonight Show," Jay Leno recently noted that policemen resent jokes about their supposed weakness for doughnuts. Then he gleefully displayed a picture of a police officer chomping into a Krispy Kreme.

All this exposure will almost certainly help the Winston-Salem, N.C., company sell stock when it holds an initial public offering, expected soon. Its underwriters have set its IPO at three million shares with a price range of $18 to $20 a share.

The big question for investors is whether Krispy Kreme can continue to generate so much buzz as its doughnuts become more widely available and less of a novelty. Coors beer, produced by **Adolph Coors** Co., provides a sobering example for the doughnut maker. In the 1970s, when Coors was available only in parts of the West, it developed a cult following on campuses in the rest of the country. After it went national in the 1980s, Coors became just another light brew. "People want what they can't get," notes Emanuel Goldman, a consumer-products analyst at Merrill Lynch & Co.

Krispy Kreme officials are aware of the Coors effect. To avoid saturating the market, they generally keep stores at least 10 miles apart. "We don't want to be on every corner," says Jennifer C. Gardner, a marketing manager.

Long managed conservatively, the company has grown so gradually that it didn't reach New York and other major cities outside the Southeast until the past few years. Today, the company has about 140 stores in 27 states, compared with 3,700 for Dunkin' Donuts, the nation's biggest doughnut chain, a unit of Britain's **Allied Domecq** PLC.

By any doughnut standard, Krispy Kreme has a distinctive product. To entertain customers, the company installs its doughnut-making machines behind picture windows in each store. Like something out of Dr. Seuss, the steel contraptions extrude raw dough in the shape of doughnuts and then float the little rings through a lake of vegetable oil at 360 degrees, before drowning them in a "waterfall" of white glaze. Served hot and gooey, just out of the fryer, the chain's signature "original glazed" doughnuts are "easily squished into your mouth in one motion," says Donna Soroczak, a nurse in Long Beach, Calif.

This combination of theater and hot doughnuts proved overpowering for the Rev. Jon Engen. A talk-show host on the KTIS Christian radio station in Roseville, Minn., Mr. Engen tried his first Krispy Kreme while traveling in Florida five years ago. Since then, he has raved about the doughnuts so frequently during his radio show that Krispy Kreme is famous in Roseville, even though the nearest outlet is a four-hour drive away in Des Moines, Iowa. During a trip to Des Moines last year, Mr. Engen says, he and his friends visited a Krispy Kreme shop five times in two days. "We were so jazzed up on sugar by the time we went home we couldn't feel our fingers," he says.

Along with hot doughnuts, Krispy Kreme shops play up the company's history with grainy black-and-white photos from the chain's early days. The taste of the doughnuts, Krispy Kreme says, hasn't changed since 1937, when Vernon Rudolph set up the original Krispy Kreme shop in Winston-Salem. He used a secret recipe his uncle had bought from Joe LeBeau, a onetime steamboat cook from Louisiana.

With the help of a few franchisees, Mr. Rudolph gradually added stores in neighboring states. When he died in 1973, there were about 50 shops.

Three years later, the Rudolph family sold the business to Beatrice Foods Co. of Chicago. Beatrice added deli-style sandwiches to the menu. But "the world's best doughnut maker was the world's worst deli-sandwich maker," says Carver Rudolph, a son of the founder. In 1982, Beatrice sold Krispy Kreme to several families that were longtime franchisees for about $22 million.

The new owners, whose descendants still control the company, ditched the sandwiches and focused on the doughnuts. Rather than expanding the chain immediately, they concentrated on paying down debt. So it was only in the mid-1990s that Krispy Kreme began a systematic drive to award franchises in major cities outside the Southeast.

Growth has accelerated. The chain rang up sales of $180.9 million in the year ended Jan. 31, 1999, up 57% from four years earlier. "We believe we are in the infancy of our growth," the company says in a registration statement for its planned IPO.

Even so, Krispy Kreme could stumble if it fails to keep quality consistently high as it

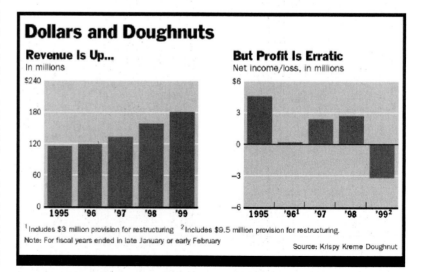

Dollars and Doughnuts

Revenue Is Up...
In millions

But Profit Is Erratic
Net income/loss, in millions

[1] Includes $3 million provision for restructuring [2] Includes $9.5 million provision for restructuring.

Note: For fiscal years ended in late January or early February

Source: Krispy Kreme Doughnut

recruits more and more franchisees. "That's probably the No. 1 risk," says Dennis Lombardi, executive vice president of Technomic Inc., a Chicago food-service consultancy.

Given the potential problems of expansion, some question the wisdom of a public offering. There have even been signs of discord at **J.P. Morgan** & Co., a co-manager of the IPO, over Krispy Kreme's potential. Damon Brundage, who recently resigned as Morgan's lead restaurant analyst, appeared skeptical about Krispy Kreme's prospects as a public company, according to people familiar with the matter.

Mr. Brundage declined to discuss the reasons for his departure from Morgan. Morgan officials said his departure wasn't related to his views on Krispy Kreme.

Despite such misgivings, Roger E. Glick-man is betting that Krispy Kreme still has a lot of mileage. A native of Los Angeles, he earned a master's degree in business administration from the Wharton School in 1996 and then took a job that involved scouting the country for potential movie-theater sites. One business trip took Mr. Glickman to Gastonia, N.C., where the owner of a shopping mall happened to suggest a meeting at the local Krispy Kreme.

"I had no idea what those two words meant," recalls Mr. Glickman.

By the end of the meeting, he had gulped down a dozen of the doughnuts. (Each glazed doughnut contains 170 calories, says Mr. Glickman, who is 6-foot-6 and weighs about 275 pounds.) He was enchanted by the taste, the glistening doughnut machines and the red neon sign reading "Hot Doughnuts Now."

Soon Mr. Glickman and his father-in-law, Richard Reinis, persuaded Krispy Kreme to award them the franchise for Southern California. So far, they have opened four stores in the Los Angeles area, and they expect the total to reach 40 or more in the next few years.

One recent afternoon, the 31-year-old Mr. Glickman slid his silver Audi up to one of the stores just in time to watch a Brownie troop take a Krispy Kreme tour. He beamed as the Brownies smeared their faces and hair with doughnut glaze. "We're trying to form indelible impressions," he said.

51

A NEANDERTHAL INDUSTRY SMARTENS UP

How the electrical-parts biz got the glitches out

John E. Haluska is a bear of a man whose gray beard makes him look more like Santa Claus than an Internet visionary. But three years ago, while the chief information officer for $2.2 billion electrical-parts maker Thomas & Betts Corp. was visiting a distributor, he passed the accounts payable office and noticed a large stack of documents with his company's name on them. When he asked about the papers, he was told: "It's T&B day." On such days, eight hours are spent crawling through the paperwork, addressing snafus between the distributor and Thomas & Betts—missed shipment dates, damaged goods, and, mostly, price discrepancies. Haluska estimates that it costs his company about $300 to straighten out each gnarly inconsistency. After learning others had the same nasty problem, "That got me thinking," he says.

Good thing. There's bedlam in the $90 billion electrical-parts industry. According to industry executives, upwards of 70% of administrative costs go into correcting order errors. Even highly automated organizations like Haluska's are struggling. In Thomas & Betts's distribution center 35 miles southeast of Memphis, 70,000 different parts—from pipe connectors to light-bulb fittings—are sorted by a mass of conveyor belts and shipped to distributors across the country. It's an efficient operation, but there's one problem: There are scores of distributors like the one Haluska visited that day, lacking the ability to quickly match items they need with the ones T&B ships. So workers instead spend time reshipping wrong orders or chasing down lost ones. The industry has "not had the good sense to back up and understand how to use technology to store and track all of our parts," explains Clyde R. Moore, Thomas & Betts CEO.

All that is about to change. Thomas & Betts and some 225 other companies are shaking their antiquated ways and working furiously to enter the Internet era. In September, the industry launched IDxchange, a cutting-edge private network linked to a massive database that catalogs parts and carries orders between manufacturers and distributors

in a snap. While the new system isn't designed to enable such market-transforming innovations as real-time auctions or comparison shopping, doing business via IDxchange is expected to cut labor and telecommunications costs by some 50% a year. "We're an industry that is certainly a bit Neanderthal," says Malcolm O'Hagan, president of the National Electrical Manufacturers Assn. "But we're taking a quantum leap from the back of the pack to the front of the pack."

The custom network puts the industry light years ahead of its traditional way of doing business. For eons, electrical parts makers and distributors have zapped important sales data to one another using a system called electronic data interchange or EDI. Information on an invoice or sales order was coded based on arcane EDI definitions, then converted to bits and transported through a maze of electronic networks. While each part or category was standardized, the actual way of conveying the categories was not. One company might identify the shipment date with dashes and another with slashes.

That led to a raft of manual errors—nearly 20% of orders had typos or other goof-ups that required at least a phone call to clear up. For example, when a worker at Crum Electric Supply Co. in Casper, Wyo., typed in the wrong part number, the distributor mistakenly ordered a $100,000 motor instead of a set of $2,200 light fixtures. Crum had to ship the motor back and was charged a 25% restocking fee. "It just killed us," says owner David Crum.

Haluska was feeling the same pain. The CIO cringed at EDI costs that hit more than $10,000 a month. Those were the charges for sending data to a kind of electronic post office that forwarded it to designated distributors and vice versa. Many others in the industry had similar, if not higher, costs. "Small players couldn't even play," Haluska says. Add to that this stinger: There was nothing real-time about the old EDI system. Electronic orders didn't automatically pop up in a virtual inbox like they do today. Instead, the EDI system required companies to dial up and fetch data out of their mailbox. That meant most transac-

tions were sent or received at the end of the day, making same-day shipments a rarity.

Haluska dreamed of a network that would bypass the expensive proprietary EDI system and simply speed data along a network using open Internet standards. With cheaper Net

(Cont.)

gear, costs could be slashed significantly. Indeed, using the new network, T&B now pays a fixed connection and usage fee of up to $2,900 a month.

Haluska's brainstorming paralleled the visions of Crum, the owner of Crum Electric. Crum had been watching enviously as retailers such as Wal-Mart Stores Inc. automated their check-out and distribution processes, while electrical wholesalers were stuck in the "dead tree" world of paper. Crum, along with Haluska, pushed members of the National Association of Electrical Distributors to meet with representatives of the National Electrical Manufacturers Assn. The goal was to synchronize the manufacturers' data with the distributors' so that errors in price and product identification would be wiped out. "We recognized the lack of technology in our business relationships," Crum says.

In March, 1998, the industry's top executives met in Arlington, Va., and pledged about $5 million to construct IDxchange. They commissioned Triad Systems Corp. in Livermore, Calif., to build a database that would store information on hundreds of thousands of parts. With IDxchange, companies like Crum's will be hooked into the database and a point-and-click ordering system, eliminating the time-consuming task of typing in parts numbers. Today, for example, a light bulb has a single part number that identifies it consistently, not by whatever method each company prefers. "Until we talk apples to apples, electronic commerce can't take off," Haluska says.

Now it can. MCIWorldcom Inc. has built the network component of IDxchange. Companies connect using Internet access gear, ranging from sluggish 54Kb modems to speedy T1 lines. The member companies pay a flat monthly fee, from $800 to $2,900, depending on the size of the company and the speed of its connection.

The new system has persuaded some companies to abandon paper forever. Moeller Electric Corp., for example, had been sending invoices and packing slips via snail mail. George Leonard, the company's manager of information systems and logistics, avoided moving documents electronically because the EDI system was too expensive. Now he figures the $840 a month he'll spend on IDxchange will beat paying someone to print an invoice, stuff the envelope, and lug bags of mail to the post office. "There's got to be money saved in that," Leonard says.

With their own private Internet, electrical manufacturers and distributors suddenly have the capability to operate at Net speed. The new network bypasses the clunky EDI network and allows companies to complete transactions in minutes. Connected via IDxchange, a distributor can now send an order at 9 a.m. and have it received by 9:03 a.m. Then, the order can be packed, shipped, and delivered the same day. "That was an impossibility before," says Jeff Kernan, vice-president for information and technology at Lithonia Lighting in Conyers, Ga.

To add even more convenience, several distributors are building Web sites that let them give customers–contractors or utilities–a much higher level of service. In the past, if a plumbing contractor came to a distributor's office to ask about a pipe fitting, the distributor either logged on to a pipemaker's Web site and browsed for a part or, if that took too long, he would pick up the phone. "When you call, the person on the other end is in the bathroom," Crum huffs. IDxchange will eliminate all that. At the touch of a key, the computer will confirm a part's availability.

NOT FAR ENOUGH? Despite the advantages, IDxchange still has its skeptics. Small shops, especially, have fretted over having to adjust to new equipment and ways of doing business. Joseph G. Schneider, president of Madison Electric Co. in Warren, Mich., supports the industry effort, but he's not convinced that it will save his company money. Madison spends about $4,000 a month for phone and data lines that link his branch offices. Schneider worries that expense might not be eliminated, even if he shells out some $2,900 a month for IDxchange. So he's cautious about signing up for the service. "I don't think you go running through the door," he says. "You peek around the corner."

Or do you? For all its merits, there are some who say that IDxchange doesn't go far enough. For starters, it's not set up for buyers and sellers to haggle fast and furiously. That bartering is still going on, but it remains the province of the phone call. Too bad, say Net futurists. John J. Sviokla, a digital strategist at Diamond Technology Partners Inc. in Chicago, says if the IDxchange remains a kind of megacatalog and ordering system, "that's a big thing, but not anything like an electronic market."

For now, the leaders of IDxchange are content to e-engineer their old-line industry this far. After all, IDxchange does catapult them well beyond paper and postage stamps–and past the frustrations of yesterday's poky old technologies.

By Roger O. Crockett

52

Trick or Treat

Hershey's Biggest Dud Has Turned Out to Be Its New Technology

At the Worst Possible Time, It Can't Fill Its Orders, Even as Inventory Grows

Kisses in the Air for Kmart

BY EMILY NELSON
AND EVAN RAMSTAD
Staff Reporters of THE WALL STREET JOURNAL

Just a few days before the biggest candy binge of the year, the Great North Foods warehouse in Alpena, Mich., displayed empty shelves where there should have been Hershey's bars. Reese's Peanut Butter Cups were missing, too. So were Rolos.

The trouble: An order for 20,000 pounds of candy that the regional distributor had placed with Hershey Foods Corp. in mid-September hadn't arrived. Great North earlier this week had to stiff 100 of the 700 stores it supplies on candy orders it couldn't fill. Only yesterday did a Hershey shipment show up at Great North – the first in five weeks – and the distributor still didn't know if Hershey had sent enough to meet its needs.

"No one seems to believe it's Hershey that's having the problem," says Bruce Steinke, Great North's candy buyer.

Spot Shortages

For the nation's largest candy maker, with revenue of $4.44 billion last year, this could turn out to be a very scary Halloween. New technology that came on line in July has gummed up its ordering-and-distribution system, leaving many stores nationwide reporting spot shortages of Kisses, Kit Kats, Twizzlers and other stalwarts of the trick-or-treating season.

In mid-July, Hershey flipped the switch on a $112 million computer system that was supposed to automate and modernize everything from taking candy orders to putting pallets on trucks. Two months later, the company announced that something was wrong. Now, an additional six weeks later – and with Halloween looming – it's still working out the kinks and says it hopes to have everything running smoothly by early December. Some

customers and industry analysts, however, think that based on what they've seen, the problems could persist through Christmas – and maybe even Valentine's Day and Easter.

Already, rivals are benefiting without making much effort. Mars Inc., based in McLean, Va., says sales are up. Nestle USA, the U.S. unit of Swiss food giant Nestle SA, says it, too, has received an unusual spurt of late requests for Halloween treats. "Orders don't typically come in this late," says Patricia Bowles, spokeswoman for the company's candy division in Glendale, Calif. Both companies say they haven't offered any special promotions to boost sales.

The Mars Option

Randall King, candy buyer for Lowes Foods, a chain of 81 supermarkets based in Winston-Salem, N.C., says the delivery delays prompted him to tell stores last month to stop reordering regular Hershey candies. His suggestion: Go with Mars brands.

Hershey says it lost about one-tenth of a percentage point of its still-dominant market share in the four weeks ended Sept. 12. But retailers predict a greater drop for October. And shelf space may be hard to win back, since a typical candy eater is loyal more to type of candy – chocolate, say, or lollipops – than to a particular brand.

"If you don't have my toothpaste, I'm walking out" of the store, says Ron Coppel, vice president of business development at Eby-Brown Co., a Naperville, Ill., candy distributor. "But for a chocolate bar, I'll pick another one." Customers are "not likely to walk out of the store because there wasn't a Hershey's bar. They'll pick another candy bar."

Hershey has taken steps to stay in touch with its largest customers and keep them flush with sweets. Kmart Corp. says it has received 98% of its Halloween orders placed with the company – some of that sent by air freight, rather than the typical and much less costly trucks. Wal-Mart Stores Inc., the nation's largest retailer, won't disclose the impact of Hershey's problems on its own inventories, but says it is talking daily with the confectioner. It also has ordered more than usual from Nestle and Mars for backup.

Information, Please

And John Moser, candy-category manager for Dallas-based 7-Eleven Inc., says a Hershey sales representative is calling him weekly, instead of monthly as usual, to ask what 7-Eleven has received because, among other things, Hershey itself can't tell what the chain has received.

Mr. Moser says that this summer, after 7-Eleven started receiving incomplete lots of everyday items like Hershey's bars, he advised stores to expand their displays of other candies. "If we ran out of Kit Kat or another Hershey item, we might expand facings of Snickers," he says. "We typically used the next-best-selling item."

Hershey officials declined requests to be interviewed for this article. But some details

of the computer glitches have come out as Hershey has spoken in recent weeks with customers and analysts. The company told analysts in a conference call earlier this week that relations with customers are "strained."

Perhaps most galling for Hershey is that it has plenty of candy on hand to fill all its orders. It just can't move some of the candy from warehouse to customer.

Hershey embarked on its computer project in 1996, partly to satisfy retailers who are demanding increasingly that suppliers fine-tune deliveries so that they can keep inventories – and thus costs – down. The company also faced year-2000 problems with its old computer system.

The project called for 5,000 personal computers, as well as network hubs and servers and several different vendors. Under the new system, software from Siebel Systems Inc., San Mateo, Calif., Manugistics Group Inc., Rockville, Md., and SAP AG, Walldorf, Germany, is used by Hershey's 1,200-person sales force and other departments for handling every step in the process, from original placement of an order to final delivery. It also runs the company's fundamental accounting and touches nearly every operation; tracking raw ingredients; scheduling production; measuring the effectiveness of promotional campaigns; setting prices; and even deciding how products ought to be stacked inside trucks. International Business Machines Corp. was hired to pull it all together.

Big-Bang Approach

Despite the complexity of the system, Hershey decided to go on line with a huge piece of it all at once – a so-called big bang that computer experts say is rare and dangerous. Initially, the confectioner planned to start up in April, a slow period. But development and testing weren't complete, and the date was pushed to July, when Halloween orders begin to come in. Retailers say, and Hershey confirms, that the problem is in getting customer orders into the system and transmitting the details of those orders to warehouses for fulfillment.

But no one is taking responsibility. Kevin McKay, chief executive officer and president of SAP's U.S. unit, says the system itself isn't at fault. "If it was a system issue, I'd point directly to a system issue," he says. Mr. McKay says he is in touch with Hershey executives almost daily, and he points out that the companies successfully installed a SAP system in Hershey's Canadian operation last year, though that operation is a tiny fraction of the size of the U.S. operation. IBM spokesman Brian Doyle says the company continues to help Hershey address "its business challenges," adding that "the business process transformation under way at Hershey is an enormously complex undertaking."

Siebel executives say that Hershey officials told them the problem wasn't with their software. "It may have turned out with the big bang kind of installation, they were maxed out there," says Paul Wahl, Siebel's president.

(Cont.)

Candy as Core

The bitter irony for Hershey is that the computer system was part of a broader overhaul intended to sharpen the company's focus on its core mass-market candy business. In early 1996, Hershey sold its Planters nut and Life Savers operations in Canada and its Beech-Nut cough-drop business, as well as stakes in a German praline maker and an Italian candy and grocery firm. In January this year, it sold its pasta business to New World Pasta LLC for $450 million.

In the meantime, it picked up Leaf North America, the maker of Good & Plenty, Heath, Jolly Rancher, Milk Duds, Payday and Whoppers, for about $450 million. While Hershey eliminated about half of Leaf's products, the purchase still boosted its number of specific product offerings by 30%.

Hershey also has been adding variations – king-size, bite-size and such – to its existing products, and has introduced ReeseSticks and reduced-fat Sweet Escapes. It also has created different wrappings and packages for different holidays. Altogether, Hershey estimates it makes 3,300 different candy products.

The proliferation of candies seemed to be working. Hershey sales in recent years have grown faster than the overall industry's, though total candy sales have slowed this year. Hershey was counting on 4% to 6% sales growth this year, but for the first nine months, they fell 2% from a year earlier to $2.84 billion, excluding the pasta business. The computer problems alone clipped sales by about $100 million during the period, the company told analysts.

Hershey had built up eight days of inventory as a cushion against any temporary troubles with the new computer system, but that wasn't enough. By early August, the company was 15 days behind in meeting orders.

In early September, the company told customers to order Halloween candy by Sept. 27. Orders for delivery in October were delayed. And customers placing new orders were told the turn-around time was at least 12 days, more than twice as long as usual. Hershey executives said earlier this week that the 12-day lead time is still in force and that it still can't fill complete orders.

Some retailers and food distributors say Hershey sent them a letter in July saying shipments might be delayed because of computer problems. McLane Co., a food distributor to convenience stores, said it began receiving incomplete shipments in August. "It wasn't any particular item. It was across the board," says Martha Kahler, director of trade relations at the Temple, Texas, unit of Wal-Mart.

Candy companies record about 40% of their annual sales between October and December. Halloween is the single biggest candy-consuming holiday, accounting for about $1.8 billion in sales, followed by Christmas, with $1.45 billion, according to the National Confectioners Association and the Chocolate Manufacturers Association, both based in McLean, Va.

Hershey told analysts that it is looking at a number of fixes, but all of them will have to be tested before they can be used. Meanwhile, the company's stock price has been hammered. In New York Stock Exchange composite trading yesterday, the stock closed at $50.25 a share, up a bit from its 52-week low of $47.50, but well below its price of around $74 a year ago.

Fortuitous Easter

Hershey executives have said they are hopeful sales will rebound in the fourth quarter. The company will get a small break from the 2000 holiday schedule: Easter is later than usual, which means chocolate eggs and the like will be shipped in January and February rather than in December. Indeed, Lowes Foods last Friday placed a Valentine's Day order.

Still, analysts think the company will have to offer retailers special promotions or discounts to win them back. Customers are likely to demand billing changes or shipment changes or other perks because "when retailers smell weakness in a manufacturer, they go for blood," says Andrew Lazar, an analyst with Lehman Brothers in New York.

Mr. Steinke of Great North in Michigan is a little more sanguine than that. He says he received a visit last Friday from his Hershey sales representative and his regional manager. "They understand the problem," he says. They told him they hope the situation improves toward the end of November, "but they wouldn't guarantee anything."

Don Clark contributed to this article.

53

How a Tighter Supply Chain Extends the Enterprise

As companies go to the Internet to cut costs, the boundary is blurring between supplier and customer. ■ *by Philip Siekman*

Many of the brightest ideas for new pieces of computer hardware emanate from companies like Adaptec, a Silicon Valley outfit that turns over most of its production to people on the opposite side of the Pacific. But in a business that can change course in a week, 105 days used to elapse between an order for computer boards from Adaptec's headquarters in Milpitas, Calif., and shipment from its Singapore assembly plant. Then Dolores Marciel, the company's vice president of materials management, saw the light. Treating her suppliers like partners and, not incidentally, installing new computer software and using the Internet, she slashed the cycle to 55 days. Not only did customers get faster delivery, but in addition Adaptec cut its work-in-process inventory, or WIP, in half.

Adaptec is part of a growing vanguard of companies benefiting financially and in other ways from closer ties in their supply chains. Unifi, the leading U.S. maker of synthetic yarn, shares production-scheduling and quality-control information daily with Du Pont, a principal supplier of raw materials. Boeing's Rocketdyne unit uses supplier expertise to help reduce the time and money it spends building engines for space vehicles. And Mercury Marine, the big boat-engine producer, is starting to use the Internet to tighten connections with boat builders and engine dealers as a way to fend off Honda, Yamaha, and Volvo.

In companies that have made such moves, executives speak with the zeal of religious converts. Rocketdyne has cut WIP by $2 million in the past year alone, says general manager Byron Wood. Bigger shrinkage lies ahead, he asserts, along with a reduction in cycle time by a whole order of magnitude. When Adaptec established close computer links with its supply chain, its chip supplier, Taiwan Semiconductor Manufacturing Corp. (TSMC), was so impressed that it created a similar setup of its own. As a result, says Monty Botkin, TSMC's director of customer support in the U.S., he can now "service more customers with fewer people."

Software sellers and consultants say you ain't seen nothing yet. One enthusiast is Dave Cope, vice president of Extricity Software, a private company in Redwood Shores, Calif., that supplied the software being used by Adaptec and TSMC. Get him started, and he paces the room, describing the promised land with the passion of a tent-meeting evangelist. As Cope and others envision it, the future belongs to giant complexes of "virtual companies," tightly integrated from raw-materials suppliers all the way to the consumer, with information flowing front to back and back to front at the blink of a video monitor. More than linear supply chains, these leviathans will be assemblies of companies, tight schools of individual fish with a few always joining and others departing, while the mass moves synchronously in perfect, immediate response to customer demand.

The terminology and details vary with the speaker. Some talk of the "extended enterprise," while others expound on the "borderless corporation." But the gospel is much the same: Integrate the supply chain into some sort of virtual keiretsu and, promises consultant Ann Gracklin, a vice president of Avicon in Natick, Mass., you'll get "lightning-speed responsiveness while cutting a layer of inventory."

More and more corporations are buying in. Extricity's sales, on the way to tripling this fiscal year, are doing the Silicon Valley quickstep. Consulting companies are gathering clients on both sides of the Atlantic. Andrew Berger, a partner in Andersen Consulting's London office, says, "Six months ago it was like talking to fish about land." But no more. Berger says the reason for the interest is simple: "Value is leaking out of the supply chain." That's blood in the water for chief financial officers. Reengineering and continuous quality improvement have already picked up the big gains on the factory floor. The remaining economies must come from cutting the cost of moving, handling, and storing whatever comes in the back door or goes out the front.

At the same time, nearly everybody's encountering the computerized, Internet-connected buyer who, says Douglas Aldrich, a

Dallas-based managing director of the A.T. Kearney consulting firm, "decides who gets to play, why they get to play, and, frankly, what price he or she is willing to pay for something." Aldrich has bad news for laggards who delay wringing out supply-chain costs. Lots of businesses, he says, are going to have to deal with "price points that are no place near the sum of costs plus a margin that most people have been used to living on."

Many companies are joining the parade for another reason: A querulous CEO wants to know what happened to the return he was promised on ERP, the enterprise resource planning computer system that took so much money to buy and so many months to install. "A lot of people thought ERP was going to enable them to have a tighter supply chain," says Robert Derocher, a senior manager at Deloitte Consulting. "A lot of them are realizing it doesn't."

ERP programs weren't designed to manage and report usefully on the hodgepodge of machinery and processes in the plant. But that's necessary if suppliers are to anticipate customers' needs and those customers, in turn, are to plan on orders arriving just in time. Dave Cone, CEO of Camstar Systems in Campbell, Calif., which sells a software program he claims does these jobs, says eight out of ten potential customers in recent months had ERP systems that they had put in about four years ago only to find that "the stuff didn't work in the factory." A year ago Camstar's customer base was mid-sized electronics companies plus the occasional early adopter like yarnmaker Unifi. Today it includes big-league players like Dell Computer and Corning.

Improving supply-chain management builds on trends that are transforming much of American manufacturing: outsourcing noncore activities, reducing the number of suppliers, and building only after orders come in rather than for inventory. But supply-chain integration still can't happen without seamless exchanges of order, marketing, and production information. That's well beyond the capabilities of electronic data interchange

(EDI), the inflexible system widely used for years to place and confirm orders but dismissed by Silicon Valley snobs as "glorified fax." Enter the Internet, the Web, e-commerce, and the almost inevitably quoted Forrester Research forecast that the annual value of business-to-business transactions over the Internet will reach $1.3 trillion by 2003.

The Internet brings hazards, of course. By making it easier for buyers to get bids from anywhere, e-commerce could mean that many are called but few are chosen. Deloitte's Derocher foresees that "where specs are tight and turnaround is critical, companies will have strong, deep relationships with partners." Other suppliers will see their products commoditized as nonstrategic items go out for Internet auction among qualified bidders. The low bid today wins this chunk of business. The lowest tomorrow wins the next.

The new environment is already on the way at Solectron, a big Milpitas, Calif., electronics contractor. Kevin Burns, vice president of global material services, says that by the end of 2000 about half of his purchases will be made under vendor-managed inventory programs that require close cooperation between supplier and Solectron. For other purchases, it's meet the takedown, that is, the quarterly price-reduction target, or, says Burns, "I'm going to explore other alternatives."

Generally, though, the streamlined supply chain is more aspiration than reality. Sandor Boyson, co-director of the Supply Chain Management Center at the University of Maryland's business school, says, "Lots of companies haven't even begun to get a handle on the supply chain, let alone fashion extended-enterprise concepts." Boyson and his associates found only a fourth of 117 companies in an e-commerce association that claimed extended trading relationships with partners.

And claims can be just that. Says Joe Bellini, president of C-Bridge Internet Solutions, a consulting firm in Cambridge, Mass.: "If you look at most supply chains, even ones that are touting that they are a fully integrated, collaborative environment, in just about every one you can find a point where they're still following the old methods: 'We'll just prebuild what we think the market's going to buy, and then we'll adjust as we get the actual demand coming in.'"

Two major roadblocks are precedent and people. Bellini explains, "The technology is there to tightly couple these supply chains on a daily basis and collaborate, but the management processes, the way contracts are written for supply and demand between the nodes in the supply chain, just aren't able to support it." Moreover, other consultants say, as information filters through any chain, each participant is sorely tempted to adjust or manipulate it for his own reasons or because of prior experience.

Even among Silicon Valley's early adopters, the flow of information from point of sale to basic suppliers like chipmakers is not what it

> **The streamlined supply chain is more aspiration than reality at most companies.**

could be. TSMC's Botkin complains: "I'm at the bottom of the food chain. We're buying millions of dollars of equipment based on information that has been filtered down to me. I'm looking back up the supply chain, and really all I have is what I've read in the newspaper and some comments here and there from customers. It's not part of the culture in electronics to share that kind of information."

For many, sharing isn't what they've been taught. Says Christopher Gopal, an Ernest & Young global director: "They still look at procurement as a semi-adversarial deal where you propose your hardball bids, come up with somebody who has the lowest price, and then try to get that price down." These tough negotiators are now being asked to cooperate and trust. "To work effectively," says Deloitte's Derocher, "you've got to believe that if you make the pie greater, everybody benefits." Accepting that will take time. Adaptec's Marciel has it right: "Although people say they like change, they only like it when it doesn't include them."

Poster children for the cause are big-box retailers like Wal-Mart, which has long required suppliers to manage their portion of its inventory, and a few Silicon Valley players like Cisco Systems, which has a vested interest in expanding Internet use. Any morning after 4 A.M., 7,000 Wal-Mart suppliers can go into Wal-Mart's database and find out which store sold how much of their products for a two-year period ended the previous midnight. In its last fiscal year, Cisco ran up revenues of more than $12 billion with only 500,000 square feet of its own manufacturing space.

Customers now call up Cisco's Website to configure, price, and order $1 billion of its networking equipment a month. Cisco then sends orders back out across the Internet to board producers and assemblers including Celestica, Flextronics, Jabil, and Solectron. Products are built and tested to Cisco standards, sometimes with procedures run remotely by Cisco. Most are drop-shipped to buyers, untouched by human hands on Cisco's payroll.

Wal-Mart and Cisco are so dominant that supply chains follow their dictates instead of functioning as completely cooperative efforts. But lots of collaborative efforts are under way elsewhere to tighten the relationship between buyers and sellers. Chevron, for example, is getting its predominantly independent gas stations to work together. Says C-Bridge's Bellini, who is helping with the project: "Chevron now has the ability to go back to the Cokes and the Pepsis and the cigarette makers, and negotiate for 8,000 locations." The aim is not to hammer down prices, says Bellini, but to raise the question, "Is there a way where everybody wins–suppliers, Chevron, and the retailers?"

Companies working at integrating frequently start by looking in the direction along the supply chain–upstream or downstream— where initial gains are easiest to get. They're in a hurry because they are under stress from new competition or new technology. What follow are the recent experiences of two companies, all stressed, and all reacting by forging closer relationships with suppliers or customers, generally with the help of the Internet.

(This article continues)

UNIFI: Tightening Starts at Home

Little known outside its industry or its home state of North Carolina, where it has its headquarters in Greensboro and plants in eight small towns, Unifi dominates a highly specialized niche in the textile industry. In the year ended last June 28, it generated revenues of $1.4 billion–and a handsome 19.5% return on equity–by "texturizing" partially oriented yarn, a stiff, first-stage polyester or nylon with the look and feel of small-diameter fishing line. Known by its acronym, POY is processed at blurred speeds using heat and tension to condition it so it can be woven. Some is sold that way; more goes through additional steps that alter the yarn's look, feel, and strength, and such characteristics as stretch. The clothes you are wearing or the upholstery on the chair you're sitting in may well have originated in a Unifi plant. The company has more than 70% of its market.

Unifi buys POY from suppliers such as Du Pont and Nanya, an Indonesian company with a plant in South Carolina. But it also makes some in Letterkenny, Ireland, and in a year-old facility in Yadkinville, near Winston-Salem, N.C., which now supplies about a fourth of what Unifi uses in the U.S. The Irish plant starts with petrochemicals. Yadkinville buys solid chips, again from suppliers such as Du Pont and Nanya. Those are melted and extruded in spiderweb-thin filaments that are hardened in air and then spun and entangled together, dozens at a time, to form a single strand of POY.

Yadkinville is close to science fiction's "lights out" factory, where everything is run by computers and there's nobody on the production floor. POY filaments stream down two stories from the melting and extrusion stations at 120 mph or faster. On the ground floor, about a football field in size, 312 winders each feed POY onto six spool-like "packages" that weigh 40 to 45 pounds. When the winder finishes six, the completed packages are automatically rotated out of the way, and six more are started. If the finished packages are not removed from the machine in eight minutes, the new ones will fill up enough to collide with them, jamming the winder and spilling the near-unstoppable flow of POY onto the floor.

Before that can happen, an automated-guided vehicle, or AGV, rolls quietly down the aisle and retrieves the completed material. With caution lights blinking, it shuttles the material to a transfer rack that in turn carries the packages off to an adjoining factory for texturing. Some 12,000 packages make the trip every 24 hours. The only human on the winding floor of the POY plant full-time is a quality-control inspector. It's a lonely job. The lights stay on, but except for the occasional visitor or maintenance person, there is nothing out there except whirring machines and eight AGVs ghosting about.

Unifi's major competitors are Indian and Indonesian companies, including supplier Nanya, that are, in some cases, integrated from oil well to textile plant. When Asia caught the economic flu, these companies aggressively cut prices for yarn, fabrics, and apparel sold in the U.S. Automation and process control systems like those at Yadkinville have helped Unifi survive in this tough climate. The company has also been evangelizing up and down its supply chain, urging everybody to cooperate as though they were vertically integrated.

Several years ago Unifi recognized that a prime requirement for supply-chain integration is to get your own house in order. Says Michael Smith, a vice president of Unifi Technologies, its information technology group: "It all depends on what happens on the shop floor." In what is now a companywide program, Unifi has not only automated processes and machines but has also linked them. Manufacturing information can be gathered continuously, consolidated, interpreted, and "exported" to the ERP system for use in managing the business. Since every batch of chips, every package of POY, and every spool of yarn is tracked and recorded, poor quality in some textured yarn was recently traced all the way back to one of the 1,872 spinnerets used to form POY in Yadkinville.

On a daily basis starting last year, Unifi has been exchanging production and quality information over the Internet with supplier Du Pont (but not with Nanya, which is a rival as well as a supplier). Says Ralph Mayes, president of Unifi Technologies: "We are able to see the inventory Du Pont has. They are able to see our inventory and our demand, so we can both optimize production." In plants where Unifi makes yarn to order, it also sends out work-in-process information daily to customers.

So far, none of these information exchanges is done computer to computer, with suppliers and customers able to peer into Unifi's database. But, says Mayes, "we see ourselves doing more and more of this and moving to Internet access, allowing partners to come in instead of pushing data out." While Mayes' group is working on that, it will also be advising other companies. Convinced that it now knows how to create and install what it calls "integrated manufacturing systems," Unifi is spinning off part of Unifi Technologies as a manufacturing-systems consultant.

(Cont.)

MERCURY MARINE: Focusing on the Demand Side

Mercury's private network is being moved to the Internet to give dealers better access.

The parent, Brunswick Corp., makes a lot of recreational and outdoor equipment: boats, bowling alleys, bikes, and its original product, pool tables. But Mercury Marine boat engines power the company. Last year the Mercury group rang up $1.4 billion in sales, 38% of Brunswick's $3.9 billion, and brought in two-thirds of the company's $340 million in operating income. Mercury makes outboard engines in Fond du Lac, Wis., which serves as group headquarters. It builds inboard, ski, and stern-drive engines, probably accounting for about a third of the group's sales, in Stillwater, Okla.

With sales estimated at 200,000 engines a year, Mercury has about 40% of the U.S. outboard market. Outboard Marine's Johnson and Evinrude brands straggle behind; more worrisome competition comes from Japan's Yamaha and Honda. Honda got a big assist when the U.S. Environmental Protection Agency ruled that emissions by new outboards must be reduced annually between 1997 and 2006, for a 78% overall decrease. The standard two-stroke outboard burning a gasoline-oil mixture won't make it under the limbo bar. But Honda has long made only clean-burning four-stroke outboard engines that meet the EPA target.

Mercury has since caught up, bringing out its own four-stroke engines and a direct-injection two-stroke that is fuel-efficient as well as low in emissions. However, the effort is hurting margins. Both designs are costlier to build, yet competition holds down the price. In the past, Honda's four-stroke had to meet the two-stroke price; now Mercury has to meet the Honda price. That is complicating the supply chain downstream. Some buyers aren't ready to give up old-style two-stroke engines, which put out a lot of power per pound. So Mercury's outboard catalog has expanded to include all three engine types, not to mention horsepower ratings from 2.5 to 250, and special versions for "blue water" and "coastal" use. Counting all variations, Fond du Lac turns out about 400 different outboards.

Until the early 1990s, outboard engines were sold mainly to dealers who mated them to boats. However, the market is changing. There's some consolidation of dealers, bringing professional management to a business that needs it. And about half the engines sold now go to boat builders that provide dealers with a boat-outboard package. Both trends make the business more predictable and manageable. Yet this, too, puts pressure on margins, since boat builders and dealer groups expect and get volume discounts.

The competitive picture is different in the stern-drive and inboard market. Mercury's share is somewhere north of 70%, enough to have made it the target of antitrust and restraint-of-trade suits from dealers and its only important competitor, Volvo. Although Mercury doesn't say, probably nearly half of the Stillwater plant's output is shipped to the two biggest pleasure- and fishing-boat builders, sister divisions of Brunswick, whose brands include Sea Ray, Bayliner, and Boston Whaler. The rest of the production goes to several hundred other boat builders. Market dominance here is not all it's cracked up to be. Business is flat. Politically, Mercury can't increase market share. Nor can it push up prices, since that makes all boats, including Brunswick's, more expensive and encourages potential buyers to do something else with their extra cash.

Anybody who thinks manufacturing has fled the U.S. ought to walk through the Fond du Lac plant. Mercury's outboard production is vertically integrated from the scrap can lids used to make aluminum alloy on down the line to the finished product. Stillwater isn't much different. The plant buys engine blocks from General Motors but modifies them for use on water and adds fuel, electric, and other components. Unswayed by gurus who encourage companies to put a narrow definition on core competency and outsource to the max, Jim Hubbard, Mercury's chief of staff, claims, "We have to have a strategy to compete long-term on cost and quality. So we want to do as much as we can that makes economic sense."

This still leaves room for tightening supplier relations. Among other items, Mercury buys the covers for its outboards, called cowls, and both its plants buy hydraulic components. Fond du Lac recently made a deal with the supplier of the hydraulic device that assists boaters in tilting outboards out of the water. To cut handling and transportation costs, the supplier is going to start consigning truckload lots to the factory rather than shipping in smaller quantities, and will get paid as they're used. The savings will be shared. Mercury says it is going to extend the consignment idea to other suppliers.

Mercury's biggest effort to date has been on the demand side, where the company is trying to make it easier for customers to do business with the company. MercNet, a private electronic network system for parts ordering, has been around since the mid-1980s. Now, says Geof Storm, Mercury's chief information officer, the group "is trying to use technology as a competitive weapon."

MercNet is being moved to the Internet so that dealers can access it with nothing more than a PC and a browser. Along with ordering parts, they can enter an engine type and get all the service bulletins for that model, or search the database for a way to fix a particular problem. Now being planned: electronically sharing forecast information and collaborating on promotions with big dealers.

One thing outboard dealers and boat builders can't do over the Net is buy engines. The reason is not technology, but resistance from Mercury's sales department. Says Gary Tomczsk, an executive charged with introducing supply-chain changes: "They want a more personal touch on that." What he means is that the sales force fears that electronic ordering will eliminate up-selling and cross-selling, that is, the ability of a salesperson to talk a customer placing an order into buying a more expensive engine or adding something else to the order, such as one of the company's inflatable boats. As Storm notes, "There are a lot of culture changes involved when tightening the supply chain."

Such barriers, however, are being overcome at Mercury's inboard operation. Tomczsk has a green light to install a system enabling Stillwater's boat-building customers to buy engines over the Internet. He hopes to prove to the outboard salespeople that "up-sale and cross-sale is not as big a problem as they expect it will be."

54

XTREME RETAILING:

Stores fight the online onslaught

Sixteen-year-old Mike Carlson of Fontana, Calif., was ready when Vans Inc., a Los Angeles-based sporting goods retailer, opened a 60,000-square-foot, $4 million skate park and off-road bicycle track at the Ontario Mills Mall near L.A. last month. Within the first two weeks, Carlson had logged a half-dozen visits, shelling out $14 each time for two hours of sheer skating bliss. "All malls should have this," says the demographically desirable teen. "They kick us out of everyplace else to skate—they might as well make it legal."

Mike may very well get his wish. The regional shopping mall, venerable symbol of suburban prosperity for the past 40 years, is in the midst of a reinvention. And in the new shopping paradigm, fun counts.

As the Christmas shopping season enters peak frenzy, online retailing is grabbing headlines. With an explosion of new Web sites, almost anything for sale in a shopping mall can be bought by computer—in many cases, faster and cheaper than in a store. That makes e-tailers a potent threat to bricks-and-mortar stores, even though online will account for less than 1% of total sales this year. But retailers are fighting back. How? With the one weapon in their arsenal their virtual counterparts simply can't match: reality. "You can't sit on Santa's lap on the Internet," notes John Konarski III, senior vice-president of the International Council of Shopping Centers, a New York City-based trade group. "Nor does Amazon.com have coffee and chairs."

But bricks-and-mortar retailers aren't stopping with a coffee bar and the occasional in-store promotion. In the new world of

> The idea: Turn bricks-and-mortar shopping into an event to keep customers flocking

Xtreme Retailing, stores are combining the speed, convenience, and immediacy of e-commerce technology with the thrills of an amusement park. How? Essentially, by taking their core product or image and turning it into an experience. Thus, Vans becomes a skate park and not just a place to buy sneakers, while Bass Pro Shops becomes a fishing pond

and archery range and not just a sporting-goods store.

EMBRACE THE FOE. Assuming it's enjoyable enough, a unique experience can be packaged and sold just like books and undershirts—or at least that's what the Xtreme retailers are banking on. B. Joseph Pine II, co-author with James H. Gilmore of *The Experience Economy,* says saleable experiences come in four varieties: entertainment, education, esthetic, and escapist. "Experience means to spend time and, increasingly, to spend money to spend time. If retailers just provide a completely mundane experience, people won't come," says Pine.

Increasingly, retailers also are beginning to embrace the enemy, making the Internet a part of their bricks-and-mortar operations. Borders Books & Music will soon offer in-store kiosks allowing shoppers access to its immense online inventory. Mall developer Simon Property Group Inc., based in Indianapolis, is testing an electronic "zapstick" as a tool to help time-squeezed shoppers find merchandise more efficiently. In the new world of retailing, stores and malls are trying to sell themselves as places to spend leisure and recreation time instead of just shopping time. Those that can't offer either a great experience or great service could well find themselves squeezed out.

Even the dot.com retailers are taking notice. eBay Inc. just signed a deal to stage live auctions in selected malls, while Gateway Inc. is building real-world stores to give its brand some three-dimensional reality. Jeffrey P. Bezos, chief executive of Amazon.com and a passionate believer in online retailing, concedes that traditional stores have a few advantages. "The physical world is still the best medium ever invented," he says. "What's going to happen is that stores are going to get more entertaining. The quality of the sales associates is going to go up. Stores are going to get cleaner. Every dimension you can imagine of making a physical store better is going to happen."

The real question, though, is whether those enhancements will induce shoppers to spend more money. Some of the earliest forays into entertainment-based selling, such as NikeTown and Planet Hollywood, have faded. Many blame the static nature of the experiences they offered. After all, once you've seen the memorabilia, what's left to

do? It's too early to tell how the newer efforts will fare, but proponents say they offer a richer, more intense, and more varied experience that will help them endure.

Indeed, at one of the earliest shopping-mall-as-theme-park creations, The Forum Shops in Las Vegas, where Atlantis rises and falls on the hour and Roman gods cavort in animatronic splendor, shoppers can't seem to get enough. The Forum has passed its seventh birthday and still is racking up a spectacular $1,200 per square foot in annual sales, compared with a national average of about $300.

In fact, the trend toward experience-based retailing—or "shoppertainment," to use a word trademarked by super-regional mall developer Mills Corp.—has been building for some time. The Internet is the latest threat, but the rise of strip malls, superstores, and giant discounters such as Wal-Mart Stores

Inc. already had made change imperative for many traditional retailers. A recent study by Deloitte & Touche reports that not only will 80% of consumers shop at discount department stores this holiday season but that they plan to spend the most money there.

All of which has led to a fundamental re-thinking of exactly what it means to "go shopping"—and what a mall should be. "The long-term players in our business should be in the 'out-of-home-entertainment' business," says Mark J. Rivers, executive vice-president and chief strategic officer at Mills, a developer noted for large, flashy malls, such as Ontario Mills. "We see ourselves more as a Disney-type venture than a mall. Vans Skatepark is to Ontario Mills what Space Mountain is to Disneyland," he says.

It is an apt comparison. In the Disneyesque lingo of the New Retail, shoppers have become "guests," shopping has become an "experience," and malls have become "entertainment centers" with "communities." Everything has become more friendly, fun, and frenetic. "We want it to be loud. We want to take it over the top. We want to get off the couch," says Rivers.

Instead of hewing to the time-honored formula of building a mall around a big department store anchor, developers have started searching for fresher, more offbeat stores that offer better opportunities for adding entertainment. "We see ourselves as retail bounty hunters," says Laurence C. Siegel, chairman and CEO of Mills. "There are no Macy's at our centers. We want to create destination retail." Siegel seeks out billboard tenants such as Bass Pro Shops Inc. and Gibson Musical Instruments' Guitar Showcase, which will open at Opryland Mills next summer. Customers there will be invited to watch their guitars being built.

Mixing entertainment and retail is hardly a new idea. The cineplex has been a mall staple for at least the past decade, and fads such as pool halls have come and gone. Then, in 1992, the same year it opened The Forum, Simon Property Group opened Mall of America, a giant three-ring circus of a megamall in Bloomington, Minn. Faced with the daunting task of filling 400 retail spaces during an economic downturn, Simon sought out offbeat retailers, many of whom would have been too small or new to have qualified for space under normal circumstances. Bolstered by such entertainment anchors as Camp Snoopy, an indoor amusement park, and Underwater World, an aquarium with walk-through tunnels, the mix proved to be a hit. The mall attracts 43 million visitors each year, and sales per square foot average $540.

THE KIDDIE CARD. So why didn't other malls and retailers copy this formula sooner? Perhaps because there was no real pressure to until now, when consumers have so many choices. Mall developers today are eager to sign leases for stores such as the Wizards of

SHOPPING IN STORES HAS SOME DRAWBACKS . . .	. . . SO RETAILERS ARE INNOVATING
➤ Driving to the mall is a pain, especially during the peak holiday season.	➤ Give 'em more than Santa. Entertainment includes electronics, games, how-to demos.
➤ If you buy it, you generally have to haul it home.	➤ More stores are delivering, or even driving you home.
➤ Want to compare products and prices at different stores? Better start walking.	➤ Scan store items you like into a Web site, then make your choices from your home PC.
➤ Limited inventory means you may not find what you're looking for.	➤ In-store terminals give you online choices beyond what the manager can stock.

the Coast. Wizards, owned by Hasbro Inc., is known for fantasy games, collectible game cards, and now Pokemon products. About a third of the space of a typical 3,000-square-foot Wizards store is devoted to a game room, complete with tables for card trading and tournaments, and a bank of networked computers where kids can play video games with one another. Although card trading is free, computer time runs $7 an hour.

For many parents, that's a bargain. Karen Robinson feels safe leaving her 10-year-old son Vaughn to play while she does a little shopping in Woodfield Mall in suburban Chicago. "He's supervised. And he's on his best behavior," she says. Thus the store gains Vaughn as a customer and the mall gains his mother.

When Robinson comes back to pick up her son, she could have a hard time leaving empty handed. The game room is strategically located at the back of the store so kids and their wallet-toting parents must first pass through a packed retail area. Wizards Senior Retail Marketing Director Karin Kriznik reports that sales at the company's 16 stores are running in the neighborhood of $1,000 per square foot. Some 50 more stores are planned for 2000. "A year and a half ago when we began opening the stores, people thought, 'What's this about?' Now we're the wave of the future," laughs Kriznik.

To make that experienced-based formula work, the experience has to reflect the brand. The Sam Ash music store in Ontario Mills offers shoppers their own in-store performance space and the instruments to use in it. The St. Louis-based Build-A-Bear Workshop chain lets "guests" spend hours creating and customizing stuffed animals. American Girl Place, the new Chicago flagship store of the

doll cataloger owned by Mattel Inc., offers its signature line of historically inspired dolls and related merchandise as well as a themed musical revue and cafe. This is shopping as an event.

It also is brilliant branding. As the Internet intensifies competition, building a strong brand identity has become more critical than ever for retailers, e-tailers, and even for malls. And brand-based entertainment isn't just for kids. Bass Pro Shops, a chain of outdoor-sports equipment stores based in Springfield, Mo., offers its grownup clientele giant aquariums, waterfalls, trout ponds, archery and rifle ranges, putting greens, and classes in everything from ice fishing to conservation—all free. "You won't see everything, even if you're here for two hours. And we change constantly," says Jeff Baars, general manager of the Bass Pro store in Gurnee Mills, outside Chicago.

Bass Pro was one of the first retailers to mix over-the-top displays and events with retail when it opened nearly 19 years ago, which speaks to the strength of the concept. However, until Mills "discovered" Bass Pro in the mid-1990s, it had opened only two stores. Since then, it has opened another seven, mostly in Mills malls, with three more planned for next year. The stores have attracted a loyal following: At the Gurnee store, customers routinely deliver trophy fish they've caught to a staff aquaculturist to add to the store's 27,000-gallon tank. The closely held company does not release sales figures, but it proudly notes that its Springfield store ranks among Missouri's top tourist attractions.

Meanwhile, San Francisco's Metreon, located next door to the Museum of Modern Art, is also shaping up as a tourist favorite. Opened last June after five years in development, it

55

Racing for Slice of a $350 Billion Pie, Online Auto-Sales Sites Retool

Strategies of Web Merchants And Conventional Dealers Are Beginning to Converge

BY FARA WARNER
Staff Reporter of THE WALL STREET JOURNAL

With a shakeout looming in the overcrowded online auto-buying industry, some of the biggest players are re-creating themselves so they don't end up as road kill.

Online car sellers have taken two approaches to selling on the Internet. Some sites let consumers buy a car directly from their computer. Other, "lead generator" sites pass on customer inquiries to dealers and offer Internet training to sales staff.

Now these business models are starting to converge – just one example of how e-commerce and bricks-and-mortar retailing are increasingly melding. Today, Autobytel.com Inc., one of the biggest of the lead generators, is expected to announce that the company will offer a "click and buy" option so consumers can purchase a car immediately at a fixed price. That's a dramatic shift from Autobytel's old model, which left it up to dealers to respond with an e-mail price quote and then haggle on the showroom floor.

"We've clearly been influenced by what goes on in the market," says Autobytel Chief Executive Mark Lorimer.

Autobytel's move is a response to direct-selling rivals such as CarsDirect.com and CarOrder.com, owned by Texas-based Trilogy Inc., and new entrant Greenlight.com, in which Amazon.com Inc. acquired a 5% stake on Friday. Direct sellers have won over a significant number of consumers by offering near-instantaneous price quotes online and allowing consumers the option of bypassing dealer sales personnel.

Meanwhile, Microsoft Corp.'s CarPoint will have a direct-sales option available on its site this year, says Lindsay Sparks, chief

Online car sellers now seem less likely to run bricks-and-mortar dealers off the road

executive of the unit that got its start as a research tool and referral service. "We've recognized for a long time that direct was a natural evolution," he says. "But we don't believe the current models work, but that a hybrid that includes the dealers is where it's headed."

Fighting back, CarsDirect is teaming up with Cars.com, a lead-generator site owned by Classified Ventures Inc., a business launched by several newspaper companies. Under a six-month deal to test the idea, CarsDirect will offer its direct-sales service to Cars.com visitors who don't want to use a dealer.

CarsDirect, which is a start-up of idealab! and funded in part by Dell Computer Corp. founder Michael Dell's venture-capital operation, is also expected to announce today that it has signed a deal with the Internet portal Earthlink. That deal will have CarsDirect featured as Earthlink's auto-buying site of choice.

All this action is heating up the biggest battle under way on the Web. With U.S. auto sales totaling $350 billion last year, a company that can grab a fraction of that market could be a colossus.

For now, the fraction is small. Despite the dot-coms' claim that they would rapidly revolutionize the business of car dealers, only 2.7% of new vehicles were actually sold via the Net in 1999, according to J.D. Power & Associates.

And all of those sales ultimately went through a traditional dealer no matter how fancy a facade the e-dealers tried to throw up. Even a company like CarsDirect, which delivers cars to a customer's driveway, buys that car at a dealer.

While online car sales are expected to almost double to 5% of total sales this year, J.D. Power estimates, there are big hurdles ahead. Lobbying by car dealers has led key states like Texas to tighten franchise laws to further restrict efforts to sell cars without involving traditional dealers. CarsDirect, CarOrder and Autobytel's new direct model aren't allowed to sell cars in Texas.

"There is a lot of buzz about direct," says Sam Hedgepeth, president and chief operating officer of lead generator Autoweb.com Inc. Autoweb has a direct-sales pilot operating to figure out what approach works. The big question, Mr. Hedgepeth says, is "how much do you hide the dealer."

That's a prickly question to answer, especially since lead generators originally based their businesses on dealers' ignorance of the Internet. Early on, many dealers were loath to do any more than take e-mail from consumers and put their salespeople through

---

---

some Internet-sales training. But some large dealer groups are now fighting back with their own versions of online direct sales.

Greenlight.com, one of the newest auto-buying sites, was created by Asbury Automotive, a big, closely held auto group in Pennsylvania, and Kleiner Perkins Caufield & Byers, the powerful Silicon Valley venture-capital firm.

In a test called Project Everest – the name reflects the scale of trying to change a business with 22,000 retail showrooms – Greenlight decided against the referral model in favor of direct sales.

Greenlight will get its cars through Asbury's dealers and other dealers with which it's signing exclusive deals. The San Mateo, Calif.-based online car company also expects to get a big jump on the competition from its association with Amazon. Greenlight is paying Amazon $82.5 million over five years to promote it, and Amazon has warrants to increase its stock holding to as much as 30% over five years.

Todd Collins, the company's chief executive, says the owners decided Greenlight had to be different from broker sites, such as CarsDirect. A broker risks losses if it can't find a dealer to sell a car for less than the price at which it sold the vehicle online. Greenlight is nailing down prices first with dealers so "we know whether we're making money or not," Mr. Collins says.

Autobytel's new direct-sales plan illustrates both the promise and the complexity of

(Cont.)

weaving together e-commerce and traditional car dealers. Autobytel won't buy cars from dealers and resell them to consumers.

Instead, 200 dealers Autobytel already works with will list vehicles from their car lots on the Web site along with a nonnegotiable price. Autobytel says it plans to add a majority of the thousands of dealers it already works with to the "click and buy" model over the next year, but will continue to offer referrals as well.

After deciding on what model car they want, potential buyers will be able to see several choices of that model and compare prices. When consumers hit the "click and buy" button, the transaction will be handled by an Autobytel salesperson, not a dealer.

Autobytel has become a licensed car dealer in California through a wholly owned subsidiary. That will allow the company to handle all the back-end details of purchasing a car for customers in much of the country. Autobytel won't take care of warranties or servicing. For that, consumers can get a referral to a dealer near them.

Autobytel will charge dealers a fee of between $150 and $300, depending on the price of the car, to list cars on its service. Mr. Lorimer, the CEO, says the company estimates dealers can cut their costs by $800 to $1,000 by not having to pay personnel and by moving inventory off their lots more quickly.

56

EN GARDE, WAL-MART

Retail rival Carrefour bulks up

All right, so it's not quite as good as winning the World Cup. But the French, dispirited after months of fruitless haggling to create Europe's largest bank, have bounced back by creating Europe's No. 1 retailer with the merger of homegrown chains Carrefour and Promodes Group. Carrefour's $16.5 billion acquisition of Promodes, announced on Aug. 30, does far more than give France a national champion, though: The merger creates a much tougher playing field for Wal-Mart Stores Inc. in its drive to expand internationally.

With 8,800 stores in 26 countries and combined revenues of $65 billion, Carrefour is set to challenge Wal-Mart around the globe. As Europe's new top dog, Carrefour can use its buying clout to extract deeper discounts from suppliers, undercutting rivals and accelerating a push toward consolidation in the industry. The Promodes deal also widens Carrefour's impressive lead in several Latin American and Asian countries. What's more, Promodes brings to the union a reputation for solid inventory and distribution systems, an area where Carrefour has long lagged behind Wal-Mart. "We're creating a worldwide retail leader," says Carrefour Chief Executive Daniel Bernard, who will head the merged company.

CRITICAL MASS. In Europe, the deal puts pressure on Wal-Mart to make another acquisition. The retailer already has holdings in Britain and Germany. But if it doesn't grab

> Buying Promodès gives Carrefour the muscle to vie with Wal-Mart globally

another partner soon, it could be left without the critical mass to become a major European player. Its biggest European holding, Britain's Asda Group PLC, is only one-fifth the size of the bulked-up Carrefour. Likewise, Wal-Mart needs to counter Carrefour's expansion in emerging markets. Only hours after unveiling the Promodes deal, Carrefour announced the acquisition of three Brazilian chains, boosting its market share there above 20%, vs. 1.4% for Wal-Mart.

Certainly, Carrefour isn't about to dethrone Wal-Mart. Now the global No. 2, Carrefour is still far behind Wal-Mart in sales and market capitalization (table). Even if Wal-Mart has trouble growing in Europe, it has room to expand in the U.S., especially in the grocery business. Carrefour, by contrast, has fewer opportunities in its saturated home market. And despite Carrefour's headstart in Asia and Latin America, Wal-Mart has plenty of openings because mass-scale retailing in many countries is only starting to develop. "The scope for growth all over the region is tremendous," says Hans Vriens, a Hong Kong-based vice-president for the U.S. consulting firm APCO Asia.

But Carrefour is a nimble competitor. Since 1963, when it opened the world's first hypermarket, selling groceries, clothing, and other merchandise under one roof, it has been a marketing pioneer. Today, a Carrefour shopper who stops in to buy groceries or a pair of tennis shoes can also get a watch repaired, order mobile-telephone service, rent a car, or book plane tickets and hotel rooms for a vacation. Wal-Mart offers few such services.

Carrefour also has been an innovator in store design, softening the look of its warehouse-size buildings by installing wood floors and nonfluorescent lights in some departments and putting service counters in the food department, where shoppers can get meat, cheese, and bread sliced to order. "Carrefour has incredible depth and breadth of range," says Philippe Kaas, a partner in Paris of OC&C Strategy Consultants. Such services also boost margins: Carrefour's 1998 profits, up 13.6% from the year before, were $755.2 million on sales of $32 billion.

Equally striking has been Carrefour's successful push into foreign markets. It began expanding across Western Europe and into Latin America during the 1970s, opening its first store in Brazil in 1975. During the past decade, it has moved into Asia and Eastern Europe. Merged with Promodes, Carrefour is the No. 1 retailer in Brazil, Argentina, and Taiwan, as well as in France, Spain, Portugal, Greece, and Belgium. True, Carrefour has had setbacks. It made a disastrous foray into

TWO GIANTS FACE OFF

CARREFOUR	WAL-MART
SALES $65 billion*	**SALES** $160.2 billion*
MARKET CAP $47 billion	**MARKET CAP** $200 billion
STRENGTHS Innovative marketer, aggressive, experienced in foreign markets	**STRENGTHS** Dominates U.S. market with superefficient supply and distribution network
WEAKNESSES Lacks strong logistical and information systems, crucial to improving efficiency	**WEAKNESSES** Spotty record on foreign expansion
LIKELY NEXT MOVE Cut costs in Europe while pushing Asian and Latin American expansion	**LIKELY NEXT MOVE** Seek more acquisitions to extend its reach in Europe

*Forecast for 1999   DATA: BUSINESS WEEK

(Cont.)

the U.S. market in the early 1980s, when it opened a handful of stores in the Philadelphia area and soon closed them because of weak sales. Emerging markets are risky business, too. Carrefour reported a net loss of $10.4 million in Asia last year. Latin America's economic woes could hit Carrefour's bottom line this year.

A key challenge for Carrefour is logistics. Wal-Mart has clobbered its U.S. competitors by creating tight links with suppliers and fine-tuning its distribution system, squeezing out costs and allowing it to keep prices low. To compete, Carrefour will have to tighten control over its operations, which have been decentralized, says Ajay Hemnani, international retail analyst at Management Ventures Inc. in Cambridge, Mass.

But Carrefour has already proved its mettle in head-to-head combat with Wal-Mart. "They're just relentless–the toughest competitor I've ever seen anywhere," says a retail executive who watched Carrefour ward off Wal-Mart in Brazil and Argentina in the mid-1990s. To counter Wal-Mart, Carrefour slashed prices, remodeled, and even relocat-ed stores. When a planned Wal-Mart store opening in one Argentine city was delayed by construction problems for four months, Carrefour seized the opportunity to renovate its closest store.

Wal-Mart, by contrast, has taken a cautious approach to foreign expansion, moving into Mexico in 1991 and then Canada before pushing into South America and Europe. It's the No. 1 retailer in Mexico, but foreign sales last year accounted for only 9% of Wal-Mart revenues, vs. 44% for Carrefour.

SHOPPING LIST. Carrefour, saying it sees greater growth potential elsewhere, has stayed out of Britain and Germany, the two European countries Wal-Mart has recently entered. Wal-Mart likewise has stayed away from Carrefour's strongholds in France and southern Europe. But that could soon change as European retailers brace for a shakeout. Governments in France, Germany, and other countries have moved to protect small merchants by placing a near-moratorium on large new stores. So the only way to grow is to acquire stores and squeeze more profits out of them.

Analysts expect Wal-Mart will look for an acquisition in France. That would not only give Wal-Mart a piece of Europe's No. 2 retail market after Germany but would also become a link in a Europewide distribution network. That's key if Wal-Mart is to compete with players such as Carrefour, whose networks are already well-established.

Wal-Mart, however, is a careful buyer and is unlikely to rush into a French acquisition. No matter. Other big European chains, including the Netherlands' Ahold, have said they are eyeing French retailers. "If Wal-Mart wants to get in, it really has to act quickly," says analyst David Shriver of Credit Suisse First Boston. Whether in Paris, Sao Paulo, or Seoul, these two global heavyweights will be duking it out for some time to come.

By Carol Matlack, with Inka Resch, in Paris and Wendy Zellner in Dallas, with bureau reports

U.S. Superstores Find Japanese Are a Hard Sell

By Yumiko Ono

Staff Reporter of The Wall Street Journal

TOKYO – When **Office Depot** Inc. and **OfficeMax** Inc. entered the Japanese market two years ago, Japan's 20,000 small stationery stores shuddered. The $13 billion stationery industry was archaic, and the stores usually charged full price. The two U.S. companies had grand plans to open hundreds of office superstores, behemoths of a type Japan had never seen, filled with cut-price pens, notebooks and fax machines.

But the U.S. stores proved to be too big and too American for Japanese consumers. Meanwhile, a nimble local competitor came out of nowhere to trounce the U.S. retailers at their own game. Stumbling, the Americans are changing course, testing store formats entirely different from their U.S. formulas.

The office superstores are among a big crowd of American retailers that have run into trouble here. During Japan's great recession of the 1990s, U.S. companies stormed in, aiming to make a killing by revolutionizing a tradition-bound retail industry. They sparked profound changes with their new products, offering better value and wider selections. But only a few, including **Toys "R" Us** Inc. and **Gap** Inc., truly succeeded. Many others are scrambling to revise their strategies, and some are even giving up.

JC Penney Co. is closing its five home-furnishing stores, in part because so many products, from curtains to bedsheets, had to be made differently for Japan. **Spiegel** Inc.'s Eddie Bauer unit, after much prodding from Japanese staffers, is straying from its strategy of selling the same products it sells in the U.S. It recently designed straight-leg pants and stretchy shirts to better fit the Japanese shape. And **Sports Authority** Inc. recently reduced its stake in a Japanese joint venture to 8.4% from 51%. Its Japanese partner, **Jusco** Co., is now opening smaller stores.

"Retailing is such a local business, it's not that easy to succeed," says Kyoichi Ikeo, a professor of marketing at Keio University's business school. However well a retailer fares in the U.S., he says, "you can't just take the same formula and expect it to work in Japan."

The travails of Office Depot and Office Max show why. Like many foreign merchants, the two office-supply giants linked up with local partners that knew the lay of the land, a strategy that permitted quick expansion but limited operational control. Office Depot, the No. 1 office-supply retailer in the U.S. in terms of revenue, negotiated a 50-50 joint venture with **Deodeo** Corp., a Hiroshima electronics chain. OfficeMax, the No. 3 U.S. office retailer, formed a joint venture with the supermarket chain Jusco. Jusco was developing suburban malls and planned to put OfficeMax stores in them. Encouraged, OfficeMax announced plans to open up to 200 stores by 2002.

But the Americans soon hit a wall. Japanese office products are so different from those in the U.S. – just for starters, loose-leaf binders here have two rings instead of three – that they had to buy most products from traditional local suppliers. Because they were selling the same products as their Japanese rivals, they also had to compete extra hard on price. But they didn't always get the best sourcing deals, with some suppliers even insisting on going through costly middlemen for fear of annoying neighborhood stores.

The stores also turned out to be simply too American. Office Depot opened two U.S.-size stores in Tokyo and Hiroshima. They were more than 20,000 square feet each, and featured wide aisles and signs in English. But with rents in Japan more than twice those in the U.S. and personnel costs sky-high, the stores were too expensive to run.

Japanese consumers were baffled by the English-language signs and put off by the warehouselike atmosphere. Tellingly, when Office Depot later reduced the size of one Tokyo store by a third and crammed the merchandise closer together, sales remained the same, the company says.

An even bigger challenge was brewing at **Plus Corp.,** Japan's No. 2 stationery maker. Striving to lift its sagging sales, Plus created a small division in 1993 called Askul to sell discounted stationery by catalog. Askul targeted exactly the same customers as its U.S. rivals: small business owners that weren't getting the discounts that big companies buying in bulk received. Askul's wide selection and catchy name – it means "it will come tomorrow" in Japanese – hooked young clerks who liked the ease of ordering from their desks.

When the U.S. retailers opened shop in late 1997, Askul slashed its prices and boosted selection. Askul also beat the Americans at pleasing core customers. Aware that most small companies put young "office ladies" in charge of ordering stationery, it ran loyalty programs aimed at them: If a company placed orders totaling 100,000 yen (about $920), it won a teddy-bear clock. A 200,000-yen purchase brought a box of chocolates.

The result: Sales continued to soar, despite the new competition and a long recession. In the year ending May 20, Askul expects sales to grow at least 77% from a year earlier to 40 billion yen ($367 million). Twenty percent of those sales are likely to come from an Internet business it started two years ago, an arena Office Depot and OfficeMax haven't yet entered. "We don't think there are a lot of reasons why we should lose" to the Americans, says Hiroyuki Komatsu, vice president of marketing and customer service at Askul.

Last year, as the challenges mounted, Office Depot reversed strategy. It severed ties with its partner, Deodeo, and closed its large store and delivery center in Hiroshima, Deodeo's hometown. That let it act more nimbly and focus more on Tokyo, where it opened four ministores that are about 5,000 square feet, or a fifth the size of its U.S. stores.

Office Depot says that this year it plans to add another four to 10 small stores to the six stores it already has. Its new Depot stores still have American radio programs blaring in the background. But the signs are in Japanese, and the shelves, lining narrow aisles, don't stock as many files or as much copy paper. To compete with Askul, the company is beefing up its two catalogs. Office Depot declines to disclose its sales in Japan but says its losses here last year probably exceeded $30 million.

Meanwhile, OfficeMax, with six large stores in the Tokyo suburbs, says it too is switching to the small-store format in Tokyo. It opened its first "business express store" in Tokyo in November. A spokesman won't provide details of future plans but hints that OfficeMax is mulling further changes in strategy.

Bruce Nelson, president of Office Depot's international business, says his company plans to decide later this year whether its small-store format is working.

The Japanese market "has enormous risk and it has the potential of enormous payout," he says. "It will just be one of the best places where we do business – or it will be one of the worst."

Home Depot Strikes at Sears In Tool Duel

By James R. Hagerty

Staff Reporter of The Wall Street Journal

ATLANTA – Does the world need a $30 hammer that comes in right-hand and left-hand models?

Home Depot Inc. hopes so. Inside the store chain's headquarters here, Mike Tracy holds up the Ridgid RoboHammer, introduced last month. "This," says the Home Depot senior vice president, "is man's oldest tool, reinvented."

At a construction site on the other side of Atlanta, Tony Wiley, a veteran builder, picks up the RoboHammer and squints at its gaudy orange-and-gray grip. "It looks weird," he says.

RoboHammer is designed to fit snugly in the user's preferred hand, absorb shocks and improve chances of hitting the nail on the head. It also is designed to help Home Depot lure tool buyers away from other retailers, notably **Sears, Roebuck** & Co.

In many respects, Home Depot has already left Sears in the sawdust. Home Depot is the world's biggest retailer of home-improvement supplies and recently replaced Sears as a constituent of the Dow Jones Industrial Average. Home Depot's stock market value of $147 billion is about 11 times that of Sears.

But Sears still has the nation's best-known line of hand tools, Craftsman, which are produced for it by a variety of manufacturers. Sears won't disclose annual sales of Craftsman tools but says the 73-year-old brand is far better known than Home Depot's Husky or Ridgid lines, a claim Home Depot executives don't dispute. Nearly nine out of 10 adult men in the U.S. own Craftsman tools, Sears says.

Craftsman is particularly strong in mechanics' tools, such as wrenches and sockets. Even Pat Farrah, Home Depot's merchandising chief, concedes that it will be difficult to beat Sears in that category.

But in other types of tools, he says, "Sears is being routed." For instance, Home Depot says it is the biggest seller of portable power tools, including drills. And Mr. Farrah says Home Depot is making headway against Sears in stationary bench tools, like routers and band saws.

A Sears spokesman declines to comment on how his company is faring against Home Depot. But he notes that Sears is experimenting with a new selling format for its tool departments. Last year, stores in Hartford, Conn., and Virginia Beach, Va., introduced the new format, dubbed Tool Territory, which lets browsers play with the power drills and other tools. The test stores also offer a broader range

of tool brands than other Sears stores do. Sears says it hasn't yet decided whether to put the format into more stores.

Both Home Depot and Sears are trying to reach toolheads by sponsoring auto racing. Sears has been a sponsor for decades and bills its Craftsman line as "the official tool" of Nascar racing. In 1999, Home Depot began sponsoring Tony Stewart, one of the hottest young stars in Nascar racing.

A Home Depot poster depicts Mr. Stewart's scowling pit crew surrounding his car with Husky mechanics tools in their hands. "You can't own their car," the ad says. "You can own their

From left :
The **Ridgid RoboHammer** *from Emerson Tool;*
The **Striker** *from Spencer Products;*
The **AntiVibe** *from Stanley Works.*

tools." **Stanley Works,** of New Britain, Conn., and other suppliers make the Husky mechanics tools exclusively for Home Depot's 900 stores.

One manufacturer eager to cooperate with Home Depot is **Emerson Electric** Co.'s Emerson Tool unit, a longtime supplier to Sears. Emerson makes the RoboGrip pliers, a huge hit for Sears since their exclusive introduction there in 1993. Home Depot wanted a similar tool. So Emerson came up with a

larger version, called RoboGrip II, which Home Depot introduced exclusively in August. Emerson also makes an exclusive line of Ridgid tabletop power tools for Home Depot, using a plant in Paris, Tenn., that used to make Craftsman bench tools for Sears.

About 18 months ago, Emerson Tool's president, Dave Pringle, approached Home Depot with his latest idea: the RoboHammer. Mr. Pringle, who describes himself as a "tinkerer," says he dreamed up the shock-

IF I HAD A HAMMER . . .

A sampling of hammers designed to reduce shock to the arm.

NAME/COMPANY	APPROX. PRICE
Ridgid RoboHammer Emerson Tool	**$30**
Steel Eagle Vaughan & Bushnell	**$18 to $32**
Striker Spencer Products	**$28 to $30**
AntiVibe Stanley Works	**$25**
Hi-Viz Pro Cooper Industries	**$20 to $28**

Source: The companies

absorbing technology for the RoboHammer one night while lying in bed.

The technology involves slicing a jagged groove, about the width of six hairs, into the head of the hammer. This redirects energy toward the nail and minimizes recoil, Emerson says. The difference between the right-hand and left-hand models is in the handles, Mr. Pringle says, so that users can hold the tool more comfortably and hit the target with greater frequency and force. "We think this is going to be the hottest tool in the market," he says.

A $30 hammer could be a tough sell. After all, people who want to hang a few pictures on the wall can easily make do with hammers costing as little as $4. Those who do lots of nailing typically use nail guns, which start at about $129.

Joe Thomas, who manages a crew that builds house frames in Atlanta, swears by his nail gun. But he always carries a hammer as a backup. Standing inside a newly framed house on a sunny winter afternoon, he takes one look at the RoboHammer and says, "It's too little – way too little."

The RoboHammer has an 18-ounce head. Mr. Thomas draws his 22-ounce Estwing hammer from a leather tool belt. "I've had good luck with them," he says of the hammers, made by **Estwing Manufacturing** Co. of Rockford, Ill. "I've had this one for two years."

Still, he agrees to try the RoboHammer, gripping it in a fist the size of a grapefruit. With four expertly aimed whacks, he sinks a 16-penny nail into a slab of Southern pine. The RoboHammer feels good in his hand and reduces the shock to his arm, he says, "so that's good." But he doesn't care for the downward curve of the hammer's claw; the claw on his Estwing juts straight back, and he finds that more useful for extracting nails or pulling apart boards. Home Depot says it eventually may offer a larger RoboHammer designed for framing houses.

Winning over people like Mr. Thomas will be vital for the RoboHammer's success: Serious amateurs love to own what the pros use.

But the RoboHammer isn't the only hammer competing for the pros' affections. Stanley Works promotes its AntiVibe hammers, introduced in 1998, as the ideal way to absorb shocks. **Spencer Products** Co., Seattle, says its new Striker hammer, with a curved fiberglass handle, virtually eliminates vibration. Spencer's president, Ernst V. Omri, rules out the idea of mimicking the RoboHammer's right-handed and left-handed models. "We don't do gimmicky things," he says.

59

Cold Comfort

Breakthrough Product Visits Funeral Homes: Partial-Casket Displays

Mr. Doody's Idea Jazzes Up The Industry, Emulating Wal-Mart and Starbucks

'First Innovation in 75 Years'

BY DAN MORSE

Staff Reporter of THE WALL STREET JOURNAL

Most people hate buying caskets, and Billy Higgs was about to find out why.

His wife, Donna, had just died of cancer at age 45. They had grown up a few houses apart and had married when they were barely adults. Now, in the summer of 1994, he found himself driving to a funeral home in Batesville, Miss. A mortician talked Mr. Higgs through options, before leading him into a showroom where he was surrounded by 14 coffins.

Mr. Higgs eased up to each one, checking prices. By the time he got to the last of them he had forgotten how much the previous ones cost. Worse, though, was his recurring thought: The next time I see one of these, it will be Donna's. He pointed to a blue metal casket at $1,150 and hurried out of the room.

Three months ago, Mr. Higgs again headed over to Wells Funeral Chapel after his father died. This time, he was taken into an entirely new kind of showroom. Gone were the intimidating rows of coffins. Instead, he saw pieces of caskets – corners, really. Prices were clearly marked, cheap to one side, expensive to the other. Kind of like cabinet samples at a hardware store, he thought. He chose a $2,245 model.

What Mr. Higgs didn't know was this: For the past 10 years, a small team of retailing experts has quietly entered the arcane world of funeral service. They stumbled upon the partial-casket concept in England, then improved the process through focus groups at mock casket rooms in an old New Orleans cotton warehouse. The result: a merchandizing method that not only makes it easier for consumers to buy caskets, but also raises the average sale by $200 to $400 per coffin.

Tommy Wells, owner of Wells Funeral Home, bought the sectional displays in 1997, one of 571 such installations now built. He has seen his casket sales jump by an average of $800 per coffin. As is the case with any merchandise, he says, when customers understand the display, and are presented with a wider range of options, they tend to spend more. Mourners can avoid the discomfort of full-size boxes. None of the more than 200 customers he has served over the past two years has asked to see complete caskets, says Mr. Wells, who has been in the business for 35 years. "This is the most tremendous, positive thing I've ever seen," he says.

New profitability isn't necessarily logical. While baby boomers are buying caskets for their parents, they also have more options to choose from, with dozens of Web sites selling caskets, many at steep discounts. Cremation is on the rise, too. And many in this group grew up watching television exposes on 500% casket markups.

Into that potential quagmire stepped Alton F. Doody, a retail consultant who helped Wal-Mart redesign its stores and has since hung out his shingle to the death-care industry. Mr. Doody applies his theories for York Group Inc., one of the "Big Three" casket manufacturers that supply funeral homes.

"If the funeral-home owners can't make the transition from doing it their way to the way people want it done, someone else will," says Mr. Doody, a 65-year-old New Orleans native.

His casket strategy is a clever blend of Wal-Mart (neat rows of accessible product) and Starbucks (premium pricing for perceived premium value). The goal: get shoppers to spend money at their comfort level. "People want to be in the middle" of the price range, he says. "They want the Honda Accord LX."

Like business owners everywhere, operators of the nation's 22,000 funeral homes have been searching for ways to increase profit. They have been holding their own against the Web and discount casket retailers, since mourners want one-stop services, so they tend to go where the body is. And consumers still spend a lot on full-service funerals: an average of $5,020 per funeral in 1998, up 5% from $4,780 in 1996, according to the most recent statistics available from the National Funeral Directors Association. Amid that increase, though, the average casket sale rose just 89 cents.

But morticians linked to York are finding that casket dollars are flowing thanks to Mr. Doody's 30-employee team.

The theory is to make the entire experience less of a crisis, in turn getting consumers to choose a more premium box. The quarter-casket system works because it "abstracts" the very object being sold, in part because the caskets remain closed. To examine the lining, shoppers pull out little drawers below the shelves that reveal swatches of material similar to what they would see when buying a sofa.

The new units can show 30, even 40 casket styles, vs. the average of 18 that fit into traditional casket rooms. The displays load up on selections in the $2,000-to-$3,000 range, where customers tend to buy caskets and where they can choose from more midrange units lined up in logical price progressions. So it's easy for customers to identity a feature or material they like in one of these caskets – and then comfort themselves by spending an additional $200 or $400, rather than the $1,000 price jumps they used to face.

The new rooms also offer more price points in the upper end caskets, which makes, say, solid cherry caskets a more inviting alternative to the even higher priced walnut and mahogany models.

At York's New Orleans warehouse on a recent day, Mr. Doody walks into a mock funeral home. He goes to the middle of the casket display, with samples ranging in suggested retail prices from a $795 particleboard veneer casket to a $6,600 solid bronze. It's easier to understand than traditional displays, where "part of the feeling of being hosed is it hasn't been organized for the consumer," Mr. Doody says.

Not surprisingly, York's big competitors contend that the strategy is flawed.

Batesville Casket Co., a Batesville, Ind., unit of Hillenbrand Industries Inc., holds that seeing full-size caskets can be crucial for dealing with a death. Batesville uses some partial caskets, but says York has gone overboard. "I don't think you can abstract death," says a spokesman. To try to turn the process into some kind of "conditioned" trip to Home Depot is to ignore the emotional shock of what's happened, he says. Batesville says what customers really want is customization. So it offers a range of personalized caskets, say, one with American flag accents to celebrate a veteran.

Aurora Casket Co., meanwhile, has linked with Dell Computer Corp. to sell computers and monitors to funeral homes. Funeral directors lead customers through point-and-click presentations to piece together personalized, virtual caskets. "We think this leapfrogs over the other two" systems,

Alton F. Doody

says Aurora's Nancy Koors.

Mr. Doody concedes that he knew nothing about funeral homes until relatively late in his career. At first, he tried to dress up full-size casket rooms, a strategy he now says was fundamentally flawed by the jarring full-size caskets.

In 1995, while working for Service Corp. International, the world-wide chain of funeral homes, Mr. Doody came across a mortician outside of Liverpool, England, who, cramped for space, had split three coffins lengthwise down the middle and hung them against a wall. It was crude but eye-opening. Mr. Doody helped install hundreds of such systems in Europe and brought his ideas back to the U.S.

He pitched the system to Batesville, his former client, but got nowhere. So he turned to York, which was struggling just to remain a distant second to Batesville. "We had to reinvent ourselves," says Fred Turner, York's marketing chief.

To Mr. Turner, who came to York after years of selling Whirlpool and Frigidaire refrigerators to Circuit City and Best Buy, the Doody marketing idea made sense. It was similar to that employed by Best Buy Co., the electronics-appliance retail chain where customers are given free range to look over well-stocked displays – and tended to buy a higher-priced mix of products, Mr. Turner says.

York, which bought Mr. Doody's consulting company, found that the concept was a hard sell to morticians. In many cases, York was trying to win over funeral directors who had literally grown up with caskets, living upstairs in small-town funeral homes. "We, as funeral directors, see the caskets and we all think they're pretty," says Casey Young, a second-generation funeral director in Ferriday, La.

In New Orleans, Mr. Doody started bringing funeral-home owners to the warehouse. One of the first to see it: Kevin Kirby of Bowling Green, Ky., who says he had tried everything to dress up his full-size casket room, from plants to paintings – and decided to buy the system. "I called back home and told my staff," he says, "and they thought I had gotten drunk at Pat O'Brien's," the famed French Quarter bar. Explaining it in person later didn't help. "They looked at me like I was a damned idiot," Mr. Kirby remembers. "I said, 'Just hold on to your britches until you see this.' This is the first new innovation in caskets in 75 years."

York says that its first 50 displays showed an average gain of $438 per retail sale since they were installed in 1997. The next batch of 175 showed a $300-$400 gain. Funeral-home operators still often balk at the initial price of $25,000 to $125,000, depending on room size and features. The York system is restrictive. Funeral directors can't use it to sell other casket brands such as Batesville, which many funeral directors believe are better made. In Strasburg, Pa., Norm Mable, who owns one of the oldest funeral homes in the nation, believes his sales declined. The reason: Under the new system, he can no longer sell Batesville's $2,395 pecan-wood casket, a popular item.

And at York, even sales of 571 partial-casket installations since 1997 haven't been enough to stop the company's share price from skidding to around $4 in recent months from a high of $26.63 in late 1997. The stock was hit hard in 1998, when Batesville took away York's largest account, Service Corp., which operates 3,800 funeral homes on five continents.

But most morticians are happy with the system. They don't have to keep an inventory of large caskets, which are instead delivered to order. In Columbus, Ohio, Mike Schoedinger says he was skeptical of York's claims before purchasing the new unit. "I've learned, in this business," he says, that casket-company salesmen can always get the statistic they are looking for. At an open house to inaugurate a Schoedinger facility, though, guests looked inside the casket room, then drifted in to touch casket pieces while holding drinks. "It was so unthreatening," says Randy Schoedinger, Mike's cousin.

And at the Brunner funeral home just outside Cleveland, owners Jim and Nancy Sanden used partial caskets as part of a total retail overhaul over a year ago. They moved all their merchandise out of a low-slung basement in their funeral home into an adjacent building – away from their memorial chapel and embalming room. Signs lead customers to the Bruner Funeral and Cremation Retail Store.

"Nothing has changed in funeral-home service for 100 years, for crying out loud," Mr. Sanden says. In the new store, customers shop for everything from guest registries to cremation urns, arranged in classic good-better-best, self-service displays. New Age water machines burble in the background, also for sale ($60-$200).

"It's kind of like a shopping mall," says Charles Bulick, sipping a cup of coffee inside the store, where he's come with his wife to shop for the caskets they want to be buried in. "It's not like you're sealing your doom in here."

Promotion

60

THE CORRUPTION OF TV HEALTH NEWS

Viewers who tune into the local news on Channel 11 (WBAL-TV) in Baltimore will see a series of reports on women's health by Donna Hamilton, the station's health news reporter. In these reports, part of a series called "The Woman's Doctor," Hamilton explains why women should get screened for cervical cancer, for example, or how they can identify the warning signs of ovarian cancer.

Careful viewers might notice that the doctors in these news reports are all from Baltimore's Mercy Medical Center. What viewers do not know is that the reports are part of a promotional deal between Mercy and WBAL. Mercy pays WBAL a hefty fee to get its doctors on these reports. And Mercy officials meet with WBAL staffers every few months to discuss story ideas for upcoming reports.

Such deals involving hospital placements in news stories are increasingly common, hospital officials and television executives say. Many hospitals buy advertising time on TV, of course, but these deals are something different: Mercy wouldn't say what it pays, but hospitals can spend hundreds of thousands of dollars per year to get their doctors and their hospitals on the news.

RIVALRY. It's difficult to know exactly how widespread such arrangements are. Hospitals being offered the deals are sometimes reluctant to talk about them for fear of angering local stations and being locked out of coverage. Hospitals compete ferociously for patients, and loss of TV coverage can be devastating. Gary N. Michael, vice-president for

> ### Consumers need unbiased medical information, not paid "news reports"

marketing and business development at Mercy, says he has received numerous calls from other stations seeking advice on setting up such programs themselves. Medstar Television, a production company in Allentown, Pa., that brokers these deals and prepares the news reports, wouldn't say how many clients it has, but it did say its clients include hospitals, health plans, and TV stations in San Diego, Denver, Hawaii, and San Francisco. A hospital promotion group within the Association of American Medical Colleges (AAMC),

concerned about these new kinds of news sponsorships, has scheduled a panel session to discuss the issue at its upcoming meeting in March.

These promotional arrangements, by creeping into news reports, violate a cardinal principle of journalism–that news and advertising should always be kept separate. Advertising should never masquerade as news. And news outlets should not share undisclosed financial involvement with the subjects of stories. That was what got the **Los Angeles Times** in trouble last fall, when it wrote about the Staples Center entertainment complex and shared ad revenues with the center. "You want the public to trust that a news organization is going to approach any story without bias or favoritism," says Barbara Cochran, president of the Radio-Television News Directors Assn. and former Washington bureau chief for CBS News. "If the content is being selected or influenced by someone who is paying for the privilege of doing that, it is no longer impartial news reporting. There would be no reason to believe that it's honest."

ALARMS. For Mercy Medical Center, the WBAL deal is valuable precisely because it gets the hospital into the newscast. "Ads are limited by the amount of time–there's only so much you can say in 30 seconds," says Michael. "We wanted to showcase our docs as real people and get into the nitty-gritty issues, and I think you do that best through a news story." Mercy spends a third of its promotional budget on its WBAL contract. It employs a full-time public-relations specialist to administer the program, and it has hired a local sportscaster to give media training to doctors before they appear on TV.

The program clearly has proved its effectiveness, Michael says. When "The Woman's Doctor" began airing in 1994, Mercy was "a distant seventh...in the metro area when you asked what hospital you would recommend to a friend for women's health," Michael says. "After one year, we were ranked No. 2, and in 1997, we became No. 1."

For WBAL, the arrangement "was a new opportunity to create revenue," says Ronald L. Briggs, an account executive who works with Michael on the program. It also helped the station attract viewers. "In the beginning, it allowed us to promote our news. We were promoting Mercy, Mercy was promoting 'The Woman's Doctor,' and it was promoting viewership," he says. Mercy "has been on the cutting edge of marketing."

Marianne Banister, a WBAL-TV anchor who sometimes introduces the Mercy reports,

says the practice has alarmed reporters. "It has a lot of people in newsrooms going 'Whoa, whoa–what's going on?'" she says. She "was not particularly comfortable with it to begin with," but she feels the station has not crossed the "fine line between advertising, promotion, and news." News Director

> "A PR agency or TV sales department can guarantee that an organization's physicians will appear on commercials . . . but they can't guarantee the physicians will be on the news, the most credible source for health information . . . "
>
> *—FROM A MEDSTAR PROPOSAL THAT PUTS A HOSPITAL'S DOCTORS ON LOCAL TELEVISION NEWS, FOR A FEE.*

Princell Hair does not think the reports compromise the station's standards, because the news staff controls the content. "We decide what story to do, what not to do," he says. "We have complete control over the editorial content. If we didn't, I wouldn't be comfortable with this." What if the relationship with Mercy became known to viewers? "I don't think this would taint our relationship with viewers at all," he says. "It's providing them valuable information."

"RELATIONSHIP." Studies by the Radio-Television News Directors Assn., however, suggest that viewers are concerned about advertisers' influence on news. A poll of 1,007 people in 1998 found that 84% believe advertisers "sometimes or often" improperly influence news content. A similar poll of 300 TV news directors found that only 43% of them agreed.

Not every hospital is eager to pursue such TV deals. L.G. Blanchard, director of Health Sciences News & Community Relations at the University of Washington and the organizer of the medical colleges' meeting on this subject, recently turned down such a proposal. "To the

(Cont.)

uninvolved observer, it would appear that we were being asked to purchase positive news coverage," he says. He says colleagues at other hospitals have told him that prices for such arrangements can range from $25,000 to $200,000 per year. He says, "I can see a day when nobody is going to get news coverage unless they've paid for it. That's a world I don't want to live in."

Medstar Television Inc. has been arranging such relationships between hospitals and TV stations for more than a decade. "We build a relationship between a local television station and an underwriter in a marketplace," says Vice-President Susan Ferrari. "It could be a TV station and a hospital, or a TV station and a health plan." The "underwriter" pays Medstar to produce two 90-second reports each week, which are given free to local stations. The stations' reporters add their voices, making it appear that the reports were produced by the local station. "It's not advertising. It's really content that's prepared for

the newscast," says Ferrari. "The TV station airs the program on its newscast." The reports are preceded or followed by brief advertising spots identifying the sponsor, but the spots do not explain that the sponsor paid for production of the news items.

NO SALE. Medstar would not say how much it charges, but a Medstar proposal obtained by BUSINESS WEEK says the yearly charge for airing two news spots per week for a year is at least $364,000. The figure rises in subsequent years of a multiyear deal. In its proposal, Medstar notes the particular value of featuring doctors on the news: "A PR agency or TV sales department can guarantee that an organization's physicians will appear on TV commercials...But they can't guarantee the physicians will be on the news, the most credible source for health information." Edward C. Dougherty, Medstar's vice-president for broadcasting, defended the company's editorial integrity. "We and the stations maintain total editorial control, from topic selection,

research, script writing, final editing," he says.

That's not quite good enough. "Total editorial control" ought to mean the ability to choose the most qualified doctors and researchers to be part of a story–without being influenced by the hospital sponsoring the report. The sponsorship of TV news stories is a problem with an easy answer: TV stations shouldn't offer to sell the news, and hospitals shouldn't buy it. Medical news affects life-and-death decisions every day. It is essential that viewers and patients believe they are getting direct, unbiased information from local TV stations. If television news is prepared for the benefit of sponsors, rather than for the public, all of its credibility is lost.

By Paul Raeburn
Raeburn is senior editor for science and technology.

61

Read Their Lips

When You Translate 'Got Milk' for Latinos, What Do You Get?

The Answer Was a Surprise For a Marketing Group Courting Hispanic Teens

The Meaning of Biculturalism

By Rick Wartzman

Staff Reporter of The Wall Street Journal

LOS ANGELES – It was late February when Jeff Manning began to focus on a phenomenon he had never had occasion to think about before: slathering peanut butter and jelly on a tortilla.

The executive director of the California Milk Processor Board, Mr. Manning was poring over a report on the Latino community, searching for a way to reverse an industry sales slump in the heavily Hispanic southern portion of the state.

And right there on page 12, the answer seemed to jump out at him: The ranks of Hispanic teenagers, it noted, are projected to swell to 18% of the U.S. teen population over the next decade, up from 12% now. "When you see that kind of number, it's like, 'Wow,'" says Mr. Manning, whose organization is behind the ubiquitous "Got Milk?" advertising campaign.

But appealing to these youngsters, he learned, isn't as simple as cutting an ad in Spanish with tried-and-true Hispanic themes. The kids often live in two worlds: one rich in traditional Latino values such as a strong commitment to family and religion, the other in which they eagerly take part in mainstream teen America. The report described how they bounce between hip-hop and Rock en Espanol; watch "Buffy the Vampire Slayer" with their friends and Spanish telenovelas (nighttime soap operas) with their parents; blend Mexican rice with spaghetti sauce – and spread PB&J on tortillas.

When it comes to "young biculturals," the "conventional model" of straight Spanish-language advertising "is irrelevant," Roxana Lissa, a Beverly Hills public-relations con-

sultant who had prepared the report, told Mr. Manning.

To Mr. Manning, who spent 25 years at major ad agencies before joining the milk board in 1993, Ms. Lissa's advice made perfect sense. Soon, he was talking up the possibility of a "cutting edge" milk ad shot in "Spanglish." He foresaw combining distinctive Latino imagery with sights and sounds that are seductive to teenagers of all backgrounds. "I want to capture both worlds," Mr. Manning declared.

Four months later, a milk spot aimed at Hispanic teens is now ready. It will be aired across California starting next week on the Spanish-language network Telemundo. But the end result is radically different from what Mr. Manning and his team first envisioned –

Jeff Manning

a turn of events that stirred passions and raised a question with broad implications: What is the smartest way to peddle products to one of the fastest-growing demographic groups in the country?

As she sits in her small office one morning in mid-March, ad agency president Anita Santiago is pumped up by the prospect of producing a new style of television commercial.

Since 1994, Ms. Santiago's client roster has included the milk board, for which her firm has generated a series of Spanish-language TV ads tailored to Latino moms. Because "Got Milk?" doesn't translate well into Spanish – it comes out as, "Are You Lactating?" – the moms have their own slogan: "And You, Have You Given Them Enough Milk Today?" With tender scenes centered around cooking flan and other milk-rich Latin classics in the family kitchen (some of the ads were directed by the cinematographer from the film "Like Water for Chocolate"), the campaign has proved popular in its own right.

Yet as Ms. Santiago contemplates the approach that Mr. Manning has in mind, she realizes there is no easy formula to follow. "The word 'bicultural' has been thrown around a lot, but I don't think anybody has really figured it out," says Ms. Santiago, who founded her Santa Monica, Calif., agency 12 years ago.

Not that others haven't recognized the dual worlds of Latino teens. A couple of years ago, for instance, McDonald's Corp. hawked its french fries in ads featuring soccer star Tab Ramos hanging out with basketball's Scottie Pippen. During the 1993 baseball All Star game, a Spanish-language ad for Nike Inc. ran on CBS with English subtitles, a strategy

other major companies have mirrored. And a Levi Strauss & Co. commercial last year fitted a pair of jeans on a hip, young Latina who asserts her independence in Spanish as well as English.

Ms. Santiago imagines pushing the concept even further. "We're going to put ourselves right into that third reality" Latino teens experience, she says.

Meanwhile, up in San Francisco, there is similar excitement at Goodby, Silverstein & Partners, a unit of Omnicom Group Inc. that in 1993 created the "Got Milk?" campaign. Jeff Goodby, the agency's co-chairman, believes that by joining with Ms. Santiago, they can create a bicultural ad that will find a home not only on Spanish television, but on general market television as well. Says Mr. Goodby, whose firm has done work for Nike, Anheuser-Busch Cos., The Wall Street Journal and other big clients: "It's a killer idea."

The next step: Convene some focus groups of Latino teens, and determine which of their buttons to push.

Mana and Korn

At an office building near the Los Angeles airport in late March, Mr. Manning, Ms. Lissa and representatives from the two ad agencies are lined up behind a giant one-way window, noshing on M&M's and observing a group of Hispanic teenage girls relating their likes and dislikes.

"You can speak Spanish or English or any mixture-however you feel comfortable," the focus-group moderator, Horacio Segal, tells the eight 13- to 15-year-old girls seated around him.

As the two-hour session gets under way, the girls move seamlessly between the two languages. They tell of how they tune in to both Spanish- and English-language television, and rock out to the Mexican band Mana and the Anglo group Korn. They characterize themselves as "Latina," while the magazines to which they relate best are Seventeen and Teen People.

They seem, in short, to be the very embodiment of biculturalism that Ms. Lissa had sketched out. But as the girls watch a string of television commercials, something surprising happens – at least in Mr. Manning's view.

Roxana Lissa

The spot they are most enthusiastic about is an ad in English for Kellogg's Corn Pops. It depicts a grunged-out teen being lectured by his parents, when all he wants to do is eat his cereal – a scene that several of the girls say they

(Cont.)

can identify with, though it contains no special message for those straddling two cultures.

At the same time, an ad in Spanish for Mountain Dew with the Chilean technorock band La Ley doesn't resonate much. And the Levi's commercial in which the heroine speaks in Spanish and English doesn't work at all; a few of the girls complain that it's unclear what the ad is even about.

For Mr. Manning, the girls' reactions are eye-opening: They may be bicultural, he thinks, but as consumers of advertising they appear to be completely acculturated. As for language, they don't seem to care – or even notice – whether the message is delivered in Spanish or English or both. They never raise the matter with Mr. Segal.

A little later, the girls' attention turns to "Got Milk?" and, again, Mr. Manning is taken aback. He had always expected that the humorous campaign, which the California milk board licenses nationally, would be well-known and even liked by Latino teens; after all, "Got Milk?" has become part of the American vernacular. But he also anticipated that some in the group would gripe that the ads don't speak at all to their bicultural existence.

Instead, the girls gush over the commercials. They "make you feel like you're thirsty," says Olga, an eighth-grader who came to the U.S. from Mexico 11 years

Anita Santiago

ago. As six different "Got Milk?" ads are played in succession, the room erupts in laughter.

Sue Smith, Goodby Silverstein's planning director, leans over to Mr. Manning and whispers: "They really love this stuff." Mr. Manning, clad in a "Got Milk?" T-shirt, beams.

A subsequent focus group, of boys the same age, is a bit less effusive about the "Got Milk?" campaign. But they still find the ads funny, and likewise don't say a word about language or lack of a bicultural perspective. Two more focus groups the next night, of 16- to 19-yearolds, do raise questions as to why more Hispanics aren't being cast in the ads.

By then, however, it's too late. Mr. Manning has all but decided to turn the notion of biculturalism on its head. His new idea: to take the existing "Got Milk?" spots and air them without any changes on Spanish-language television.

What's the Problem?

"Am I missing something? Tell me if I'm missing something."

A week has passed since the focus groups, and Mr. Manning's voice is booming from a speaker-phone on Ms. Santiago's conference table. She and several associates gather around. Ms. Lissa and Ms. Smith are also patched in.

In order to justify a brand-new campaign for Latino teens, "you've got to start with problems, guys," says Mr. Manning, back in his own office in Berkeley. "Where were the big problems with 'Got Milk?'"

The line falls silent for a moment before Ms. Lissa offers up an answer: The teens "didn't think the ads were speaking to them."

"But they did," Mr. Manning says, cutting her off quickly. "They liked them. They laughed at them."

By now, everybody knows where things are headed. Before the meeting, Ms. Santiago had proclaimed Mr. Manning's plan to introduce "Got Milk?" – in English – on Spanish-language television a "disaster." "I have to find a diplomatic way of telling him," she had said.

Yet there is no way. Mr. Manning can't get past the fact that most of the teens loved the "Got Milk?" ads, and showed no special affinity for the spots that were supposed to reflect their bicultural lives. Ms. Smith agrees, chiming in with a strong British accent that, when it comes to advertising, "these teenagers are just like any other teenagers."

Ms. Santiago looks up at the skull mask and other Mexican folk art hanging on the wall and rolls her eyes.

"Got Milk?" is "a very Anglo campaign," she counters. She voices concern that its appearance on Spanish television could conflict with her commercials for the moms. Being deprived of milk – the basis for the humor throughout the "Got Milk?" ads – "is not funny to" an older Hispanic audience, she says. "They've been there too often."

Ms. Lissa raises concerns, too. Unlike previous immigrant groups, she says, many Latinos embrace their language and heritage more strongly as they get older and become more established in America; advertising in English, therefore, may be a lousy way to foster long-term product loyalty. Beyond that, she worries that sticking "Got Milk?" on Spanish-language television could well be perceived as an insult, especially among Latino community leaders. "It shows a lack of commitment," says the energetic Argentine native.

Mostly, she and Ms. Santiago argue that they're letting a tremendous opportunity slip away and that, at a minimum, a lot more research into bicultural teens is needed. "You can say these teens are the same as everybody else, but they're not," Ms. Santiago says after the meeting. "They don't look the same. They don't talk the same."

But Mr. Manning won't budge. He says that he'll certainly look to place more Latino actors in the regular "Got Milk?" campaign.

And he may further explore a bicultural ad at some point. But any urgency he had to develop a whole new campaign has waned.

Broadcast Views

"I don't want to look like we're backing off this group of people," he says. "But as a marketer, I can't find a rationale" for launching a bunch of new ads. He is confident that his alternative scheme will "extend the reach" of "Got Milk?" – without having to shell out hundreds of thousands of dollars for new creative work.

As it happens, Ms. Santiago and Ms. Lissa aren't the only ones with doubts about airing "Got Milk?" on Spanish-language television.

Univision, the leading Spanish-language network (and the fifth-largest network in the U.S.), swiftly rejects the ads. It cites a policy against showing a commercial "as it currently airs on English-language television." Univision doesn't even accept general-market commercials with Spanish dubbed in, finding the money-saving technique a slap to its viewers.

Telemundo, a distant No. 2 in the Spanish TV wars, has squishier guidelines. But officials there also express some reluctance. "It seems counterproductive" for the milk board to go on Spanish-language television with commercials that "do not feature Latinos or are in nonrelevant scenarios to a Latino consumer," Eduardo Dominguez, the station manager at Telemundo's Los Angeles affiliate, writes to Ms. Santiago. Instead, he urges Mr. Manning's outfit to devise original ads "reflecting the lives and nuances which Latinos can associate with intimately."

In late April, despite its misgivings, Telemundo warily accepts one ad with no dialogue, save for a voice at the end intoning, "Got Milk?" In the spot, which first ran in 1994, a priest stuffs a hunk of chocolate cake into his mouth and then becomes frantic when he can't get a carton of milk out of a vending machine. Two nuns stumble across him as he flails wildly. Mr. Dominguez says he'll be watching to make sure that, given the Latino community's reverence for the church, there is no "significant public protest."

But Mr. Manning – who held additional focus groups with moms to see if they'd be put off by the ad – isn't worried about a possible backlash. Indeed, he hopes that once this first ad appears on Telemundo next week, additional "Got Milk?" commercials with even more English will follow.

For Ms. Santiago, that's a sour prospect. "This is taking a step backwards," she says. For Mr. Manning, it's something else entirely: "We're breaking new ground."

62

THE NAME'S THE THING

Dot.com's are spending like mad to establish an identity

Picture this: Thanksgiving morning, and the family gathers around the TV for the Macy's parade. There are all the famous cartoon characters bobbing down Broadway: Bullwinkle and Mickey Mouse and Spiderman and, look, it's...Jeeves? Who? The pin-striped butler–the make-believe spokesperson for the Ask Jeeves Inc. Internet search service–is elbowing his way into the pantheon of commercial icons, the first time a company has tried to buy instant brand awareness with a giant parade float.

The rolling Jeeves ploy is just one sign of the times as newly minted Net companies scramble to become national brands, alongside Coca-Cola, Kodak, and McDonald's. Scores of companies that you never heard of are spending tens of millions on advertising and marketing to establish their brands. For example, the little dot.com startup behind

Jeeves has also hired Hollywood superagent Michael Ovitz to put it on the marketing map.

According to Forrester Research Inc., dot.coms will double their spending on national ad campaigns this year, to $1.7 billion. Startups routinely devote as much as 90% of the capital they raise in public offerings to advertising and marketing. "A lot of companies are saying, 'We have to make it big, fast, or we're not going to make it at all,'" says Jay S. Walker, vice-chairman of Priceline.com Inc., a heavy advertiser.

CLUTTER. And it's not just the upstarts. Amazon.com Inc., the online bookseller whose brand is recognized around the globe, announced on Oct. 27 that it may triple ad spending, to more than $100 million, for the fourth quarter–just to keep its brand name on top as the clutter of messages from wannabes piles up. Now, Amazon says it will rack up

$1 billion in cumulative losses before it sees a profit.

America Online Inc., the biggest brand in cyberspace, has always invested heavily in brand marketing and has no plans to lighten up. Analysts say it will spend more than $900 million, or roughly 14% of its revenues, next year to keep its name out there. But, even AOL execs are startled by the frenzy now under way. "The AOL brand was a decade in the making," says Stephen M. Case, chairman of America Online Inc. "What's happening now is a dramatic compression of that process."

AOL, Amazon, and Yahoo!, the "first movers" among Internet brands, have broken the top ranks–all among the top 60 of global brands, according to Interbrand Group. But how many of the dot.com masses can make the cut? "The early success of Yahoo! and Amazon set a level of expectation about branding on the Web that proved to be ephemeral," says Roger McNamee, a general partner at Silicon Valley venture firm Integral Capital Partners. Two years ago, he says, it was possible to build a Net brand for $10 million to $30 million. Today, McNamee says, "it can cost hundreds of millions. That's scary."

"TOO MUCH NOISE." And, notes Shelly Lazarus, chairwoman and CEO of Ogilvy & Mather Worldwide Inc., advertising alone won't do the trick. Building a real brand takes years of effort that involves creating an identity for a product or service at every point of contact with the customer. "There's nothing as expensive and as difficult as imbuing meaning into a brand," she says.

Even now, seasoned ad executives, venture capitalists, analysts, and brand consultants say a big chunk of the money is being wasted. The ad campaigns might give a Web company's name a momentary buzz, but it's quickly drowned out by the rising

The Cost of Building a Brand

The cost of establishing and sustaining an Internet brand is high by traditional standards, even for the lucky few that have broken into the world's most recognized brands

RANK	BRAND NAME	BRAND VALUE $ MILLIONS	1999 MARKETING BUDGET $ MILLIONS	MARKETING AS A PERCENT OF REVENUE
ESTABLISHED BRANDERS				
1	COCA-COLA	$83,845	$4,000	20.5%
2	MICROSOFT	$56,654	3,752*	16.7
3	IBM	$43,781	1,000	1.1
INTERNET BRANDERS				
35	AMERICA ONLINE	$4,329	807*	16.9
53	YAHOO!	$1,761	206*	35.9
57	AMAZON.COM	$1,361	402*	25.9

*Sales and Marketing

Data: Interbrand Group, Analysts' Estimates

(Cont.)

cacophony. Meanwhile, scores of wannabes keep crowding into e-biz markets. In the third quarter alone, $5 billion in venture funding was pumped into Web businesses, double the amount for all of 1998. The result: multiple brands fighting for dominance in every possible category, from home furnishings to pet care to drugstores. Says Henry Blodget, an Internet analyst at Merrill Lynch & Co.: "You won't see a lot of brands built...There's too much noise."

But you will see brands die. On the Web, brands are born, force-fed to maturity at a terrifying rate, and then vanish. For bamboo.com Inc., the arc from promising startup to disposable brand was a scant nine months. The Palo Alto (Calif.) provider of interactive video tours of real estate merged with InteractivePictures Corp. on Oct. 26. Both companies are losing money hand over fist as they promote their brands. But despite spending a combined $25 million on marketing for the first nine months of the year, the new company may wind up dumping both brands and picking a new name, says bamboo.com founder and Executive Vice-President Kevin B. McCurdy.

It's not like bamboo.com and its executives are making up their own marketing rules as they go along. The company's advisers include Peter Sealey, former director of global marketing for Coca-Cola Co. "I never would have considered throwing a brand away at Coke," says Sealey, who spent a decade building up Sprite. But Net companies can justify scrapping their investments in brands and starting all over, he says, because franchises are being established at a much faster pace.

There's no question that building brands in cyberspace is a daunting challenge. Dot.coms can't reinforce their advertising the way traditional companies do–through the Crest toothpaste tube you see in the morning or the Buick logo on the steering wheel.

How do you put across a cyber-brand's advantages? E*Trade Group Inc.'s strategy, for example, is built around the need to shine in the overcrowded e-broker market. To stand out, the company has fashioned itself into a financial portal, complete with stock quotes, financial news, and company releases–for free. The core idea? Be the place that empowers the small investor to trade like a pro. But to pound that idea into the minds of consumers, E*Trade–which lost $54.4 million on sales of $621.4 million in fiscal 1999–spent $200 million on marketing. "It's really the experience on the site that defines the brand," says Jerry Gramaglia, chief marketing officer at E*Trade.

Indeed, technology alone won't do it. Ask AltaVista Co. Savvy Internet users praised its search engine's superior capabilities, but its former corporate parents, Digital Equipment Corp., then Compaq Computer Corp., did not follow up with sufficient marketing. Yahoo! quickly dominated, and AltaVista languished. Now, Net holding company CMGI Inc. will spend $120 million on marketing in 10 U.S. cities over the next nine months to put AltaVista back on the digital map.

So, the e-brands keep buying up ad time, sometimes squeezing out the traditional consumer brands. "There's increased demand to get onto shows where companies can reach very large audiences," says Timothy M. Callahan, a vice-president for beverages and

---

COMMENTARY

By Peter Coy

NYNEX, WE HARDLY KNEW YE

Somwhere up in corporate heaven, Studebaker is still making cars. You can still make a deposit at Chemical Bank, get a Digital Equipment Corp. computer, fly a new McDonnell Douglas jet, ride the Atchison, Topeka & Santa Fe Railway, and buy shares from Shearson Loeb Rhoades.

But not here on earth. All of those corporate brands, once household names that limned daily life, died when the companies that bore them were acquired. Boeing bought McDonnell Douglas and expunged its name. Shearson disappeared inside American Express. And so on.

Mergers are hell on corporate brands. And that puts an interesting perspective on the image-building efforts of young e-commerce companies such as Yahoo!, Priceline.com, and eBay. Many of those names won't be on their own in five years. While some may survive as brands, others will be extinguished entirely. In other words, immense sums are going to build brand skyscrapers that will be torn down before their time. This is creative destruction with a vengeance.

Killing a corporate name, much as it pains the copywriters who nurtured it, is often the sensible thing to do. Economists remind us to ignore sunk costs—all those Super Bowl ad extravaganzas—in determining a brand's fate. The money is spent, and there's no getting it back. What's more, some venerable names, such as New York's Chemical Bank, just don't cut it after awhile. When it bought Chase Manhattan in 1996, Chemical assumed Chase's identity in a maneuver that recalls the movie *Invasion of the Body Snatchers.* Ditto for Westinghouse's acquisition of CBS Corp.

NO RESPECT. Still, brand gurus say many merger-happy CEOs don't show enough respect for the brands they acquire. One of their cases in point is Bernard J. Ebbers, the cowboy chairman of MCI WorldCom who bought MCI Communications last year and is lassoing Sprint Corp. for a record $130 billion, including assumption of debt.

MCI and Sprint are two powerful brands. Competitive Media Reporting, an ad-tracking firm, ranked MCI No. 2 in the nation and Sprint No. 9 among 1998's top 100 brands. Ebbers paid about $25 billion over book value for MCI and is paying about $100 billion over book value for Sprint. Much of the premium is for the brands. Yet Ebbers hasn't decided exactly how to use them. Probably, they will be applied to different market segments. What's sure is that the corporate name will be reduced to its least-recognized element, WorldCom. "They're damaging brands that have taken years and years to develop," says James R. Gregory, CEO of Corporate Branding, a Stamford (Conn.) consultancy.

Companies that continually change are bound to have a hard time creating an identity. Take Nynex Corp., a phone company that sounded like a stock exchange. Few tears fell in 1998 when it disappeared into Bell Atlantic Corp. Next year, Bell Atlantic will vanish, dropping its name after buying GTE Corp. Odds are, its new name will lack both history (Bell) or geography (Atlantic). And it will start life with zero brand equity. Then again, it only has to last until the next megamerger.

Coy is associate economics editor.

(Cont.)

business development at Campbell Soup Co. Gary Stibel, founder and principal at brand consultants New England Consulting Group, has advised some of its old-line clients to drop out, at least until after cyber-Christmas, and make a little money by selling slots to the dot.coms. "Between now and the Super Bowl, more money will be misspent on advertising than any of us have seen in our lifetime," he says.

But the upstarts do have something to aim at. AOL's brand value–the contribution to market capitalization that's attributed to brand–is greater than that of Apple Computer, Chanel, or Burger King, according to Interbrand. Yahoo! and Amazon rate ahead of Guinness and Hilton Hotels. And remember: Yahoo! and Amazon didn't even exist five years ago. "When you can market the message directly to the individual customer, you can establish a brand presence much more rapidly," says Christopher E. Vroom, an analyst at investment bank Thomas Weisel Partners.

Does the flood of aspiring Net brands with money to burn mean the rules of marketing are being rewritten? Not likely. And so far there's not much evidence that traditional companies with established brands have ceded any ground to the upstarts. Indeed, the thing to watch now is how traditional companies can transfer their brands to the Net. Says Dan Latimore, a consultant at Mainspring Communications Inc., which advises companies on e-commerce strategies: "We tell our clients: 'When you look at what some of the Net players are spending to establish a brand, you're sitting on a gold mine.'" And it's getting more valuable every day.

By Paul C. Judge in Boston and Heather Green in New York, with Amy Barrett in Philadelphia, Catherine Yang in Washington, and bureau reports

Cough Syrup Touts 'Awful' Taste in U.S.

By Joel A. Baglole

Staff Reporter of The Wall Street Journal

W . K . Buckley is proud to say Canadians have hated its cough syrup for 80 years. And now, the company thinks it should be the U.S.'s turn.

Buckley has used a blunt eight-word slogan, "Buckley's Mixture. It tastes awful. And it works," in its advertising campaign to become a household name in Canada.

Buckley, based in Mississauga, Ontario, is trying to stretch a thin ad budget to launch its first national entry into the U.S. Previously, it has run only bus and bus-shelter ads in the New York City area. With just 2.3 million Canadian dollars (US$1.6 million) to spend on ads this winter-cold season, the company is using low-cost tactics, including contests, giveaways and product placements to build a *bad* name for Buckley's brew.

Ads running in the National Enquirer supermarket tabloid, for example, ask people to mail in pictures of their faces as they taste Buckley's Mixture. At the end of January, the company will select the best grimace. The winner will receive US$500 and get his or her picture published in an ad in the paper.

For fans of Buckley's, grimaces come naturally enough. Unlike most cough syrups, Buckley's Mixture contains no sugar or alcohol, the ingredients used to mask the taste. The company says it could improve the taste (and has done so with its Jack & Jill children's brand), but shuns the idea for its main brand. If the taste improved, "nobody would know us anymore," says John Meehan, general manager of the closely held company.

In another bid to get out the word in the U.S. as cheaply as possible, Buckley is giving away samples over its Web site. Also on offer are free T-shirts, refrigerator magnets and coffee cups to Americans who tell six friends or family members about Buckley's and get them to write to the company.

To get Buckley's Mixture showcased on the television game show "The Price Is Right," where contestants guess the cough syrup's retail price, and in other venues, the company has hired **Premier Entertainment Services,** a Hollywood product-placement firm. So far, Buckley's Mixture has landed appearances on 38 TV shows, including prime-time hits "ER" and "The X-Files," and it will be included in a film starring Julia Roberts.

In addition, Buckley said it is spending US$99,000 to run a 10-second TV ad featuring a man shoving cotton up his nose, tasting Buckley's Mixture, and then screaming. The ad will run 23 times over the next two months on shows such as "Jeopardy" and "Wheel of Fortune."

A larger radio-ad campaign, which cost US$435,000, features company President Frank Buckley joking about the elixir's bad taste.

Buckley's *hopes to win over American consumers by not hiding its awful taste.*

Over the years, plenty of other campaigns attracted attention by focusing on the negative attributes of products. Ads for Listerine mouthwash used to trumpet "the taste you love to hate." Campaigns for the Volkswagen Beetle portrayed it as the ugly duckling of cars.

Ads for Heinz ketchup in the 1980s played on the time it takes for the ketchup to slide out of the bottle. But it stressed the product is so good, it is worth the wait, notes Patrick Dickinson, managing director of Toronto ad agency Publicis SMW, a unit of France's **Publicis,** which is running the current campaign.

Buckley's has a long history of dwelling on the negative, with past ads containing such promises as, "Relief is just a yuck away," and "Not new. Not improved." Those efforts have helped make the company Canada's No. 3 cough-syrup maker, with a 12% market share, according to Advertising Age magazine.

But it trails far behind Benylin, produced by giant **Warner-Lambert,** with 22% of the Canadian market, and Robitussin, made by **Whitehall-Robins Healthcare,** with an 18% Canadian share. According to market-research firm ACNielsen, cough medicine sales in Canada last year totaled C$70 million.

In the U.S., where cough-syrup sales total US$418 million a year, Robitussin dominates with a 52.7% share, according to Information Resources, Chicago. Buckley aims for a 5% market share in five years, the company's Mr. Meehan says.

The U.S. market will be a challenge for Buckley's, where even an audacious but small campaign might simply get lost. Buckley, which has only 28 employees, projects revenue of C$15 million in the fiscal year ending March 31. The company doesn't release profit figures.

Stephen Greyser, a professor of marketing at Harvard University's Business School, says the success of the Buckley ads will ultimately depend on their humor. For a small company trying to gain brand recognition, being funny is probably the best hope, he says.

The Users:
Making the Sale

Salespeople are using software and the Web to make their jobs a lot easier

BY ANDREA PETERSEN

Staff Reporter of THE WALL STREET JOURNAL

Tina Damron doesn't consider herself a computer person. And just one year ago, Ms. Damron, who sells office furniture to businesses in Silicon Valley, didn't need to be one.

But today, the 38-year-old impresses chief executives with cool three-dimensional renderings of desks, chairs and cubicles. She chats with salespeople across the country, beats back the competition with real-time information and sends her orders – all from the laptop that is her constant companion.

Ms. Damron is among the thousands of salespeople who use mobile computer software and the Web to make their jobs easier – and to help them sell more stuff. Revenue from sales-force-automation tools is expected to surge to $4.8 billion in 2003 from $887.6 million last year, according to International Data Corp., a Framingham, Mass., market-research firm.

On a recent afternoon in Menlo Park, Calif., Ms. Damron demonstrates the power of mobile sales resources. During a sales call at an Internet company, Ms. Damron talks up some new cubicles distributed by her company, Coordinated Resources Inc. of San Jose. Ms. Damron works for CRI's SQA division, which sells low-cost furniture. She also points out some of the downsides of a product that one of CRI's competitors sells.

Although the Internet company in the end decided to buy used furniture, Ms. Damron is confident that she did her best sales job. And she thanks the Web. That is because before Ms. Damron went on the sales call she had already learned that the Internet company was interested in her competitor's cubicles. So she fired up her laptop and cruised onto the Internet to do some opposition research. She headed to a site called youknowit.com that details the attributes of the products that Ms. Damron's company sells and gives tips on how to sell them against specific competing products.

'A Great Selling Point'

"Their cubicles can't be powered," Ms. Damron says of the competition. "You can't plug anything into the bottom of the panel. That was a great selling point for me. I would have never known if I hadn't gotten the information from the Internet."

The Web site Ms. Damron used was produced by Herman Miller Inc., the Zeeland, Mich., office-furniture maker. Ms. Damron's employer – known as CRI – is a dealer of Herman Miller furniture, which accounts for about 80% of Ms. Damron's total monthly sales. Herman Miller created the site to help its salespeople from around the country get information on new products, tips on placing orders, help with tracking sales – and get an edge against competitors.

All 250 of the company's dealers use the program. "We take people through the features of a product and how to best position it against the competition," says Cathy Lawrence, a Herman Miller communications specialist. "Our salespeople can know the best way to attack the competition."

Salespeople like Ms. Damron also trade information with one another. Herman Miller has set up a series of online bulletin boards where salespeople can exchange tips. The company also offers training about new products and sales techniques over the Internet.

"There is this great network of sharing," says a Herman Miller spokesman. "We use the network to build literacy across the organization."

CRI has also brought in other mobile sales tools beyond what Herman Miller gives to its dealers. CRI's salespeople use a Web-based program created by UpShot.com Inc., Mountain View, Calif., to track new customer leads. When a salesperson gets a lead on new business, he or she enters the name and contact information into UpShot. All salespeople can go online and consult UpShot to make sure they don't duplicate efforts.

"You don't waste your time," Ms. Damron says. "And you don't look silly by having two people from the same company working on a deal."

UpShot also helped when Ms. Damron inherited some accounts from a salesperson who had left the company. That salesperson had included helpful notes about the customers. "He wrote things like, 'So and so is really serious, so don't joke around,'" Ms. Damron says.

Before UpShot, Ms. Damron made all of her notes about a client in pen on a folder. In those days, a lost folder could mean a lost client. But now, all of Ms. Damron's client information is online, and accessible from anywhere. That allows her to add new information to UpShot from home. "I do it at night when my son is watching TV," she says.

Upshot also allows CRI's managers to keep better tabs on their salespeople. "We can measure how much sales activity our people are doing," says Barbara Carlyle, a CRI founder. "Salespeople will say they are working on it, but we can find out how hard they actually are working."

Quicker Service

Bringing more of its sales activities online has also allowed CRI to get products to

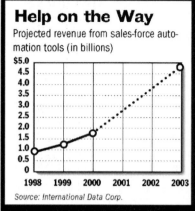

Help on the Way

Projected revenue from sales-force automation tools (in billions)

Source: International Data Corp.

customers more quickly. Salespeople now submit most of their orders directly on the Internet, and their requests are instantly processed by Herman Miller's back-office system. That has cut the time it takes for a customer to get their cubicles and furniture from five weeks to a little as five days.

"Internet companies operate at Internet speed," says Ken Baugh, president of Space Designs Inc., a Mountain View, Calif., furniture dealer that recently merged with CRI. "Our speed and capability is becoming a differentiator for us." The ability to deliver quickly is increasingly important in the office-furniture business, where hundreds of dealers sell the same products from the handful of major manufacturers.

Speed is critical for Dana Waldman, president and chief executive of Centerpoint Broadband Technologies Inc., a high-speed Internet access provider in San Jose that is less than a year old. Mr. Waldman recently needed more than a dozen cubicles – and fast – for his growing work force. "We were running out of room," Mr. Waldman says. "There were people who had no place to sit." Thanks to the online order processing, Centerpoint got its furniture from CRI within two weeks.

Ms. Damron says that ordering online also helps cut down on human error. At her previous job, she says, she had to do everything by hand. "We used to use three sheets of carbon paper," she recalls. "If you had a change in your order you would have to recopy the whole thing."

But speed and accuracy aren't the most important things that moving online has brought her, she says. What she really relishes is the freedom. "I have the flexibility to dial up and work from home," she says. "As a single mom, that's important. I can spend more time with my son."

Pitching Saturns to Your Classmates— for Credit

BY ANNE MARIE CHAKER

Staff Report of THE WALL STREET JOURNAL

SANTA ROSA, Calif. – The 18 men and women huddled in a conference room at a Saturn car dealership on a Saturday afternoon are brainstorming intensely. Winding up a pitch for a new marketing slogan – "We Never Sounded So Good" – Tony Emerson says, "You know what? It's a new company that's getting better and better every year." Christina Vorrises expounds on Saturn's "no-hassle, no-haggle 30-day money-back guarantee." Elizabeth Sadlier exclaims, "I'm ready to promote!"

They sound like pumped-up Saturn marketers. In fact, they are students from Sonoma State University in Rohnert Park, Calif., in a marketing class funded by the Saturn dealership, and they will be graded on just how well they promote the cars to their peers.

The long arm of corporate marketing has reached onto campuses in many ways, but corporate underwriting of college classes is a new twist. Saturn's parent, **General Motors** Corp., has funded classes at more than 200 colleges. Others who have paid to have college classes spend a term pitching their products include **Time Warner Inc., Wells Fargo** & Co., **Bristol-Myers Squibb** Co. and Ameritech Advertising Services (now part of **SBC Communications** Inc.).

"One reason we signed on was to get in touch with talented college kids who might like to work with our company," says Ken Godshall, senior vice president of partnership marketing and new business development for Time Consumer Marketing Inc., which underwrote marketing classes at five schools last semester. Another goal: to sell a total of 375 subscriptions per school.

For schools, the program typically means money: **EdVenture Partners,** a closely held firm in Berkeley, Calif., that brokers relationships between companies and colleges, says the schools get $2,500 for costs related to the marketing project plus a $500 contribution to the faculty department. Companies also pay EdVenture $12,500 to $17,500 a school.

"A large number of our 106 colleges are engaged in these kinds of relationships," says Christopher Cabaldon, vice chancellor of the California Community Colleges. "A real-world client for students to work with enhances the quality and practicability" of their classes, he says.

Once the class is set up, students typically use their $2,500 budget to plan a promotional party complete with food, games, prizes, music and, of course, marketing come-ons. The end result looks like a corporate-sponsored fraternity bash (minus the liquor) and typically attracts hundreds of students.

At Sonoma State, students began the semester by conducting market research on their classmates. They passed out surveys to 200 fellow students, which revealed that 81% didn't know the name of their local Saturn dealership, Saturn of Santa Rosa. Worse, only 28% rated Saturn an "excellent" car company, compared with 57% who said they thought the same of Honda.

Since Saturn of Santa Rosa wanted the class to throw a party advertising the dealership and its cars, the class began to plan a "Pardi Gras" featuring free food and prizes. Over the next several weeks, students went to work promoting their party by hanging fliers throughout the school and passing them out at campus hangouts.

The class threw the party on a Tuesday afternoon ("Phat Tuesday"), and featured six Saturns parked on Salazar Plaza, one of the busiest spots on campus. About 400 students showed up for free hot dogs, giveaways such as frisbees and compact disks, and a scavenger hunt played inside the racier-looking car models, so that students could get a good look at features like the eight-speaker sound system. Through it all, a GM finance and insurance specialist was on hand, ready to answer students' queries about car loans and credit.

Within two days after the party, the class again polled 200 randomly picked students. Of the students who attended the party, 43% rated Saturn an excellent company. And the students' ability to name Saturn of Santa Rosa as their local car dealership increased to 88% among the students who attended (and even increased to 51% among those who did not attend).

Small wonder, then, that GM considers the program "a bargain," the term used by William Palace, who oversees the company's youth marketing on the West Coast. Students, he says, "are the opinion leaders of the future." Right now, their "aspirational vehicles" tend to be imports such as Mercedes-Benz or BMW. But having them market to their peers can lend GM makes like Chevrolet and Pontiac the cool they now lack. "We see it as a huge competitive advantage," Mr. Palace says.

The underwriting programs outrage critics like Richard Randall, who teaches at North Idaho College. In the spring semester of 1998, when Mr. Randall was an instructor in the philosophy department at Washington State University in Pullman, he protested a campus promotion for Chevrolet run by students in a marketing class. He recalls standing for over two hours clutching a picketing sign that read: "Internships OK – but We Are a University, Not a Car Dealership."

"It was the use of a state, taxpayer-supported institution which was very obviously being used to sell products," Mr. Randall now says. "If this was an academic exercise, then what in the hell were the salespeople doing there?"

The professor of that class at Washington State, David Sprott, is in his third year with

---

BIRTH OF A SALES FORCE

Some classes with corporate sponsors

SCHOOL:	CLASS:	PROMOTION THEME:
Colorado State U. Fort Collins	BK 492 Marketing Seminar	Norwest Cash Cube Contest (Wells Fargo)
Washington State U. Pullman	Marketing 496 Special Topics	Spring into Great Deal! with Chipman & Taylor Chevrolet
Diablo Valley College Pleasant Hill, Calif.	Business 257 Applied Advertising and Promotions	Lehmer's (GMC Trucks) Luau

Sources: EdVenture Partners, Wall Street Journal reports

(Cont.)

the GM program in his marketing class and defends it. "There's never enough funds provided by the state," he says. "Any type of external support that comes without work on our part is a good thing." Every spring semester, his students throw a promotional party for a local Chevrolet dealership. He maintains that a program like this is useful in teaching a less theoretical subject such as marketing. "We teach how to sell stuff," he says.

Elsewhere, the program has recently taken a new turn with a different kind of

One college professor complains that for-profit corporations are just using taxpayer-supported institutions to sell their products. He has picketed against such underwriting programs.

sponsor: the Immigration and Naturalization Service, which has just begun classes at four universities. The marketing project for the students: to interest their classmates in working for the U.S. Border Patrol, whose recruiting efforts have suffered because of the strong economy.

Republished with permission of Dow Jones, Inc. from *The Wall Street Journal,* January 31, 2000; permission conveyed through Copyright Clearance Center, Inc.

NOW THAT'S A HAIL MARY PLAY

Inside a dot.com betting $5 million on the Super Bowl

To find the headquarters of OurBeginning.com Inc., head west from downtown Orlando about five miles until the neighborhood turns, uh, more interesting. OurBeginning's nondescript industrial building is easy to overlook among the shabby storefronts. So maybe this will help: It's across the street from the Pooch & Purr Grooming Salon and a few doors down from God's Miracle House of Prayer.

It's about the last place you'd expect to find a company that will share the stage with BMW, Visa, and other corporate giants that have purchased commercials on Super Bowl Sunday, Jan. 30. Ad time for the top-rated TV show of the year–the audience is expected to hit 135 million–runs as high as $3 million for a 30-second spot. At those prices, you would think that only companies with the flushest marketing budgets would give it a thought.

Yet OurBeginning, an online stationery e-tailer that launched its Web site only last April, is right in there with the big boys. So what if it has just 12 full-time employees and, according to Chief Executive Michael E. Budowski, has

> **"I consider myself a visionary," says Budowski, who launched the stationery site last spring**

thus far racked up revenues of a little over $1 million? OurBeginning is paying to produce and air three pregame ads and a fourth spot to run during the game at a cost of about $4 million (plus $1 million for tech upgrades to handle the expected surge in site traffic).

"NOT NUTS." There's no doubting Budowski's nerve. But what about his sanity? "This is a risky move. It's certainly an aggressive strategy. But I'm not nuts," says the stocky 34-year-old with a grin. In fact, he admits to only one regret: "I wish I'd thought about buying more."

It's big talk from a small company. But OurBeginning isn't the first dot.com to use the Super Bowl to break out of the cyberclutter. Last year, job sites HotJobs.com (HOTJ) and Monster.com (TMPW) made big splashes with clever commercials. Monster averaged 600 job searches per minute before the game, compared with 2,900 after. "There aren't many places to establish a brand as quickly to a mass audience," says Charlene Li, who tracks dot.com advertisers for Forrester Research Inc., a Cambridge (Mass.) Internet research firm.

The exposure is, presumably, still paying off for Monster and HotJobs. Both are back this year as Super Bowl advertisers, and HotJobs is a hot stock–its share price has tripled since its initial public offering in August.

It may not be as easy for this year's larger class of dot.com advertisers, however: As many as 12 will be competing for the attention of beer-sloshed fans. For advertisers who cut through the haze, though, the rewards can be enormous. Some 8% of the audience–almost 11 million viewers–concede that they actually tune in to watch the commercials, according to a study by Eisner Communications, a Baltimore-based firm that conducts Super Bowl research.

That helps explain why Budowski is laying down the biggest bet of his life. Already, the move has lifted OurBeginning from obscurity onto the radar screen of Wall Street investors, a major objective since the company plans an IPO this year. At the same time, it's a warning shot to competitors in the fragmented online-printing category. "It sends a very clear message: 'I am taking this very seriously,'" says Li of Forrester Research.

The Super Bowl ad campaign also has given Budowski his 15 minutes of fame, which he is wearing comfortably. Tooling around Orlando at the wheel of his 1995 GMC Yukon last week, he said offhandedly: "I consider myself a visionary." Budowski has had the vision thing before, though on a smaller scale. At 20, he left community college to start an exterminating company that he ran out of his parents' garage in Crofton, Md. He still owns that business, which has since expanded to eight states, and several other enterprises, including a steakhouse.

OurBeginning began in the Budowski's Orlando home, where his wife, Susan ran a small business as a wedding consultant. Budowski persuaded her to expand into cyberspace and last spring launched a Web site. Customers click through pages showing wedding invitations, thank-you notes, birth announcements, and starting soon, business cards and letterheads. OurBeginning forwards the orders to outside printers that ship to customers under the OurBeginning label.

Budowski's Super Bowl dream revealed itself as he lay in bed last September. He remembers thinking: "Here's a way to put a turbocharger in this company." He quickly shared the idea with investor and Chief Operating Officer Michael C. Brandenberg and Susan. "The Super Bowl is huge," recalls Susan. "I thought he was kidding."

SNEAK PEEK. To pay for the spots, Budowski and Brandenberg spent the next three weeks raising $5 million through loans and sell-offs of equity positions. They bulked up the site so it could handle 2 million users a day, compared with the average of 10,000. And they hired Disney i.d.e.a.s., a unit of Walt Disney Co., to create slick comedy out of the seemingly humorless topics of stationery and personalized Post-It notes.

OurBeginning paid Disney $1 million for its four spots and a fifth that Super Bowl viewers won't see. ABC's censors found its language offensive and rejected it, citing "antisocial behavior," Budowski notes. For OurBeginning, it's a case either of exquisite luck or shrewd marketing, because the company plans to post the banned ad on its Web site as a means of generating additional traffic. "It never hurts for people to be talking about an ad too risque for TV," says David Blum, a vice-president at Eisner Communications. In another effort to drive traffic, OurBeginning will pay $250,000 to a lucky Web surfer who registers at its site. Budowski says he hopes to create a data base of 5 million customers, including many who heard about the site on the big game.

If a tiny fraction uses OurBeginning to buy business cards and party invitations, Budowski's bet will have paid off. And if they don't? "It doesn't fold the company," he says. "I like living on the edge, but not that close to the edge."

By Mark Hyman in Orlando

Agencies Get Dot-Com Stock For Hot Spots

BY SUEIN L. HWANG

Staff Reporter of THE WALL STREET JOURNAL

The advertising industry has a new deal to offer Internet start-ups: deluxe treatment normally reserved for top clients, in exchange for stock.

Leading the charge is Madison Avenue giant **Interpublic Group**'s Western Trading unit, which has quietly launched an initiative that's turning the advertising industry on its ear. Wielding the clout of its massive media-buying affiliate, Western is promising dot-coms top-level attention and access to some of the best advertising space on television and radio across the country. In return, it's seeking – and getting – equity stakes from a carefully selected handful of Internet start-ups.

It's a striking departure from standard ad-industry practice, and it shows how important image-making has become in the Internet world. For many start-ups, getting desirable time slots for their ads is tougher than raising money. "We are the secret weapon in a dot-com's marketing arsenal," says Robert Ingram, Western Trading's president and a 25-year industry veteran.

Not just any dot-com, though. When Mr. Ingram got wind of start-up MortgageIT.com from an investment banking friend, he and his team of analysts thoroughly scrutinized the start-up's funding, management team and business plan before negotiating to exchange services, including ad placements, for equity.

Western is hardly the only company swapping services for stock. Ad agencies, tired of watching the images they create turn their clients into overnight millionaires, have joined a long list, including publicists, accountants, attorneys, and even real-estate agents and contractors.

But Western's eAdvantage program goes much further than those of other ad agencies, which worry about alienating their traditional clientele. Western provides its chosen start-ups with the kind of high-level talent and choice advertising space usually reserved for bigger clients. "Our top management is focused on it," says Mr. Ingram, who adds that he may try to sign up as many as 30 dot-coms.

In the case of MortgageIT.com, Western has assigned an eAdvantage executive to the account to help the start-up grab any coveted last-minute ad slots that pop up. Doug Naidus, MortgageIT.com's chief executive, says the company is getting the "good stuff" – the ad spots that aren't sandwiched between four other commercials and spots at peak listening hours on news-formatted radio stations.

Mr. Ingram has also introduced MortgageIT.com to an affiliated ad agency, Boston-based **Hill, Holliday, Connors, Cosmopulos,** and even helped recruit some executives to the start-up.

Though MortgageIT.com has committed to spend only $20 million on advertising – a ho-hum amount by dot-com standards – Hill Holliday's president and chief creative officer, Fred Bertino, will oversee the development of the ads himself. "I don't know if a smallish media account would normally get that level of attention," concedes Brian Carty, managing director at Hill Holliday. But "we want to make sure we get it off in the right way. The more successful they are, the more successful we are."

Not surprisingly, Western's bold strategy is being greeted skeptically by others in the ad world. In the old days, agencies were paid a percentage of the amount a client spent on a campaign. The theory was that the better the ad, the bigger the campaign and the fatter the fees. Recently, more clients have forced agencies to accept largely flat fees, no matter how big or effective the campaign is.

But in an industry built on pleasing many different clients, ad executives at other agencies argue that playing favorites with a small dot-com is professional suicide. "If I were the other clients, I'd be awfully angry," warns Rich Silverstein of **Omnicom Group**'s Goodby, Silverstein & Partners. "You can't put all your efforts and your top people on one client in hopes of making more money on it. It would be irresponsible, and bad business."

For traditional clients, the agencies' shifting loyalties are yet another potential problem resulting from the deluge of dot-com advertisers. "It's harder to get media, do production work or even try to get an agency," says Maura Rearden, director of advertising for **Allied Domecq**'s Dunkin' Donuts, a Hill Holliday client. "This is one more thing to look out for."

After considerable internal debate, executives at **True North Communications'** Foote Cone & Belding agreed to accept some compensation from dot-coms in equity. But it immediately transfers the options to key employees in an effort to keep them from leaving for start-ups themselves.

> *Other ad agencies are greeting Western's strategy skeptically.*

Chairman Geoffrey Thompson argues that agencies, which must serve many different accounts, can't be viewed as beholden to a few dot-coms because it is unfair to traditional clients that aren't gearing up for a big IPO. "If an agency becomes an investor in a company, it's almost a conflict of interest," he says. "We want all of our clients to feel we're invested in them."

Now that numerous Web companies are clamoring for their services, advertising agencies are in a more powerful bargaining position than they were before. In their race toward that critical initial public offering, Internet start-ups are increasingly seeking a big-name ad agency to add credibility to their efforts. "For a start-up going to market, being able to say its agency is Hill Holliday, its buyer is Western Media and its investment banker is Goldman Sachs helps a lot," says Mr. Carty.

Western's Mr. Ingram says his strategy reflects the changing times. "It's common sense," he says. "We're among the leaders in [media buying], and to use it in the exciting dot-com arena didn't take a lot of thought."

Some ad agencies have learned hard lessons in performing due diligence on Web companies. A San Francisco boutique agency, Odiorne Wilde Narraway & Partners, cut an equity deal with a dot-com start-up last year, agreeing to forgo roughly a quarter of its profit in return for a stake in the client.

But Odiorne says the start-up burned through so much capital that it couldn't even come up with the cash to pay the agency's already reduced fees. Now Odiorne is considering taking its client, which it declines to identify, to court. "They were a bunch of kids with no business sensibilities, and we fell hook, line, and sinker," says Wayne Buder, an Odiorne partner.

As a result, Odiorne won't take on any Web-company client until its law firm, **Heller Ehrman White & McAuliffe,** has thoroughly investigated the start-up's funding sources. "They find out how good is the money, who are the sources of the money, whether there are any restrictions on the money," Mr. Buder says.

Just For Feet's 'Kenya' spot during last year's Super Bowl sparked a $10 mil lawsuit and raised a troubling question:

CAN AN AGENCY BE GUILTY OF MALPRACTICE?

by Alice Z. Cuneo

When the fans went home and the lights went out for the 1999 Super Bowl, one image remained for many TV viewers: that of a barefoot African runner fleeing hunters in a Humvee, who captured and drugged their victim to force him into a pair of shoes from Just For Feet.

Amid criticism of racial insensitivity, retailer Just For Feet sued its agency, Saatchi & Saatchi Business Communications, Rochester, N.Y., for more than $10 million in damages for advertising malpractice.

While the status of the case was uncertain at press time, following Just For Feet's move to liquidate last week, the suit has raised a troubling question for the advertising community: Can advertising agencies be held liable for the ads they produce?

'A FRIGHTENING SPECTER'

"It's a frightening specter," said Grant Richards, co-founder and creative director of San Francisco shop Grant, Scott & Hurley. Mr. Richards points out the daunting effect a malpractice threat would have on an agency's creative limits.

Court Crandall, co-partner at Ground Zero, Marina del Rey, Calif., said such considerations would dim the creative spark. For example, he said, beer ads often use beautiful women to sell their product. But Goodby, Silverstein & Partners used lizards, "one of the ugliest creatures on earth," Mr. Crandall said.

The agency gave them a voice and turned them into one of the most effective ways of selling product, he said, adding that the threat of malpractice could change that.

"People would have no choice but to follow what's always been done to avoid a lawsuit," Mr. Crandall said. "Advertising is still an imperfect science."

The case raises concerns in the industry's creative community at a time when agencies have been flooded with requests from dot-com companies for cutting-edge campaigns to build quick awareness in a crowded market.

"With the clutter that is out there, there is certainly an increased exposure for someone [in the agency business]

getting a claim," said Jeffrey Michel, associate general counsel, True North Communications, Chicago.

A MUTUAL MISTAKE

Several executives said the Just For Feet lawsuit is really limited to a mistake made by the client and the agency.

"The agency was a fool for proposing such a thing, and the client was a fool for paying for it," Mr. Richards said. "We live in politically correct times. You have to be careful what you do."

In its lawsuit, Just For Feet said the finished spot, called "Kenya," was entirely different from the concept Saatchi first presented.

The original spot, the company said, would have showed a Just For Feet team coming up to a runner whose shoelace had become untied. The Just For Feet team would tie the runner's shoelace and give him water and a towel, the company said.

The spot was one of two that Saatchi and Just For Feet had been considering using until immediately before Super Bowl XXXIII.

A second spot showed a gymnasium in a school with the fictional name "Ruttenberg High," apparently a reference to Just For Feet CEO Harold Ruttenberg. There, a geeky boy played dodge ball, a school yard game where a player stands alone and tries to dodge a ball thrown at him by other players; the Just for Feet team came in and rescued him by giving him better shoes.

Just for Feet preferred this spot, the company claimed in its suit, but one network rejected it, saying it was "mean-spirited and promotes antisocial behavior."

COST, TIME CONSIDERATIONS

As the clock ticked down toward the big game, Saatchi presented the final "Kenya" spot to the client. Just For Feet said it "expressed strong misgivings and dissatisfaction" over the spot, according to the lawsuit, but Saatchi "then reassured Just For Feet that the commercial would be well received based on Saatchi's expertise and

(Cont.)

experience with national advertising and marketing, and that having committed to advertise in the Super Bowl it was too late to develop and produce another commercial or to reshoot the dodge ball commercial."

The company, out $900,000 in production costs and $2 million for the Super Bowl time slot, said in court documents it had no choice but to run the "Kenya" spot.

But creative wasn't the retailer's only problem.

Just For Feet also planned a sweepstake promotion, the "Just For Feet Third Quarter Super Bowl Win a Hummer Contest." In the weeks leading up to the game, Just For Feet spent $800,000 on promotional teaser spots during the National Football League and American Football League conference championship games.

> **"This is not a doctor who removes the wrong foot. [Advertising] is a shared expertise and a shared responsibility."**

Those spots urged viewers to watch the third quarter and find out how many times the Just For Feet name was mentioned. Viewers wishing to participate in the contest were to telephone or go to the Just For Feet Web site with their answer to enter the sweepstakes.

The spot, however, ran in the fourth quarter, making the contest's correct answer zero. The company's Web site would not accept zero as the answer, so "customers were left with the mistaken impression that Just For Feet was attempting to trick or deceive them," the lawsuit said. Saatchi's sibling, Zenith Media, bought the ad time.

INEFFECTIVE BRAND BUILDING?

Following the Super Bowl, critics lashed out at the "Kenya" spot. Some said it was not only ineffective in building the company's brand, it may even have been viewed as promoting drug use. Advertising Age's Bob Garfield said the spot was "probably racist."

It all came as the retailer was trying to move away from its "Where the 13th pair is free" tagline from agency Rogers Advertising, Birmingham, Ala., and break out as a national advertiser appealing to its core customer base of minorities and women with small children.

The shoe store chain, the second-largest in the nation, also was under duress because of a fashion shift from sweatsuits and white athletic shoes to khakis and brown shoes. It also had been expanding at a rapid rate, buying the Athletic Attic and Sneaker Stadium chains to the concern of some analysts, who questioned the fast

pace of growth.

Just as the dust from the Kenyan runner's shoes settled, Saatchi sued Just For Feet in U.S. District Court in Rochester in late February for failing to pay its $3 million media bill. On March 1, Just For Feet filed its own case in Jefferson County Circuit Court in Birmingham, against Saatchi and Fox Broadcasting Co.

'PROFESSIONAL NEGLIGENCE'

The retailer charged Saatchi with breach of guaranty and warranty, misrepresentation, breach of contract and "professional negligence and malpractice."

"As a direct consequence of Saatchi's appalling, unacceptable and shockingly unprofessional performance, Just For Feet's favorable reputation has come under attack, its business has suffered and it has been subjected to the entirely unfounded and unintended public perception that it is a racist or racially insensitive company," the company said in its lawsuit.

At press time, executives for Just For Feet had not returned phone calls for comment. A spokesman for Saatchi said neither the agency nor its attorneys would comment on the pending litigation. In its legal papers, however, the agency claims advertising is a business that has no explicit guidelines and standards, and therefore, it cannot have committed malpractice.

Still, the litigation and publicity have become an embarrassment to other Saatchi offices, said one executive familiar with the situation. The executive blames Advertising Age's Mr. Garfield for Monday morning quarterbacking the spot in print and in TV interviews and stirring up the controversy.

Before the spot aired, "No one ever mentioned racial overtones," the executive said, noting the client selected the agency and its work in a pitch that included DDB Needham Worldwide, FCB Worldwide and TBWA/Chiat/Day.

"Kenya" "was presented to the networks and it was not rejected. This issue never surfaced," he said.

The executive also said the hunters depicted in the spot were a multiracial group, though it was difficult to determine through the camouflage gear.

The executive also denied that Just For Feet and Saatchi planned to go the "controversy as cheap advertising" route, that is, creating a controversy around the "Kenya" spot to generate talk and subsequent publicity. Such tactics can multiply the reach of a spot far beyond the price paid for its original audience.

Many advertising executives and their legal advisers would agree with the non-culpability of the agency.

"This is not a doctor who removes the wrong foot. It is not a big mistake in auditing," said True North's Mr.

Of contracts and claims:
Agencies face liability issues

While the threat of malpractice may be new, advertising agencies have long protected themselves from other legal and ethical perils.

Many liability issues are handled in agency-client contracts. For example, agencies generally use information provided by clients for advertising claims. In standard contracts, the agency is protected from suits involving the accuracy of those claims.

The contract absolves the agency of responsibility if something goes wrong with the advertised product and consumers suffer damages or other product and liability claims arise.

Agencies also buy insurance to protect themselves from claims brought by third parties. For example, if the music or words of a broadcast spot infringe on a copyright or trademark, the agency's indemnity policy would kick in. It also covers ads that might be libelous, slanderous or might violate the privacy of a living individual or the right of publicity held by the estate of a deceased person.

In addition to legal and financial precautions, agencies can take other steps to protect themselves, attorneys say. For one, attorneys suggest agencies talk with clients to set a clear definition of responsibilities. In addition, agencies can hire attorneys, either as consultants or as part of the agency staff, to screen proposed ads before they run.

At True North Communications' FCB Worldwide, all advertising is reviewed by the company's legal department. "We want to see it all," said Jeffrey Michel, associate general council at True North.

The required broadcast network approval of spots before they run is a good stop gap, as well.

Finally, focus groups and other methods of testing a campaign can alert agencies to potential problems.

"You have the vehicles to test it before you put it on the Super Bowl," Mr. Michel said.

—Alice Z. Cuneo

Michel. Advertising, he said, "is a shared expertise and a shared responsibility."

TAKING RESPONSIBILITY

Many clients wouldn't even consider the responsibility shared, but believe it is firmly in their laps.

"I think the client is ultimately responsible," said John Lauck, senior VP-marketing of shoe retailer Footaction, a shoe store chain. "I don't agree with laying the blame on the agency. It speaks poorly of your ability and skills to manage."

Although agencies do carry some legal protection for things that can go wrong (see story at top), most agency executives believe that, ultimately, the client approves the ad and therefore takes responsibility for it. Standing industry philosophy also strongly backs an unfettered creative department.

"How far do we have to go? Build something in [the contract] which says, 'Warning, this advertising might not work'?" asked one attorney who works for agencies and asked not to be identified.

New York attorney David Lehv, whose firm handles the McManus Group, Omnicom Group and WPP Group, said it is "inappropriate for an advertiser to disclaim responsibility for its message," adding a client "cannot be compelled to do advertising that is illegal, immoral or in bad taste." However, Mr. Lehv said, the agency has a responsibility to tell its clients that "their advertising message may be perceived as in bad taste."

Just For Feet attorney Robert Brodegaard said that's just not the case. "Just about everybody else who holds themselves out as an expert, is," Mr. Brodegaard said. "The agency does have a responsibility . . . And somebody should have said stop."

For an agency to claim it doesn't have any responsibility is the equivalent of saying "we have no expertise," he said.

The issue Mr. Brodegaard raises, along with the "Kenya" spot, may take its place in advertising history. For the retailer, the controversy appears to be a small pebble in the Just For Feet shoe.

BANKRUPTCY FILING

In September, Helen Rockey replaced Mr. Ruttenberg as president-CEO; she left four months later.

By November, the company filed for bankruptcy and began liquidating inventory and closing some stores.

The Alabama Securities Commission also has begun a probe of possible financial irregularities.

Last week, Just For Feet filed a motion in U.S. Bankruptcy Court in Wilmington, Del., to liquidate its assets.

69

A New Model

Online Persuaders

The one thing everybody agrees on is this: Web advertising is different; Now, as to what that means...

By John Buskin

Staff Reporter of The Wall Street Journal

When it comes to the Web, advertisers shell out first and ask questions later.

According to figures cited in Adweek magazine, ad spending on the Web reached $917 million in 1997. Last year, the total more than doubled to $1.9 billion. To put that in perspective, in 1998, for the first time, Web ad spending surpassed outdoor billboard spending, which totaled $1.58 billion.

For all those bucks, there's still no consensus on the crucial question: What exactly should Web advertising *be,* anyway? Many agencies apply lessons learned in other media, and use saturation to get their message across: hence, the banner ads slapped across the top of nearly every Web destination.

Others argue that such approaches won't work because surfers aren't as passive as, say, TV viewers. Subtler methods are called for, they say – if you expect Web users to read an ad, you've got to give them some content in return. But such approaches often blur the line between advertising and editorial.

The Theories

The first question to ask when looking at Net ads is what they assume about surfers – are users "active" or "passive" viewers of the Web?

The "passive" tack comes down to thinking of the Web as a variation on television – and of surfers as a variation on TV viewers. Take the most visible kind of Web ad, the banner. These rectangular messages often use animation, sound or other high-tech trickery to try to get you to quit surfing long enough to read them, or click on them. That's basically the approach that TV commercials take: If they're clever enough, the logic goes, the audience can be lured into paying attention.

The "active" camp says those rules simply won't work on the Web. And that's because "we don't *watch* the Internet, we use the Internet," says G.M. O'Connell, chairman and CEO of **True North Communications'** Modem Media.Poppe Tyson operation, one of the first Internet-oriented ad agencies. "No matter how much bandwidth is available, the Web will never be 'watched.'"

What *will* work down the road, Mr.

O'Connell and others say, is a series of approaches that look nothing at all like traditional ads.

For one, this camp sees the Web crunching functions together so that advertising, promotion, marketing, public relations, retailing, distribution and customer retention all reside at the same address. That means that, say, a drug company might sponsor an informational site or forum about illnesses – where surfers would find a link to order the company's products.

Then there's the idea of *giving* users something in exchange for looking at an ad. Mr. O'Connell spelled out this approach in an address at this year's Clios, advertising's version of the Oscars.

"We build brands by providing services to consumers," he told the assembled ad professionals. He says Web advertising is "about what you can do as an advertiser to enable the user at that moment."

In other words, Internet users will never sit still long enough to watch, say, a bunny with Barry White's voice singing about salad dressing – but they might take advantage of an offer like that made by **Yahoo!** Inc. Vice President Seth Godin. Click on an ad for Mr. Godin's book, "Permission Marketing," and you get four chapters e-mailed to you free.

The gap between the two sides in the argument – the active and the passive models – is huge. For an idea of *how* huge, consider the Clios again. For the first time, event organizers had a separate interactive-awards presentation for the best Internet ads.

Asked if creativity alone can sell to large numbers of people on the Web – the idea Mr. O'Connell blasted – one winner in the banner-ad category said, "It works in broadcast."

BANNERS

Catching the Eye

The most popular type of Internet ad is unquestionably the banner. It's also the most controversial in the ad community. Critics say banners are window dressing, as easy to tune out as beer logos at a rock concert. Supporters say the ads are cheap and help distinguish broad-based brands whose products are similar to the competition – products, that is, that depend on brand imagery.

Moreover, they fit the traditional ad-agency formula. They're essentially headlines, and according to the ad manual "Ogilvy on Advertising," five times as many people read the headlines as read body copy.

Even Yahoo's Mr. Godin, who sees Web surfers as "active," thinks banners have value. "Enough banners," he says, "will create a footprint."

Banners *did* get results – at first. Two years ago, Jupiter Communications, a New York research firm, estimated banner ads had a 2% click-through rate, meaning for every 100 "page views" (the number of surfers who visit a page with a banner ad), two people would click on the ad logo. That's better than

most estimates for the response to direct mail.

But now, the click-through rate for banner ads is only about 0.5%, Jupiter says.

That means, according to Jupiter spokeswoman Marissa Gluck, that "banners' dominance will wane."

That assessment seems to be confirmed by at least one academic study. An assistant marketing professor from Rutgers University, Patrali Chatterjee, argues the ads aren't effective because of an important difference between advertising on the Web and on television.

While banner ads don't look like TV commercials, they're designed on the same principle – repetition, says Ms. Chatterjee in "Modeling the Clickstream: Implications for Web-Based Advertising Efforts," a paper published as part of Vanderbilt University's Project 2000, a study of business and media.

> *'There are new [ad] models to be created, new value propositions to be invented,' says one entrepreneur*

Broadcast viewers have no control over their exposure to ad images and consequently need to view them many times to become aware of them, understand their message and finally form an opinion. Ms. Chatterjee calls this progressive understanding "wearin."

In theory, seeing the same banner every time you go to a Web page should have the same effect: You may ignore a banner the first time around, the logic goes, but by the fifth or six time you'll be ready to click and buy.

In reality, it doesn't exactly work like that, Ms. Chatterjee argues. Because Web users can control the amount of time they spend on a page, they can absorb an ad the first time around and make the decision to click or not to click. Response drops steeply thereafter.

CO-BRANDING

Spot the Ad!

After banners come more-complex types of selling, such as co-branded sites. In these arrangements, advertisers form a partnership with a site that provides content. The advertiser then gets to offer information about its own products along with the other, ostensibly objective, information on the site.

"Would I design an ad campaign that just used banners?" asks Robert Levitan, a founder of **iVillage** Inc., an online community that uses co-branding. "No. As a business model, I don't believe in selling just space. Traditional ad values miss the true value of the Web.... There are new models to be created, new value propositions to be invented."

True, he does use *some* traditional ads: Mr. Levitan led the team that sold every pixel's worth of ad space that the iVillage sites had available. Along the way, however, he also invented what he calls the Value Triangle sponsorship model of co-branding. At one point of the triangle is the advertiser, at the second point is the hosting site (iVillage in this case). Balanced on the third point are the "members." (Mr. Levitan uses "members" rather than "users" because iVillage requires users to register to gain access to all community areas.)

The action takes place within the triangle. Consider a triangle sponsorship involving **Merck** & Co. The drug company wanted people with coronary concerns to learn about a new heart medicine; it also wanted to collect data about how patients talk to their doctors. For iVillage, the goal was to attract and serve users who would become repeat visitors. And members wanted information they could use.

So, Merck and iVillage set up a site that provided facts and figures on heart disease, such as a heart-risk calculator and other therapeutic devices.

Health-conscious users flocked to the site. Many requested free brochures from Merck and agreed to be queried by iVillage about whether they made appointments with their doctors to address heart issues. The result: Many of the respondents said they asked their doctors about the Merck product.

Co-branding can also involve more than one advertiser, such as Armchair Millionare, a personal-finance area launched by iVillage in partnership with **Intuit** Inc.'s Quicken.com and **Charles Schwab** Corp., the online broker.

Users were attracted to the pitch: a site loaded with information about how to get rich through a combination of investing and saving. For a co-branding fee, Intuit got to put up links to content on its Quicken.com site, and Schwab could offer links that let users open an interactive investment account. Schwab won many new accounts, mostly from youthful customers with a lifetime of investing ahead of them. And those new investors tracked all their finances using Quicken.

But is co-branding a dangerous mixing of objective information and promotional message? It certainly kicks at the wall between advertising and editorial. Media pundits love to throw around phrases like "commoditized information" or "branded news." Though banners may be less effective, they're more clearly recognized as ads.

Lee Peeler, associate director of the Division of Advertising Practices for the Federal Trade Commission, explains that the organization has two rules with respect to advertising: Advertisements can't be deceptive, and objective claims in ads must be substantiated.

"We are very interested in consumers knowing the difference between objective presentation and presentation with financial interest," Mr. Peeler says.

The agency does random surfing to evaluate advertising on the Internet. As to commercial representations in any media, Mr. Peeler says, "It's got to be clear that it's paid-for content."

The FTC recently held an extensive workshop, "Application of Rules and Guides to Electronic Commerce." Participants – a diverse group of institutions and advertisers from AARP to QVC – discussed different aspects of mock advertisements that were created specifically for the workshop and touched on issues of disclosure and analysis.

Public comment had been solicited well in advance of the workshop and is posted on the FTC Web site. Not surprisingly, groups such as the Direct Marketing Association posted long statements including comments like, "in the laudable pursuit of consumer protection, we urge the Commission to be mindful of the potential for inadvertent stifling of commercial expression and the imposition of unnecessarily burdensome restrictions."

America Online Inc. urged caution in the face of changing technology: "Given the unique and still-developing characteristics of the Internet, the Commission should proceed very carefully and deliberately in any proposed application of the rules and guides themselves in this new medium."

PERMISSION MARKETING

Getting Personal

There's another school of thought on cyber-advertising that sidesteps many of the co-branding concerns. In "Permission Marketing," Yahoo's Mr. Godin advocates the title concept: bartering for the attention of consumers, offering them some product in exchange for listening to a pitch.

"Time is worth more than money," he says. "People won't give up time unless they're going to get something back." Case in point: the four free chapters of Mr. Godin's book.

In contrast, he characterizes nearly all conventional advertising and promotion as "interruption marketing."

The Internet is a natural environment for permission marketing, he writes, because of e-mail communication and its growing ability to close sales and, in the case of informational products, fulfill them.

But Mr. Godin argues that once an advertiser has the consumer hooked, there's a next step to the process. Instead of pouring resources into growing market share, Mr. Godin argues, a business should try to sell as much product as it can to existing customers. Mr. Godin calls this "driving for share of customer" – something like the growth of Amazon.com, a service that began with just books, but continues to absorb smaller companies and expand its line of different products. Because the bookstore established trust with its customer base, he argues, those customers will stick around and use Amazon as a one-stop shopping source.

"The true value of any one customer is a function of the customer's future purchases, across all the product lines, brands and services offered by you," he argues.

THE FUTURE

I, Bot

While the direct approach of permission marketing may be a counterpoint to advertising's sly "Hidden Persuaders" of the 1950s (reed-thin ballerinas plugging gooey chocolates, for example), the battle for consumers may ultimately be swayed by something even more sinister: hidden technology.

In "Bots," his book about the automated software programs that prowl the Web, Andrew Leonard warns that these virtual rascals may come to influence our buying habits, without our knowing it. A company might send a bot into a chat room, say, to talk up the business, while programming the thing to masquerade as an ordinary human being.

"That chat room participant singing the praises of Apple's new operating system?" writes Mr. Leonard. It could be "a lying, no-good propagandabot."

And, according to Mr. Leonard, that's just the tip of the iceberg. "Bots will begin constructing profiles of human behavior that dwarf what is currently possible from reviewing a credit-card trail or a bar-code-generated record...." Bigbrotherbot?

So if bots and agents can hone a Web advertiser's ability to cumulatively fine-tune your profile, you and your family will become an entire target market. They'll know the rate of your consumption and the storage capacity of your house so accurately that they'll sell you a year's worth of toilet paper, toothpaste or Q-tips all at once. If they do that with large groups of Mr. Godin's "collected customers," they, and we, can reap huge savings of scale.

So, what does that do to the argument about active and passive viewers? Maybe the next step up from us using the Internet is the Internet using *us*.

Shopper Turns Lots of Pudding Into Free Miles

BY JANE COSTELLO

Staff Reporter of THE WALL STREET JOURNAL

David Phillips found a lifetime of free plane trips in a cup of chocolate pudding.

Last May, Mr. Phillips was shopping in the frozen-food aisle of his local supermarket when he noticed a frequent-flier offer on the package of a Healthy Choice frozen entree: Earn 500 miles for every 10 Universal Product Codes from Healthy Choice products sent in to Healthy Choice by Dec. 31. Any "early birds" who submitted the UPCs, or bar codes, by May 31 would receive double the mileage – 1,000 miles for every 10 bar codes.

Mr. Phillips, a 35-year-old civil engineer with the University of California at Davis, flies only sporadically each year. Until he made that fateful trip to the grocery store, his largest frequent-flier account had a 40,000-mile balance. "I quickly did the math and realized what this could mean," he says.

With an investment of $3,140 and 50 hours of his time, Mr. Phillips is the proud owner of 1.25 million frequent-flier miles, good for about $25,000 worth of airline tickets. "He's got a lifetime of free travel now," says Mark Kienzle, a spokesman for **AMR** Corp.'s American Airlines.

It's common for consumers to stock up on products to acquire frequent-flier miles. Susan Michael, a real-estate broker from suburban Chicago, bought between 200 and 300 liters of Diet Coke last year to earn frequent-flier miles from Delta Air Lines. "The trunk was so full I'd get worried about the tires on my car," she says. And David Fisher, a computer salesman from Issaquah, Wash., racked up an additional 12,000 **Northwest Airlines** miles by participating in the Healthy Choice promotion last year.

Mr. Phillips, however, is in his own stratosphere. Here's how he did it.

With only three weeks to take advantage of the early-bird offer, Mr. Phillips calculated the best way to maximize his mileage. He contemplated buying an additional freezer to hold the frozen entrees but decided to shop around for cheaper products from Healthy Choice, a brand of **ConAgra** Inc., Omaha, Neb.

While scouring the city for cans of Healthy Choice soup on special, Mr. Phillips happened upon **Grocery Outlet,** a supermarket chain that sells excess inventory to consumers at a discount. He emerged from the store with a full shopping cart and a new identity: Pudding Guy.

"I found the gold mine: cups of chocolate pudding selling for 25 cents apiece," says Mr. Phillips, who subsequently began using the handle Pudding Guy for his online correspondence. "That's when I started to get serious," he says.

He obtained a list of Grocery Outlets from the store manager and set out with his mother-in-law to wipe out the inventory between Davis and Fresno. They went to 10 stores, filling a van with thousands of cups of Healthy Choice chocolate pudding. The manager of the Grocery Outlet in Davis ordered him an additional 60 cases, bringing the final tally to 12,150 cups of pudding.

When it became apparent that he and his wife couldn't possibly remove the labels in time to meet the double-mileage deadline, Mr. Phillips decided to donate the pudding to local food banks. In exchange for globs of free pudding, workers at the Salvation Army in Sacramento and other local charities agreed to peel off the UPC symbols as they dished out the desserts at breakfast, lunch and dinner.

Mr. Phillips incurs no tax obligation from his mileage, which isn't considered income because it derived from a purchase. In fact, he plans to claim the entire $3,140 pudding purchase as a charitable deduction, yielding a tax savings of about $815, bringing down his total cost to $2,325.

A former Internal Revenue Service commissioner, Don Alexander, says writing off the entire purchase might be too aggressive. "Technically, an allocation should be made between the value of the pudding and the value of the frequent-flier miles," he says. "Had he given the charities the frequent-flier miles along with the pudding, he would be entitled to the full deduction."

Another caveat from the ex-commissioner: "Naturally, he can't deduct the cost of the puddings he ate."

A federal tax official declined to comment on whether Mr. Phillips's efforts will fly come April 15. "There is no specific ruling that would address the facts in this case," said a spokesman for the Internal Revenue Service.

Last week, American Airlines posted the last of 1.04 million miles to Mr. Phillips's AAdvantage account. He divided the remaining 216,000 miles between Northwest, Delta and **UAL** Corp.'s United Airlines. He could sell some of these miles to other fliers but says he has no plans to do that. He is planning to take his wife and two children to Europe this spring (flying coach) and is looking forward to a later trip to New Zealand (business class).

Joan Lukas, a spokeswoman for Healthy Choice, declined to comment on the promotion's sales or participant data, except to say that the frequent-flier offer "met and even exceeded expectations."

Healthy Choice purchased the miles in advance from the airlines, as is customary. Most carriers sell blocks of frequent-flier miles to companies for two cents a mile. United has set up a special Web site to spur sales of "Reward Miles." Continental Airlines has a special "Miles of Thanks" section on its Web site to encourage businesses to reward customers with OnePass miles.

American Airlines has more than 3,000 businesses participating in its "American Airlines Incentive Miles" program, which it markets to large and small companies alike. Although officials at the airline maintain silence on the number of miles awarded in total to Healthy Choice participants in last year's promotion, they say they are pleased with the results.

"We're looking forward to working with Healthy Choice again," Mr. Kienzle says. He points out that American benefits twice: companies pay it for the miles and some consumers buy extra tickets for family or friends.

In most instances, miles earned through nonflight-related activities don't qualify travelers for an airline's coveted elite status. But Pudding Guy is now golden at American: The airline confers lifetime AAdvantage Gold status on people who accumulate a million miles, regardless of how they are earned. Gold privileges include access to a special reservations number, priority boarding, upgrades and bonus miles.

All that's enough for Mr. Phillips, who realizes the extraordinary nature of his tale. "It was like a harmonic convergence of pudding and promotion," he says. "That doesn't happen every day."

Price

GIVING AWAY THE E-STORE

The Web has become a freebie fest. Can firms make money offering something for nothing?

by Karl Taro Greenfeld

Yaron Zilberman, 33, and Guy Blachman, 28, have made all the right moves. They have M.B.A.s from top business schools, $8 million in venture capital and a snazzy Trump Place apartment and office suite on Manhattan's West Side. They also have Gooey, an innovative Web application that allows visitors to any website to chat with other Gooey users at the same site. Zilberman and Blachman will tell you it's a killer app, one that will turn the whole Internet into a billion-voice AOL chat room. So how much is Hypernix, their company, charging for this product?

Nothing. Like hundreds of high-tech and Internet companies, Hypernix has embraced the business of free. You name the product, and someone out there wants you to have it gratis. There are at least five companies giving away PCs, five offering Internet access, a couple promising long-distance calls at zero cents a minute, three passing out voice-mail boxes, one seeking the privilege of doing your faxing and another that wants to give you postage. You want e-mail? Pick from a dozen companies that would love to be your no-cost provider. Once you're online with your free PC, you may want to trade stocks–American Express Brokerage will provide free trading for accounts over $100,000. Amex won't do your taxes, but H.D. Vest, another financial planner, has just volunteered. Other software needs? Linux is a free operating system, and Sun Microsystems' StarOffice is a complimentary office suite.

Why the proliferation of businesses that are literally giving away the store? "We're moving from an economy where people pay directly for services to an attention-based economy," says Joe Krause, senior vice president of content at Excite@Home. "What's valuable for businesses is not necessarily the money being directly paid but rather the consumer's attention." Most of these businesses–like Free-PC, which offers a free computer in exchange for a constant ad presence on your desktop, and NetZero, an Internet provider–are relying on advertisers and marketers to provide their income. They subscribe to the old Net mantra: Get Big Fast. Gather enough eyeballs, aggregate enough consumer-shopping habits and click-through tendencies, and sellers will pay a premium to get at your customers.

One might rightly ask: How much does all this free stuff cost? In the case of PCs, some firms, like InterSquid and PeoplePC, provide quality computers that come with multiyear contracts requiring the user to sign for dial-up Internet access at somewhat pricey rates–a deal many consumers might regret when high-speed Internet access becomes widely available. AltaVista, a free Internet service provider, runs a narrow, scrolling banner across your screen that requires you to click through–interact with the ad–every hour.

Although free everything seems like another Internet innovation, it's actually a century-old strategy. King Gillette gave away his safety razor and made a fortune selling the blades. Perhaps you remember something called broadcast television, which was preceded, in

YES, A FREE LAUNCH

New companies are popping up to give away stuff that others still sell

HARDWARE

■ **FREE** Free-PC, InterSquid and PeoplePC give away computers, but there are strings attached

■ **PAY** You can spend up to $5,000 for computers from IBM, Dell and other makers

OPERATING SYSTEMS

■ **FREE** Linux, the OS of the Web proletariat, is popular with programmers and other digerati

■ **PAY** Microsoft's monopoly on the for-profit OS has hurt consumers and slowed innovation, say feds

INTERNET-SERVICE PROVIDERS

■ **FREE** If you will click on demand, such sites as AltaVista, NetZero and WorldSpy will give you Net access

■ **PAY** In the land of the free you still pay Earthlink, WorldNet and AOL, three of the biggest ISPs, for a hookup

E-COMMERCE

■ **FREE** *Bigstep.com* and *OLB.com* will set up your e-store and design your e-commerce site

■ **PAY** Yahoo, IBM and Razorfish have for-profit businesses in e-commerce development

(Cont.)

the 1920s, by broadcast radio. RCA created the NBC network to sell radios.

These classic business models are being embraced by an Internet industry that can't dispense money fast enough. "With $60 billion in uninvested capital in the hands of venture capitalists, every gimmick ever thought of will be funded," says Ann Winblad, partner with Hummer Winblad, one of the best-known venture-capital firms. "We have seen free everything walk through our office. Still waiting for Free House."

The Net has always been conducive to giving away high-tech gewgaws. Browsers like Netscape's Navigator and Microsoft's Explorer have long been free. And in 1997 RealNetworks became a new media power by handing out its media player to build market share. Then Sabir Bhatia, co-founder of free e-mail provider Hotmail, sold his company in 1997 to Microsoft for $400 million, or $44 per user. "What hit people when Microsoft bought Hotmail was how much they paid per user," says Diane Greene, CEO of VMware, a Palo Alto, Calif., software firm. "All of a sudden, eyeballs were worth a lot of money."

Entrepreneurs of the pro bono model worship Hotmail—even though the company never made a profit. They overlook the fact that what made Hotmail hot was one of the stickiest applications out there—once you have an e-mail address, you tend to keep visiting the site—and a one-year ramp up to 5 million users. Start-up founders fantasize about that 400 mil. "Now there are so many companies, and you ask them what their revenue model is and they say, 'I don't know. We just want to get big fast and get acquired, like Hotmail,'" says Bhatia. "That's scary when entrepreneurs don't think through how they are going to make money."

Zilberman vows that Gooey will be profitable—he's just not sure when. He says Gooey needs a minimum of 3 million users within a year. Today he's got about 300,000. "Nobody has ever done our business model successfully," he concedes as he heads into Hypernix's next round of fund raising. "But we are talking about really high-quality reach media."

That's another word for targeted advertising. The two-way nature of the Net makes it possible for advertisers to know a lot about you (sometimes without your knowing it) so they can deliver more effective ads. Web entrepreneurs are counting on advertisers paying a higher CPM (cost per thousand) for this rifle-shot data than they do for the old shotgun approach. "We charge more than average because each advertiser can see how their ad is performing with each demographic and can then focus their campaign," says Steve Chadima, founder of Free-PC. Forrester Research estimates that Internet advertising will grow from $2.8 billion in 1999 to $22 billion in 2004. But with click-through rates hovering at under 1%, those ad dollars will support only a handful of the many businesses that are making a go of the giveaway. "It'll be a dogfight," says Chan Suh, CEO of Net advertising operation Agency.com. "People who think that advertising makes up for the lack of a biz model and execution are going to fall by the wayside."

The Gooey guys have no doubts about their model. But neither does their competitor, Third Voice, another free client that allows users to post on websites. These two Internet software firms will be battling it out for eyeballs, advertisers and traffic. One thing you can bet on, however: no price wars.

With reporting by Susan Kuchinskas/San Francisco and Julie Rawe/New York City

73

LEMONADE STANDS ON ELECTRIC AVENUE

Net sales booths sell everything from staplers to pet products

You won't find many shops on Main Street that sell strictly refrigerator magnets. The items are cheap, and demand for them is rarely strong enough to justify renting an entire storefront. They're the ultimate in a niche business. On the Internet, however, none of that matters.

Just ask Chris Gwynn of Quincy, Mass. His two-year-old online magnet store, Fridge-door.com, which he started as a part-time gig, has allowed him to quit a well-paying job and focus exclusively on his startup.

The Web is spawning a world of just such virtual lemonade stands–home-based businesses that hawk everything from staplers to accessories for Jack Russell terriers. Thanks to the Net's global reach, these tiny sales booths can appeal to a highly dispersed group of customers–and prosper. Gwynn is making 200 to 400 sales a week: Austin Powers and Scooby-Doo! are hot right now. "An inch wide and a mile deep," says Gwynn, who was formerly an analyst at Yankee Group Research Inc. "That's what I'm going after."

If 1998 was the year that mainstream Corporate America discovered E-commerce, 1999 may well be the year that all the Toms, Dicks, and Harriets with dreams of being their own bosses hang out a shingle in cyberspace. "There are a lot of people who have a passion," says Bo Peabody, co-founder of Tripod, an online community hosting the home pages of 3.7 million members. "Now they're turning that passion into a business."

And they're doing it in droves. Around 30,000 small businesses–outfits with annual revenues of less than $10 million–now take orders over the Web, according to Keenan Vision Inc., a San Francisco consulting firm. That's up from just 200 companies in 1996–and should grow to 400,000 by 2003. Already, some 3 million more people make a living from home than was the case in 1995, according to International Data Corp. And experts believe many of them soon will start selling via the Web.

It all adds up to one of the few big exceptions to the massive consolidation trend of the past decade. Large numbers of people who have full-time jobs can experiment with E-commerce businesses on the side, boosting their income or living out a fantasy. A subset of them will even quit their day jobs. "This is a fundamental transformation," says Steve Westly, vice-president for marketing at auction site eBay Inc.

Perhaps–but these lemonade stands still face huge questions of sustainability. After all, some of the nation's biggest sellers of goods–from supermarkets to Wal-Mart Stores to Sears Roebuck–have barely begun to dabble in E-commerce. When they go whole hog, a lot of small-time Web merchants could find their niches swallowed up. The pressure is on them to establish a position now and become big enough to fend off competition.

It's surprisingly easy to get started. You don't need to keep any inventory–or even sell your own products. The least sophisticated way that people are adding to their income is by becoming "affiliates" of larger businesses, such as the Amazon.com Inc. shopping site. Its 260,000 affiliates position an Amazon banner or button on their home pages. When a visitor clicks on the link and buys something from Amazon, the affiliate gets a cut ranging from 5% to 15%.

The key to being a successful affiliate is offering content so compelling that Web surfers not only flock to your site but also click through it to buy related products. In Britain, David Campion has built a Web site that includes the lyrics to every Nirvana song, a time line on the grunge band, speculation on lead singer Kurt Cobain's suicide–and a link via an affiliate button to CDNow. He makes a 7% commission or more on every CD sale that originates from his site.

Alison Yoshikawa, however, can tell you what happens when your Web site has little to do with the affiliate link. The business-products broker, selling mainly electrical and janitorial supplies to companies near her Northern California home, has increased sales three- or fourfold by putting her business on the Net. But she hasn't made a single cent off of the link to barnesandnoble.com that her 25-year-old daughter installed on the Web site 10 months ago. After all, how many people who are ordering a mop are inclined

to buy a copy of *The Iliad* at the same time?

Another way to join the game is by selling goods on one of the big auction sites, such as eBay and Amazon. While most of the people who sell items at auctions are trying to clear out their attics, others are making real businesses out of it. Indeed, eBay says more than 10,000 people now make all or a big chunk of their salary through its site alone.

One of them is Wendy Gem Davis, a 30-year-old Alabamian with five children,

---

Help for Mom-and-Pop E-Shops

What Internet companies are doing to help the small fry set up their virtual lemonade stands

LYCOS On July 12, the No. 2 portal announced that it would allow members of its Tripod community to link online auctions to their home pages–the first such program.

HYPERMART The largest community of small businesses—some 360,000—will add full E-commerce capability later this year. That means Mom-and-Pop shops won't have to build their own security or electronic shopping carts.

SHOPNOW.COM The E-commerce company has created a massive online catalog and a warehouse of products, called MyShopNow.com, allowing individuals to create ministores without having to worry about inventory or shipping. Individuals get a 5% cut of any sales made off of their sites.

EBAY Starting in July, sellers and buyers using the eBay online auction site will be able to get updates on their offers and bids via Skytel pagers. Later this year: the same service via telephones.

(Cont.)

including 5-year-old quadruplets. About 2 1/2 years ago, she logged onto then-obscure eBay to see if she could buy any porcelain figurines for her collection. When she saw all the buying and selling going on, she realized it could be the perfect way to supplement her husband's salary without leaving her kids. "I felt like I could do this," Davis says, "and it just started taking off."

She has gone from trading figurines to selling clothing her kids had grown out of to driving to the nearby Walt Disney discount outlet and stocking up on cut-rate goods. She then marks them up–usually by 100%–and sells them to people as far away as Australia and Kuwait. She brings in a profit between $1,000 and $5,000 a month, and the extra income has allowed her family to move to a bigger house.

Now, the Internet community sites plan on making it even easier for small fry to get a flying start. Later this year, HyperMart Inc. will launch a service allowing Netrepreneurs to sell goods over the Web without building their own security or electronic shopping

Some people are starting online businesses by becoming affiliates of sites such as Amazon.com

carts. They'll simply pay $100 or so a month and link up with HyperMart's technology.

Major Internet companies also are lending a helping hand, hoping to build their own traffic in the process. They're enabling merchants to set up a store from scratch in a few days, with almost no technical savvy and for about $500 in startup costs and $150 to $350 per month after that. Web portal Lycos Inc., for example, just connected its members' Web sites to its auction listings. That enables merchants to present much more information about a product than they could on the auction site itself–and still show real-time updates on the bidding.

That's a boon to people like Davis. But it can't shield her if one day Disney decides to start selling its outlet goods online and leaves her without a niche. "These small, scrappy

folks can do well," says Tim Brady, vice-president for production at the Yahoo! Inc. portal. "But it's also very easy on the Internet for Wal-Mart to see what's popular and why someone's doing well."

That's what happened to Paula Jagemann, a part-time executive assistant who last year set up a Web site to sell office supplies. Things started well enough, but then Staples and Office Depot got into the act. Jagemann quickly refocused on helping established stationers set up E-businesses.

And that's the rub. While it's true that there are enormous opportunities for entrepreneurs on the Web, they can disappear quickly. Flexibility is the watchword. Otherwise, mom-and-pop shops can be left with little more than a bitter taste in their mouths.

By David Leonhardt
Contributing: David Rocks

'BUILD A BETTER MOUSETRAP' IS NO CLAPTRAP

Yes, companies can hike prices—if they reinvent their products

When Gillette Co. unveiled Mach3, the world's first triple-blade razor, it took a bold gamble. While deflationary pressure was making it impossible for most companies to charge high prices for new products, Mach3 cartridges were to sell for around $1.60 each, a 50% premium over Gillette's then-priciest blade, the SensorExcel. Skeptics predicted the personal-care giant would soon be forced to cut that price. But six months after Mach3 hit U.S. stores, the price is holding and Mach3 has become the No. 1 blade and razor. Gillette had 70.7% of the U.S. market in December, its highest share since 1962.

Most companies would kill for a product with this kind of pricing power. In a new survey by the Financial Executives Institute and Duke University, chief financial officers from all industries said they expect price hikes to average just 1.4% in 1999. Manufacturers say they'll manage a gain of only 0.2%. And some 25% of U.S. companies, in industries from breakfast cereal to autos, will have to cut prices, figures Gary Stibel, a founder and principal of the New England Consulting Group.

REALLY BIG SHOE PADS. But an elite few are bucking the trend by introducing "new products that provide benefits people think are worth paying for," says Gillette CEO Alfred M. Zeien. Colgate-Palmolive Co., for example, priced Colgate Total 25% above mainstream brands because Total is the first paste approved by the Food & Drug

> Pricey toothbrushes are appealing to aging baby boomers who want to enter old age with their own choppers

Administration to help prevent gingivitis. After a year, Total is the No. 1 brand, with a nearly 10% share. Dr. Scholl's, a unit of Schering-Plough Corp., has taken the lowly shoe-insert pad and used biomechanics to transform it into a remedy for leg and back pain. The new product, Dynastep, sells for as much as $14 per insert, twice as much as older inserts—and since 1997, it has become the No. 1 device, with 29% of the market.

What's the secret to pricing power? For starters, a commitment to innovation. Gillette spent nearly $1 billion on the development and initial marketing of Mach3. Similarly, a stream of breakthroughs allows Sony Corp. to command a premium even for TVs, where prices have been falling. Thanks in part to the Wega, the world's first conventional flat-screen TV, Sony's TV sales rocketed 24% in the first half of its fiscal 1998.

Of course, pricing power is often fleeting. Intel Corp., for one, has had to cut prices of low-end chips as rivals have brought out similar products. But Intel remains "the only game in town" for high-end chips, says Ashok Kumar, senior research analyst for Piper Jaffray Inc. Intel is charging $3,692 for its latest Pentium II Xeon processor—or $3,271 above the production cost, according to MicroDesign Resources. "It's a license to print money," says Kumar.

It also helps to aim products at the affluent. They "are willing to pay a lot more to save time or obtain other significant benefits," says Christopher Hoyt, a marketing consultant in Stamford, Conn. Maytag Corp.'s environment-friendly Neptune washer is a hit among well-off consumers, even though at $1,100, it costs twice as much as conventional washers. Over the course of a year, it uses $100 less electricity than other washers and saves 7,000 gallons of water—as much as a person drinks in a lifetime.

BLITZKRIEG. Even the humble toothbrush has undergone a price-boosting metamorphosis—thanks to aging baby boomers who want to keep their choppers. Gillette's Oral-B Laboratories is betting that it can charge $5—50% more than current top-line rivals—for its new CrossAction brush, due in February. Oral-B claims its unique design will remove 25% more plaque than today's best-selling brush.

The pricing elite also back their products with lavish ad spending. Gillette is sinking $300 million into marketing Mach3 in its first year. Ian Cook, president of Colgate North America, boasts that an "unprecedented"

> **WHERE THE PRICING POWER IS**
>
> **COLGATE TOTAL TOOTHPASTE**
> 25% higher than conventional toothpaste, now No. 1 brand
>
> **GILLETTE'S MACH3 RAZOR**
> $1.60 per cartridge, 50% more than SensorExcel, now top seller
>
> **MAYTAG'S NEPTUNE WASHER**
> $1,100, double the average washer, now No. 2

blitzkrieg on dentist's offices made Total "the toothpaste most recommended by dentists and hygienists" in its first four months.

Inevitably, some pricing power champs lose muscle. "Three years ago, Nike was a controlling factor," says Chet James, owner of Super Jock 'n Jill, a Seattle running-shoe store. But thanks to a style shift to brown shoes, a plunge in Asian demand, and Michael Jordan's retirement, "right now, it's not pricing power but buying power" that's at the forefront. In autos, a global capacity glut has meant that "prices have actually gone down," says DaimlerChrysler Co-Chairman Robert J. Eaton.

The message seems clear. While competing on price can work, the success of the pricing elite suggests there may be a better way. "Most companies don't take a bold enough position to invest in the development of superior products that can command a premium price," argues Jeffrey M. Hill, managing director of Meridian Consulting Group. Given the potential rewards, perhaps they should.

By William C. Symonds in Boston, with bureau reports

Competing Online, Drugstore Chains Virtually Undersell Themselves

Their Web Sites Charge Less Than Their Own Stores, With Some Strings Attached

By Laura Johannes
Staff Reporter of The Wall Street Journal

Cecil Powell Grant didn't want to pay a lot for his cholesterol-lowering medication, so he went online to price shop.

A few mouse clicks later, he discovered that CVS.com, a Web site owned by **CVS** Corp., the big drugstore chain, would sell him his monthly ration of Lipitor for only $78.68 – with free mail delivery. At his neighborhood CVS store, it costs $99.

Waging war in one of the scrappiest battles under way on the Web, the biggest drugstore chains – CVS, **Walgreen** Co., **Rite Aid** Corp. and the Eckerd unit of **J.C. Penney** Co. – have begun offering medicines online at prices 10% to 30% cheaper than those in their own stores. Other drugstore items, from shaving cream to diapers, are also sold at bargain prices online.

"I was shocked to find out that CVS is underselling its own retail stores online," says the 56-year-old Mr. Grant, who lives in Cincinnati. "Why would anybody go to a drugstore when they can get it cheaper from the same company online?"

Many of those who might be beneficiaries of cut-rate prescription prices online lack access to the Internet.

Asking a similar question, retailers of all kinds with a Web presence have approached the Internet gingerly, carefully avoiding online discounts that could ultimately drive down in-store prices.

But there are some notable exceptions. In May, after **Amazon.com** Inc. started offering bestsellers at half the publishers' list prices, **barnesandnoble.com** Inc. matched the discount – even though that meant it was massively underselling stores run by **Barnes & Noble** Inc., which has a 40% stake in barnesandnoble.com.

J&R Music & Computer World, a New York City music and electronics retailer, offers a handful of special bargains to lure Internet surfers to its Web site. If a customer walks into J&R and asks for the Internet discount, employees are instructed to give him the cheaper price. "We don't want the Web to be a venue that will undercut our bricks-and-mortar stores," says J&R spokesman Abe Brown.

Among the retailers that do undersell their own stores online, none do so as aggressively as the pharmacy chains, where competition is particularly intense. The Web's drug retailers monitor rivals' prices and often adjust their own to match others' discounts. "Prices on the Web are so visible, that you have to be competitive with online providers," says Jim Smith, vice president of electronic commerce at Eckerd.

People with insurance pay the same amount whether they buy the drugs online or in stores. The price differentials apply only to the 70 million Americans who don't have prescription-drug insurance benefits. They account for 10% to 20% of retail medicine sales, but cash customers' prescriptions are high-profit-margin purchases that help offset the discounts given to managed-care and government buyers.

Internet prescription sales in 1999 represented a small slice – about $160 million – of the $101 billion U.S. market, according to Forrester Research Inc., an Internet research firm in Cambridge, Mass. Eckerd, CVS and Walgreen say they have no evidence of cash business defecting from their stores to the Internet. A Rite Aid spokeswoman says that the company's deal with drugstore.com leaves online pricing decisions to the Internet company, while giving Rite Aid a prominent online presence. In most cases, customers must use mail delivery to get the discounts. But Rite Aid, under a deal with Internet start-up **drugstore.com** Inc., allows customers to buy online at Internet prices and pick up their purchases the same day at a Rite Aid store.

Scrambling to Catch Up

Internet start-ups such as Soma.com and drugstore.com launched the first major e-drugstores last year, verifying prescriptions by phone or fax. Conventional drugstore chains scrambled to catch up. In June, CVS bought Soma. That same month, Rite Aid bought a large minority stake, now 22%, in drugstore.com. Eckerd, going it alone, started selling prescription drugs online in August. Walgreen followed in October.

For now, this isn't a price break that's helping the majority of elderly and uninsured cash customers, whose plight has become a major issue with legislators in Washington and state capitals.

Tricia Smith, a health lobbyist at AARP, the big advocacy group for retirees, explains: "Older Americans and those who have no insurance are the stand-alone groups paying higher prices, and they can least afford it. Ironically, they are among the least likely to access Internet prices so they are left out of the opportunity."

Nationwide, 38.5% of all households have access to the Internet, says Kenneth B. Clemmer, an analyst at Forrester Research. But only 8% of households headed by someone over the age of 65 are online, he says.

The Web Drug Price Gap

A sampling of drug-price savings offered online to cash customers

- ◆ **Claritin** (allergy)
  Dosage: 30 pills, 10 mg.
  Walgreen.com price: $58.99, with free mail delivery
  Price at Walgreen store in Newark, N.J.: $67.19
  Internet savings: $8.20, or 12%

- ◆ **Fossamax** (osteoporosis)
  Dosage: 30 pills, 10 mg.
  CVS.com price: $53.76, with free mail delivery
  Price at CVS store in Akron, Ohio: $69.99
  Internet savings: $16.23, or 23%

- ◆ **Lipitor** (cholestrol)
  Dosage: 30 pills, 20 mg.
  Drugstore.com price: $74.94, with free mail delivery or pickup at Rite Aid stores
  Price at Rite Aid store in Albany, N.Y.: $105.98
  Internet savings: $31.04, or 29%

- ◆ **Zantac** (ulcer)
  Dosage: 30 pills, 300 mg.
  Eckerd.com price: $82.15
  Price at Eckerd store in Dallas: $92.60
  Internet savings: $10.45, or 11%

(Cont.)

A Matter of Convenience

Other patients, even those with Internet access, won't shop online because they like the convenience of drugstore pickup, says Lawrence J. Zigerelli, CVS's vice president for corporate development. Half of CVS's prescriptions are for urgently needed medications, such as antibiotics or painkillers, he says.

CVS.com's Chief Executive Tom Pigott says the Web site is bringing in customers from areas such as California, where CVS does not have stores. Still, Mr. Zigerelli says the company will carefully monitor whether CVS.com is eroding store sales and will adjust online prices – now an average 15% lower than CVS's store prices – if needed.

"We expect there will be fallout and consolidation among smaller players," CVS.com's Mr. Pigott says.

Marie Toulantis, chief financial officer of barnesandnoble.com's, defends the online discounts. "People have to eat the shipping charges and make an investment in a computer. It's a lot of work," she says.

Besides, Ms. Toulantis adds, while online retailers are losing money now, in the long run, it is a cheaper way to conduct business.

For now, the competition is brutal. Mr. Grant ultimately ended up getting his Lipitor at **PlanetRx.com** Inc.'s Web site for $73.97 – $5 less than the CVS.com price.

Vaccine's Price Drives a Debate About Its Use

By Gardiner Harris

Staff Reporter of The Wall Street Journal

When an influential government health panel meets today, it will face a wrenching question: Should it recommend scaling back the use of a major new childhood vaccine simply because of its unusually high price?

Hopes are still high that the vaccine, called Prevenar, will prevent scores of deaths and millions of illnesses in the U.S. from meningitis, pneumonia, blood poisoning and ear infections. But at $232 for a four-dose series, Prevenar will cost as much as all other approved childhood vaccinations combined.

That price is just too high, say some doctors advising the government. So instead of giving the vaccine to all children up to age five, as it had voted to do in October, the Centers for Disease Control and Prevention's Advisory Committee on Immunization Practices is expected to recommend that Prevenar be given just to the children at highest risk: those under the age of two.

Today's vote also portends a looming problem for government vaccine experts, who rarely worry about price. For decades, research has proved that vaccines save more money than they cost by preventing expensive and deadly illnesses. As most new vaccines came along, government panels readily recommended that all American children get them. And the government has picked up much of the tab, paying for half of all childhood immunizations in the U.S.

But as manufacturers increasingly target less-severe illnesses with pricey medications, government experts will be forced to begin debating if the cure is worth the cost. This same debate has for years roiled adult medical care – and has emerged as central in discussions over the future of Medicare – but it is only now making its way into childhood vaccines.

"In the past the ACIP has not focused heavily on vaccine cost," says John Modlin, chairman of the CDC committee. "I think we are being forced to do so now." He notes: "Government largesse isn't bottomless."

Many in the medical community don't like making such choices. "A lot of us are very uncomfortable" balancing medical benefits with economic considerations, notes Jon Abramson, chairman of the committee of infectious diseases for the American Academy of Pediatrics and a non-voting member of the ACIP.

No one is disputing Prevenar's medical value. The vaccine targets pneumococcal bacteria that cause about 3,000 cases of meningitis, thousands more cases of blood poisoning, 100,000 to 135,000 hospitalizations for pneumonia and millions of infant ear infections every year in the U.S.

A narrower age range would be a disappointment to **American Home Products** Corp., which manufactures Prevenar. The company expects to receive approval this week from the U.S. Food and Drug Administration to market the vaccine, based on clinical trials on children under the age of two. It says that Prevenar is worth its high price.

While the outcome of today's ACIP vote isn't certain, some prominent committee members predict that Prevenar's price will lead to a change in the recommendation.

The FDA concerns itself only with whether a vaccine is safe and effective. The CDC debates whether a vaccine is needed and, more recently, whether it's worth the price. Critics worry that the government's vaccine committees aren't set up to engage in this kind of cost-benefit assessment.

"The ACIP is mostly made up of infectious-disease experts who see the people who die and suffer from infectious disease. There are not enough people thinking in terms of health economics, where to put health-care dollars," says Richard K. Zimmerman, an associate professor at the University of Pittsburgh and a non-voting member of the ACIP.

Several nonvoting members of the CDC's vaccine committee grumbled in October when the committee granted a conditional recommendation of Prevenar before the manufacturer had told any of them what the price would be.

This meant, these members argued, that the CDC had surrendered any power in negotiating a lower price. The CDC should instead insist that manufacturers provide their suggested price with their application, so price can be part of the discussions from the beginning, these members say.

Peter Paradiso, vice president for scientific affairs and research strategy for the Wyeth-Ayerst Laboratories division of American Home, says the price of Prevenar simply wasn't available earlier.

Dr. Modlin says that the ACIP voted in October to recommend the vaccine before it knew the price in part because each week's delay means more preventable infant deaths. "The desire is to have as little delay as possible," Dr. Modlin says. "I don't know whether playing cat and mouse with the company affects the price."

The vaccine has been under development since 1986, and it has seven different types of the pneumococcal bacteria. "That costs a lot of money," Dr. Paradiso says. He also notes that immunizing older kids is more cost-effective than immunizing infants, because children two and older need just one shot, not four. Each shot costs $58.

However, experts concerned about the overall cost of a vaccination program argue that vaccinating kids ages two and older – who aren't as susceptible to illness – isn't nearly as beneficial.

Promotions for Cut-Rate Long Distance Draw Fire

Deluged by Complaints, Regulators to Investigate If Fine Print Is Too Fine

By Kathy Chen

Staff Reporter of The Wall Street Journal

WASHINGTON – When Charles Harris saw a television ad touting a special number that would let him make a 20-minute long-distance call for 99 cents, he thought he saw a sweet deal.

Until he got his phone bill, that is. The 58-year-old retiree from Ooltewah, Tenn., had made some 20 calls to his children out of state using the 10-10-220 number, from **MCI WorldCom** Corp., but got their answering machines. Though each call lasted just a few seconds, he was billed the full 99 cents each time.

"It's not false advertising, but they're not telling you everything," Mr. Harris grumbles. "To me, it's misrepresentative."

Consumers have flooded the Federal Communications Commission with nearly 3,000 complaints since January 1998 about what they view as misleading or confusing promotions of discounted long-distance services from upstarts and giants like MCI and AT&T Corp. The FCC has launched an investigation into such practices, and today it will air the issue in a joint hearing with the Federal Trade Commission, which regulates deceptive advertising.

The companies offer an array of new services from the 10-10 numbers that let callers "dial around" their regular carriers for cheaper rates, to deeply discounted calling plans, such as AT&T's new seven-cents-a-minute offering.

But in the battle to sign up customers, some push too far – often with ads that don't paint a clear or complete picture of the offer, regulators say. "Information that matters to consumers needs to be disclosed in a clear and conspicuous way," says Eileen Harrington, the FTC's director of marketing practices. "What we've found is the ads are all wanting."

In the last three years, the FTC has cracked down on car-lease advertisers, charging them with deceptive advertising and forcing them to revise their marketing and not hide added fees in the fine print. Regulators are looking into the same issues in long-distance phone advertising.

Many "10-10" ads, for example, play up their rates in screaming bold type, then add conditions in tiny print to the side. A billboard sponsored by PT-1 Communications Inc., a subsidiary of **Star Telecommunications** Inc. in Santa Barbara, Cal., proclaims a 7.9-cents-per-minute rate for "long distance, 24 hours, 7 days" in big letters on an orange background. Only by following an asterisk to the fine print in the poster's upper corner does the viewer find that federal tax will be added and that potentially different rates apply for long-distance calls within certain states.

Jerry Ginsberg, Star Telecommunications' vice president of marketing, says the company is "very careful in providing full disclosure and letting consumers know what the offer is." He adds that it has been careful to use a size print that "the average person with average eyesight can read in an average amount of time."

A study last year by the AARP, which represents retired people, suggests many consumers are reluctant to try new long-distance options because of confusion over their terms. One barrier for older consumers is the small print carriers often use to notify consumers of added terms or conditions related to promotions made on TV or in print ads, says AARP legislative representative Jeff Kramer.

"On TV ads, it's difficult to see because they flash it. With print ads, you have to spend time looking at it," Mr. Kramer says.

Mr. Harris, the MCI customer who complained about the cost of calling his kids answering machines, got his money back. But

---

Many large-type ads detail conditions in tiny print on the side

---

an MCI spokesman, Brad Burns, says that the company is confident its ads, including the one Mr. Harris saw, are clear.

"More than 85% of our customers on a monthly basis are repeat users" of the dial-around service, he says. "That is our best evidence." He says it's in MCI's best interest to make sure its ads are clear because "at the end of the day, if there's sticker shock, customers won't dial the number again."

One source of confusion is that big carriers like MCI and AT&T, which enjoy a big share of the dial-around market, offer such services under different brand names. That's not only misleading, regulators say, but it also makes it difficult for consumers to figure out where to turn if they have a complaint.

When Ray Lippman of Scottsdale, Ariz., got an unexpectedly high phone bill for a call he placed to Taiwan in June using a 10-10 number offered by Lucky Dog Phone Co., he called the toll-free number listed on the company's flier to complain. He followed up with

---

PHONE TIPS FROM THE FEDS

Advice from the Federal Communications Commission on choosing long-distance service.

■ **Beware of Additional Charges**

Ask if there are monthly, minimum or per-call fees in addition to the per-minute rates. For example, if a dial-around service charges a $5 monthly fee and you make only one 10-minute call that month, then you pay an extra 50 cents a minute for that call.

■ **Be Careful of Comparison Rates in Advertisements**

Consumers should be careful about comparison rates in ads, such as 50% off of a carrier's basic rates, because such basic rates are often not the lowest available.

■ **Check Out the Phone Companies' Web Sites**

Their sites should have specific information on their rates and calling plans.

■ **Tie-Ins and Other Discounts**

Ask your long-distance carrier about mileage tie-ins that they may offer. Many companies now offer frequent-flier miles for the amount you spend on your long-distance bill. Also, some phone carriers provide discounts if you have your long-distance charges billed to your credit card.

(Cont.)

a letter to Lucky Dog but got no response. Neither the flier nor the representative informed him that the 10-10 number is actually offered by AT&T.

Howard McNally, president of AT&T Transition Services, which oversees AT&T's dial-around business, says AT&T decided to offer the service under a different name when it entered the market last year because "some people don't want to buy a brand, they think [10-10] is a better bargain." In addition, he adds, "It allows us to be different...a little cute, very humorous, which isn't in AT&T's brand image."

But Mr. McNally said that while AT&T strives for simplicity in its ads, it can't afford to offer consumers using its 10-10 number the same level of customer service as its core business. He says AT&T will look into Mr. Lippman's case and consider a refund.

Federal officials hope the forum today will bring industry and regulators together to improve long-distance advertising, but are prepared to take enforcement action if needed.

"There's no question any consumer in America today can get cheaper long distance rates than three years ago," says Bill Kennard, the FCC chairman. "But you can only shop around if you get the information you need, and not all customers are getting that information."

78

In Europe, Surfing a Web of Red Tape

Even on Internet, Ancient Rules Inflate Prices, Block Path To 'Borderless Commerce'

BY NEAL E. BOUDETTE

Staff Reporter of THE WALL STREET JOURNAL

BERLIN – Byson Dalgleish is a Web retailer's dream. Sitting at the desk in his apartment here, the 46-year-old teacher of foreign languages cruises the Internet every week buying books. He figures he has coughed up about $1,100 so far this year at **Amazon.com** Inc. But none of his money goes to Amazon's German Web site.

"If you buy from the U.K. site, it's much cheaper," he says. "Even if you include the shipping, it's a better deal in the U.K. I don't know why people go to bookshops in Germany. The whole thing with the prices is crazy," he says.

Why? Germany, France and several other European states allow publishing cartels through which groups of book publishers can legally dictate retail prices to booksellers – both online and on the ground. "Galileo's Daughter," the popular new biography by Dava Sobel, for example, sells at the list price of 50.24 marks ($26.99) on Germany's Amazon.de. At Amazon.co.uk, it costs 40% less.

That's the state of e-commerce in Europe right now. Despite Europe's ambitious goals of borderless commerce and recent hype from politicians claiming to embrace the "new Internet economy," the old habits of the brick-and-mortar economy are severely restraining online business.

Even as a growing number of Europeans go online – about 16% of them are now hooked up to the Internet, compared with 6% only two years ago – e-commerce is burdened with a Byzantine maze of rules, regulations and tax laws from another era.

Online auto sales are inhibited by an exemption from European Union rules that allows auto makers to dictate retail prices and to bar dealers from competing with each other. German regulations, in a nod to mom-and-pop stores, prohibit most price discounting on consumer goods except for two fortnights a year. The same law keeps airlines from dumping empty seats at the last minute with fire-sale fares. Online auctions run into legal tangles over laws requiring the physical display of goods to be sold at auction.

So far, there have been few efforts by governments to attack obstacles to e-commerce. Moreover, some established industries are fighting to preserve their advantages under the old system. But even as such 19th century relics frustrate would-be online entrepreneurs, consumers like Mr. Dalgleish are fighting back. Indeed, enterprising Europeans have found an array of Internet tricks to short-circuit economic regulations that inflate the prices of products ranging from software and clothes to plane tickets and hotel rooms. Internet companies, meanwhile, are fighting in the courts to crack barriers to Internet business.

"E-commerce should be borderless and it isn't in Europe. It's a regulatory nightmare," says Peter Bradshaw, an Internet stock analyst at Merrill Lynch in London. "But if the politicians don't get their act together, the market will make the rules for them. People will find a way around the rules. It's happening all the time."

Just ask David Butler, a recently retired medical-equipment sales manager in West Yorkshire, England. He turned to the Internet to get a better deal when he was looking for a new car in March. Car prices in the U.K. are as much as 40% higher than elsewhere in Europe, largely as a result of anticompetitive regulations.

After going online, Mr. Butler paid **Garage Canada,** a Belgian car dealer, just $19,933 for a 1999 Ford Focus and saved $5,150 – even after paying for a weekend at a floating hotel in Bruges. He came away feeling he was part of a bigger movement. "It is universal knowledge that we are getting ripped off in the U.K.," he says. "I've done my little part to bring these prices down."

Many top European leaders, including British Prime Minister Tony Blair, German Chancellor Gerhard Schroeder and French Prime Minister Lionel Jospin, say they want to support the rise of an Internet economy in Europe. But few barriers have fallen. Indeed, Messrs. Schroeder and Jospin support fixed book pricing. Earlier this month, the German minister of culture defended book cartels in clear terms. The EU, he said, shouldn't turn "weak, German book retailers into an experiment for an unfettered market economy."

Book cartels have flourished in Germany, France, the Netherlands and Austria for more than 100 years. Publishers maintain that guaranteed profits on bestsellers enable them to take risks on unknown authors, "literary" books that have limited audiences and books written in less widely spoken languages. They also say it protects small bookstores from the type of chain-store and Internet competition which has staggered thousands

WHICH PRICE IS RIGHT?

A thicket of economic regulations is restricting Europe's Internet economy and producing a wide range of prices for the same product.

	AMAZON.DE GERMANY	AMAZON.CO.UK BRITAIN	AMAZON.COM US
Galileo's Daughter by Dava Sobel	$27 (50.24 DM)	$13.52 (8.33 pounds)	$16.20

	EUROPEAN DEALER AT WWW.TOTALISE.NET	UK DEALER
Ford Focus 1.6i ZETEC	$18,102 (11,151 pounds)	$22,519 (13,750 pounds)

	DOWNLOADED FROM U.S. WEB SITE	CD-ROM, SHIPPED TO EUROPE, WITH TAX
FX Razor Special effects software from Ulead System	$89.95	$113.34

(Cont.)

> *In Germany, it is against
> the law to operate reverse
> auctions like Priceline.com*

of independent bookshops in the U.S.

The EU, which is supposed to eliminate barriers to trade, has attacked international price-fixing schemes between Austrian and German publishers. But it has no power to dissolve cartels within countries because book pricing is considered an internal, cultural matter.

Curtis Kopf, books general manager of Amazon.co.uk, scoffs at the justification offered for fixing prices. "I don't think anyone would complain in the U.S. or U.K. market that great works are not being published," Mr. Kopf says.

Although the Internet can help European consumers get English-language books at a discount from British sites, it can't do much right now about the prices of books from German, French and Dutch publishers – which provide their books only to resellers that respect the fixed price. (So far, Amazon and other online sellers have abided by the cartel prices.)

Many traditional European businesses don't want to see things change. Even Amazon rival BOL.com, a unit of Germany's **Bertelsmann** AG with sites in six European countries, supports the cartel system. Auto makers have pressured dealers in countries with lower car prices not to sell vehicles across the borders.

Ricardo.de, a German auction site that offers computers, cameras, appliances and clothing, was hauled into a Hamburg court by an association of traditional auctioneers. The auctioneers cited a paragraph in a 100-year-old law that requires auctioneers to, among other things, obtain a permit for each auction and make a public exhibition of goods on the block – conditions that Internet sites would be hard pressed to meet. The court split a razor-thin hair to allow Ricardo to operate. "The court said that online auctions, in a legal sense, are not auctions at all, but are sales to the highest bidder," says Ricardo Chief Executive Stephan Glaenzer. "That is something different, in the court's view."

Other types of e-commerce remain entirely prohibited. Germany, for example, has a Rabattgesetz, or discount law, that forbids special offers to individual customers. "The price of a product has to be the same for everybody," says Marc Samwer, one of the founders of a German auction site, alando.de, that was acquired earlier this year by **eBay** Inc.

As a result, it is against the law in Germany to operate a reverse auction like **Priceline.com** Inc., where customers name a price they are willing to pay for cars, airline tickets, hotel rooms and other items. "The whole concept of Priceline is not allowed," Mr. Samwer says. One side effect is that unlike in the U.S., where online competition pushed airlines to offer advanced ticket systems on the Web, major European airlines still have only limited Internet buying options.

Many consumers aren't waiting for European e-commerce to catch up. Mr. Dalgleish, the Berlin English teacher, uses the Internet to order reference works, texts and software for his language institute's Web site. "I recently bought a Web site development kit online from a company in the United States. I just downloaded it from the Web," he says. "If you have them ship you the CD-ROM, you pay customs and value-added tax. If you just download it, it's like you bought it in the U.S."

Jola Thatcher, a Frankfurt mother of a one-year-old with another child on the way, has found a way around the German rule that prevents stores from slashing prices except during one two-week period in the summer and another in the winter. She buys brand-new Baby Gap and Baby Dior clothing at the U.S. site of eBay.com, the online auctioneer. She also avoids paying taxes and customs duties because the sellers on eBay are often private dealers, not online stores.

Mr. Butler, the Englishman who bought his Ford Focus online, is now shopping for a video camera – at U.S. online retailers. "It's incredible," Mr. Butler says. "They're 40% to 50% cheaper over there. Even with shipping and customs, I could still save money."

79

GOOD-BYE TO FIXED PRICING?

How the wired economy could create the most efficient market of them all

Coca-Cola Co. has a bold idea: Why should the price of a can of Coke be the same all the time? Would people pay more for a cola fix on a sweltering summer day than they would on a cold, rainy one? The beverage giant may soon find out when it begins experimenting with "smart" vending machines that hook up to Coke's internal computer network, letting the company monitor inventory in distant locales—and change prices on the fly.

Sure, consumers might balk if Coke's prices were suddenly raised. But they also might be persuaded to buy a cold soda on a chilly day if the vending machine flashed a special promotion, say 20 cents off—the digital equivalent of the blue-light special. Says Sameer Dholarka, director of pricing solutions for Austin-based software maker Trilogy Systems: "List pricing is basically irrelevant."

Forget sticker prices. Forget sales clerks, too. There's a revolution brewing in pricing that promises to profoundly alter the way goods are marketed and sold. In the future, marketers will offer special deals—tailored just for you, just for the moment—on everything from theater tickets to bank loans to camcorders.

Behind this sweeping change is the wiring of the economy. The Internet, corporate networks, and wireless setups are linking people, machines, and companies around the globe—and connecting sellers and buyers as never before. This is enabling buyers to quickly and easily compare products and prices, putting them in a better bargaining position. At the same time, the technology allows sellers to collect detailed data about customers' buying habits, preferences—even spending limits—so they can tailor their products and prices. This raises hopes of a more efficient marketplace.

Today, the first signs of this new fluid pricing can be found mostly on the Internet. Online auctions allow cybershoppers to bid on everything from collectibles to treadmills. Electronic exchanges, on the other hand, act as middlemen, representing a group of sellers of one type of product or service—say, long-distance service—that is matched with buyers.

The pricing revolution, though, goes beyond the Net. Companies also are creating private networks, or "extranets," that link them with their suppliers and customers. These systems make it possible to get a precise handle on inventory, costs, and demand at any given moment—and adjust prices instantly. In the past, there was a significant cost associated with changing prices, known as the "menu cost." For a company with a large product line, it could take months for price adjustments to filter down to distributors, retailers, and salespeople. Streamlined networks reduce menu cost and time to near zero.

This will clearly benefit consumers. Already, many are finding bargains at the hundreds of online auction sites that have cropped up. And on the Net, it's a cinch to check out product information and compare prices—thanks to a growing army of shopping helpers called "bots" (page 188). That, says Erik Brynjolfsson, a management-science professor at Massachusetts Institute of Technology, "shifts bargaining power to consumers."

But that doesn't mean sellers get a raw deal. Businesses can gather more detailed information than ever before about their customers and run it through powerful database systems to glean insights into buying behavior. While the concept of point-of-sale promotions, such as Coke's, is not new, in a wired world, it takes on a whole new dimension. Suddenly, marketers can communicate directly with prospective buyers, offering them targeted promotions on an individual basis. Says Yanni Bakos, a visiting professor at MIT's Sloan School of Management: "It's like an arms race, where you give a more powerful weapon to both sides."

As buyers and sellers do battle in the electronic world, the struggle should result in prices that more closely reflect their true market value. "The future of electronic commerce is an implicit one-to-one negotiation between buyer and seller," says Jerry Kaplan, founder of Onsale Inc., a Net auction site. "You will get an individual spot price on everything."

The notion of fixed costs is a relatively

recent development. A couple of hundred years ago, when a person went to the cobbler to order a pair of shoes, they negotiated the price face-to-face. It wasn't until the arrival of railroads and canal systems, which allowed products to be distributed widely, that uniform prices came into being.

The Net brings us full circle. "We've suddenly made the interaction cost so cheap, there's no pragmatic reason not to have competitive bidding on everything," says Stuart I. Feldman, director of IBM's Institute for Advanced Commerce based in Hawthorne, N.Y. Someday, you might haggle over the price of just about anything, the way you would negotiate the price of a carpet in a Turkish bazaar. Except it's likely to take place on an electronic exchange, and it may be a computer bidding against another computer on your behalf.

WIN-WIN. For a preview of what's to come, just look to the financial markets. Take the NASDAQ stock market, or Instinet's even more automated system, after which many Net entrepreneurs are modeling their businesses. NASDAQ, for example, uses a system of dealers, or market makers, who trade shares of stock for brokers or individuals. The dealers are linked by an electronic network that matches buy orders with sell orders, arriving at the value of a stock for that moment in time.

Like NASDAQ dealers, the new Internet market makers must set up mechanisms for clearing transactions and for making sure that both buyers and sellers are satisfied. As electronic exchanges are established to trade everything from advertising space to spare parts, the true market value of products will emerge. "All of this brings you closer and closer to the efficient market," says Robert MacAvoy, president of Easton Consulting in Stamford, Conn.

The most widely used form of this today is online auctions. In the world of virtual gavels, Kaplan's Onsale is the kingpin. The Web site runs seven live auctions a week where people outbid one another for computer gear, electronics equipment, even steaks. Onsale buys surplus or distressed goods from companies at fire-sale prices so they can weather low bids. And customer love it. Grant Crowley, president of Crowley's Yacht Yard Inc. in Chicago, bought 14 old-model desktop PCs for his business via Onsale. He figures he saved 40% over what he would have paid in a store. "It's a great deal for people in small businesses like mine," Crowley says.

So far, the lure of a bargain has proved powerful: More than 4 million bids have been placed since Onsale opened its doors three years ago. It sold $115 million worth of goods last year, up nearly 300% from 1996. "Suddenly, consumers are active participants in price-setting," says Onsale founder Kaplan. "It's infinite economic democracy."

For every couple dozen online auctions, though, there is an entrepreneur applying the new Net economics in ways that will ultimately transform entire industries—from telecommunications to energy. These companies are setting up exchanges for trading things such as phone minutes, gas supplies, and electronic components, a market Forrester Research projects will grow to $52 billion by 2002. Their approach is such a departure from the past that analyst Vernon Keenan of Zona Research Inc. says they represent the "third wave" of commerce on the Net—companies that are moving beyond simple marketing and online order-taking to creating entirely new electronic marketplaces.

EQUAL FOOTING. Who are these trailblazers? Some are established companies, while others are born of the Net. But they all share a radical new vision of electronic commerce. "This is the model of the future," says Eric Baty, business-information manager at Southern California Gas Co.

You might not think of a stodgy utility as being in the vanguard of cyberspace, but that's exactly where Southern California Gas is. A couple of years ago, it saw an opportunity in the dovetailing of two sweeping trends—the deregulation of the energy industry, which lets customers shop for energy suppliers the way they shop for long-distance phone service, and the rise of the Web. So, last fall, it launched Energy Marketplace, a Web-based exchange that lets customers shop for the best gas prices.

The system has something for everyone. Small and midsize gas providers list their prices on the exchange. That lowers their marketing costs and gives them access to a broader market—putting them on equal footing with big energy suppliers. Customers, mostly businesses, save money by shopping for the best price, or locking in long-term deals when prices are low. And Southern California Gas, as a distributor, increases its volume of business and collects a subscription fee from gas providers that use the exchange. In coming months, SoCalGas will offer residential customers the same opportunity and expand the service to include electricity.

Does it work? Using Energy Marketplace, Sumiden Wire Products Corp. in Stockton, Calif., found a new supplier, Intermarket Trading Co., and now saves $500 a month—about 20% of its $3,000 a month energy bill. "They're cheaper than the other guys," says Wayne Manna, plant manager at Sumiden. "It's much simpler and easier than before."

Energy Marketplace is typical of the early electronic bazaars. Like the pork bellies or wheat traded in the financial markets, the first goods to be bartered in the new electronic markets are commodities. Whether No.2 steel or No.2 pencils, price—not features or how something looks, feels, or fits—is the determining factor in a sale. And if the commodity happens to be perishable—such as airline seats, oranges, or electricity—the Net is even more compelling: Suppliers have to get rid of their inventory fast or lose the sale.

Alex Mashinsky sees similar qualities in long-distance phone minutes. A former commodities trader, Mashinsky's New York-based

ArbiNet (short for Arbitrage Networks) is building an exchange for routing phone calls over the lowest-cost networks—on the fly.

Most telecommunications carriers have built massive networks to handle peak loads. The problem is, much of the capacity goes unused. AT&T, for example, typically uses just 20% of its global network capacity. In a fiercely competitive market that has seen margins erode, "that excess capacity is becoming

(Cont.)

extremely sensitive," says Mashinsky. "It can be the difference between making money and losing money." ArbiNet's exchange lets carriers optimize their capacity by accepting lower-cost calls over their networks during off-peak hours. There are other companies that broker long-distance minutes. But Arbi-Net is the only one attempting it in real time.

The ArbiNet Clearing Network works this way: Network carriers, such as AT&T, supply information about their network availability and price at a given time. Carrier customers send calls through ArbiNet's clearinghouse—say, a phone call from New York to Hong Kong that must travel over secure lines. ArbiNet's powerful computers and phone switches match the request with the lowest-cost carrier for that particular call, check to make sure the capacity is in fact available, and route the call—all in a millisecond. "We arbitrage the capacity available at any given time," says Mashinsky.

ArbiNet's focus today is on the wholesale, or carrier-to-carrier, business. But Mashinsky thinks that two years from now, the market will be ripe for consumers. A "smart" phone, for example, could automatically check for the lowest carrier on each call that is placed. Such a scenario could be unnerving to the giant phone companies. "The

---

A CYBERSHOPPER'S BEST FRIEND

Amy Rommel uses the Web a lot at work. But the 25-year-old public-relations director doesn't have time to compare prices when buying CDs online. Not, that is, until she discovered Lycos Inc.'s shopping service. Using the search engine's technology to scour the Web, Rommel found a way to come up with deals at the click of a mouse button. "I knew there were other music sites, but the Web is so big, it's hard to keep up," she says.

Shopping services, which include helpers, or "bots," are popping up all over the Web. They range from true bots—such as the one Lycos uses—that comb sites for prices each time a request is made, to hybrids, such as Compare.Net, a Web site that lists comparative product information.

These clever programs promise plenty of bargains for consumers—and headaches for merchants. Early online merchants often charged higher prices than physical stores because customers would pay for convenience. But bots undercut the convenience premium. A recent Ernst & Young study found that 87% of the 30 consumer products tracked could be bought online at the same price or cheaper than in retail stores. "Margins are going to be pushed down and down," says Walter A. Forbes, chairman of Cendant Corp., which runs an online shopping club.

The timing is right. Web shopping is on the rise—10.3 million people bought online last year, up from 6.3 million in 1996, according to Jupiter Communications Co. That's prompting Web sites to add bots to their lineups. Search engines Yahoo! and Lycos offer shopping bots through partnerships with Junglee and InfoSpace. Last fall, Excite Inc. acquired shopping service Netbot. And this month, Microsoft Corp. bought Firefly, which recommends products based on a consumer's tastes.

How do they work? Once a request is made, the agents hunt down product information as well as prices and reviews. Excite, for example, tracks products from 500 merchants. Consumers visiting the Excite shopping area type in the name of a specific product. The service then goes to different merchants' sites and hunts for current data and prices.

Yet bots have flaws. These first-generation agents can sometimes misidentify data on retailers' sites. A search for a Tickle Me Elmo doll on Yahoo! Inc. brought back information on that toy—as well as Elmo sheets, Barbie dolls, and Tickle Me Cookie Monster. Accuracy will improve in the coming months with a new language called XML, which lets site designers create "tags" to define data on a site, making it easier for bots to pick out the right information.

And there's a new generation of bots in the works. Massachusetts Institute of Technology's Kasbah can negotiate based on price and time constraints that it is given. And companies such as AgentSoft Ltd. create software that lets corporations build their own bots.

So what will happen when bots are really let loose on the Net? Sure, there will be bargains. But in computer simulations at IBM's Institute for Advanced Commerce, bots set off price wars. Some concerned companies already are blocking bots' access to their sites. But experts say the best solution is product differentiation and bots that take into account more than price. If that doesn't work well, bots may just turn out to be too much of a good thing.

By Heather Green in New York

WHERE THE BOTS ARE

In Web parlance, "bots" are software "robots" that do your bidding. Among the more sophisticated are digital bargain-hunters.

JUNGLEE Searches databases and Web sites, including job listings from 450 employers, such as AT&T and IBM. Also lists prices and products from 70 merchants. Partners Yahoo! and America Online offer the service for free and share with Junglee a percentage of the revenue they get from merchants.

EXCITE'S SHOPPING SEARCH Available on Excite's site, the free service seeks out products, prices, and reviews from 500 merchants. The technology is Netbot's Jango, which Excite bought for $35 million last October.

AGENTSOFT Develops software that lets companies build their own agents for comparison shopping of suppliers and subcontractors. It has four test services on the Web, including book shopping on the Amazon.com and Barnes & Noble sites.

(Cont.)

big carriers don't want to do this," says Mashinsky. "It would undercut their prices."

Indeed, big businesses are sensitive about falling prices. Some entrenched companies already are fighting the idea of electronic markets that make it easy for customers to compare products and prices. Houston-based energy giant Enron Corp., for example, last month filed suit against SoCalGas and its Energy Marketplace. Enron, which plans to enter the California market, alleges that Energy Marketplace unfairly favors local suppliers that are better known. SoCalGas calls the suit a blocking tactic.

BEYOND SURPLUS. Other big players are embracing the Net, but half-heartedly—using it to dispose of surplus goods while protecting margins on their core products. Not that surplus inventory is anything to sneeze at. Chicago-based FastParts Inc. and FairMarket Inc. in Woburn, Mass., operate thriving exchanges where computer electronics companies swap excess parts. All told, U.S. industries generate some $18 billion in excess inventory a year—around 10% of all finished goods, says Anne Perlman, CEO of Moai Technologies Inc., a Net startup that makes software for creating online bartering sites. "Excess and obsolete equipment is a big and painful problem," she says.

Or a huge opportunity. Perlman knows firsthand about surplus goods. Before joining Moai, she ran Tandem Computer Inc.'s personal computer business. When Intel Corp.'s 386 microprocessor came out, she found herself with a boatload of earlier-generation 286 chips that were instantly obsolete. Afraid that she might have to write off the inventory as a loss, Perlman made some calls and found a customer willing to buy the stock—though she was left with the nagging feeling that she could have gotten a better price. Now, at Moai, along with co-founders Deva Hazarika and Frank Kang, she sells a $100,000-plus package to companies that want to run their own auctions to generate revenue from aging merchandise.

Most of the Net pioneers had to build their own systems—a time-consuming and costly task. The availability of off-the-shelf software packages from Moai and others should help jump-start more electronic exchanges.

"THIRD WAVE." That could pave the way for fluid pricing to reach beyond commodity products and surplus goods to popular, even premium-priced items. Electronic markets could be just as effective selling unique items, such as a Van Gogh painting or a company's core product line. "The move away from surplus goods to primary goods will be the real thrust of the third wave," says Zona's Keenan.

There's just one snag: When anyone on the Net can easily compare prices and features, some high-margin products could fall in price. And a strong brand name alone may not be enough to make a premium price tag stick. Some branded products may even prove to be interchangeable. You might not trust your phone service to an outfit you have never heard of on the basis of price alone. But you might be willing to swap among AT&T, MCI, or Sprint for a better deal. And do you really care if your credit card is from MasterCard or Visa? "There's a commoditization at the top level of brands," contends Jay Walker, CEO of Priceline, a new Web service that lets consumers name their price.

One way companies can respond is by cooking up creative ploys to distinguish their products. That could include personalizing products or offering loyalty programs that reward frequent customers. "Inventiveness in marketing is going to be very important in this world where people can go out and compete on price," says IBM's Feldman. That's happening in online brokerage services, a cutthroat market. Thanks to Internet brokers, trading fees are already rock-bottom. Now, companies such as E*trade are mulling loyalty programs that reward frequent traders.

There are other ways to sidestep the effects of the ultra-efficient Net market. Just look at the airline industry. It was one of the first industries to go online, starting with American Airlines Inc.'s Sabre automated-reservation system in the 1960s. When other airlines followed suit, American introduced the frequent-flier program to keep customers loyal.

Three decades after Sabre, airlines still manage to get many passengers to pay rich fares. The secret: knowing whom to gouge—in this case, the business customer who has to get somewhere and is less price-sensitive. Airlines also have perfected the science of yield management, concocting complicated pricing schemes that defy comparison. The price for an airline seat can change several times an hour, making it virtually certain that the person sitting next to you paid a different fare. "Airlines are using the Internet to raise the average price of a fare," says Ken Orton, CEO of Preview Travel, an online ticketing site.

Now, airlines are tapping into the Net—but mainly as a way to sell unfilled seats. They routinely send out E-mail alerts of last-minute fare specials. And several major airlines have signed up with Priceline, which lets consumers specify when and where they want to travel, and name their price. Priceline then forwards the bids to participating airlines, which can choose to accept the request or not. The company makes its money on the spread between the bid and the lower airline price. "It empowers the buyer," says Walker, "but also the seller. They can plug in demand to empty flights."

As long as Priceline is clearly targeted at the leisure—not the business—traveler, airlines are willing to go along. "It's not for frequent fliers but to get people out of cars without affecting the airlines' retail price structure," says Walker.

In the end, such tactics may simply delay the inevitable march of the Internet. And the truth is, Net-based markets may not be such a bad thing for sellers. They produce a price that fairly reflects demand. Some companies may be surprised by the results.

Look at AucNet, an online auction for used cars. Dealers and wholesalers flock to AucNet's Web site to buy and sell some 6,000 cars a month. Surprisingly, sellers fetch more for their used cars than they might on a physical lot. That's partly because of the larger audience they get on the Net. But dealers also have come to trust the quality ratings that AucNet inspectors assign to each car after physically examining them, and they are willing to pay more for that seal of approval. Moai's Perlman has seen similar results in other online marketplaces. Most of the time, she says, "the market will bid a better price than the vendor was expecting."

Or at least, the right price. So why fight the perfect market?

By Amy E. Cortese, with Marcia Stepanek in New York

80

Soft Money

Private Internet "currencies" and other increasingly abstract forms of exchange may replace government notes

By Sarah Lueck

Staff Reporter of The Wall Street Journal

The global monetary system of the next millennium may amount to a hill of "beenz."

Sure, plenty of dollars, yen and euros will be floating around as paper bills, coins and electronic transfers. But government-backed notes increasingly will vie for wallet space – or its cyberspace equivalent – with private Internet "currencies" that already are cropping up, like the beenz created by beenz.com, along with similar units like "Flooz" and "Ubarter dollars."

"Digicash paracurrencies" is how Internet writer and artist Mark Amerika dubs these emerging coins of the virtual realm. Companies and future celebrities could become the basis for tradable computerized value units backed by their fame and fortune, he believes – like General Electric dollars or Michael Jordan dollars or Picasso dollars. "There are going to be all forms of currencies that coexist with each other," Mr. Amerika says.

That evolution of money over the next millennium would, at one level, mark a logical continuation of the development of cash over the past 3,000 years, from concrete to ever more abstract and diverse. But in taking those trends to a new extreme, the change will raise intriguing questions about the true role and meaning of money in an economy and in society. Why does money exist? Does the system require anything concrete to make legitimate the universe of floating bits and bytes greasing the wheels of exchange? What are the limits of faith that people will place in a promise that they hold something of value? When anybody can issue cash, is anybody in control?

Forward and Back

In some ways, the grand technofuture may look a lot like the past. And it may not be a smooth ride – reminiscent, perhaps, of the chaotic early 1800s, when wildcat banks issued their own currencies.

"People are going to have to be more aware of who handles their money," says Jack Weatherford, author of "The History of Money." "For 100 years, we've been so accustomed to the government taking responsibility. In the old days, people had to weigh coins or bite them to make sure they were real."

Of course, the main purpose of money has always been – and always will be – the same: to facilitate commerce. Business started as barter, when people traded goods of relatively equal tangible worth. But that system had obvious limits. Short-lived items such as food couldn't keep their value for long. Transporting goods, whether five cows or five bags of salt, was difficult. Values varied from region to region.

The first solution was coins, which emerged in Lydia near the Aegean Sea, in 640 B.C. Metal pieces were weighed and stamped with their value, making transactions more convenient and values more standardized – but heavy. Clearly, people needed something lighter as they traveled more frequently. Many began to see advantages to storing money with a money lender and taking away a paper note in exchange.

Paper currency was used in 11th-century China and 14th-century Italy. Yet for centuries after that, people still believed the paper should be fully backed by stores of metal. Through succeeding centuries, there was increasing public trust in gold- and silver-backed paper notes as a form of currency. But in 1933 the U.S. government stopped tying currency to a fixed price in gold, and instead moved to the dollar standard and the elusive notion that the credibility of the U.S. Treasury backed up the notes.

"When you could no longer trust in gold, they invited you to trust in God," says currency artist J.S.G. Boggs, alluding to the phrase on the back of U.S. notes. Quoted in Lawrence Weschler's book "Boggs: A Comedy of Values," Mr. Boggs says "it was like a Freudian slip."

Small Change

Checks and credit cards came into wide use by the 1970s, quickly replacing cash for most large transactions. By the mid-1990s, bills and coins in the U.S. were largely relegated to the smallest of transactions, such as paying cab fare or buying a newspaper. Three-fourths of all cash is now used for transactions valued at $20 or less, says Mr. Weatherford, the author.

With the development of Internet commerce and electronic cash, money has become even more ethereal. U.S. consumers, who spent about $20.2 billion online in 1999, will spend $184 billion in 2004, according to Forrester Research Inc.

Children growing up now are becoming increasingly comfortable with cashless commerce. Several Web sites allow parents to create allowance accounts, which their kids use online.

Convenience is the main advantage of the future system, in which the transfer of money will be effortless. A world traveler may never again have to exchange dollars for euros or pesos for yen, since "value" won't be confined to national borders; instead, international "smart" cards will hold value in a microchip. And workers will be able to say goodbye to being handed a paycheck. Just as spending in the future will deal in intangibles, so will earning – just a slick transfer of data from one account to another.

The touch of a button, or even just a quick scan of the microchip embedded in one's finger, may open the door to the vault that holds their "money." Even pickpockets may have to use new techniques. If they can break the codes that conceal passwords and financial information, they can drain accounts from any distance.

"In 200 years we'll see the elimination of cash in almost all areas," says Tod Maffin, a business-technology consultant in Vancouver, British Columbia.

Technology will facilitate not just the replacement of cold hard cash, but the proliferation of all different sorts of "money." These are the next generation of long-existing reward programs issued by businesses to encourage customer loyalty, like S&H Green Stamps, airline frequent-flier miles and supermarket coupons. But their impact is magnified by e-commerce, which allows for the quick, mass creation and trading of "units" of value.

One such currency is being spread by New York-based Flooz.com, a kind of one-step-removed variation of official U.S. currency. Customers use conventional dollar-backed credit cards to purchase Flooz, then e-mail them to someone else as a gift. This "gift currency" can be spent at 75 businesses, and Flooz.com says it currently has about 150,000 users.

Beenz, launched in March 1999 in the U.S. and U.K., stray even further from the official currency system. People can't buy beenz but must earn them as an alternative form of compensation by performing "e-work," such as providing e-mail or demographic information, reading a document or, in the case of one musical group's site, listening to a song. The businesses awarding beenz pay beenz.com one cent each for them. Beenz are then stored in the user's account and can be spent at retail sites, which receive a half cent for each beenz they honor.

There are even exchange possibilities. Internet users may convert beenz into Flooz, with 200 beenz equaling roughly one Flooz, or about $1. Flooz, however, can't be converted back into beenz.

In the typical setup, a user would have to do, say, about two hours of e-work, such as filling out forms and answering surveys, at about 10 sites to earn the 3,250 beenz, or about $16.25, it takes to buy a compact disk. Users of beenz so far have conducted about 12 million transactions, according to Glenn Jasper, a beenz.com spokesman.

The company says it is mindful of its role

in creating a parallel currency universe. Mr. Jasper ambitiously describes the venture as a kind of "central bank of the Internet."

Then there are Ubarter dollars, a back-to-the-future blend of third-millennium digital cash and prehistoric bartering. At Ubarter.com, businesses unload their excess inventory and get Ubarter dollars in return, which they can use to buy excess goods other companies post on the site.

"Everybody has something in their garage, and its value diminishes over time and they've gotten their use out of it," says Steve White, chief executive of Ubarter.com. Bartering "is a way for them to recoup part of that asset."

Rough Transition

It sounds like a grand technofuture of unprecedented efficiency. But the transition to that world may not be so easy. The last time America saw such a broad proliferation of currencies was before the National Banking Act of 1863. Back then, any bank that set up shop could issue its own paper exchange notes, backed by whatever it decided was appropriate collateral.

Since many so-called wildcat banks sprang up at that time, they flooded the market with notes, and their value sank. In addition, the banks often had such short lives that a traveler from California, for example, wouldn't know whether the bank note issued to him by one frontier bank would be accepted upon his arrival in Texas.

The Internet could spawn its own wildcats: cyberbanks and companies handling transactions and issuing currencies without regulations or a central bank to guide them.

Take beenz, for example. If 1,000 years from now it is still a popular Internet currency, many people will have accounts holding hundreds or thousands of beenz. Mr. Jasper says beenz will be on safe ground so long as businesses believe consumers should be rewarded for e-work. Indeed, banks might even start allowing borrowers to use beenz as collateral, and the currency, if enough people are confident of its value, could trade with other forms of money.

But what if several large vendors decide to stop honoring the stuff? Panic could ensue. Banks would call in their loans, and consumers with piles of worthless beenz would lose faith in other paracurrencies. Since national borders wouldn't confine the new currencies, the ripple effect would reach international proportions.

"The thing that has always scared me is a bunch of people issuing digital money who aren't insured and aren't backed up," says Elinor Harris Solomon, author of the book "Virtual Money" and a former Federal Reserve economist.

Indeed, such fears – and other visceral feelings about money – may make the dawning of a digital-cash age less inevitable than experts think. For all the momentum toward replacing coins and bills, there also are plenty of factors to keep them around. Money, after all, has endured to a degree unexplained by the limits of technology alone. It isn't just about exchange. It's about culture. About national identity. About faith.

Limits of Faith

Mr. Boggs, the artist, has, in a sense, made a career out of testing the limits of faith embodied in money – with mixed results. He creates altered versions of national currencies and then attempts to use them to buy things, explaining at museums, restaurants and shops that it isn't traditional money but has its own inherent value. As if mocking the "full faith and credit" claims of government notes, he sometimes labels his bank notes, "I promise to promise to promise." Mr. Boggs amplifies the test by offering a bill with a larger "face value" than the good he is purchasing, so that he must get change back in "real" money.

At times, Mr. Boggs succeeds in persuading vendors to take his version of cash – transactions aided by the fact that some dealers have valued his money as art worth upward of $100,000.

There are other reasons tangible money may never be fully eliminated. Some may always be needed to legitimize all the digital cash replicating that currency.

"Going way back in the ages, money has always become money because of philosophical and tangible attachments," Ms. Solomon says. "Trust is really at the bottom of any currency.... There has to be something behind it or people won't use it."

"People are very concerned about money," adds Douglas Mudd, manager of the Smithsonian Institution's numismatic collection. "It's hard to convince people to change, even when a change makes sense."

And there are still times when traditional money is useful, even essential. The tooth fairy, for now, deals in quarters, not smart cards. The Salvation Army's bell ringers require coins in their Christmas kettles. And few panhandlers will be accessing digital wallets.

Mr. Boggs thinks people will always want to have cash in some form, especially for making anonymous purchases that can't be picked up by computers. "People will always want some form of private currency," he says. "People do things they just don't want to be on record, like buying dirty magazines."

81

Renovations of grandeur

Upscale superstore makes home improvement easy — and pricey

By Lorrie Grant
USA TODAY

BOYNTON BEACH, Fla. – Expo, the chain of glitzy interior design and remodeling stores popping up across the USA, illustrates just how turbocharged the economy really is.

Dolphin Flamingo water faucets go for $2,057; Schonbek 15-light chandeliers, $5,595; Viking four-burner ranges with griddle, simmer plate, grill and two ovens, $8,414; 30-foot U-shaped kitchens with maple wood cabinets, plate-warming drawers and Dacor cooktops, $42,639.

The concept resembles a discount superstore, but the goods in these massive shopping venues are anything but.

Hansgrohe bathroom fixtures, Shivakashy granite countertops and Bates & Bates hammertone basins are displayed across eight elegant showrooms. Everything for an upscale home redo is available in one place – like a top-shelf Home Depot.

In fact, it is Home Depot.

The Atlanta-based home-improvement retailer that redefined the do-it-yourself market and built a $30 billion empire owns Expo and is trying to transfer its proven strategy – lots of choices, competitive prices and knowledgeable salespeople – to the top end.

Home Depot, which kicked off its 20th anniversary last month, is exploiting a void in the home-improvement market, says Wayne Hood, retail analyst at Prudential Securities.

"Consumers had to go to a number of home decorator shops, especially for high-end merchandise, but Expo puts that under one roof," Hood adds.

And unlike Home Depot, Expo offers an interior designer and project manager to handle the details, down to hiring and overseeing contractors.

It was that access to a project manager that clinched the deal for Amy and Jordan Estra of Ocean Ridge, Fla. They were frustrated after working with several independent contractors on previous home-remodeling projects.

"You have to coordinate the craftspeople so everything gets done on time. For the lack of an electrician getting there, the walls get held up. Without the walls up on time, the painter gets held up," says Jordan, 52, head of research at institutional broker Ryan Beck.

"The whole process...can be an absolute nightmare."

NIGHTMARE ENDS

So to restyle the 10-year-old home they recently bought, the couple tried Expo. They replaced ceramic tile on the 2,800-square-foot first floor with Jerusalem stone, changed the layout and fixtures in two bathrooms and swapped Corian kitchen countertops for granite. No nightmare.

The tab: $55,000 and running. Expo is renovating the second floor, including moving some walls.

"We believe you have to be deep in a category. If you're going to just stick your toe in the water, you don't need to be in it," says Expo President Bryant Scott, 43. He started with Home Depot as a "lot engineer," helping customers load their cars and retrieving shopping carts to earn money while in college. Asked on his application whether he wanted a career at the fledgling retailer, he checked "no."

Nineteen years later, he steers its fastest-growing division:

▲ There are 12 Expo stores. Plans call for 14 more by the end of next year; 200 by 2005.

Store locations

Expo plans to have 200 stores in North America by 2005. It currently has 12 across the USA.

Already open	**Opening by Jan. 30**
San Diego	Alpharetta, Ga.
Atlanta	Richland Hills, Texas
Westbury, N.Y.	Houston
Dallas	
Miami	**Planned for 2000**
Davie, Fla.	Eleven stores, including
Boynton Beach, Fla.	these locations:
Plano, Texas	Laguna Niguel, Calif.
Houston	Smithtown, N.Y.
Fairfax, Va.	Union, N.J.
Monrovia, Calif.	Bloomfield Hills, Mich.
Huntington Beach, Calif.	Troy, Mich.

(Cont.)

▲ Its closest national competitor, Sears' Great Indoors, has one store in Denver and another planned for Phoenix in November. So Expo has the field almost to itself for now.

The bustling U.S. economy that is fueling booming home sales and remodeling projects bodes well for Expo and parent Home Depot.

"All I see in front of us is all kinds of ways that we can dig deeper in this industry to capitalize on trends," says Home Depot co-founder and CEO Arthur Blank, 56.

Neither he nor Scott seems worried about an economic reversal.

"We are in the business of selling the American Dream. If the economy did turn down, people are still going to invest in their homes," Scott says. "We're not recession-proof, but we're recession-resistant."

While kitchens and bathrooms are Expo's heart and soul, consumers also can pick from an array of brands, styles and finishes in carpet, patio equipment, barbecue grills, lighting, tile and wall and window coverings. A separate area of in-stock items is aimed at keeping consumers from leaving empty-handed.

PLEASING RESULTS

Expo revenue is not separated from Home Depot's. But analysts estimate the Expo stores account for 2% of Home Depot's revenue, which rose 27% the first half of the year to $19.4 billion. Net income was up 45% at $1.2 billion, or 76 cents a share. The stock is up 5% in the period.

Says Blank: "We would not have anointed this as a roll-out if we had not been pleased with the results."

The first Expo, which opened in San Diego in 1991, struggled. It was selling the wrong products: towels, bed linen and such. And they were stacked sky high, consistent with Home Depot's warehouse atmosphere.

"The stores needed work in terms of focus and concept," Scott says.

The next battle was persuading manufacturers accustomed to placing their elegant wares in small, upscale showrooms to sell them in the new store. Vendors dismissed Expo as another Home Depot, with little commitment to price integrity. "We had to assure them that we wouldn't sell below cost. That was a pivotal point," Scott says.

Today, Expo executives say they have the formula right. The average store is 92,000 square feet, down from 140,000, which is the size of a Home Depot store. Ceilings are lower. The stacks are gone. Each showroom has pizazz.

"We're selling home design, not just pieces for the home," says Sergio Del Pino, head of display at the Boynton Beach store. "We show the public what you

---

THE EXPO REMODELING PROCESS

1 Customers browse the showroom for items related to the project and to determine a budget range. Services are explained by a design services representative.

2 A $750 retainer is paid before an in-store appointment with a project designer. The retainer can be applied toward a minimum of $3,000 worth of bath merchandise or $5,000 worth of kitchen merchandise, excluding appliances.

3 Designer and/or measurer visit job site to blueprint preliminary design.

4 Customer and designer meet in store to review plans and select products.

5 Contractor and project manager visit the site to review the project and make an installation bid.

6 After the designer receives contractors' bids, a final bid is compiled.

7 A meeting is set for bid review and approval. Total cost of installation is discussed. Expo has a lifetime warranty on all installations, but customers can get bids from independent contractors.

8 All merchandise and labor are paid for.

9 Merchandise is ordered and checked by project manager. Pre-construction meeting is set with homeowner, project manager, contractor and designer for final review.

10 Construction begins. Project manager takes charge.

---

can do with our product in your own home."

In lighting, for example, crystal lamps sit on Louis XVI-style furniture – also for sale.

Merchandise is made by some of the same companies supplying Home Depot, but only about 10% of the products are the same. "Expo decor lines begin where Home Depot ends," Scott says.

But primarily Expo's style and prices are several rungs above its humbler siblings.

"This is the fashion business. You have to stay on the cutting edge," Scott says.

Designers and project consultants pull it all together.

Sid and Deborah Goodman needed ideas for remodeling a 35-year-old home they bought in Boca

Raton, Fla., in December. Most important was keeping its oceanside feel.

"I don't have the vision of how to get all of the pieces tied together," says Sid, 52, executive director of Renaissance Institute of Palm Beach, a drug rehabilitation center.

But he is learning while working with designers Jerry Natale and Paula Draluck to enlarge the master bathroom.

Selecting the materials called for some expertise. The Goodmans had agreed on marble floors and countertops before salesman Irwin Adler warned about what happens when certain stone encounters moisture. The ex-Navy man, whose store ID badge reads "Guru of Granite," swayed their decision: "You know why granite is used for tombstones?" he asks. "It can take the water and keep its sheen."

The Goodmans say the whole process is supportive.

"They give shape to your ideas and almost hold you by the hand," Sid says.

Marketing Strategies: Planning, Implementation, and Control

Siberian Soft-Drink Queen Outmarkets Coke and Pepsi

BY BETSY MCKAY

Staff Reporter of THE WALL STREET JOURNAL

KRASNOYARSK, Russia – Yevgeniya Kuznetsova, 60 years old, is a former communist factory director who now espouses capitalism. Does she ever.

As head of beer and soft-drink maker OAO **Pikra**, based in this gray Siberian city of 875,000, she competes with **Coca-Cola** Co. and **PepsiCo** Inc. and airily dismisses both. Coke and Pepsi "are not a problem for us," she declares. "We're a problem for them."

Her weapon: Crazy Cola, an aromatic fizzy concoction meant to ape the global giants. Lighter brown than a Coke or a Pepsi and with a slightly grassy taste, it has a 48% share of cola sales volume in Krasnoyarsk, according to ACNielsen Russia in Moscow.

The success of Pikra illustrates how hard it is for even the world's most experienced marketers to expand in markets with poor and unstable economies. But it also is a testament to the business skills of Ms. Kuznetsova, who was beating Coke and Pepsi at their own marketing game even before the ruble's crash.

In fact, she picked up most of her management and manufacturing techniques from Pepsi, which began bottling its drinks at her state-run plant in 1989. Pepsi even sent her to an executive-education program at Duke University's Fuqua School of Business. "Pepsi was my business school," she says. "They lost out because they taught me so well."

A large part of the U.S. companies' problem stems from last summer's financial implosion, which diminished millions of Russians' savings and paychecks, making price particularly important. At a local grocery, a two-liter bottle of Coke or Pepsi costs the equivalent of 77 U.S. cents; a 1.5-liter bottle of Crazy Cola is 39 cents. The premium is beyond the reach of most consumers.

With these problems, Coke is expected to operate in Russia at about 50% of capacity this year; Pepsi last year took a $218 million charge to restructure its Russian business. Meanwhile, Ms. Kuznetsova's sales volume has doubled since last summer. "Coke may be the world leader," she says, "but we're No. 1 here."

One of only a few female company heads in Russia, Ms. Kuznetsova is also among the very few Soviet-era factory directors who successfully switched gears from the communist to the capitalist system. She took

charge of Pikra in 1986, when it was plagued by outdated equipment and, she says, "450 low-paid employees, a third of them drunks." She privatized the plant as soon as the Soviet government would allow her to, in 1990, "so no one else would get it."

Ms. Kuznetsova then set about overhauling the plant and its management. She returned from business studies in the U.S. with "entire notebooks" full of ideas, she says. Among them: Creating a modern marketing department and teaching salesmanship. "I spent a year fighting with my employees," she says. "They didn't know how to sell."

Despite the schooling she got from Pepsi, Ms. Kuznetsova parted abruptly with the company in 1997. The two sides failed to renew their contract in a dispute over expanding distribution of their respective products. Ms. Kuznetsova claims Pepsi wanted her local brands to "die their own death."

Pepsi, which declined to comment on any aspect of its activities in Krasnoyarsk, was left without a local bottler. Now the company has to bring its drinks in from other Siberian regions.

Ms. Kuznetsova's real wake-up call was Coke's sudden arrival in 1996. So eager was Coke to enter the market here in this former prisoners' outpost that it airlifted an entire bottling plant across 12 time zones. Ms. Kuznetsova, a former regional legislator and one of Krasnoyarsk's most prominent captains of industry, had virtually controlled her local market at the time, but Coke's presence threatened all that. Fresh-faced managers began working the stores. They filled shop shelves with Coke and plastered windows with big red signs. Pepsi did the same.

The factory director, unfazed, struck back. She ordered a cola concentrate from a German manufacturer and crafted a new drink that, she says, would "parody" Coke. Calling the concoction Crazy Cola, she drew up an ad campaign that targeted youth with photo contests, prize giveaways and hip advertising: One ad showed teens in gaudy hip-huggers drinking Crazy Cola as they danced in a disco. Another featured two young lovers caught in a kitchen sipping Crazy Cola between smooches.

Then Ms. Kuznetsova followed the lead of Coke and Pepsi and got 20 supermarkets

to agree to exclusive deals. Her associates say some of those deals remain to this day.

Ms. Kuznetsova says she rarely thinks about Coke or Pepsi anymore. Her mind is on Pikra's newest recipe for kvas, a Russian traditional fermented drink, and Flash, a new vitamin-laced energy drink.

But the cola wars go on in Russia. Coke introduced a Russian-made, fruit-flavored soda of its own this summer in southern Russia, aimed at consumers who can't afford the premium brands. Both Coke and Pepsi are also cutting prices as much as 50% and running promotions.

"For us, the issue is to make sure we stay highly relevant, and we're being as innovative as we can," says Paul Pendergrass, Coca-Cola's communications director for Europe. "We want the Russian consumer to know we're going to stick by them as they work

Nonstop promotions *have made Crazy Cola's label ubiquitous in Krasnoyarsk*

through the tough economic times."

When times get better, Coke and Pepsi can only hope that Viktoria Pimenova, a 25-year-old graduate student here, is a representative consumer. Ms. Pimenova keeps her eye on the Western brands and hopes one day to be able to afford them again. "Crazy Cola is fun, and it's our local product," she says. "But it's a drink for people who don't have money. Coke and Pepsi taste better."

SUDDENLY, AMAZON'S BOOKS LOOK BETTER

The e-tailer is raking in a bundle—from other merchants

No sooner had Amazon.com Inc. reported its fourth-quarter earnings on Feb. 2 than the squabbles erupted on online-investor message boards. "The Amazon numbers were great!" gushed William Harmond, a trader on the Silicon Investor site. Retorted another, identified as Lucretius Taurus: "I'll be shocked if this piggy is even around in a couple years." Even the pros are betwixt and between. "I'm still a believer in Amazon in the long term," says David D. Alger, chief executive of money manager Fred Alger Management Inc.–yet he recently dumped most of the Amazon shares in his Enterprise Internet Fund.

It's easy to understand why there's so much confusion about the pioneer e-tailer's prospects. Each year, its sales have rocketed far beyond expectations. But so have losses, now at nearly $900 million and counting. As CEO Jeffrey P. Bezos has moved Amazon far beyond books to music, Pokemon cards, drill presses–and, ultimately, anything people want to buy–doubts have intensified about whether it will ever turn a profit. Those doubts were fueled on Jan. 28 when Amazon fired 150 employees, or 2% of its staff. Now its stock languishes at 83, about 27% below its Dec. 9 high of 113. Says J.P. Morgan analyst Thomas H. Wyman: "There's a fear on Wall Street that maybe e-tail business models aren't working."

But suddenly, that fear is starting to wane. Once again, Amazon's model is looking sweet–and showing a path to that most elusive of dot-commodities, profits. The turnaround started on Jan. 21, when Amazon announced the latest in a series of deals to rent some of its Web-site space to other e-tailers–in return for a stunning $606.5 million in cash. Then, on Feb. 2, it announced that its original books business is profitable–a sign that its core e-tailing model might just have legs after all. The kicker: Some analysts now think Amazon will be profitable in 2002, a year earlier than expected. Says Goldman, Sachs & Co. analyst Anthony Noto: "These guys are really poised to take off in 2000."

Positive signs aside, though, it's far from certain that Amazon's core e-tailing business is viable. It had to write down $39 million in inventory in the fourth quarter, mostly toys and consumer electronics–which Amazon said it purposely overstocked to avoid disappointing customers during the holidays. But since Bezos plans to keep adding new products–more this year than ever–balancing demand and inventory is a ticklish problem that may plague Amazon for a long time to come. **SNAFU SPECTER.** And the stakes are higher than ever. Insiders say the company, even though it has ballooned to $1.6 billion in annual sales and 7,500 employees, is stretched to the breaking point. Over the holidays, hundreds of administrative workers had to help out in distribution centers and customer service to keep up with demand, raising the specter of execution snafus as Amazon keeps growing. And now that Bezos has stuck his neck out by predicting better results to come, there's no room to disappoint. If he misses the mark, the stock may crater, reducing his ability to expand. Bezos concedes Amazon has taxed some investors' patience but insists the long wait was worth it. "This year, we expect our model to visibly demonstrate its inherent operating leverage and its long-term potential."

Indeed, Amazon may finally have hit a historic milestone in e-commerce: critical mass. With 17 million customers, Amazon has an asset unmatched in all of e-commerce–one that may finally be primed to deliver on the Web pioneer's promise. "We have reached a tipping point as a business," Bezos says. "When you reach a certain critical mass of customers, you very quickly have a long line of people who want to associate with you." In other words, people who give you boatloads of money for nothing more than a few square centimeters of your Web page.

Once again, Amazon's hyperkinetic leader has changed the rules of the game almost overnight. First, he showed the world he could sell stuff online to millions of people worldwide with almost none of the costly stores and inventory of traditional retailers. But he quickly recognized that as he added more products and customers, the virtual model would not work. To offer not just the biggest selection but the nearly instant gratification customers demanded, he needed to stock and ship his own inventory. So he spent an unprecedented $300 million to build five new distribution centers last year, and hired hundreds of customer-service operators.

Investors blanched, but Amazon aced the holidays: More than 99% of Amazon's holiday deliveries arrived on time. That earned the unswerving loyalty of Amazon's customers, whose repeat purchases now make up 73% of its sales. "Amazon's biggest asset is its customer base," says Alex Nesbitt, CEO of Sameday.com, a Los Angeles e-commerce distribution company. "Customers who are satisfied and keep coming back are very valuable."

That's the key to Bezos' latest shift. He's flipping e-tailing itself on its head—not just selling more and more products to his customers, but selling the attention of those customers to other e-tailers. It's a page from the playbook of Internet portals such as America Online Inc. and Yahoo! Inc.–with one big difference. Amazon's customers aren't just surfers and chatters. They're people primed to buy and experienced in how to do it online. That's why the deals are especially attractive to other e-tailers, such as Drugstore.com and Visa issuer NextCard Inc. "We're going to the sweet spot of online shoppers," says Shaun Holliday, CEO of Living.com, which will open a store within Amazon in return for paying $145 million over five years.

BUY, BUY. Already, this rich new lode— which carries 85% gross profit margins, more than six times Amazon's current level—has helped turn around many analysts who had been wary of the stock. Several have upgraded their ratings recently so that now, 16 analysts have a strong or weak buy and 10 have a hold. Some have even moved up by a full year their timetable for Amazon to turn a profit, to 2002. Goldman analyst Noto sees the six deals so far cutting operating losses by $110 million in operating income this year, or about 25%. And more are on the way. "We've had hundreds of companies that have approached us to work with us in this way," says Amazon President Joseph Galli. "We're the power that takes the customer and delivers him to the suppliers."

Becoming a landlord isn't the only new role Amazon can play. Bezos reckons he has built an e-commerce "platform"–made up of its customers, its brand, technology, e-commerce expertise, and distribution capabilities–on which it's far easier and cheaper to build new businesses. Boasts Bezos: "The platform allows us to launch new e-commerce businesses faster, with a higher quality of customer experience, a lower incremental cost, a higher chance of success, and a faster path to scale and profitability than any other company."

In short: Amazon may be poised to add a raft of other revenue streams if it so chooses. It could accept traditional advertising, a $4.7

billion market. It could offer membership clubs, giving those who pay a fee access to more in-depth reviews or discounts. It could offer Internet service subsidized by advertising–as a new rival e-tailer, the Kmart Corp.-backed Bluelight.com, just started doing. Amazon could even offer distribution services to other e-tailers. Says Jeffrey A. Wilke, Amazon's vice-president for operations: "I want to have people lining up out the door begging, begging, begging us to fulfill their operations." Bezos says he has no immediate plans for such moves, but he also doesn't rule anything out.

Despite these new and potential riches, e-tailing will continue to comprise the bulk of Amazon's business. But that's a business that depends on execution more than vision–and Amazon's executives and employees have a lot to learn about retailing basics like balancing demand and inventories. Some skeptics say Amazon was forced to become a landlord because the underlying model doesn't work. "They had to give merchandise away in order to get customers," says Prudential Securities analyst Mark Rowen. "It's not clear if costs will come down or they'll be able to raise prices."

PINK SLIPS. Indeed, Amazon's profit picture in the fourth quarter looked grim. It lost $184.9 million, its biggest quarterly loss ever. Gross margins fell by more than a third, to 13%, thanks largely to the inventory writedown. As Amazon continues to expand, that could remain a chronic problem. "They have a lot of room for improvement," says Robert A. Bowman, CEO of online computer seller Outpost.com.

That's where the layoffs came in. The need to tighten up operations–not a drive to cut costs, according to Amazon insiders–led to the recent purge. Those fired were largely veteran employees whose jobs outgrew their skills, say insiders, who peg the layoffs to more rigorous management instituted by two managers hired last year: former Black & Decker exec Galli and Chief Financial Officer Warren C. Jenson from Delta Air Lines. While the layoffs pained Amazonians, investors applauded. "It was a very healthy sign," says Andrew S. Cupps, portfolio manager with mutual fund firm Strong Capital Management Inc.

It's up to Wilke, who oversaw AlliedSignal's manufacturing quality drive, to polish up the back end. He's deep into analyzing

each step of the fulfillment process, from delivery by suppliers to shipping the product out the door. He hopes to persuade suppliers to cut unnecessary steps–such as wrapping toys in packaging geared to physical store needs. If such moves can reduce the time it takes to receive a product from a supplier to perhaps a day, Wilke says, then inventory falls to almost zero–for a huge jump in efficiency. "We should start to see gains within six months," he says.

That's one reason the fourth quarter may have been the low-water mark for Amazon's finances. Another plus: The biggest capital costs are over for now. The distribution centers, which can handle up to $10 billion worth of annual sales, are all built. Actually, the costs never were that much relative to traditional retailers, whose biggest expenses by far are building and staffing stores. Amazon's fixed assets, such as warehouses, for instance, on average produce double the sales of Wal-Mart Stores Inc. and Barnes & Noble stores.

Now that the warehouses are built, some analysts see the attractive cash flow of Amazon's business model becoming more obvious. But even with the added inventory it now carries, on average, it gets paid about a month before it must pay suppliers–because it charges credit cards as soon as buyers click but doesn't have to pay suppliers until up to 45 days later. That's one reason that the underlying business, before equity investments and capital costs, generated $32 million in cash in the fourth quarter.

Marketing efficiencies also are beginning to kick in as Amazon's brand recognition and customer base grow. Some 118 million U.S. adults recognize its name, more than any other e-commerce company. And the more customers Amazon serves without a hitch, generating chummy word-of-mouth, the less it has to spend to get more.

As a result, Amazon's marketing cost to acquire a customer is only $19, less than any other e-tailer. As Amazon's sales grow from $1.6 billion in 1999 to an expected $2.8 billion this year and $6 billion in 2002, marketing costs will fall from 25% of sales now to 13% in 2002, according to Goldman Sachs. At the same time, as Amazon adds more products, each customer is starting to buy more–from $106 annually in 1998 to $116 in 1999, and by Noto's estimate, $150 by 2002.

With traditional retailers from Barnes & Noble to Wal-Mart all breathing down their neck, Amazon will have to keep those trends heading in the right direction. Brick-and-mortar retailers can apply their formidable brands and the ability to offer pickups and returns at stores. By using the Web as a broadcast channel for stores, vows Barnesandnoble.com Chairman Steven Riggio, "we are going to create a network of tens of millions of customers."

But with Amazon asserting its newfound power, traditional retailers' gains may come

(Cont.)

more at the expense of other e-tailers. Amazon has bought nine companies, from cataloger Tool Crib of the North to technology providers such as shopping software maker Junglee Corp., and taken stakes in 10 others, including category leaders such as Drugstore.com and NextCard. With its $28 billion market capitalization and $706 million in cash and short-term investments, it can afford to keep plucking off rivals–or playing kingmaker with partnership deals. "The pure-play e-tailers are going to be forced to reinvent themselves," says Mark H. Goldstein, CEO of BlueLight.com. But they had better hurry before Amazon once again reinvents itself.

By Robert D. Hof in San Mateo, Calif., with Heather Green and Diane Brady in New York

INSIDE IBM: INTERNET BUSINESS MACHINES

Big Blue is doing a boffo Net business—some $20 billion is driven by demand for e-business. 'They get it,' says a rival. 'Every day they tell a better story'

To prepare for his annual meeting with Wall Street last May, IBM Chairman Louis V. Gerstner Jr. had an assistant pull the financial reports on 25 of the "real Internet standard bearers"–companies like Yahoo!, America Online, Amazon.com, eBay, and E*Trade. Last year, those companies generated combined revenues of about $5 billion–and lost $1 billion. Yet the market value of the Internet 25 together was 50% greater than that of IBM. "Go figure," Gerstner deadpanned when he delivered the news to analysts. "Now, I am not suggesting that you view us as an Internet company, but I think it is worth noting that IBM is already generating more [e-business] revenue and certainly more profit than all of the top Internet companies combined."

Get ready to adjust your thinking. The marquee names of the Internet Age may be dot.com companies, but the big dot in the New Economy these days is IBM. While Amazon's Jeffrey P. Bezos and Yahoo!'s Timothy Koogle get all the Internet kudos, Gerstner has been quietly zipping past competitors, large and small, to emerge as a leading arms supplier to the Information Age. Today, IBM is doing it all: helping merchants hang their shingles online, advising corporate chieftains on how to reshape their businesses top-to-bottom, even wiring local courthouses. "They get it," concedes Edward J. Zander, president of rival Sun Microsystems Inc. "Every day they're telling a better story."

NO CHOICE. And it's one that Zander and other rivals don't much enjoy hearing. Big Blue, despite its dinosaur image, is doing a boffo business from the Net. IBM estimates that 25% of its revenue–some $20 billion–is driven by e-business demand. That's nearly 50% more than Internet darling Sun, whose servers are de rigeur for most Web businesses. Even sweeter: About 75% of IBM's e-business revenue comes from sales of Net technology, software, and services–fast-growth, fat-margin businesses–and not the old mainframe computers for which IBM is so well known.

Just as surprising is how Gerstner is seizing the Internet inside IBM. The 57-year-old CEO, once jeered for his lack of computer industry experience, has done an extraordinary job of weaving the Web's vast reach into every corridor of the company–its products, its practices, its marketing. The results have been stunning: Online sales, mostly of PCs, are expected to top $12 billion for the year, skyrocketing nearly 400% from $3.3 billion last year. The productivity gains from using the Net have been just as profound. The company figures it will save $750 million by letting customers find answers to technical questions on its Web site. And by handling a portion of its internal training over the Net instead of in classrooms, IBM will save $120 million. All told, IBM will whack nearly $1 billion out of its costs this year by taking advantage of the Web.

Suddenly, International Business Machines is looking a lot more like Internet Business Machines. Surprised? Don't be. Gerstner doesn't have a choice. Every company from the tiniest dot.com startup to IBM's biggest rival is using the Net to skin costs to the bone and to reach new customers. And even though Gerstner has been hard at work doing just that, IBM's gargantuan size has made a wholesale Internet conversion tough. PC and server sales, for one, are going nowhere. While competitors Dell Computer Corp. and Sun rack up Internet-fueled sales growth of 25% and 40%, respectively, IBM's revenues have been stuck at an Old Economy rate of 7%. This year, analysts estimate, Big Blue will grow a tad faster–9%, bringing revenue to around $90 billion.

That's not nearly fast enough in the New Economy. But if Gerstner can hook more of IBM's revenue to the Net, he may be able to pull IBM out of the slow lane. With $15

(continued)

IBM's e-Business Strategy

E-IBM   The best way to learn is by doing. So IBM is becoming an e-business. By moving purchasing onto the Web, the company expects to save $240 million on the $11 billion in goods and services it will buy this year. Similar moves to put customer support online will save another $750 million.

Competitive Landscape: The field is split here. IBM is clearly ahead of rivals such as HP, Sun and Compaq. Others such as Dell, Cisco and Intel have been on Internet time longer than IBM.

E-SERVICES   IBM has 130,000 consultants and an e-service business expected to hit $3 billion this year. IBM has handled 18,000 jobs over the last three years—from Web-site design to hooking older corporate databases into new online systems—for companies such as DHL and Payless ShoeSource.

Competitive Landscape: The giants are plunging ahead—Sun, HP, Intel and EDS—along with upstarts Scient and Lante. Still, IBM has the advantage with corporate databases that need to be hooked into online systems.

E-ENGINEERING   This is where IBM sees e-business heading. Companies will use the Net to cut costs, turning for help on how to do it. United Technologies Corp. has already turned over procurement via the Web to IBM.

Competitive Landscape: Not the usual crowd. Companies with specific skills such as Federal Express will get into logistics, while Andersen Consulting and other Big 4 consultants will help e-engineer business tasks.

IBM's e-Business Strategy
(concluded)

PRODUCTS IBM offers everything from laptop PCs to mainframes that plug easily into the Net. Its software, such as MQ Series, is becoming the glue that allows machines from different makers to pass messages over the Net. Other programs such as Net.Commerce handle huge amounts of e-commerce transactions.
Competitive Landscape: IBM continues to stumble in PCs and servers, as pesky Dell Computer and Sun Microsystems roar ahead. In software, Microsoft looms, while upstarts such as BroadVision have been knocking Big Blue out of some key accounts, such as Ford and Sears.

RESEARCH IBM pumps half of its $5 billion R&D budget into Internet-related areas. Gerstner isn't stopping there: He has created the Institute for Advanced Commerce, a think tank that includes outside consultants and academics as well as 50 IBM scientists—all working on electronic commerce. Initial focus: Auction software.
Competitive Landscape: Growing your own takes time. Meanwhile, rivals Microsoft, Cisco and Intel are using their sky-high stock valuations to buy what they need.

E-OUTSOURCING Don't want to run your Web business? Let IBM host it for you at one of their mega data centers. IBM does the works. At Lego, for example, it runs everything, including contracting the Danish post office to handle shipping.
Competitive Landscape: EDS is big, but it has been slow to move its business to the Net. New outsourcing players like Intel and Exodus are piling in. But IBM remains in the lead.

billion of IBM's Net-driven revenues growing at more than 30%, the time may not be too far away when the company's slow-growth businesses such as mainframes and storage systems are no longer a drag.

This is Gerstner's chance for IBM to reclaim the mantle of leadership, and it may be his last. If IBM blows the Internet, which is becoming more pervasive with every mouse click, it blows its franchise–perhaps once and for all–as the leading high-tech supplier to Corporate America. In the Internet Age, it's not just Sun, Microsoft, Hewlett-Packard, or Compaq that Big Blue frets about. Every day, nimbler challengers, ranging from e-consultant Scient Corp. to Net software maker BroadVision Inc., keep chipping away at Big Blue's turf. Says IBM senior vice-president and longtime Gerstner confidant Lawrence R. Ricciardi: "We had to be ready to respond, or we would be dinosaur bones."

Y2K FREEZE. In some markets, IBM is playing catch-up. The company has been slow to woo the dot.com crowd, for instance, leaving that to Sun, HP, and a slew of startups that sell PCs, servers, and software. The trouble is, Web companies will soon buy as much computer gear as traditional companies. "We've had to adapt our model to them," concedes Gerstner. "We were late."

The events of the past couple of months underscore IBM's urgency to focus on e-business. In early October, the company disclosed that it will yank its Aptiva home PC off retail shelves in North America, making them available only through its Web site. IBM also will lay off up to 10% of its PC workforce. The moves, IBM hopes, will stanch the flow of red ink in a unit that lost nearly $1 billion last year. Analysts expect IBM to lose approximately $400 million in PCs this year.

Then on Oct. 20, the company shocked Wall Street with news that sales of large computers–one of its slowest-growth areas, but among the most profitable–had dried up because customers were locking down their operations for the rest of the year to prepare for Y2K. The buying freeze, IBM told analysts, will hurt the company through the first quarter of next year. The news sent IBM's stock tumbling 15%, to 91 from 107. The company also announced another layoff of up to 6% of the workers in its computer server group.

And now IBM's accounting method has come under scrutiny. On Nov. 24 it was disclosed that Big Blue is being criticized for its policy of bundling one-time gains, such as the $4 billion earned from the sale of its Global Network business to AT&T, into operating income. That, critics claim, makes it difficult for the average investor to assess the company's performance because operating income is typically used as an indicator of pure sales success since it excludes taxes, interest and other items.

"VERY AGGRESSIVE." Nonsense, the company says. IBM maintains that it's following Securities & Exchange Commission guidelines and provides analysts with all the data they need to evaluate the company's efficiency. As for Y2K, IBM says, that's a temporary hit on its big iron computers while customers sort out last-minute changes before the new millennium. But Gerstner says demand for e-services and software is strong. And analysts agree. They expect sales for online systems to gain momentum sometime after the first quarter, when companies will have finished wrestling with Y2K. "E-business is the next big thing on the road map for a lot of companies," says Gartner Group Inc. analyst Tom Bittman.

If Gerstner is right, after years of upheaval, Big Blue could once again be on solid terrain. Gerstner believes that the advent of the Internet will befuddle execs already struggling to take advantage of the new technologies. Companies around the globe will spend $600 billion a year by 2003 on e-business, according to market researcher International Data Corp. More importantly, some 62% of that amount will go to consultants and the like who can sort out how to use all the bedeviling technology. By contrast, just 29% will be spent on hardware and 9% on software. "The real leadership in the industry is moving away from the creation of the technology to the application of the technology," says Gerstner. "The explosive growth is in services."

That couldn't be better for IBM. Building powerful computers and software that don't fail, as well as providing tons of services–especially tons of service–is second nature to IBM. Its army of 130,000 consultants in its Global Services unit is unmatched in the industry and does three times more Net work than the $1.9 billion combined revenues of Andersen Consulting, Electronic Data Systems, and Computer Sciences, according to IT Services Advisory LLC, a research and advisory firm in Hillside, N.J. In the past three years, IBM has handled 18,000 Internet jobs for its customers, from shaping an Internet strategy to Web page design to hosting entire online storefronts.

Now IBM's e-business client roster is stoked with the biggest names in industry—from Ford Motor to Charles Schwab, and from Prudential Insurance to the New York Stock Exchange. In a Merrill Lynch & Co. survey last month, 53 chief information officers at major corporations cited IBM as one of only two computer companies–the other was Sun–that are best positioned to handle their Internet projects. "They are very aggressive about building their expertise in the online world," says Rhonda Wells, director of e-commerce for Payless ShoeSource Inc., which chose IBM when it wanted to build a full-fledged e-commerce hub–in three months. "IBM has a strong knowledge of brick-and-mortar businesses, not just Internet businesses."

How did Big Blue catapult itself to such heights after such lows? Credit Gerstner. He recognized as early as 1994 that the killer app for the Internet was going to be transactions–not simply having the best browser or the coolest search engine. One of Gerstner's first moves was to shift 25% of IBM's research and development budget into Net projects. He declared that every IBM product must be Internet-friendly. And he began to push all software development toward the Java programming language. There was also a crash effort to tie Lotus Notes software tightly to the Web. "The Internet was a major change and opportunity for IBM. The first person who saw its value was Lou," says G. Richard Thoman, chief executive of Xerox Corp., who worked with Gerstner at IBM, RJR Nabisco, and American Express.

MUSHROOMING SERVICES. To get the massive, 225,000-person organization focused, Gerstner shook things up. He set up the Internet Div. and appointed Irving Wladawsky-Berger, a respected IBM exec and computer scientist by training, to head it. Wladawsky-Berger made sure that every product in IBM would work with the Web. Then he sat down with his staff and figured out what IBM calls the "white spaces"–the empty spots where the company needs to develop products. Indeed, Gerstner looks back on his move as a "bet-the-company decision."

Gerstner's smartest move, though, may be e-business services. Today it seems like a no-brainer, but in 1995, the industry was obsessed with snazzy new products, from network computers to superfast search engines. Gerstner could have focused on trying to gain leadership in Web cruisers or browsers–after all, IBM had its own browser, which it wound up scrapping. Instead, Gerstner decided to use services to distinguish IBM from the pack. "We concluded this [the Internet] was not an information superhighway," says Gerstner. "This was all about business, doing transactions, not looking up information."

Now service is paying huge dividends. The company's e-business services revenue is growing at a galloping 60% and is expected to hit $3 billion this year. And Gerstner says that number could easily double if you include (as he says competitors do) portions of IBM's huge outsourcing jobs that use the Net to deliver software and services. "They have an incredible pool of professional services," says Jeff F. Lucchesi, chief information officer for DHL Airways Inc. IBM helped create DHL Connect, an online shipment scheduling and tracking system that uses IBM software to connect a variety of computers so that customers can get estimated shipping charges immediately. When Lucchesi needed a special Java program, IBM had a team on the job within 24 hours. "That's something that tells me I'll use them again," says Lucchesi.

No wonder Gerstner is adding services as fast as he can. In the past year, IBM has launched 20 new Net-related services including privacy consulting and an online service designed for small to medium-sized business.

For as little as $99 a month, IBM will provide all the hardware, software, and services that small businesses need to get online. Big Blue is even in the application service provider (ASP) market, delivering enterprise software from companies such as PeopleSoft, Great Plains Software, and ebank.com over the Net.

Still, the big money is in IBM's traditional customer base–the thousands of big companies that have yet to tap the Net and transform their businesses. IBM refers to such companies as below the e-line. Gerstner isn't just out to help them set up cybershops, he's zeroing in on Web-izing all of their business operations–their supply chains, customer service, logistics, procurement, and even training. "The Internet is ultimately about innovation and integration," says Gerstner. "But you don't get the innovation unless you integrate Web technology into the processes by which you run your business."

Above the e-line, IBM is a straggler. That's why in April, Gerstner created a swat team to focus exclusively on selling IBM products and services to Web companies. It's also trying a novel sales approach. Together with Conxion Corp., an Internet service provider, and the Silicon Valley Bank, IBM is

offering up to $1 million in technology and services free of charge for six months to 24 Net startups. The idea is to help incubate startups without them burning through all their funding. At the end of six months, the startup can buy or lease the equipment or simply take a hike.

For all these efforts, IBM's pole position in the Internet race isn't guaranteed. For one, Gerstner hasn't been able to solve his hardware problem. Sure, once companies get past Y2K they'll want more mainframe power to handle massive online businesses. But mainframe prices are falling faster than sales are rising. And in the white-hot Web server business, made up mostly of Unix computers, IBM has been a no-show. That's why its computer business looks anemic compared with Sun's 25% growth. For the year, IBM's sales of Unix systems are expected to reach $3.2 billion, up 7%, says Sanford C. Bernstein & Co. Says Sun Chairman Scott G. McNealy: "They're not nearly the systems provider they used to be."

"UNINSPIRING COMPETITOR." That has left IBM on the sidelines during one of the biggest boom periods for Web servers. "We have been an uninspiring competitor

---

How IBM Uses The Net

e-Care   Getting customers to use the Net to help themselves means big savings. For every service call handled through ibm.com, the company saves 70% to 90% of the cost of having a person take that call. This year, IBM expects to handle 35 million online service requests, saving an estimated $750 million in customer support costs.

---

e-Commerce   Through the first three quarters of 1999, e-commerce revenue–from sales of everything from PCs to mainframe software–totaled $9.7 billion, up from $977 million during the same period last year. By yearend, e-commerce revenue is expected to be between $10 billion and $15 billion, vs. $3.3 billion in 1998.

---

e-Learning   IBM estimates that for every 1,000 classroom days converted to electronic courses delivered via the Web, more than $400,000 can be saved. For the year, the company expects 30% of its internal training materials will be delivered online, with anticipated savings of more than $120 million.

---

e-Procurement   In 1999, IBM expects to buy $11 billion in goods and services over the Web, saving at least $240 million. So far this year, IBM has plugged more than 6,700 suppliers into its online procurement system. Now, IBM can cut out rogue buying–employees who buy from suppliers that aren't pre-approved.

against Sun and HP," admits Gerstner. "We're behind in that arena, and we have to take that share back."

Even so, hardware may be the least of Gerstner's worries. The e-biz field is no longer Big Blue's to romp in virtually uncontested. Sun and Microsoft are beefing up their focus on servicing e-biz customers. A revitalized HP is zeroing in too. Even chip giant Intel Corp. is steering its considerable might there, spending $1 billion to set up rooms of servers to host Web sites. And then there is the raft of hot startups that claim IBM and other big companies are just too bloated to work on Net time. "We have the look and feel of a speedboat," says Rudy Puryear, the former head of Andersen Consulting's e-business practice who now heads Chicago-based e-consultant Lante Corp. IBM, he says, is a "battleship."

Some rivals are even taking a page from IBM's playbook–and using it against them. Earlier this year, HP emulated IBM's hugely successful e-business marketing campaign with its own e-services campaign–even hiring a member of the team that launched the e-business campaign to do it. HP's e-services strategy could be a danger to IBM, if it works. That's because HP, which lacks IBM's consulting muscle, is trying to create do-it-yourself Net technologies. In HP's view, companies should easily be able to add new features and services onto their Web sites, no big consulting contracts necessary. Says Nick Earle, chief marketing officer for HP's enterprise computing unit: "We always bristle when people say we copied IBM. We learned from the good things that they did, but that was over three years ago. In Internet time, that's a lifetime."

That's why Gerstner isn't letting up. He's pumping more than 50% of IBM's huge $5 billion R&D budget into Net projects, up from 25% in 1996. What's next? IBM wants to be the supplier of technology and services to link all manner of digital devices such as pagers, cell phones, and handheld computers. IBM will either license the technology to others or build the infrastructure and rent the capability.

MASSAGE CHAIRS. To present this vision to customers–and within IBM–Gerstner is up to his old tricks. In Feb. of 1998, IBM set up the Pervasive Computing Div., headed by Mark F. Bregman, another former IBM research scientist. Much like Wladawsky-Berger did in the Internet Div., Bregman has spent the past 18 months analyzing the market and working with other areas of IBM to develop strategies centered on devices, software, and services that make the Net accessible anywhere, anytime.

The first offering: software that lets any type of digital device, say a cell phone or Palm handheld, fetch content off the Net. Sounds simple, but it isn't. Right now companies are struggling to deliver pages to screens of any size. Bregman's group has put together a service that companies can rent that will translate content from any Web site and deliver it to any screen. "The idea," says Bregman, "is to offer infrastructure as a service. It's more like a utility. You just pay the bill."

Already IBM is lining up customers. On Nov. 29, PlanetRx, an online pharmacy, will go live with a service that allows virtual shopping via Palm handheld devices. Telecom companies Nokia, Ericsson, and Sprint PCS have signed on, too. "Moving information from 17-inch screens on your desk to where it can be used on the Web from anywhere is an important trend," says John F. Yuzdepski, a vice-president at Sprint PCS. "IBM's technology allows a ubiquity of access to information."

The technology is one thing, but if Gerstner is going to build a new IBM, he has to create an Internet culture. That work began in Atlanta four years ago. When you walk in the door at IBM's Atlanta Web design office–dubbed the "Artz Cafe"–dogs are camped out alongside Web designers and an iguana. Four workers sit astride massage chairs getting worked over by masseuses. Ping-pong tables double as conference tables, and there's a billiard table upstairs where workers can go to clear their heads after long hours toiling at–gasp–Macintosh computers. "To attract the cool, younger people in the Internet business we had to break with the whole IBM culture," says Kerry Kenemer, a creative director who sports a goatee. "We're the only creative bone in the entire IBM body."

Now, IBM is trying to spread the culture throughout its organization. On Nov. 15, the company launched Project Springboard. After pouring $100 million into its four-year-old Atlanta Web design center, it's broadening that approach and opening e-business integration centers around the world. Instead of just design services, these centers will offer customers a place to tap IBM specialists and outside experts to set up next-generation e-business solutions.

The centers reflect a hipper IBM that the company hopes will be able to attract Web-savvy employees. In some areas, IBM is angling to siphon off creative types by setting up shop in cool areas of the country. In Los Angeles, for example, the center will be near the MTV and Sony studios. The company is even lightening up on job titles. One worker in Chicago goes by the title "concept

architect and paradoxiologist." (Translation: Someone who works on tough Internet strategies.)

That's not the only Silicon Valley-ish move the company is taking. Like Intel and Cisco, IBM has quietly invested $60 million in venture funds that focus on Web technologies. Of course the company wouldn't mind a big IPO payday, but it is mostly using these deals to provide "headlights" into cutting-edge technologies. IBM has hit pay dirt on at least one investment so far: In August, it invested $45 million in Internet Capital Group, a holding company that funds business-to-business Web companies. That was just before its public offering. Now IBM's investment is worth $619 million.

NEW HORIZON. What's the next e-business frontier for Big Blue? It's getting companies to turn over entire business processes to IBM that are conducted over the Web. "The way we think of e-business is that it's really the opportunity to do the next level of transformation," says Richard B. Anderson, who has been given the task of taking IBM to the Web.

Consider what IBM is doing for United Technologies Corp. IBM uses the Net to handle $5.8 billion worth of general procurement for Carrier Corp., UTC's Farmington (Conn.) subsidiary. The company won't talk about the actual savings of the system, but says it has been a phenomenal success–increasing efficiency, cutting costs, and becoming a gold mine for collecting information about purchasing habits. Now UTC has the data that will allow the company to talk to suppliers and get better discounts. But UTC insists it's not about cutting costs. "This is all about turning data into information and turning that information into action," says Kent L. Brittan, vice-president for supply management for UTC.

That's the sort of phrase Gerstner might coin for his next analyst's meeting. Back in May, for just a few hours after Gerstner's Wall Street meeting, IBM was like a dot.com company: Its shares shot up 20 points, the kind of movement associated with Web giants eBay or Yahoo. But if Gerstner can continue to convince customers that he has truly remade IBM into Internet Business Machines, he may yet join the Internet 25.

By Ira Sager
Contributing: Peter Burrows in Santa Clara, Calif., David Rocks in Atlanta, and Diane Brady in Greenwich, Conn.

(This article continues)

(Cont.)

INKTOMI . . . GETTING MONEY FROM CLICKS AND CACHES

Inktomi's revenues could jump fourfold between 1998 and 2000 if its new products live up to their billing. Here's how:

	FISCAL YEAR		
	1998	1999+	2000+
	Revenue (in millions)		
INKTOMI'S TRAFFIC SERVER: Now Inktomi's biggest moneymaker, Traffic Server is software sold at a starting price of $24,000. The software, licensed by nearly 100 companies, allows Internet service providers such as America Online and Excite@Home to speed up the delivery of content over the Internet by caching, or storing, frequently requested Web pages or sites in their high-speed computers. That way they can be dished up instantly.	$8	$40.3	$83.9
SEARCH: If you thought that Yahoo and AOL delivered what you needed based solely on their own homegrown search capabilities, think again. Operating behind the scenes is Inktomi's search service. Sold to more than 50 companies and portals, Inktomi generates revenue by charging every time it returns a page requested by a search query.	$12.5	$25.2	$39.5
SHOPPING: About 20 Web sites offer Inktomi's new shopping service, which allows Web surfers to compare the products of 350 merchants that have partnerships with Inktomi, including J. Crew and Barnes & Noble. When customers buy something found through the shopping service, Inktomi takes a percentage of the sale from the merchant and splits the money with the portal. Inktomi plans to add auctions, local merchants, and classified advertising to this service.	$0	$1.8	$4.1
DIRECTORY: A new portal service launched this summer, Inktomi Directory Engine builds off its popular search to provide portals with neatly packaged subject categories. The directory, for example, will let customer GoTo.com offer cybersurfers categories of information, like health, rather than just bits of information. Inktomi charges the portal every time it serves up a page. So far, it's signed up seven clients, including Knight Ridder.	$0	$1	$4

+Revenue estimates

DATA: Bear, Stearns & Co. Inc.

tsunami of data, Inktomi this summer introduced a new directory of Web pages, called the Inktomi Directory Engine, designed to help speed and improve the accuracy of searches.

WAKE-UP CALL. With the explosive growth in the number of Web pages, though, it's no surprise that new search-engine companies are intent on stealing some of Inktomi's lucre. Earlier this year, Inktomi got a major wake-up call when its first customer, the HotBot Web site, announced it was adding a second search service from Direct

Hit Inc., a year-old Wellesley (Mass.) startup. The reason? While Inktomi is considered good at getting results from basic queries, Direct Hit's analysis of many similar searches improves the relevancy of search results. According to market researcher Media Metrix, 53% of all Web searches now use Direct Hit's technology in addition to traditional search engines.

Now comes Google, a new search-technology provider that claims its searches are faster and more accurate than Inktomi's. "We think that there is a lot of room for

innovation in the world of search," says Larry Page, co-founder of Google, which is based in Mountain View, Calif. Google has raised $25 million from backers, including the influential Kleiner Perkins Caufield & Byers.

Inktomi isn't running scared. It plans on continually beefing up its search technology. And with the competition in search heating up, Peterschmidt's diversification push is starting to look smart, indeed. Early last year, the company introduced its Traffic Server software, which lets Internet service providers (ISPs) store often-viewed Web pages on

(Cont.)

computers scattered around the world where they're just a quick click from consumers' screens–a practice called caching. Already, more than a half-dozen companies have signed on, including Net video leader Real Networks Inc.

Caching radically improves the performance of Web sites. For Excite@Home, which is using Inktomi's software, at least half of the traffic running on the network doesn't have to travel across the Internet backbone, says Milo Medin, Excite@Home's chief technology officer. On a busy day, that can shave crucial seconds off the time it takes for a viewer to see a Web page.

TROJAN HORSE. Unfortunately for Inktomi, this market is under attack from competitors, too. And they're the giants like Cisco Systems and Novell Inc., which tower over Inktomi in size and resources. The market for caching is now about $100 million and is expected to grow to $1.6 billion by the year 2002, according to the Internet Research Group. So chances are Inktomi will have more adversaries in the future. Even Microsoft is expected to add some basic caching capabilities to its Web server software, some-thing that it bundles for free with Windows NT software.

Wary of all the competitive threats, Peterschmidt is hoping to improve Inktomi's prospects by targeting new kinds of customers–not just the large ISPs and mega-portals. Recently, he has inked deals with dozens of smaller, niche players like music site kadoodle.com, set to launch in October. The rationale, say Inktomi executives, is that because the search technology is so flexible, it can be tailored for specialized searches. A music site like kadoodle.com can get a search engine designed by Inktomi to filter out any unrelated Web pages. A search for the rock group REM, for instance, wouldn't return any pages related to dreaming and rapid eye movement, also known as REM.

Peterschmidt's hope is that search is the Trojan horse that gets Inktomi's foot in the door of new customers–making it easier to sell them the rest of the company's portfolio of products. Especially promising in this market are the new shopping service and technology that helps sites build and maintain their own Web site directories. For example, when someone does a search on a site focused on backpacking, not only would the search engine deliver a long list of Web pages based on the key words supplied, but it could also dish up a list of backpack merchants, plus a directory that lists related sites or subjects.

The way the Net is expanding, there's no end in demand for the basic network plumbing that Inktomi supplies. The question is: How quickly can it expand into new markets? For its founders, the pace has been dizzying. "When you hire folks, especially in the early days, you sell them a bill of goods and a promise," Brewer says. "Then you have the on-going burden of making that vision come true." Brewer and Peterschmidt have kept their promises so far. And they no longer stumble over homeless people when they go to work. Now they just have to worry about tripping over themselves as they race to capitalize on what may be some of the sweetest of sweetspots on the Web.

By Michael Moeller

Reprinted from the September 27, 1999 issue of *Business Week* by special permission. Copyright © 1999 by the McGraw-Hill Companies, Inc.

86

WHY OFFICE DEPOT LOVES THE NET

Its brick-and-mortar network is a big plus

Warehouses, stores, and inventory are all the kiss of death when it comes to Internet economics, right? If so, someone forgot to tell David I. Fuente, chairman of Office Depot Inc. Since getting into e-commerce nearly four years ago, Fuente has used Office Depot's nationwide network of 750 superstores, 30 warehouses, and $1.3 billion in goods to build the largest office-supply retailer on the Internet, with $250 million in sales. And unlike high-flying Web-based companies that have yet to turn a profit, he gloats over the fact that Office Depot's Net business is in the black. "For us, this has been profitable from virtually the day we opened," says the 54-year-old Fuente.

As the Internet matures, it may be the old brick-and-mortar retailers like Office Depot that have the last laugh. But only if they develop a Web strategy not unlike Office Depot, which is leveraging its strengths in terra firma for success in cyberspace. The necessary ingredients: a solid brand name, extensive local distribution, and hefty purchasing power to match–or even undercut–discount-minded cyber-rivals. "If the traditional retailers would only wake up and use their stores and distribution power, it would be a phenomenal opportunity," says PaineWebber Inc. retailing analyst Aram Rubinson.

Office Depot is a case study in how to avoid being Amazoned. The Delray Beach (Fla.) company is tightly integrating the Net into the heart of its operations. Focusing primarily on business-to-business, it has set up customized Web pages for 37,000 corporate clients, including Procter & Gamble Co. and MCI WorldCom Inc. For each customer, Depot has designed a site with parameters that allow different employees various degrees of freedom to buy supplies: A stockroom clerk might only be able to order pencils, paper, and toner cartridges, while the assistant to the CEO might have carte blanche to order everything the company sells.

Customers also can use the Net to check up-to-the-minute inventory at the nearest store or warehouse to see what's available for delivery the next day. "Office Depot seems to really get it," says Chuck Martin, chairman of the Net Future Institute, a New Hampshire think tank that studies e-commerce. "Rather than just extending their business to the Net, they've used it to leverage their bricks and mortar."

There's a sweet financial incentive for doing it: Electronic sales cost less than those made in stores or from catalogs. Processing an order taken over the Net costs Depot less than $1 per $100 of goods sold, vs. twice that for phone orders. And since no customer-service representative has to key in the transaction, order-entry errors are virtually eliminated and returns are cut in half. The Web now accounts for some 20% of Depot's sales to corporations–and the company aims to raise that to 30% by yearend. That would help: Last month, the company told analysts that its second-half earnings would come in more than 20% below the Street's estimates, primarily because of rising inventories of outdated office-technology products and the costs of closing underperforming stores.

Office Depot isn't the only one that wins by moving to the Web–so, too, do its customers. The Depot's Web operations help corporate clients reduce their need for costly purchase orders since billing is handled electronically. While the average order for supplies is about $125 at Office Depot, many customers report costs of more than $100 to simply process a purchase order and pay an invoice. Using the Web, that can be slashed to $15 to $25. "We went to Office Depot primarily because of their Web systems, which translated to greater efficiency in ordering," says Urban Sommer, director of procurement at MCI WorldCom. The phone company has seen its $3.5 million annual bill for office supplies shaved by more than 10%.

To be sure, Office Depot isn't the only seller of office supplies on the Net. Staples Inc. in Framingham, Mass., has a site that many experts believe rivals Depot's–and even has certain advantages, such as a partnership with Register.com, a Web site that lets businesses sign up for Net domain names. The third player in the real-world office supply business, Office Max Inc. of Shaker Heights, Ohio, was first to the Web, beating Office Depot by a year. But thanks to Depot's sophisticated approach, it's leading the pack with Web sales that are 25% higher than Staples' $200 million. Office Max doesn't report its Web revenues, but concedes its sales are smaller than the other

---

OFFICE DEPOT'S E-STRATEGY

How it Benefits Office Depot:

Cuts in half the cost of processing an order. Typically, it costs about $2 to process a $100 phone order, but over the Web that drops to less than $1.

Wins new customers. Consumers who weren't close to an Office Depot store can now use the company's Web site to order goods.

Keeps customers. Those that might defect to online competitors can now stick with Office Depot. Less than 1% of sales in the $200 billion office-supply market are generated by Web-only companies.

How it Benefits Office Depot's Customers:

Reduces the cost of purchasing goods. Corporations spend $75 to $175 to issue a purchase order for an item and then pay for it. The Net slices that to $15 to $25.

Businesspeople can place orders from their chairs. Customers tell Office Depot that ordering over the Net reduces phone calls to the purchasing department by 60%

Provides a peek into Office Depot's inventory. Why is that important? If you have a presentation tomorrow, you may want to know whether Office Depot has 40 purple binders on hand.

Lets workers do away with inventory. Because customers can get supplies when they want them, they can ditch the old supply cabinet.

(Cont.)

two. "Depot has done the best job, hands down," analyst Rubinson says.

SMART FRIENDS. Together, the three have occupied the Web early and forcefully enough to neutralize any serious threat from Internet startups, such as At Your Office.com and Online Office Supplies.com. Consider this: Online Office Supplies started operating a year ago and has logged less than $1 million in sales. Anybody would "have a difficult time becoming the Amazon of office supplies," says Paula Jagemann, CEO of Online Office Supplies.com.

Office Depot can credit smart friends for its success. Its push into e-commerce began at the behest of one of the more tech-savvy institutions: the Massachusetts Institute of Technology. The school was looking to ditch an archaic system of requisitioning office supplies from campus stockrooms and outside vendors. "We wanted the school community to use the Internet in a way that would eliminate having to make a call, generate a purchase order, and pay an invoice. Yet they could still have the item the very next day or sooner," says Diane Devlin, who led the MIT team developing the operation.

Depot won the contract and opened the system in January, 1996. Soon, MIT had rid

> With its site for big companies thriving, Office Depot is turning its attention to small business

itself of five stockrooms and a warehouse, allowing redeployment of much of the $1.2 million it had tied up in inventory. And through the Office Depot initiative and other Internet-ordering systems, MIT has reduced employment in its procurement department by roughly half.

Since Office Depot started building similar sites for corporate clients in the autumn of 1996, it has found that the cost of operating on the Web is minuscule compared to the benefits. Because Depot built its Net business on an existing network of warehouses, 2,000 delivery trucks, and phone-order sales to many of the same customers, the upfront cost was less than $10 million. "Our incremental investment to become a Web-based company was almost zero," Fuente says. "We didn't need to buy any different products, we didn't need to build any new distribution centers or order-entry systems. All we needed was a Web site. It's very cheap."

Now, Office Depot is turning its attention

to a public Web site for small businesses and consumers. Individuals can order any of the company's products. Small companies get a poor man's version of the big corporate sites. For example, each visitor can set up lists of authorized users with the ability to purchase specific types of supplies or goods up to a certain dollar value. A company can also authorize a lower-level worker to place orders that will only be submitted after a supervisor, who is notified by e-mail, approves them. The site is catching on: It attracted more than 800,000 visitors in July.

Even though Depot's Net operations are growing 50% per quarter, Fuente believes they will not displace the company's traditional business anytime soon. Even now, the Web accounts for only 3% of the company's total revenues. Besides, he knows how critical brick-and-mortar assets like warehouses are to Depot's Internet future.

By David Rocks
Contributing: Peter Galuszka

87

HOW AN INTRANET OPENED UP THE DOOR TO PROFITS

Weyerhaeuser's door plant was on its last legs—until an in-house information network showed people how to work better and smarter

From its drab, corrugated-metal exterior, Weyerhaeuser Co.'s Marshfield (Wis.) door factory, deep in America's dairy belt, doesn't look like much. But inside, the 100-year-old timber giant is carving out its own piece of the Internet revolution.

Four years ago, the plant was on its last legs–what Weyerhaeuser Vice-President Jerry Mannigel had called a "dead dog" of a door plant, besieged by bloated costs, flagging sales, and bad morale. Even Mannigel, a Marshfield native who initiated a factory redesign in the mid-1980s, had to be begged to return from his job at another facility to see if things could be turned around. "The situation had gotten so bad that Marshfield was operating at half capacity but costing us the equivalent of full capacity," he says. And morale couldn't have been worse. Says Mannigel, whose father also used to work at the plant: "You had to practically beat people with a stick to get them to come back to work every morning."

What a difference the Internet has made. Today, the plant–which cuts, glues, drills, and shapes customized doors according to each buyer's desire–is profitable again, and revenues are growing at an annual 10%-to-15% pace. Better management has been key. But productivity experts give much credit to Weyerhaeuser's installation of a state-of-the-art in-house communications network that uses the Internet to compare prices in a heartbeat, boost on-time deliveries, and track orders as they move through the plant.

NEW RULES. Since phase-in began in late 1995, the technology, dubbed DoorBuilder, has helped the plant to double production–to more than 800,000 doors annually. Tracking software has improved the plant's record for complete and on-time deliveries–up from 40% to 97%. The plant's share of the U.S. commercial door market has zoomed from 12% to 26%. And since 1993, the year Weyerhaeuser thought to shut down the plant, the factory's return on net assets has grown from -2% to 27%–well beyond this year's companywide goal of 17%.

Now, Weyerhaeuser is taking DoorBuilder even further, rewriting the rules of the doormaking industry. In the past year, Weyerhaeuser has begun to experiment with extending its DoorBuilder network beyond the plant's borders to some of its most valued customers–key distributors. That communications link is speeding up the ordering process for customers, while eliminating costly errors, waste, and delivery snafus. The result: Weyerhaeuser can offer faster turn-around and, in some cases, lower prices that rival doormakers may have to match. At the same time, distributors that want to get in on the improvements are being forced to automate their shops so they can hook into Weyerhaeuser's network.

For many of Weyerhaeuser's distributors, the arrival of the Internet to their old-line businesses is jarring, and not altogether welcome. Charles Hummel, CEO of Pleasants Hardware Co. in Winston-Salem, N.C., the nation's largest door distributor and one of Weyerhaeuser's biggest customers, gripes that DoorBuilder will require him to put computers, extra phone lines, and trained tech staff in his 15 branch offices. Hummel is hoping he can hold out but concedes he may have to bite the bullet because of Weyerhaeuser's clout. "It's a love-hate relationship with Weyerhaeuser right now," he says. "If you're not on DoorBuilder, your lead times may actually increase."

Such upheaval is the inevitable by-product of E-engineering in the timber industry and just about everywhere else these days. High-tech and low-tech companies alike are scrambling to remake their businesses from top to bottom so they can tap into the power of the Net. At the heart of these efforts are communications networks much like Weyerhaeuser's, called intranets, that link all the workers in the company while plugging into vast databases of information, factory-floor operations, supplier inventory, price lists, and order-taking. According to International Data Corp., an estimated 52% or more of manufacturing companies with revenues of $1 billion or higher are considering, or already have, intranets. "From its original role as a data repository, the intranet has rapidly grown to become the central nervous system of the enterprise," says a May report from Concours Group, a research and consulting firm in Kingwood, Tex.

As essential as that may sound, not all intranets have paid off. Some companies have stopped with a Web site or have failed to exert the type of leadership and flexibility needed for the technology and the cultural changes it brings. Or, says Ernst & Young consulting's chief technologist, John Parkinson, "they end up costing far more than expected and drown managers in too much information." Even at Marshfield, Vice-President William Blankenship–who persuaded Weyerhaeuser's top brass to O.K. the plant's intranet, admits that "it has been a long haul." Weyerhaeuser's initial $2 million investment has more than quadrupled. And when Mannigel made the system fully operational last February, glitches and worker errors temporarily slowed deliveries and hampered production.

CUSTOM CRAFT. Executives remain committed to Marshfield as one of a handful of examples of E-engineering that is working in the U.S. And Blankenship says Weyerhaeuser is just beginning to discover what DoorBuilder can do.

To understand just how dynamic DoorBuilder is, consider the dramatic changes it has brought to the single task of order-taking. At Weyerhaeuser, this has long been a painstakingly complex job, since each door is custom-built, according to an amazing 2 million different configurations–from size, style, and color to the veneer and hardware options. One door might have a round window and a core to withstand 40 minutes of fire; another could be laminated with white plastic stars, destined for a theater on Broadway. Before DoorBuilder, says Mannigel, "we had been buried in information, and our inability to handle it had become the bottleneck of this business. Every six or seven doors or so that we make here are likely to be different from those that come before and those that come after."

DoorBuilder sorts through all that information and calculates the math in seconds. The days when distributors, builders, and Weyerhaeuser reps would haggle for weeks, if not months, to hammer out an order are gone. And, if customers are plugged into Weyerhaeuser's network, they can bypass Weyerhaeuser's reps altogether by typing in their order on the Marshfield plant's Web site. All orders are final once the customer pushes the "submit" button on their computer. Sometimes, handwritten substitutions were slipped into the process at the last minute, as a special favor to a particular customer. "Today, there are no special favors," Mannigel says. "Now, every order is equal."

Indeed, DoorBuilder's order-entry software is so sophisticated that it is based on the same system Boeing Co. uses to configure its complex 777 airplane wings. "If a certain hinge can't be used on a certain door in a certain city, then DoorBuilder will reject that as an option and tell you why," says Mannigel.

Converting orders from paper to bits also has reduced the number of errors. Previously, orders were stapled to each door and would inevitably get torn off or lost at various times during production. "We had one guy who used to collect these off the floor and put them in a big bin, and every two weeks or so, he would throw them out. We were having to redo orders like crazy," says Mannigel. Weyerhaeuser figures DoorBuilder has reduced errors drastically, cutting two to three weeks off turnaround times.

The new system is making the company a lot smarter—and tougher—about pricing, too. In the past, prices were based on hunches, special relationships, and haggling with customers and suppliers. "The questions of cost and price every month were a crapshoot," says

Mannigel. With Doorbuilder, there is no more guesswork or favoritism. Thanks to more precise information about costs and lead times, doors are now priced according to what each option actually adds to the total cost of manufacture. Executives who had once prided themselves on their pricing prowess discovered that some of their generations-old calculations were faulty. In one case, Mannigel says, "a distributor who we thought was one of our best customers was actually costing us money." Says Lee Kirchman, the plant's vice-president for marketing and sales: "The machine knew more than we did."

The result: Weyerhaeuser now charges some customers more. If they balk, DoorBuilder can instantly offer up different options that are cheaper. "No way that would have worked without the data we got from DoorBuilder," Mannigel says. "For the first time, we had proof some orders weren't making any money, so we set out to fix that. Now we can show a customer precisely why we're asking for a higher price."

Ditto suppliers. Kirchman recalls that in the days before DoorBuilder, the company considered Columbia Forest Products Co. one of its best suppliers of veneers, both on price and quality. "But we did an analysis of them with DoorBuilder, and—surprise—they ranked way, way down on the chain," says

Kirchman. So Weyerhaeuser went back to Columbia, showed the company the data and gave them six months to improve—or it would start buying most of its veneers elsewhere. Now, each quarter, Marshfield's purchasing staff sits down with each key supplier and shows them how they stack up on the value chart, hammering out prices accordingly.

The biggest surprise of all: Armed with this information, Weyerhaeuser actually refuses some customer orders now or redirects them to competitors–unimaginable before. Customers also are ranked by their creditworthiness, price demands, average order size, and their willingness to go along with the company's new way of doing things. That has weaned Weyerhaeuser's roster of door distributors down from roughly 500 in 1995 to approximately 200 this year–but with more volume and profit coming from each of the mostly larger customers that remain. "This idea of 'whatever the customer wants' is gone now," says Mannigel.

What's more, customers now have to "put some skinny on the table," Kirchman says–just to be able to use DoorBuilder to place their orders. The 12 distributors starting to experiment with having a direct link to DoorBuilder have each shelled out between $3,000 and $5,000 for the software, a dedicated phone line, training, or the hiring of

How Technology Opened the Door to Profits

	Problem	Solution	Payoff
Orders	**Packages of customized** doors were configured manually from more than 2 million options. The process could take months, with time spent on phone, fax, and mail—haggling with suppliers, distributors and buyers. For the distributor, placing an order could take weeks.	**Customers assemble** their own door packages through a "virtual distributor"—a Web site on the Net or direct link by extranet that allows them to tap into suppliers' lists and get instant packages and pricing.	**Orders get placed** in minutes, with fewer errors, faster delivery times, and lower costs to Weyerhaeuser. Turnaround time has shrunk by three weeks or more.
Pricing	**Pricing was based on hunches** and individual relationships between customers, suppliers and distributors.	**A computerized** cost-tracking system now bases prices on customer value profiles—from creditworthiness to volumes ordered over a period of time—and the cost of every option that gets built into a finished door.	**Some prices went up;** some went down. Weyerhaeuser stopped losing money on the production of unprofitable doors, saving millions of dollars.
Customers	**Accepted almost any customer** and order—even though some customers cost Weyerhaeuser money.	**Using new database** and DoorBuilder software, the plant now knows its customers better and can be more choosy about which orders it bids for and which distributors it chooses to do business with.	**At least 50%** fewer customers, but a doubling in order volumes, to more than 800,000 doors this year. That boosted the plant's return on net assets from −2% five years ago to +24% this year.
Tracking Orders	**Handwritten notes** and printed forms stapled to each door for tracking orders through the factory were easily lost, inaccurate, and confusing.	**Computer system** tracks progress in real-time, with no changes in orders allowed after they are submitted by customers.	**Fewer errors,** better scheduling, faster delivery, more precise inventory control.
Delivery	**On schedule** and complete only 40 to 50% of the time.	**Using tracking and scheduling** software and a communications network inside the plant, Marshfield is able to deliver complete orders on time 97 to 100% of the time.	**Door deliveries** are speeded up—and Weyerhaeuser gets paid faster when performance is faster and more consistent.

in-house order-placers. According to some, DoorBuilder has added an extra hour or two to the order-taking process on their end. "What Weyerhaeuser is doing is transferring some of its order work to the distributor," grumbles Hummel.

Other distributors see their investment in DoorBuilder as money well-spent. David Dirtzu, president of Glewwe Door in Eagan, Minn., says the extra expenses are a small price to pay to get on-time deliveries. "You can easily lose what we spent on DoorBuilder if your orders get delivered wrong or are late," says Dirtzu. "We figure DoorBuilder will pay for itself within the year." And it could help make distributors more efficient. Says Gerald Lenger, executive vice-president at H&G Sales Inc., a St. Louis distributor using Door-Builder: "What DoorBuilder has started is like dominoes in this industry. And those who don't keep up will probably be left behind."

> **"For the first time, we had proof some orders were not making any money, so we set out to fix that"**

DoorBuilder has even had a hand in wiping out niggling problems with inventories. Previously, a shipment of, say, the wrong veneer couldn't be traced back to its supplier. Now, DoorBuilder can pinpoint which manager sold it–along with when and in what condition it arrived. Kirchman, for example, recalls that before the intranet, the plant had been buying 100 very expensive mahogany door veneers each year when they hadn't used up a single sheet of their old supply. "All that our old inventory system told us was that these items were gone and so we ordered some more," says Kirchman. "It's incredible how much this technology can challenge your basic assumptions about things." And DoorBuilder won't schedule any door for production unless the raw materials are available to build it.

Ultimately, E-business is changing the door business. It's not the first industry to feel the power of E-business. But Weyerhaeuser's experience suggests that even the most unlikely candidates for an E-engineering overhaul will have to open their doors to the information revolution–and maybe sooner than they'd like.

By Marcia Stepanek

88

AOL angles for TV viewers

AOLTV marries Net, TV in first salvo of battle for interactive services

By David Lieberman
USA TODAY

NEW YORK — When America Online announced its plan last month to buy Time Warner, everyone saw that joining the No. 1 Internet provider and No. 1 media and entertainment conglomerate would rock the Web.

But many executives and analysts are just now seeing how the deal could fundamentally reshape an emerging business that will touch more people in more ways than the computer-accessed Internet: interactive television.

AOL takes its first step toward this blending of TV and the Internet this year when it launches AOLTV.

The service, expected this summer, could be "profoundly important," says Merrill Lynch's Internet specialist Henry Blodget. If the service is a hit, the company's clout over interactive communications might become "analogous to Microsoft's control of the PC operating system."

"The more ways a subscriber interacts with AOL," Blodget says, "the less likely the subscriber will be to pull up stakes and go with a different provider — especially when the entire family has programmed the service with individual buddy lists, calendars and e- mail accounts."

That prospect terrifies rivals that also want to be interactive TV powers, such as Microsoft, which owns WebTV, and Excite At Home, a cable high-speed Internet service. Their battle could split the cable industry.

"We're sitting on a fault line," says Worldgate Communications CEO Hal Krisbergh, whose company provides Internet access to cable TV viewers. "It clearly portends earthquakes."

AOL declined to discuss AOLTV, although it recently briefed Wall Street analysts and demonstrated the service at a consumer electronics trade show.

What wows observers is the proven appeal of the services AOLTV harnesses. AOL subscribers, now 21 million, wouldn't have to boot up their computers to access e-mail, instant messaging, chats, calendars, and online shopping or investment services.

People could use them while watching, say, Who Wants to Be a Millionaire by pointing a remote or wireless keyboard at a set-top decoder that splits the screen to show online content and the TV show.

Initially, people wanting AOLTV would need a special set-top box to connect the TV to a phone line.

But the deal with Time Warner, the No. 1 cable operator with more than 13 million customers, opens the way for AOLTV to dominate interactive TV. It could become a seamless part of the cable TV package, eliminating the need for a separate set-top box and a phone line.

When AOL and Time Warner announced their merger, "we very quickly had a lot of dialogues with the AOL guys," says Jim McDonald, CEO of Scientific-Atlanta, Time Warner's chief supplier of decoder boxes and systems. "What we want to do now is to port their software into our system as quickly as we can."

They aren't alone.

"Nothing has so excited the (cable hardware) industry in the last year as the AOL-Time Warner deal," says Richard Doherty of The Envisioneering Group. "It's that big a buzz. . . . AOL is out talking to everybody."

Cable operators, who have 66 million subscribers, are just starting to negotiate interactive TV deals. Tests will begin this summer on some systems. Commercial rollout will begin in earnest in 2001.

Key points in the talks include whose name is on the service, who controls the initial online screen users see, and where and how often data and ads appear.

AOL could meet resistance on branding. "AOL wants to be your start page," says Tim Bajarin, president of Creative Strategies. "That's one of the big reasons AOL went ahead with the Time Warner deal."

By contrast, Microsoft and Excite At Home are willing to do software and services and let the cable owner control the face shown to users.

"AOL is its own brand," says Excite At Home Vice President Paul Salzinger. "But in Philadelphia, Comcast is its own brand and it means a lot to them."

The stakes are enormous. Revenue from interactive TV — subscriptions, advertising and electronic commerce — could soar to $20 billion in 2004 from $700 million in 1999, Forrester Research says.

Forecasters are enthusiastic about interactive TV because the country is so addicted to the tube.

"The numbers are staggering," says CIBC World Markets' John Corcoran. "There are still 65 million homes not connected to the Internet, and TV is well-positioned to move into that connectivity gap."

What's more, the average adult spends 126 hours in front of a TV screen each month, while the typical AOL user is online for just 26 hours.

No wonder enthusiasts say cable operators could reap a windfall.

Consider one way it could work. An operator might charge advertisers 40 cents each time a subscriber used the remote control to go to the Web for more information on a product. If a customer clicked on two ads a day, just 1% of the 180 spots airing in a typical home, that subscriber would generate an additional $24 a month.

"That's more than an operator collects from basic cable subscriptions," says Krisbergh. "And that's not a hopeful number. It's a conservative number, and the largest growth opportunity facing the industry today."

OVERHYPED PROMISE?

If it sounds like you've heard this tune before, well, you have. For decades, interactive TV has been one of cable's most over-hyped promises — and embarrassing bombs.

That's why the Yankee Group's James Penhune is "amazed at the degree of attention AOL has gotten for — I don't want to call it vaporware, but something that's pre-market."

> *Television's future?* **AOLTV marries TV and the Internet, allowing subscribers to access e-mail, instant messaging, chats, calendars, and online shopping or investment services while watching TV.**

Interactive TV could run aground again if viewers see a privacy threat. The tension is there because advertisers relish its potential for tailoring pitches to different viewers.

"We can actually send two different ads to two different TVs in the same house," says McDonald.

Cable operators could also monitor what programs you watch. "There are a few privacy issues there, but the answer is we can technically do that," he says.

Privacy laws may prove insufficient for interactive TV. Most were written for specific media and are ambiguous when applied to hybrids.

"It's problematic when the provisions are applied to old business models," says Dierdre Mulligan, counsel for the Center for Democracy and Technology.

Still, executives and analysts say that interactive TV is finally ready for prime time. People are more at ease with the Web and cable operators are completing long-term upgrades to two-way-capable systems.

To harness that power, they also are deploying more than 30,000 digital set-top decoders a week that can communicate over cable wires. The capacity for advanced services is "ubiquitous across the country pretty much now," says CEO Edward Breen of General Instrument, the leading maker of set-top decoders that is being bought by Motorola.

AOL salivated to reach the all-important cable market, but it was mostly out of reach until its deal for Time Warner. Operators resented AOL's role as leader of an effort to force cable systems to be open to competing high-speed Internet services.

In defense, AOL invested $1.5 billion last year in Hughes Electronics and got a deal to launch AOLTV on its DirecTv satellite service, using phone lines to connect with AOL through a set-top box. The deal to buy Time Warner put AOLTV on fast-forward. And it's a plus for Time Warner's cable systems.

"Beyond offering video on demand, Time Warner has no interactive TV strategy," says Paul Kagan Associates' Leslie Ellis.

Although the launch plans are still unclear, few expect AOL to offer AOLTV only on DirecTv.

"Obviously, Time Warner's going to try to put it up as soon as they can," says Scientific-Atlanta's McDonald. If the service catches on, then "most (operators) will see demand that they'll have to respond to."

Here's where the battle with other interactive TV companies — particularly Microsoft — is joined.

INTERACTIVE BATTLEGROUND

Microsoft says its experience with WebTV gives it a better insight into what consumers want from interactive TV.

"Initially we looked at a TV set as an available monitor," says WebTV marketing director Rob Schoeben. "But we realized that we missed a fundamental point. That monitor is a TV set and people want it to be a better TV, not an alternative to a PC."

That pitch will appeal to cable operators, many of whom already have financial ties to Microsoft.

Last year, Microsoft invested $5 billion in AT&T, which hopes to soon complete its deal to buy Media-One, making AT&T the No. 1 cable operator. In 1997, Microsoft reawakened Wall Street's interest in all cable companies by investing $1 billion in Comcast, the No. 3 operator.

In addition, Microsoft co-founder Paul Allen has recently gone on a buying spree to make his Charter Communications the No. 4 operator. Microsoft also has a satellite alliance with Echostar, which incorporates

Deal boosts maker of set-top boxes

By David Lieberman
USA TODAY

NEW YORK — Scientific-Atlanta CEO Jim McDonald was as surprised as everyone else by America Online's Jan. 10 deal to buy Time Warner. but few benefited more than the maker of cable systems and set-top boxes, 40% of which go to Time Warner.

Scientific-Atlanta stock is up 115% since before the deal, lifting market value to $8.4 billion. This week it announced a 2-for-1 stock split.

To McDonald, the deal vindicated his focus on robust interactive systems, where most of the computing power and memory is at the cable office, instead of set-top boxes that quickly can become obsolete.

"Interactive TV got moved up a couple of years" because of the deal, McDonald says.

His message has resonated with cable operators who put S-A systems in 100 cities passing 30 million homes.

McDonald says S-A will keep growing: "We don't know of anybody else who has even deployed a system."

Not so, says Motorola, which is buying industry leader General Instrument. "We're relying on the infrastructure that all cable operators are using" as they develop a single communications standard, says digital network manager Dave Robinson. S-A's boxes "don't include the (industry standard) high-speed modem."

But McDonald insists his company will have the interactive TV edge. His boxes include the Web's HTML language, which AOLTV uses.

"Our networks and our products can run this unchanged," he says. "No one else can make that claim."

Next up: boxes that control computers and phones as well as TV sets.

"In 18 months, I'll have twice the performance in semiconductors. And in fiber optics, the bandwidth doubles every nine months," McDonald says. "We're in for an extremely rapid rise in what you can do with these networks."

WebTV on some receivers.

Many large cable operators also are friends with Excite At Home, the high-speed Internet service that is controlled by AT&T. And Excite At Home may have some leverage by claiming that interactive TV is part of its multiyear deals to provide high-speed Internet services.

"The most important thing is, we are established today to deliver these services" via cable, says Excite At Home's Salzinger. "We are big promoters of the cable operators offering a service that ties across to the PC. It's all about convenience."

Microsoft and Excite At Home said in December that they're talking about a possible partnership. Those conversations are still under way.

Still, operators know that it would be dangerous to snub AOL and its huge subscriber base.

If they do, then AOLTV could encourage its customers to cut cable operators out of the interactive TV picture altogether. Use of AOLTV's set-top decoder would keep operators from controlling "many of the next-generation cable services that cable operators had expected to control, including e-mail, the program guide, chat and 'click-to-buy' e-commerce," says Sanford C. Bernstein analyst Tom Wolzien.

The set-top box also could be configured to handle high-speed phone lines — and AOL is exploring accepting data from wireless providers.

Everyone is positioning for a fight that will revolutionize communications and entertainment. "Right now, there's a wall 3 feet thick between the TV and the Internet," says Krisbergh. "And the opportunity to marry the two is awesome."

89

For Sale: Japanese Plants In The U.S.

Some of Japan's biggest names in electronics products are selling out to American contract manufacturers. ■ *by Gene Bylinsky*

Only yesterday, it seems, a choir of journalists, college professors, and management consultants was telling how the Japanese, through their superior manufacturing techniques, would subjugate the world economy by the start of the new millennium. Now, in the biggest flip-flop in recent industrial history, the Japanese–Mitsubishi, NEC, Fujitsu, and soon Sony–are quietly selling some of their treasured U.S. factories to the supposedly backward Americans, who will make Japanese products in them.

Japanese turning to Americans to manufacture Japanese products? Have Eskimos suddenly forgotten how to make igloos? One answer is that, after seven years of recession and poor stock performance, the Japanese have finally begun to give up their cherished dream of keeping everything in the family. They can no longer ignore outsourcing–and outright sale of plants–as a better financial model.

There's a lot more to it. Japan's rigidity has finally caught up with it in manufacturing, at least in electronics industries that require flexible production and fast product introduction to accommodate rapidly shifting demand. An executive of a Silicon Valley diskmaker boasts that, when it comes to speed in turning out a wide variety of complex products, such as computer servers and hard drives, and changing the product mix almost daily, "we can turn on a dime. The Japanese can't do that."

Don't get the wrong idea. Sony, Panasonic, and other Japanese giants still excel at cranking out high-quality consumer electronics products–such as camcorders and TVs–by the millions. And Japanese auto manufacturers still make outstanding vehicles. But it's a different story in industries with short product cycles and factories that must build what customers order instead of churning out products in anticipation of demand. Here Japan's great strength–repetitive manufacturing–is

becoming its greatest weakness.

Listen to John Costanza, president of the John Costanza Institute of Technology in Englewood, Colo., and a leading expert on manufacturing: "The Japanese are terrible at building on demand–terrible, terrible, terrible. Repetitive manufacturing works fine if you can sell everything you can build. But the day when they could tell a customer, 'I'll make a product and you'll buy it,' is gone. Building variable products to demand is the requirement for manufacturing today. So now the Japanese are saying, 'We're going to contract manufacturing by selling plants because we don't know how to change our manufacturing culture.'"

This is where a new breed of American supermanufacturers–you could call them the new Japanese–comes in. They are the so-called contract electronics manufacturers (CEMs), which are gobbling up those Japanese plants in the U.S. as well as abroad. A far cry from the grimy job shops found on the bleak back streets of suburban Detroit or Chicago, CEMs use production techniques that top those of the Japanese, in huge, surgically clean, highly automated plants employing thousands of workers. The CEMs now make products more cheaply in San Jose than the Japanese can in Tokyo.

Through supply chains linking dozens of plants around the world, the big CEMs have become the new providers to so-called original equipment manufacturers (OEMs). Though OEM brand names appear on a vast array of products–from computer servers to PCs to cell phones–a growing proportion of the wares emanates from CEMs. The term OEM, in fact, has become dated; today these companies could more accurately be called OBHs (original brand holders).

According to a recent report by the Banc-Boston Robertson Stephens investment firm, the largest brand owners using CEMs include

Hewlett-Packard, which relies on ten different CEMs to make its products, Cisco (with nine CEMs), IBM (eight), and Lucent (seven). Technology Forecasters of Alameda, Calif., estimates that 9.5% of the electronic goods sold by the world's OEMs are now put together in CEM plants, and expects this percentage to reach 17% by 2003. Japanese brand owners are just starting to get on the bandwagon.

Thus, the CEMs are the new tailors, shoemakers, butlers, and chambermaids of the brand-holder elite, whose members concentrate increasingly on R&D, product design, and marketing. The biggest contract manufacturers are Solectron of Milpitas, Calif., with projected sales this year of $13 billion, SCI Systems of Huntsville, Ala. ($8 billion), Celestica of Toronto ($6 billion), and Flextronics International of San Jose ($3 billion).

CEMs are one of the fastest-growing industrial segments. Technology Forecasters predicts that their revenues, already $60 billion a year, will hit $150 billion in 2003. Just how good the CEMs are is indicated by the fact that Solectron is the only company that has twice won the Baldrige award for manufacturing excellence. And CEMs excel at running global supply chains and using the Internet.

As the CEMs' stock market performance shows, they are not engaged in a marginal, low-profit activity. Since Solectron went public in 1989, its stock has soared 16,000%, vs. a 7,000% rise for Microsoft and 4,000% for Intel during the same period.

The CEMs' profit margins are not as impressive as those of the brand owners, averaging 4% of sales. But their return on investment, as BancBoston Robertson Stephens puts it, has been "splendid." ROI has averaged more than 20% for the big CEMs, vs. an average of only 6% to 9% for companies that make up Standard & Poor's industrials. The reason is that the CEMs' plants, operating at a high percentage of capacity, are efficient.

The growth of the CEMs has been fueled in large part by their purchases of OEM plants, for which they often bid aggressively against one another. They have turned those plants into more efficient producers by upgrading equipment and by making products for more than one client under the same roof. In 1998 alone, CEMs bought 47 manufacturing plants in the U.S., in the process keeping thousands of manufacturing jobs from leaving the country. Abroad, CEMs run dozens of plants in places like Oulu, Finland; Hortolandia, Brazil; Guadalajara, Mexico; and Kunshan, China. Generally the CEMs make more complex products in their U.S. plants than they do at foreign sites where labor costs are lower.

A big goal of many CEM executives, helped to no small extent by John Costanza's institute, has been to return U.S. manufacturing to its former preeminence. Many who have led this drive are Asian Americans, among them Solectron's former president, Winston Chen, a Chinese American, and its current CEO, Koichi "Ko" Nishimura, a California-born Nisei who spent his boyhood in a World War II internment camp.

Buying Japanese plants in the U.S. could put the CEMs on a new growth spurt. "There's a certain irony in this," says Flextronics CEO Michael Marks. The Japanese plant sales began in 1998, when Mitsubishi sold its cell-phone manufacturing facility in Braselton, Ga., to Solectron. In addition to taking over the manufacture of Mitsubishi cell phones sold in North America–the phones are being made in a new 100,000-square-foot leased facility that it has set up on the Mitsubishi campus–Solectron also manages printed-circuitboard assembly for the phones and new-product introduction. Mitsubishi, for its part, now concentrates on advanced engineering and product development.

Solectron declined to be interviewed for this article, perhaps because of the sensitivity of the subject with both buyers and sellers. But CEO Nishimura is known to be urging Japanese OEMs to sell their plants. "He tells them how Solectron would modernize the plants, reduce their costs, and improve their antiquated distribution system," says a source close to the company. The fact that Nishimura speaks fluent Japanese doesn't hurt.

The changes CEMs make in newly acquired plants, Japanese or otherwise, can be dramatic. Says Flextronics' Marks: "All factories are different. But in nearly every case, we improve the housekeeping and change some information technology functions. We almost always invest in new production equipment."

The CEMs pick their acquisitions carefully, Marks notes: "We buy plants with appropriate geographic locations, to increase customer penetration and to give us technical capabilities we don't have." Flextronics passed on NEC's Hillsboro, Ore., telecom equipment plant, which is on the block, but the company is bidding on another NEC telecom production facility in Sao Paulo. A few weeks ago, Flextronics also acquired a computer-server factory in Paderborn, Germany, which had been jointly owned by Fujitsu and Siemens.

Late last year another big CEM, SCI Systems, bought a NEC Computers manufacturing plant in Sacramento and shipped some of the production tools to Huntsville, Ala., where it has set up a plant that makes laptops and desktops for NEC. SCI will also handle the complete supply chain for NEC Computers in North America. CEO A. Eugene Sapp of SCI hailed the acquisition as providing "the basis for a range of future initiatives between the [two] companies."

What really makes CEM bosses drool is a tsunami of Japanese plant sales expected at the end of March. That's when, according to a spokesman, Sony will announce plans to dispose of 22 of its 70 plants worldwide, selling some and shutting down others. Many other Japanese manufacturing companies are expected to follow suit. "They will be saying, 'If Sony's doing it, we should be doing it too,'" says Sheridan Tatsuno, a Harvard-educated Sansei (fourth-generation Japanese American) who consults with Japanese companies from his Northern California base in Aptos.

The trend is about to accelerate because of pressure from an unexpected source. Says Tatsuno: "Even MITI [Japan's Ministry of International Trade and Industry] is now telling Japanese companies to get into e-business and to sell manufacturing plants." Yes, that's the same MITI that helped engineer Japan's assault on U.S. manufacturing companies in the 1960s and 1970s.

Selling the family jewels–Tatsuno's term

for the plants–is a traumatic experience for older Japanese executives, many of whom made their names in manufacturing. "It's a huge loss of face," says Tatsuno, "because they literally grew up on the plant floor. But the younger executives don't seem to care who makes their products."

Handel Jones, a Ph.D. economist and semiconductor engineer who runs a Japan-oriented consulting and data-gathering firm, International Business Strategies, in Los Gatos, Calif., sees nothing but black clouds over the factories of the Land of the Rising Sun. "When we project Japanese strengths and weaknesses out to 2010," says Jones, "it looks very negative for them. They remain strong in the old-style electromechanical, or repetitive, manufacturing. But when it comes to using software intelligence inside new, flexible production systems, they're very weak."

Recognizing a new need, some Japanese companies are now seeking help from American manufacturing experts such as Costanza. Fujitsu, Sharp, and Hitachi are trying to introduce demand-flow manufacturing, a concept he pioneered, in their U. S. plants. Costanza and his staff have installed it in hundreds of U.S. companies, from AT&T to GE to U.S. Robotics.

Demand-flow manufacturing works on principles diametrically opposed to those of conventional manufacturing based on scheduling and forecasts. Not only does demand flow rearrange linear production lines into semicircular cells for more efficient production, but it also does away with that mainstay of Japanese manufacturing, the just-in-time (JIT) delivery of components such as automobile seats or tires. Demand flow substitutes its own concept–raw-in-process inventory, or RIP. This calls for keeping a reasonable quantity of varied raw materials or components on hand to meet changing demand.

Sheridan Tatsuno sums it up: "John Costanza and the CEMs have totally changed the game on the Japanese." Americans teaching the Japanese that it's time for just-in-time to rest in peace? That's how far the world has turned in manufacturing.

Ethical Marketing in a Consumer-Oriented World: Appraisal and Challenges

90

The Omnipresent Persuaders:

Marketing in the future will be everywhere— including your head

By Jonathan Kaufman

Staff Reporter of The Wall Street Journal

As you settle in this weekend to watch the Southwestern Bell Cotton Bowl, the Tostitos Fiesta Bowl and the FedEx Orange Bowl, brace yourself: Pervasive, intrusive, annoying marketing is destined to get worse in the next 1,000 years.

Already, marketers are rolling out technology that attaches to your computer and sprays the smell of a new-car interior or a charbroiled hamburger into your home or cubicle. A Pittsburgh advertising firm is lobbying city officials to turn abandoned buildings into giant outdoor billboards for Iron City beer. And Pizza Hut is planning to put its logo on the rocket that will launch the international space station.

Call it "marketism"–the quest by companies to take every last space that might be commercial-free and brand it with their name and product.

Where will it all end? Inside your brain, if some marketers have their way. As technology advances, futurists imagine a world in which advertisers will "narrowcast" messages directly into consumers' brains, stirring emotional responses that impel us to buy their products.

"The thing you are going to worry about in the future is not Big Brother–the government watching you–but Little Brother–tens of thousands of companies using technology to hijack your attention," says Christopher Meyer, director of Ernst & Young's Center for Business Innovation. He thinks the only way for consumers to fight back will be forcing the government to pass laws treating the expropriation of human attention as a form of theft.

"People will rise up and say, 'They don't have the right to interrupt my brainwaves!'" predicts Mr. Meyer. "Book 'em on Distraction One."

Always in Your Face

The growing intrusiveness of advertising and marketing messages reflects an escalating late-20th-century arms race between marketers and consumers, with technology the weapon of choice on either side. Marketers harnessed the technology of television to beam commercials into people's homes. Consumers fought back by using the remote-control button to channel-surf and the VCR to fast-forward through commercials. Marketers escalated by inserting products into shows and digitally implanting messages into the backgrounds of televised sporting events.

Similarly, consumers armed with caller-identification hookups have pushed back the telemarketing offensive, while computers' filtering software struggles to stymie the ever-more-resourceful e-mail spammers.

In public spaces, consumers have been able to put up far fewer defenses than they can at home. In just the past five years, the number of sports stadiums bearing brand names has soared to 50 from six, according to IEG Inc., a Chicago-based company that tracks corporate sponsorships.

Paradoxically, the more pervasive advertising and branding becomes, the more effective people have become in tuning it out. Several years ago, Coca-Cola Co. did a survey following a race-car event that was festooned with Coca-Cola signs, giant inflatable Coke bottles and the Coke logo painted across the middle of the race track. Only one-third of the attendees named Coke as the sponsor of the event.

"People are so used to seeing Coke everywhere that when they were asked to associate a specific event with the brand, they couldn't tell us," says Scott Jacobson, a Coke spokesman. "That's when we knew it was time to change the paradigm."

'Tune It Out'

"All this signage becomes like wallpaper –you just tune it out," says Lesa Ukman, president of IEG. "The other night, my husband and I went to see something at the new Ford Theatre in Chicago," refurbished and named after the car company. "On the way home my husband asked me, 'Who was Ford in Chicago?' He thought it was named after a local family."

As a result, marketers say, companies may spend the next 1,000 years trying to cut through the clutter they have created in the past 50.

The first wave, already unfolding, is even more invasive marketing. Nowhere is going to be safe, marketers indicate. As companies sell more goods on the Internet, they will try to reach consumers in previously ad-free locations to allow people to see, smell, and touch their physical products. So, watch for auto makers to set up exhibits showcasing a new-car model in a popular dog-walking spot. Look out for mobile "tasting vans" at bus stops and outside schools after parents drop off their children.

Next will be "ambient advertising"–marketing that jumps out of its medium, such as a billboard that speaks to you as you walk by, or a computer that spews the smell of doughnuts into your face when you click on a banner ad. That's the plan of DigiScents Inc., an Oakland, Calif., company marketing a peripheral device to release scents from computers–and eventually from movie houses, television sets and other media outlets.

"Smell is probably one of the most powerful senses in respect to emotion and memory," says company co-founder Dexster Smith. "If a picture is worth a thousand words, a smell is worth a thousand pictures." He envisions a world in which technology begins to replicate touch and other senses with such authenticity that marketers place customers in "full immersion, simulating reality at more and more powerful levels."

Mr. Smith points out that computers are becoming better able to reproduce tactile sensations through the computer mouse, and that visual and auditory stimulation can be taken "far beyond where we are right now." Michael Grzymkowski, lead strategist with Idea Mill Inc., a Pittsburgh advertising firm, envisions companies taking over entire streets and creating a simulated three-dimensional world that consumers will walk through while going from one point in town to another. "More than an advertisement, it will be an experience," he says.

Such immersion will be especially powerful as companies increasingly tailor messages to each consumer, harnessing the massive amounts of information gained from watching people shop online.

Poked by Technology

"More and more, we are going to have software that looks at you as an individual and predicts what else you will like," says Ernst & Young's Mr. Meyer. Over time, he says, this software will merge with technology that allows people to stimulate their brains and recreate memories and emotions–enabling marketers to associate a car, say, with a drive alongside a sunny beach or the thrill you get from bungee jumping.

"Every person is going to be an information wave-front," says Mr. Meyer. "People will want these experiences. Companies will customize responses and give it to them. If it's done wrong, it will feel like 'The Truman Show'–an artificial world that has nothing to do with you. If it's done right, you'll feel like Louis XIV. The market, *c'est moi.* It'll feel like everything is being done for you at your command."

If such a world sounds like nightmarish science fiction, some are betting that consumers will fuel a backlash, responding favorably to marketers who don't bother them. Will it become cool in the new millennium to be discreet?

"One of these days, you won't hear the voice of James Earl Jones everywhere," says Theodore Levitt, the venerable marketing theorist now retired from Harvard Business School. "You'll have promotions that won't intrude."

Jed Pearsall, a marketing consultant, says, "People are telling us they're tired of having advertising in their face. They want it to do something for them. Marketing will become a field that solves people's problems."

Instead of companies relentlessly marketing products, Mr. Pearsall envisions them

(Cont.)

sponsoring environmental cleanups, paying for school systems, funding hospitals. "People will know that Coca-Cola is doing something for them," says Mr. Pearsall, the head of Performance Research Inc. in Newport, R.I. "They'll be driving down the highway and see a sign saying, 'This road toll-free because of General Motors.'"

But to others, the thought of attending Coca-Cola High School is further evidence of marketism run amok.

"Maybe what's going to happen is that those of us who get into a mentally disturbed state induced by brand assault will take vacations in designated market-free zones that will cleanse us for a week," says Philip Kotler, a professor of marketing at Northwestern University's Kellogg Graduate School of Management. "We'll pay for camps, to be cleaned out of brand assault."

Or maybe the camps will be free–paid for by your local sponsor.

91

RUNNING RINGS AROUND SATURN

Rivals are stealing the carmaker's once-loyal customers. Is the magic gone?

No one has to tell Russell E. Hand how badly Saturn Corp. needs new models to sell. The Torrance (Calif.) Saturn dealer has been watching helplessly as rival Toyota Motor Sales USA Inc. and American Honda Motor Co. lure his once-happy small-car customers into roomier Camry and Accord family sedans. "If someone really needed a bigger car, we didn't have a way for them to go," laments Hand.

Small wonder, then, that when the General Motors Corp. division finally delivered the new L-Series midsize car to its long-suffering dealers last summer, hopes were high. After all, Saturn dealers have had a one-car lineup for 10 years. While GM was investing in its other established brands, Saturn was repeatedly passed over for a new model. Even a redesign of its aging S-Series compact was turned down. As a result, the brands' once-legendary popularity has plummeted as Saturn owners defected to the competition's larger cars, sport-utility vehicles, and newly designed small cars.

> The new midsize car was to be a savior. Now, GM is slashing production plans

Falling behind on new models has cost Saturn and its parent dearly. While just 5.6% of GM's sales at its height in 1994, Saturn, with its fresh image and huge customer following, represented one of the few bright spots on the auto giant's horizon. Since then, however, sales have fallen 20%. Last year alone, small-car sales plunged 10%, even though small-car sales industrywide rose 7%. And in J.D. Power & Associates' 1999 sales-satisfaction index, consumers ranked Saturn sixth–the first time in four years the brand wasn't on top.

If all that weren't troubling enough, now comes the lukewarm reception of the new L-Series midsize car. It was to be Saturn's savior, designed to lure new buyers and bring back its old customers. But when dealers finally got an ample supply of LS sedans and LW wagons, the crowds never showed up. "The bloom is off the Saturn rose," says

former dealer David McDavid of Dallas.

Since July, L-Series sales have averaged fewer than 5,000 cars a month, falling far short of GM's projections of 15,000 monthly sales. That forced Saturn, glutted with inventory, to halt production at its Wilmington (Del.) plant for two weeks in January. Meanwhile, Saturn competitors continue to rack up sales in the midsize car market. In January, Toyota Camry sales of 40,285 and Honda Accord sales of 24,241 dwarfed the 4,381 L-Series cars sold. Those numbers are even more startling considering both the Camry and the Accord sell for a few thousand dollars more than the $16,000 to $22,000 price range for an LS sedan. "We get a lot of Saturn trade-ins," says George Black, general manager of Mile High Honda in Denver.

So what's the problem? Uninspired styling of the L-Series hasn't helped matters, analysts insist. But last fall's $82 million-plus "Next Big Thing" advertising campaign somehow failed to make clear the car's roomy midsize dimensions–one of its major selling points. The ads portrayed the car as a fun family sedan, but did little to show that the car was larger than the Saturn compact.

Now, as the L-Series' problems linger, Saturn has quietly moved to slash its production. Suppliers say the company told them in recent weeks it will crank out just 150,000 cars annually, instead of the 200,000-plus originally planned. That means GM will likely have to pay suppliers more for parts, cutting already thin margins–about $2,000 per car. That's only about one-fifth of what auto makers can gross on their bigger sport-utility vehicles, says Rod Lache, a Deutsche Bank analyst in New York who estimates that the Saturn Div. is at best "marginally profitable."
DISHEARTENING. It's all a huge comedown since the days when Saturn was GM's hottest unit and one of the true success stories of U.S. auto makers in the early 1990s. But what bothers Saturn fans most is that clear signs of trouble went ignored for years. "It's been a great franchise, so it's disheartening to see things go awry," says Dallas Saturn retailer Randy Hiley. "The market changed, and Saturn wasn't ready for it."

Saturn's customers and dealers have, in fact, long clamored for more models. But early on, cash-strapped GM was forced to

> ### A BUMPY RIDE...
>
> - By selling only compact cars for 10 years, Saturn has lost ground to foreign car companies
> - Production snafus slowed its launch and limited supply of new midsize sedans and wagons
> - Lured by a generous spate of rebates from competitors last fall, consumers have been slow to warm to the new Saturn
> - A confusing ad campaign late last year failed to attract buyers to the new, bigger models

make tough choices about where to invest its capital. Saturn lost out to Oldsmobile in a debate among executives over whether to kill Olds or revive it at Saturn's expense, says retired Saturn President Richard G. "Skip" Lefauve. "We were a small subsidiary trying to work our way to profitability," he says. "That was more risk than [GM] wanted to take." Instead of giving Saturn a new car when the brand was hot in the mid-1990s, Olds and other divisions got new product money.

Many of the L-Series' current woes stem from the way GM finally agreed to grant Saturn a new model. To save on costs, GM had Saturn share the basic chassis undercarriage with the Vectra sold in Europe by the company's Adam Opel AG unit. The car was designed by the two units at GM's European engineering center in Russelheim, Germany. Saturn, however, didn't do enough early dry runs with workers to iron out bugs in the assembly process. The result was poorly fitting parts and slowed assembly time. There were also shortcomings in adapting the European design for the U.S. market. Tiny cup holders, for example, had to be quickly redesigned to accommodate Big Gulps. By the time Saturn

(Cont.)

92

Foodstuff:

'Genetically Modified' On the Label Means...Well, It's Hard to Say

Attempt at Clarity in U.K. Brings Much Confusion; FDA Studies the Issue

'Non-GM' Isn't 'GM-Free'

BY STEVE STECKLOW

Staff Reporter of THE WALL STREET JOURNAL

LONDON – It seems simple enough: Let consumers know when they're buying bio-engineered food by requiring a label. It's an idea being promoted heavily in the U.S. by groups such as Greenpeace and Friends of the Earth, and even by some members of Congress.

But a trip up and down the supermarket aisles of Britain, which has required such labeling since March, shows the new law hasn't exactly made things easier for discerning shoppers. Rather, it has spawned a bewildering array of marketing claims, counterclaims and outright contradictions that only a food scientist possibly could unravel.

Take cheese. One supermarket chain here labels its cheese as being "made using genetic modification," the European catchword for bioengineering. But other supermarket chains, whose cheese is made exactly the same way, haven't changed their labels, saying the cheese itself contains no genetically modified ingredients.

Then there's Birds Eye frozen beef burgers. The label on a box purchased last week states that one ingredient, soya protein, is "produced from genetically modified soya." But a spokesman for maker Unilever PLC insists that the soya isn't genetically modified . The company has reformulated the product, he explains, but has yet to replace the box.

Yes or No?

Confused yet? Then scan over the small print on a Haagen-Dazs chocolate-covered ice-cream bar. No genetically modified ingredients listed there. But consumers who question the company about it are sent a letter stating that the bar's chocolate coatings, in fact, contain soya oil that "may have been derived from genetically modified soya, but it is identical to any other soya oil and therefore does not contain any genetically modified material." The

letter adds, "We are, however, investigating whether there are suitable alternative oils."

All of this may seem puzzling to American shoppers, who so far aren't up in arms over whether the food they buy includes ingredients that have been tinkered with in a laboratory. After all, that's already the case with many U.S. products. But European consumers, who have lived through such recent food scares as beef linked to "mad cow" disease, salmonella-contaminated eggs and dioxin-tainted animal feed, are taking no chances, even though there's no proof that bioengineered foods pose any health risks.

Monster Mash

The result has been a biotech backlash that at times borders on hysteria. In Britain, tabloid newspapers routinely refer to genetically modified products as "Frankenstein food." One prisoner even went on a hunger strike demanding that no genetically modified food be served to inmates.

Critics say bioengineered foods offer consumers no obvious benefit and that despite industry and government assurances, not enough research has been done to assure they are safe. Environmental groups have expressed concern that genetically modified plants could have unintended side effects, including killing beneficial insects and, through the spread of pollen, promoting growth of herbicide-resistant "super weeds" and antibiotic-resistant "super bugs." Others fear genetically modified foods could cause dangerous allergic reactions in some people.

In response to widespread consumer outcry, the European Union last year approved legislation that required its 15 member countries to begin labeling all foods that contain genetically modified ingredients, namely corn and soybean in which new genes have been added to provide traits such as insect resistance.

American Reverberations

While no such plans have been announced in the U.S., the Food and Drug Administration said last week that it plans hearings around the country this fall to gauge public opinion on the issue. Already, several American health-food companies have begun slapping labels on their products declaring that they contain no genetically modified ingredients.

But before America leaps into mandatory labeling, the government, retailers and consumer groups might want to take a look at the far-reaching impact such a law has had in Britain.

When the European Union introduced its legislation last year, Britain's agriculture minister called it "a triumph for consumer rights to better information." Britain went on to enact the toughest labeling standards in Europe, requiring even restaurants, caterers and bakers to list genetically modified ingredients. Violations are punishable by fines of as much as $8,400, and the government says it intends to conduct surveillance, including independent lab testing.

"This is not a health issue in any way," says J. R. Bell, head of the government's additives and novel-foods division, adding that his ministry believes the latest bioengineered products are safe. "This is a question of choice, of consumer choice."

But, in fact, as a direct result of the labeling law, there's hardly any choice now at all. That's because Britain's new law sparked a mad rush by manufacturers, retailers and restaurant chains to rid their products of any genetically modified ingredients so they wouldn't have to alter their labels and risk losing sales. Even some pet-food manufacturers are claiming their products contain no genetically modified ingredients.

Among the thousands of products sold in Britain that now claim not to contain any GM ingredients are Pillsbury UK Ltd.'s Green Giant vegetables and Old El Paso Mexican food, Kellogg cereals and Unilever's Van den Bergh Foods Beanfeast line. A spokesman for McDonald's Restaurants Ltd., which operates 1,000 restaurants in the United Kingdom, says, "We do not use any genetically modified products or ingredients that contain genetically modified material." He adds, however, that some ingredients, such as soya oil used in hamburger buns, "could have come from a source which itself is genetically modified at some point."

The rush to keep products from being branded as bioengineered is hardly surprising. When J. Sainsbury PLC, a supermarket chain, began selling a bioengineered tomato puree under its own brand in 1996, sales initially exceeded other, more expensive brands by 30%, though the product's label voluntarily teered that it was genetically modified. But as the GM controversy heated up, sales slowed and, by the end of last year, "absolutely fell through the floor," says Alison Austin, Sainsbury's environmental manager. The product has since been taken off the market by its creator and distributor, Zeneca Plant Science, a unit of AstraZeneca PLC.

Having gotten the message that consumers don't want bioengineered foods, Sainsbury's and other supermarket chains, as well as food manufacturers that sell in Britain, launched extensive, month-long reviews of their product formulations. They began changing recipes to eliminate soya and corn derivatives and ordered their suppliers to find new sources of nonbioengineered raw materials in places such as South America and Asia.

"We poured over something like 5,000 ingredients . . . and made changes to 1,800 recipes as part of this process," says Bob Mitchell, manager of food technical policy at Marks & Spencer PLC, which operates specialty food shops. "It was a colossal task."

Supermarkets soon began declaring in advertising that their own house brands, which in Britain can constitute more than half of all sales, no longer contained genetically modified ingredients.

But a close examination of stores' claims,

(Cont.)

based on interviews with supermarket executives, shows that one chain's definition of removing genetically modified ingredients isn't necessarily the same as another's.

Sainsbury's, for example, says on its Web site that it is "the first major U.K. supermarket to eliminate genetically modified ingredients from its own-brand products." Does that include food additives, such as sweeteners and flavorings, which may be genetically modified? Alison Austin, the company's environmental manager, replies, "To be honest, we have focused in on major ingredients" such as soya and maize proteins and oils, as well as lecithin, an emulsifier. As for other bioengineered ingredients, she says, "It takes time for the supply chain to provide alternatives."

'We Mean Zero GM'

Tesco PLC, Britain's leading supermarket chain, says it makes no distinction between major and minor genetically modified ingredients. As a result, 150 of its house-brand products are still labeled as containing GM ingredients. "When we say zero GM, we mean zero GM," says Simon Soffe, a Tesco spokesman.

Maybe so, but laboratories that test for genetically modified ingredients say it is almost impossible to guarantee that a product line contains absolutely no genetically modified ingredients. Many growers don't segregate bioengineered and nonbioengineered soybeans and corn. Moreover, genetically modified materials in highly processed additives or oils often can't be detected in testing. "If there's no way to test, then people are going to bend the rules and they're going to bend the truth," says Bruce Ferguson, president of EnviroLogix Inc., an environmental-testing company in Portland, Maine.

Some inconsistencies in supermarket claims can be attributed to the labeling law itself. At the moment, the European Union and British regulations require labeling only if genetically modified material is detectable in DNA or protein. Additives and flavorings are exempt.

Cheese-Making

That has led to some strange labeling dilemmas in items as simple as cheese. Traditionally, cheese was set using an enzyme called rennet, taken from the lining of calves' stomachs. But to appease vegetarians, many European cheese makers in recent years switched to an enzyme called chymosin that is produced from genetically modified bacteria.

There's no evidence that any genetically modified ingredient remains in the cheese after production. Still, one supermarket chain, Co-Op, decided to place labels on its cheese that say "made using genetic modification and so free from animal rennet." "It's a question of whether the retailer is honest or open in labeling it," says a Co-Op spokesman.

Meantime, Iceland, a small but scrappy convenience-store chain whose chairman coined the term "Frankenstein food," says it has switched to making its cheese with another enzyme that doesn't come from animals and isn't produced from genetically modified bacteria. "We've done them one better," says Bill Wadsworth, the chain's technical director.

European Union officials say they are hoping to clear up some of the confusion in the marketplace. Last week, a panel of government representatives voted to extend the labeling law to cover additives and flavorings, a change that is expected to take effect next year and could force many manufacturers and fast-food restaurants to either change recipes, switch suppliers or begin labeling.

The EU also decided to address the problem of products "contaminated" with trace amounts of genetically modified material despite the best intentions of manufacturers. In a controversial decision, the panel recommended that products don't require labeling if each of the ingredients contains 1% bioengineered material or less. Consumer groups had argued that the limit should be one-tenth of that.

In the future, the EU may also try to define when a retailer or manufacturer may claim that a product is "GM-free," a phrase that already has sprung up in some advertising and promotional material. Many retailers, such as Marks & Spencer, instead use the term "non-GM," which they insist is different. "We would never call it GM-free because you could never guarantee that," Mr. Mitchell says.

And thornier labeling issues loom. In their competitive frenzy, some British supermarkets have begun introducing raw and frozen chicken that they claim was raised on feed containing no genetically modified ingredients–even though there isn't evidence that bioengineered material ends up in the meat. To accomplish this, Iceland convenience stores say they now buy their chickens in Brazil, instead of Britain. Marks & Spencer says it is about to introduce a new line of free-range, non-GM poultry, egg and pork products.

Sainsbury's has yet to join the non-GM chicken and pork parade, but Mrs. Austin says it's probably "inevitable" and adds it may only be a first step. "We are utterly adamant that if you wish to claim you are GM-free, then you are ultimately going to have to go as far as GM-free veterinary medicines," she says.

93

PRIVACY

The Internet wants your personal info. *What's in it for you?*

Rima Berzin recently inherited a laptop computer from her husband and began an intense two-day honeymoon with the Internet. She went all the way: buying jeans at Gap, browsing for books at Barnesandnoble.com, and registering for Martha Stewart's online journal. While Berzin was shopping, something very un-Martha happened: Her spree left muddy digital footprints all over the Net.

Berzin, a Manhattan mother of two, is like a lot of other Americans just stepping onto the Web. When a friend told her how much personal information she had swapped for the convenience of home shopping, she was angry at first, then confused. On Berzin's first visit to Gap, hidden files called "cookies" were deposited on her computer. Other software programs whirred into action to track and analyze her online behavior. Marketers didn't know her name at first, but the anonymity evaporated when Berzin made her first purchase. "You can say no to being tracked," says the former strategic planning executive, "but it takes a great deal of work, and sometimes it pays to say yes."

"GET OVER IT." No one hacked Berzin's credit card or stole her identity. Such crimes are still rare on the Net. The apprehensions that engulfed Berzin are more far-reaching than fear of theft and resonate across society. Personal details are acquiring enormous financial value. They are the new currency of the digital economy. Indeed, a $50 billion freight train called electronic commerce is bearing down on Berzin and millions of consumers now venturing forth on the Net. That train is powered by an insatiable need for personal information–details about what individuals do online that help businesses zero in on customers.

This train is on a collision course with consumer sensibilities. Personal information is vulnerable to abuse. Failure to apply checks and balances today will change our lives and our notions of what belongs to us as individuals. "The ability to establish a digital trail is unlike anything we've had so far in history," says Constance E. Bagley, a Stanford University lecturer in law.

As companies race to collect personal data and exploit them, consumers are being confronted with urgent trade-offs and choices about how to cover their tracks in cyberspace–or whether they should. If they decide not to hide, how should they be compensated for the information they reveal? Businesses also face arduous trade-offs. Rightly, they fear a backlash over breaches of privacy. Cries for regulation have already reached Washington. If consumers like Berzin opt to conceal themselves or bolt from the Net or bind it in new laws, E-commerce could choke in its infancy.

By slapping high prices on personal information, E-business adds a frightening new dimension to the privacy debate. That fear extends across society. Hospitals and schools, for example, are constructing vast national databases with everything from your child's fourth-grade report card to the unique twists and turns of your DNA. Businesses want that information, and in the online world–where virtually every piece of data is for sale–they will probably get it. "You already have zero privacy. Get over it," Sun Microsystems Inc. CEO Scott G. McNealy glibly noted at a recent computer-fest.

Most Americans might find that hard to swallow. Many are starting to understand that what companies discover can hurt them. First comes the nuisance: a blizzard of junk mail. Then come the real dangers: Companies on the Web that know consumers' shopping habits and history can engage in sophisticated kinds of discrimination. If a business finds out that you, for example, are not a big spender, it may leave you dangling on help lines, refuse to notify you of juicy deals and discounts, or cut you off as a customer. And you won't even know you've been a victim. "It's very hard to show the discrimination occurred because somebody had access to personal information," says Deirdre Mulligan, staff counsel at the Center for Democracy & Technology in Washington.

Then there's the danger that the discrimination could be based on information that is false or out of date. "There hasn't been a data system built yet that is not fraught with inaccuracy," warns privacy activist Robert Ellis Smith. Even when information is correct, it may be damaging–and none of anyone's business. Digital trails that imply or prove that you have AIDS, for example, could cause employers or insurers to snub you. Suppose you're a college student accused of date rape, says Jason Catlett, a privacy advocate. "What happens when the prosecutor finds out that you were on a porno site the night before?"

To get consumers protection, privacy

advocates have been mobilizing politicians, leading to scores of federal and state privacy bills. A few are calling for tight government controls on personal information. (Europe stiffened such safeguards last fall.) E-businesses can't abide these regulations, worrying that such steps will cost them money. So they are trying to police themselves. Many popular sites post privacy policies and increasingly sport seals of approval from the Better Business Bureau and others, which purport to verify adherence.

But all these efforts come up short–in part because life on the Net is so complex. Information you willingly share with one company may be sold without your knowledge to somebody else. Privacy pledges posted on Web sites have limits and may not be enforced. Your personal data can become the property of strangers through subpoenas, corporate mergers, police investigations, or hacker attacks. And the results of your latest medical exam could turn up in the hands of a potential employer.

One reason simple protective measures fail is that consumers aren't sure they want them. Although they are worried that their privacy may be violated, they realize that personalized service on the Web can be very attractive. A Web site that recalls your tastes and buying habits can save you time and find bargains that suit you. What you see may depend on where you live, where you browse, what images tend to hold your eyeballs, and whether you have the loot to do more than look.

THE HOOK. As a result, consumers send confusing signals. One day, they are up in arms over Intel Corp.'s ability to track Web surfers through identifying codes on their new Pentium chips. The next, thousands race to trade their names, income levels, and hobbies in return for a Free-PC with built-in "market to one" advertising.

E-commerce, more than conventional business, needs this personal connection for several reasons. First, despite their lofty stock valuations, Web-based businesses with little or no earnings can't afford to constantly solicit new customers. They need repeat business. At Excite Inc., for example, customers who exchange tidbits about themselves in return for a personalized experience–in the form of selected news, movie listings, local weather, etc.–return to the site roughly 20 times more often than those who don't, says Joe Kraus, Excite's co-founder and senior vice-president.

Armed with loyal customers, Excite can then pile on additional services and boost its income. It can offer advertisers banner ads and "pop-ups" aimed only at the customers deemed most likely to respond. Sites can also earn commissions for routing customers to other locales. For example, visitors to technology review pages at CNET Inc., a news site, may click through to a computer company and purchase a PC. CNET gets a flat fee for each customer.

Customers' data will become more valu-

THE PRICE OF PRIVACY: YOUR MONEY

Somewhere, a network has more personal data about you than you probably ever imagined. Some of those are valuable data about yourself that you have given away. Some are data you thought were confidential but are now public. They might have been sold, auctioned off in a bankruptcy, or subpoenaed in a legal proceeding. New technologies and laws may soon give you the ability to put a crimp on the collecting or to get something in return for your personal data. Here are some of the risks, remedies, and trade-offs:

RISK You think your financial records are private. Then your bank merges with a securities firm and its online arm blitzes you with dubious investment offers.

REMEDY A bill co-sponsored by Senator Paul Sarbanes (D-Md.) would prohibit companies from sharing your personal data with a third party or affiliate unless you give approval.

TRADE-OFF You should always have the right to say no to data sharing, but some of the sales pitches are things you might want to see.

THE POLITICIAN "Privacy laws cover video rentals and cable-TV selections, yet we don't protect citizens' basic financial information from being shared," says Senator Paul Sarbanes.

---

able as databases from various sites are linked. That includes information from cookies, the files that many sites deposit on your hard drive when you visit. These files, which identify you when you log on, were initially designed to communicate only with the site that deposits them. Now, though, online marketing firms with names like DoubleClick, AdKnowledge, MatchLogic, and Engage may merge data from multiple cookies. That, in turn, can be collated with personal information scattered among census and motor-vehicle databases, credit reports, education and health records, and toll systems such as E-Z Pass.

As they consolidate their reach across these offline databases, Web sites may also apply powerful software tools to monitor and make money from the buying and browsing habits of their visitors. For years, banks and telecom companies have been using technology called data mining to track customer trends and spot fraud. Now, the tools are getting more powerful, and they are moving onto the Web.

These tools are becoming available just as massive databases are consolidating. Experian Information Solutions Inc., the giant credit-report company, has a stake in online marketer AdForce Inc. Meanwhile, an information aggregator, Acxiom Corp., is hawking data on more than 176 million individuals and 96 million households. "They follow you more closely than the U.S. government," says Anthony Picardi, top software analyst at International Data Corp. Adds Thomas F. Kelly, president and CEO of Neuron Data Inc., a Silicon Valley maker of customer-tracking software: "The privacy trade-off is the dirty little secret that everyone in the

business thinks about and talks about to each other but never brings up in public."

Consumers have caught a whiff of these secrets and don't like the smell. In a November Louis Harris & Associates Inc./Alan F. Westin survey of 1,000 adults, 82% complained they had lost all control over how their personal information is used by companies. Three out of four said businesses asked for too much information. And though millions of consumers bought gifts on the Web last Christmas, a BUSINESS WEEK/Harris poll last month showed that two-thirds of American adults are "not willing at all" to share personal and financial information about themselves online in return for more targeted advertising.

Even when it isn't threatening, personalization on the Net can get a little crass. Imagine if people fawned over you as much offline as they do online: Say you went to a restaurant with a date, had burgers, paid with a credit card, and left. It's over. But if it were online, the next time you showed up, the waitress, searching her file of private information, would say, "Hey Joe, how are you? Fran is over there; would you like to sit with her again?" Never mind that you're with another date. Then you would find out they've already cooked your burger and are ready to charge your card. When it comes to this kind of personalization online, says Tara Lemmey, executive director of the Electronic Frontier Foundation, "there's a fine line between good service and stalking."

Web startups aren't the only ones that know how to stalk. In January, Intel came under fire for designing its Pentium III chips with serial numbers that can be identified remotely on the Web. That makes it easier

THE PRICE OF PRIVACY: YOUR HEALTH

RISK Private information collected by your doctors and nurses can be passed on to insurers, employers, medical researchers, courts, and private eyes. Police and hackers might decide to take a peek, too.

REMEDY Senator Patrick Leahy (D-Vt.) is pushing a bill forcing doctors to notify you each time your data is requested and to justify disclosure.

TRADE-OFF In emergencies, the ability to zip your records over the Net may save your life. Medical science also gains by drawing on vast pools of patient data.

THE DOCTOR "If people can't trust their doctors to keep secrets," says psychiatrist Richard Epstein, "patients won't talk about sexual abuse or mental illness. The failure to disclose information could harm other people."

for users to be tracked. Two months later, privacy buffs hammered Microsoft Corp. because its Windows 98 software, used on a network, creates identifiers that are collected during registration. The result is a vast database of personal information about Microsoft customers.

"GOOD BUSINESS." Microsoft insists that the features it added were designed to improve services. But fearing a backlash, it has promised to modify the feature. It claims customers can bow out when they register for Win98, and it promises to expunge personal data it collected improperly. "This isn't just an ethical issue. Privacy is good business," says Saul Klein, a Microsoft senior manager of Web services.

GeoCities learned that lesson last year when the Federal Trade Commission accused the owners of this booming online community of selling personal information without members' consent. The site admitted no wrongdoing but agreed to implement tougher privacy policies. Says privacy activist Marc Rotenberg: "It's too easy for Web pages to turn into trick mirrors. The marketer gets to see through to you, but all you get to see is your own reflection."

When consumers see a big payoff, however, some of them are more than willing to trade their personal information. "As long as you give people something in return, they're thrilled," says Bill Gross, the Pasadena (Calif.) entrepreneur who founded idealab!, an incubator for Internet startups. In February, he unveiled Free-PC Inc. on the premise that people would part with detailed personal information and put up with a constant barrage of ads in exchange for a $500 computer. Privacy advocates mocked the proposition as a loser. But within days of announcing registration, the company fielded more than 1.2 million applications.

PECKING ORDER. Some companies use the gold mine of consumer data to discriminate against customers who don't make the grade. You might call it "Weblining." At Sanwa Bank in California, customer-service reps use Net-based programs to classify customers into A, B, and C categories. The least-valued Cs are the ones most likely to end up on hold when they call in for service. Angie Blackburn, who oversees Sanwa's phone and online banking, defends the practice. "Obviously, if we have a customer...who has a significant amount invested, you want [him or her] to be treated extra special," she says.

Weblining's grim implications are clear, however–and can be part of the software sales pitch. Makers of these tools say the onus lies with the company that uses them, not the creator. With data-mining software, "people can be segmented any way a company wants to slice and dice them," including creed, color, and religion, says Kenneth Volpe, an executive at Boston-based Art Technology Group, which sells such programs.

So far, Web marketers haven't broadened their quest for personal data to schools or hospitals. But it may be inevitable. Think of the advantages if they could hit you with ads for special foods for your diabetic aunt or Web-based tutoring for your struggling teenager. "If you are a business, data in

health records add up to one big sales opportunity," says Dr. Richard Epstein, a psychiatrist in Bethesda, Md.

School districts from New York to Oregon have begun replacing old stand-alone computers with high-speed networks, each with the ability to profile and track students. One day, these networks will connect to a nationwide data-exchange program organized by the Education Dept. to boost school efficiency and pinpoint the sources of learning problems. The program will make student information available to other schools, universities, government agencies, and, potentially, to employers. It's not just the three Rs. Now, it can be parent income, health problems, and meetings with the school shrink. Gayle Cloud, a mother of six in Riverside, Calif., finds this alarming. "They want to track my children from cradle to grave," she says.

The medical parallel to this is even more disturbing. Pressed by health-maintenance organizations, hospitals are struggling to rein in costs, and they are loading up on information technology to help. As health records are linked to financial, employment, and managed-care databases, they can be hacked or transferred to outsiders when HMOs or hospitals merge or are dismembered by creditors. "If you have a medical record, you have a medical privacy problem," says Senator Patrick Leahy (D-Vt.), the chief architect of a closely watched medical privacy bill.

Consolidating this data in one place makes it more vulnerable to theft or abuse. Says Joe Pellegrino, manager of database administration for New York Presbyterian Hospital: "There's no question this is leading to a national universal medical database." Already, hospitals exchange data on individual patients, he says. "The next step is to take these statewide databases, containing details on your allergies, your mental health, or your sexually transmitted diseases, and make them accessible."

INFO BROKERS. There are, however, many

THE PRICE OF PRIVACY: YOUR FAMILY

RISK Are your children on the Net? Do you know who they chat with and what information they surrender when they answer surveys or make purchases? And what about school? Once they're in a database, report cards from kindergarten can follow your kids for life.

REMEDY Stiff laws are being considered that would curb requests for personal data from children.

TRADE-OFF Your child can survey the entire world on the Net. Be careful you don't erect walls just when you should be tearing them down.

THE MOTHER Under pressure to cut costs, schools are building new databases, says Gayle Cloud. "They snoop your credit and medical records–and now your kids. Where is it going to stop?"

(Cont.)

jarring trade-offs in the medical-privacy debate. When managed right, medical data in digital form cut health-care costs, hasten and improve diagnoses, and reduce cases of prescription mix-ups. Computers also help administrators track doctors and spot unprofessional behavior. In genetics, digitized DNA repositories help scientists searching for links among genes and diseases–just as they help the FBI collaborate on manhunts across continents. Down the road, doctors will tailor drug treatments to patients' total medical profile, including their genetic makeup.

Even so, many Americans are deeply concerned about medical-data abuses. Neither doctors nor patients want records to leave the doctor's office except where necessary for insurance purposes. "Your doctor took the Hippocratic oath," says Robert Gellman, a privacy consultant in Washington. "The CEO of your health plan did not."

These concerns now have Washington's ear. Leahy's medical bill would give patients the right to limit disclosure of their medical records to those with a need to know. And in the financial arena, Senator Paul S. Sarbanes (D-Md.) and others are trying to regulate the sale of customers' records and the swapping of records in mergers.

E-businesses see regulation as the wolf at the door. The Online Privacy Alliance has mobilized more than 80 companies and trade associations to fight back. About 500 companies are already displaying a "trustmark" seal of approval from TRUSTe. Recently, the Better Business Bureau added its own seal of approval. In addition, the Net is spawning the "infomediary"–an information broker that protects Web users' privacy or barters it to find them bargains. The trouble is, infomediaries, like other Web businesses, must cough up their lists as soon as a cop or bankruptcy judge comes knocking.

Techies are at work on solutions to protect privacy. None of these efforts seems a silver bullet. David J. Farber, Moore Professor of Telecommunications at the University of Pennsylvania, believes nothing short of Europe's privacy directive will suffice. "Maybe you don't feel threatened in today's political climate," he says, "but imagine if this type of information and the tools to tap it were in the hands of a Joe McCarthy."

Sure enough, the secret codes, cookies, and digital trails are proliferating by the millisecond. Most of us have already surrendered more personal details than we could ever imagine. Cybernauts have one thing on Joe, though: The Net is a grand communications channel that returns a modicum of power to consumers. If you doubt it, note how quickly Microsoft and Intel backed off when a cry went out on the Web. Now comes the hard part: figuring out what we can get for the information we give.

By Edward C. Baig, Marcia Stepanek, and Neil Gross in New York, with bureau reports

94

Selling Birth Control to India's Poor

Medicine Men Market an Array Of Contraceptives

By Miriam Jordan

Staff Reporter of The Wall Street Journal

Mirzafari, India – From his outpost behind a wobbly desk under a tree, medicine man Sushil Bharati dispenses everything from cough remedies to advice on bad karma. Like thousands of other medicine men throughout the country, he is at the very heart of village life.

Now he is also part of an elaborate new medicine-man marketing network. Known as "Butterfly," its goal is to revolutionize the way the world's second-largest country curbs its soaring population. In return for advocating a formalized birth-control program, Mr. Bharati receives free radio ads and other benefits, like customer referrals. He also profits from selling condoms, prominently displayed in a jar on his little table, and birth-control pills.

It's a revolutionary concept for a village that is far removed from the modern world. Mirzafari's 10,000 citizens have no electricity, and women are confined to the home. Most men earn about $10 a month, mainly farming or weaving cotton. The average couple has eight children.

Plastered on the wall of Mr. Bharati's makeshift clinic are posters with the bright Butterfly logo–the same one that is displayed on billboards and village walls across the giant state of Bihar. There are butterflies, too, on Mr. Bharati's stationery, referral notes and prescription pad.

"We've gone for total branding," says K. Gopalakrishan, the network's director. "This is not only about serving humanity; it's about making money."

That is a significant philosophical shift. For decades, stabilizing population in India amounted to government-ordered sterilization. Policy makers set annual sterilization quotas, which were sometimes achieved by threatening, bribing or otherwise coercing women to participate, other times by fudging the figures. Under pressure from human-rights groups, New Delhi abolished that system three years ago.

Currently, India's census bureau estimates that on May 11, 2000, the nation's population will top one billion. Only China, with 1.2 billion people, is bigger; India is on track to surpass China within four decades. That prospect has spawned Butterfly and other programs–many funded by the U.S. government and U.S. private money–that aim to create networks out of existing commercial enterprises such as the medicine men. In neighboring Uttar Pradesh state, another program recruits milkmaids at village dairy cooperatives to spread the word on family planning.

The hurdles are huge. "Pills collect in your stomach and cause a cancer to grow," declares Lukoh, a pregnant woman in a pink and orange sari at Kharik village in Bihar, who already has had four children and five miscarriages. Another villager, Bebi, chimes in as she cradles her third child: "I have never taken contraceptives. My husband is my master–he will decide."

The northern states of Uttar Pradesh and Bihar are immense and poor. With 165 million people, if Uttar Pradesh were a nation, it would be the world's fifth largest. In neighboring Bihar, 100 million people eke out a living on 5% of India's land, and more than half live under the poverty line. Fewer than two out of 10 women can read and write.

India has made remarkable strides in slowing population growth in southern states, where female literacy is higher and states devote more money to health and education. Three southern states have achieved a replacement-level fertility rate–2.1 children per couple–or lower.

The risk to India is that soaring northern populations will swallow the economic advances made since India introduced market-oriented reforms earlier this decade. "If Uttar

Pradesh and Bihar don't curb their population, India as a nation will no longer be viable," cautions Gadde Narayana, an adviser to Futures Group International, Washington, D.C., which does population research in India.

Butterfly was born two years ago when DKT International, a Washington, D.C., non-profit group, created an Indian affiliate, Janani, which hatched the idea of using village medical practitioners. DKT invested $1 million and raised another $4 million from private Indian and U.S. groups.

Eight months ago, Mr. Bharati the medicine man and his wife, Sanju, signed on. They boarded an overnight train to the state capital, Patna, for a crash course on reproductive health at Janani's headquarters, where they learned about basic anatomy and the menstrual cycle. Armed with several tall jars of condoms and birth-control pills, supplied by Janani at cost, the couple returned four days later to northern Bihar.

Standing outside his brick hovel in Mirzafari, Mohammed Khurshid, father of 12, says he would prefer not to have any more children. But he won't countenance birth control. "It's in God's hands," he says. His third wife, Birwira, the mother of four of his children, seems to agree. Later, however, Mr. Bharati says that Birwira, 27 years old, regularly buys birth-control pills: "She doesn't skip a cycle."

That some villagers are even aware of birth-control methods other than sterilization is a tribute to Mr. Bharati and his wife. Typically, it takes several encounters to get a woman to consider birth control, so Mrs. Bharati broaches the subject subtly as she performs her daily chores with other women, such as fetching water at a well.

She is openly proud of her new knowledge. "Word is spreading that I have training," says Mrs. Bharati, who is one of the relatively few women who can read here. "Many women are seeking me to help them have fewer children," she says. Some ask to speak with her in the privacy of her family's dirt-floor home. She encourages the women to bring their husbands to Mr. Bharati.

Mr. Bharati, meanwhile, says he discusses family planning with nearly every customer. The condom jar on his desk stands next to another jar full of birth-control pills, in full view of patients, as required by Janani. "Family planning is my new responsibility," says Mr. Bharati, in his sixth year as a medicine man. "It is good for the village and it is good for my business," he says. A woman in a pink and blue sari steps up to buy a pack of pills.

Mr. Bharati charges about 20 cents a customer consultation, and 40 cents for bandaging a cut, but he doesn't charge separately for family-planning advice. In fact he even has to pay an annual $12 fee to be affiliated with Janani. But he makes a tiny profit from selling Janani's Bull brand condoms and Divine Dancer pills. He also receives a $1 commission for every patient he refers to Janani-endorsed doctors for intrauterine devices or abortions.

His practice, which earns him $70 to $90 a month, most of which comes from selling medicine, is thriving thanks to the free radio ads. He claims he is even winning business away from two competing medicine men. To preserve the brand's cachet, Janani affiliates with no more than one medicine man per village.

Janani has trained about 5,400 rural practitioners in 38 of Bihar's 55 districts. That's a drop in the bucket: There are 150,000 to 200,000 medicine men statewide. But

(Cont.)

encouraging results, such as that about 45% of the condoms and oral pills sold in the state are Janani brands, have prompted the organization to lay the groundwork for similar programs in two other northern states, Madhya Pradesh and Uttar Pradesh.

"We thought that if we could make this work in Bihar, we could make it work anywhere in India," says Mr. Gopalakrishan, the program director.

In neighboring Uttar Pradesh, another approach is under way at one of the world's biggest U.S.-funded population projects. The U.S. Agency for International Development is devoting $325 million over 10 years to an array of grass-roots programs to educate people about birth control. Among them is the milkmaid project.

Looking for an avenue into village society, USAID spotted opportunity in the state's countless dairy cooperatives, which provide a livelihood for women and also serve as de facto social centers. "The cooperative has always offered health care for the cows and buffalo of its members," declares Sumitra Singh, chairwoman of Pradeshik Dairy Co-op in Revri village. "Now, it's taking care of the women themselves."

As the early morning sun warms Revri's

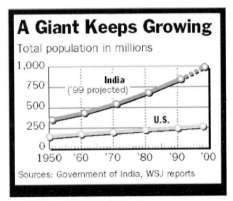

A Giant Keeps Growing

Total population in millions

India ('99 projected)

U.S.

1950 '60 '70 '80 '90 '00

Sources: Government of India, WSJ reports

mud huts, women with cans of buffalo milk line up at the co-op, and Sita Kumari, a co-op member and health worker, canvasses the crowd. Carrying a supply of pills and condoms in her shoulder bag, along with flip charts showing how to use them, she quickly identifies women who might need to restock.

The goods Ms. Kumari gives away are supplied by the government free of charge, though recently she started selling private brands, too.

USAID has trained 4,300 volunteers like Ms. Kumari, and pays them $8 month. In 15

districts of Uttar Pradesh where USAID is operating, the number of couples using family-planning services, such as pills, condoms and IUDs, has nearly doubled in three years.

A few years down the road, the co-op is expected to share the cost of the program by pooling a few pennies each month from members. In the long run, the idea is for each co-op to run the program on its own, and in fact make a profit by sourcing contraceptives for its members to sell.

"Dealing with population in India requires dynamism, flexibility and entrepreneurship," asserts Mr. Narayana of Futures Group. Nevertheless, it may take years before the success of the soft-sell approach can be accurately gauged.

Meanwhile, Ms. Kumari perseveres. Three years into the project, she supplies contraceptives to about 220 out of the 510 couples she has contacted. As for the others, she says, "I keep going back to them with my message."

95

BIG CARDS ON CAMPUS

Affinity-card issuers are stepping in with megabucks

You might say that Joseph E. Johnson, president emeritus of the University of Tennessee, thinks like any savvy chief executive officer. When the university hit what he called "a point of crisis" last year because of inadequate state fiscal support, Johnson forged one of the most lucrative corporate sponsor deals ever.

In a $16 million arrangement with First USA, the credit-card division of Bank One Corp., the bank is the sole marketer of the university's Visa "affinity" credit card–a card adorned with the school's picture and logo–to the university's students and alumni. "A lot are concerned that we're soaking our students, but we decided to do this in a reputable way rather than to let just any issuer on campus to solicit. Plus we needed the funds," says Johnson, who retired last month. In addition to the $16 million, divvied up over the course of seven years, the university receives 0.5% of every transaction charge, which could amount to an estimated $4 million annually.

More colleges and universities face similar budgetary problems, and credit-card companies are rushing in to fill the gap. Card companies pay for everything from mentoring programs to lecture series to cap-and-gown rentals. "You're finding much more of a willingness for schools to cut all kinds of creative sweetheart deals with corporations for big money," says Lewis Mandell, dean of the State University of New York at Buffalo's management school and the author of three books on credit cards.

The deals obviously benefit schools, but the real winners are card companies. Credit-hungry students are often a card issuer's best customers, despite the fact that most don't have a credit history or even a job. "If it's the first card you get, chances are you'll hold on to it for a long time," says Robert B. McKinley, CEO of CardWeb.com Inc., a credit-card tracking service. Studies show that students keep their first credit card for an average of 15 years.

Card marketers also like students because 70% of those with cards at four-year colleges have $2,000 or more of revolving debt, according to the Consumer Federation. And ironically, students are less of a credit risk than the general population because their parents often pay their bills.

TOO FAR? Once a bank secures a captive student audience, it can market other products such as first mortgages, car loans, and, in a sinister twist, debt-consolidation loans to help students repay credit-card debt. "They've got

'em and they know it," says Robert Manning, a sociology professor at Georgetown University and author of a recent study on students and credit cards.

Indeed, a growing concern is that affinity-card programs have encroached too far into academia's supposedly hallowed halls. At the University of Ottawa, MBNA Corp., the largest affinity-card issuer, started an alumni-student mentoring program last year. At the University of Hawaii, MBNA provides video production services and airtime to "ensure continuance" of the weekly UH Today radio and TV show. Says Manning: "You can't tell me that having a credit-card issuer controlling student media won't impact editorial decisions." Manning's Georgetown University gets paid an undisclosed sum by MBNA for rights to the Georgetown affinity card. Also, MBNA contributed $2 million several years ago to fund what is officially called the MBNA Career Education Center.

"DANGEROUS." In the face of all of this, student credit-card debt is mounting, due

primarily to aggressive card marketing and students' lack of credit knowledge. According to the Consumer Federation study, debt among college students has almost tripled since 1990. "That's why these mega credit-card deals are more dangerous than, say, whether a college chooses to be a Coke campus or a Pepsi campus or give all of its athletes Nike shoes," says Mandell.

Because of worry over student debt, a growing number of colleges and universities are restricting or banning campus-card marketing by non-affinity-card issuers. Still, most schools, especially large state schools, are not nearly as quick to turn down blockbuster affinity-card deals. "Colleges will say they've done a deal with a single issuer in order to get competing card marketers off campus and to control the process. But what difference does it make if you're a student with $10,000 of debt on an affinity card vs. another type of card?" asks Manning.

One of the reasons affinity cards have become so popular and lucrative for both

The Plastic Invasion		
SCHOOL	**BANK**	**DEAL**
Georgetown University	MBNA	$2 million for career counseling center
Michigan State University	MBNA	$5.5 million for athletic and academic scholarship program
University of Hawaii	MBNA	$1.5 million for TV and radio shows; athletics
University of Ottawa	MBNA	$0.3 million for alumni mentoring program
University of Tennessee	First USA	$16 million for athletics; scholarships; other needs

Data: Business Week

colleges and credit-card issuers is that the cardholders are more loyal. "If you've got a card with your college on it, it's like being part of a club. There's pride involved," says McKinley. Part of that loyalty stems from the idea that the cardholder is donating to his or her school or alma mater each time the card is used. In most affinity-card deals, in addition to an up-front flat fee sometimes as much as several million dollars, a college receives half of a percent of the purchase value of each transaction made with the card.

In addition, schools are often paid anywhere from $5 to $20 on each new account that is opened and sometimes a small percentage of loans outstanding. But card issuers emphasize that each deal they make is unique. "We make proposals to schools based on their particular needs and the information they give us," says Jeff Unkle, a First USA spokesman.

For their part, card issuers and schools often argue that affinity cards are tied to the alumni association, not the school itself, but

> **"If you've got a card with your college on it, it's like being part of a club. There's pride involved"**

this can be misleading. "In these deals, the contracts typically specify that issuers have access to student mailing lists and can solicit directly on campus," says Manning.

In a typical First USA or MBNA deal, for example, the bank is the only issuer allowed to market on campus and through student and alumni mailing lists–a coup for any card issuer in these days of cutthroat competition for the college market. At the University of Tennessee, for instance, there are some 270,000 alumni and 26,000 students, in addition to untold numbers of UT fans who are also solicited at sporting events.

Although schools and card companies are pleased with the deals, some factions are not.

This spring, the Tennessee state legislature nearly passed a bill that would have prohibited credit-card solicitations on campuses altogether, thus terminating the university's deal. The bill will be reintroduced next year. As part of the pending bankruptcy bill, Congress is considering a proposal that would allow credit cards to go to people under 21 only if they have parental approval or are financially independent.

"We realize that students may lack credit experience, but most of them are extremely responsible and handle credit cards as well or better than most adults," says Brian Dalphon, a spokesman for MBNA.

As affinity-card programs remain highly lucrative for both colleges and card companies, they will likely continue to remain BMOC–big money on campus.

By Marcia Vickers in New York

96

WRESTLING WITH YOUR CONSCIENCE

Wal-Mart wants to avoid controversy on its shelves, but consumers won't let it

Bill Saporito/Bentonville

Walk into most any Wal-Mart in the U.S. and here are a few of the things you can buy: condoms, birth control pills, hunting rifles, "Western" style toy guns, the movie *There's Something About Mary,* the *National Enquirer,* cigarettes, the video game South Park, the hard-rocking Powerman 5000's hit *Tonight the Stars Revolt.* And here are a few of the things you can't buy: a "day-after" birth control kit, handguns, authentic-looking plastic guns, *Playboy,* rolling papers, the movie *South Park,* the video game Grand Theft Auto and any number of rap CDs.

Inconsistent? Absolutely, and deliberately so. "We're a family store," says Wal-Mart CEO David Glass, and "we try to have something for everyone." And just as in real families, there is conflict about who gets what. Last week the company was pinned by a consumer who demanded that a World Wrestling Federation action doll be yanked from the shelves because both the wrestler it depicted, Al Snow, and the doll carry a prop that looks like a woman's severed head.

It was the latest in a series of controversies in which the company, by virtue of its enormous size and reach, has played an unwanted role as a sort of national conscience, discount division. Wal-Mart has been accused of being both censor and nanny, condemned as a promoter of demon rum and slave labor, and cited as both a friend and a foe of the environment. "We don't want to be America's moral conscience," says Don Soderquist, senior vice chairman. "The watchword for all of our people is 'Do what is right.' That's what we really preach and teach and we want, but there's so much gray."

And wherever there's gray, black, as in ink, is not far behind. Earlier this year, Wal-Mart infuriated some women's groups when it declined to stock Preven, an emergency day-after contraception kit available by prescription. Antiabortion groups hailed the decision as one for their side. But Wal-Mart's rationale was simpler–perhaps too much so: its pharmacies don't stock every drug available; Preven was going to be a small seller, customers were not clamoring for it, and the item was pricey ($25). "You can't carry everything. Sometimes you get credit for making a moral judgment when you're not," says Glass. Similarly, when Glass pulled handguns from the shelves in 1994, the company cited sales

more than ethics, although he notes that by then there were more negatives in stocking handguns than positives.

Glass is certain that some of the books, videos and other products in the stores he would personally find offensive. He just doesn't know what they are. "When you have 100,000 unique SKUs," he says, using the retailer's term for an item–a stock keeping unit– "something is going to irritate somebody."

That would be, for instance, Kevin Clarke, a mild-mannered carpet salesman from Mentor, Ohio, and a loyal Wal-Mart customer, who went ballistic after his son bought a CD by a band named Godsmack that he thought God-awful, particularly a ditty called *Voodoo,* which seemed to be about suicide. Wal-Mart has long had a policy of banning so-called stickered CDs, those carrying a warning label that the content might not be suitable for children. But Godsmack was stickerless, so Wal-Mart stocked it, until Clarke hollered.

The music industry doesn't like Wal-Mart's policy, muttering under its collective breath about censorship and artistic freedom, but it won't buck the system. That's because Wal-Mart's reach is enormous, representing 10% to 15% of all U.S. CD sales. "It's very difficult to have a No. 1" without Wal-Mart, says a record-company executive. That's why even the biggest, baddest acts–Nirvana, Snoop Dogg–often clean up their acts to play Wal-Mart. But even that kind of screen isn't enough for parents such as Clarke, who hold Wal-Mart accountable for everything that ends up on the shelves: "They tout a policy that their stores are a safe haven, but they didn't honor it."

Wal-Mart has a clearly articulated view of its role in society and the economy–to be an "agent" for the consumer. The company views its job as finding out exactly what folks want and getting those products into the stores at the lowest possible cost. It's a strategy that has worked superbly. Wal-Mart earned $4.4 billion last year on sales of $139 billion. It serves 90 million to 100 million customers each week. So while Wal-Mart is a conservative company born of the rural South, it hasn't let that get in the way of some basic considerations of commerce. Years ago, church leaders were unhappy, and unavailing, when the company began to open its stores on Sundays. The customers, not any

other authority, would be obeyed.

This kind of practical morality operates on a larger scale too. Take the sale of alcoholic beverages. Wal-Mart does not sell beer and wine in its traditional discount stores. Yet if you walk into many Wal-Mart supercenters, stores as big as 220,000 sq. ft. that combine a supermarket with a traditional Wal-Mart, you'll find plenty of Budweiser to put in the coolers being sold in sporting goods. Wine and beer are also sold in Sam's Clubs and in the company's new chain of downsized Neighborhood Markets, a.k.a. "small marts."

Why the distinction? Wal-Mart executives attribute the decision to the customers, who say they expect to be able to buy beer and wine in supercenters just as they do at competitors' stores of a similar type. Yet booze will remain verboten in fuddy-duddy old Wal-Mart discount stores. Explains Glass: "What's the difference between selling in a supercenter and a Wal-Mart? I can't tell you I can give you a definite answer. But I can tell you that I have a rationale for it." Nevertheless, within the company and without, there was muttering that Sam–Wal-Mart's late founder, Sam Walton–wouldn't stand for such a thing. Wrong, says Glass. Sam knew better than to buck the customers.

Hence, Wal-Mart is well stocked in inconsistencies. *South Park,* the cartoon television series and recent movie, features a funny but foulmouthed cast of characters and an infinite collection of toilet jokes. The South Park video game got to the shelves but not the film. Reason: Wal-Mart's game buyer figured that customers who purchase it are already familiar with the characters. The video buyer, on the other hand, believed that customers associate animated films with movies such as *Bambi* and not with Cartman and his profane pals. (No doubt the boys would have joyously killed and consumed Bambi.)

In Wal-Mart's world, there is accounting for taste. For instance, the video section stocks the risque comedy *There's Something About Mary.* And there's something in it that more than a few folks would find objectionable. Says movie buyer Eddie Tutt: "It's pretty crude, but [the movie] did $175 million in sales, which kind of tells you that most of the public looked at it and probably felt good about it." Which tells Tutt that unlike, say, Howard Stern's crude movie, *Private Parts,* which Wal-Mart did not carry, *Mary* will light

(Cont.)

up the cash registers.

Yet Wal-Mart customers are not of one mind on some of society's more complicated matters, as it learned with Preven. The primary ingredient in Preven is ethinyl estradiol/levonorgestrel–the same as in birth control pills–given in a high dose. The package also contains a pregnancy test. Although Wal-Mart wouldn't stock Preven, it has always sold birth control pills.

Earlier this year, Planned Parenthood sent women to Wal-Mart stores with "emergency" prescriptions for birth control pills, not Preven by name. A few pharmacists refused to fill them, some apparently under the false impression that these drugs will terminate a pregnancy, as opposed to preventing one.

Planned Parenthood pressed the company for a clarification on its pharmacy policy. Wal-Mart then sent a directive to each of its pharmacists requiring them to fulfill any emergency prescription, which is consistent with the American Pharmaceutical Association's code of ethics. Any pharmacist whose personal beliefs prevented him from filling such a prescription must find someone who will. So day-after contraception is available, even if, for business reasons, Preven is not. "We don't care what their motivation is," says Gloria Feldt, president of Planned Parenthood, who gives the company good marks for its responsiveness. "Our concern is that women can get emergency contraception."

The Preven controversy, among others, has prompted Wal-Mart to reconsider some of its laissez-faire policies. The company recently established an ethics committee, to which buyers and other Wal-Mart employees can refer any knotty issue. As Wal-Mart continues to grow internationally, the committee will no doubt get busier. Certainly the medical-ethics front will get murkier. "We are only at the tip of the iceberg," says Soderquist. "There will be lots of issues that will come up: suicide pills, genetic engineering. Can they prescribe pills that alter the genes?"

And even before we get there, the nation's biggest shopkeeper will be less able to stick to its preferred role as an agnostic buyer for the masses. There's a world full of outraged parents, students, environmentalists, activists, politicians and stockholders complaining with equal fervor about the silly and the serious. Says Glass: "The public in general becomes a little harder to serve all the time. But you have to respond to that." In other words, Wal-Mart is no longer a free agent.

With reporting by David E. Thigpen

WHAT'S ON—AND NOT ON— WAL-MART'S SHOPPING LIST

GUNS
Handguns were booted in 1994. Sales were insignificant. The publicity wasn't.
BUT . . . It sells hunting rifles, part of a strategy to create a dominant sporting-goods department for guys.

MAGAZINES
No adult, or rock titles like Cream. Has pulled individual issues of some mags.
BUT . . . Sells the *National Enquirer* and alien-heavy scandal sheets.

MUSIC
Stocks Top 100 hits, except for "stickered" CDs. Previews lyrics.
BUT . . . Bands will change lyrics to get in. Customers are ever vigilant.

MOVIES/GAMES
Top-seller focus. *South Park,* the movie, is too lewd.
BUT . . . The game is O.K. The company gets an early look at all games, but it's not fussy.

CONTRACEPTION
Won't sell Preven, emergency birth control kit, citing low sales potential.
BUT . . . Sells condoms, birth control pills and spermicides.

ALCOHOL
Not in traditional Wal-Mart stores. Customers don't expect it there.
BUT . . . Superstores are different, so beer and wine are sold where legal.

TOYS
Pulled the World Wrestling Federation Road Rage doll after charges that the character, Al Snow, promoted violence against women.
BUT . . . Still has Stone Cold Steve Austin and others. No complaints.

97

$45 MILLION FOR ONE BUCK

TV, cereal boxes—they're pushing the 'Golden Dollar' like mad

As soon as he heard the new U.S. dollar coins were available at his local Charlotte (N.C.) Wal-Mart, Ron Feuer rushed out to exchange a $20 bill for a handful of the gold-colored coins. "I was one of the first," he says proudly. Feuer, an avid collector, might be more excited than most over the coin's arrival, but that may change.

Starting Mar. 6, the U.S. Mint will unleash a $45 million marketing blitz to sell the new coin to the public. "We want to get everyone talking," says U.S. Mint Director Philip N. Diehl. The mint has dubbed the coin the Golden Dollar, even though it's really a copper and brass alloy. But it might as well be gold, given the glittering launch the mint has planned.

The new dollar has its own public-relations firm, a cereal-box promotional tie-in, and even a catchy slogan: "The Golden Dollar: The Right Change for the New Millennium." Already there are about 200 million of the new coins in circulation and the mint, which projects that number will grow to 1 billion by year-end, just doubled production to keep up with demand.

SUSAN B. FLOP. Still, the mint isn't taking any chances. Its lavish advertising campaign will hit TV, radio, and the Internet. The coins are already "prizes" in Cheerios boxes and next month, mint officials plan a multi-city coin giveaway, handing out Golden Dollars in front of rail and subway stations.

It might seem like overkill. But the mint is determined not to end up with another Susan B. Anthony, the dollar coin that was introduced in 1979 and quickly flopped. The vending machine industry spent $200 million retooling its machines to accept the Anthony dollar, according to the National Automatic Merchandising Assn. (NAMA). Still, the public shunned the coin because it was often mistaken for a quarter.

Clearly, vending machine operators, including the postal service and mass transit operators, have the most riding on the new coin. NAMA estimates that the industry loses $3 billion a year when consumers try to slip a tattered bill into a vending machine to no avail. "Those are sales that would have happened" if a coin were used, says Thomas E. McMahon, vice-president of NAMA. The mint, on the other hand, didn't lose money on the Susan B. Anthony because it made the coin for only 9 cents, then transferred it to the Federal Reserve for $1. "What the Mint lost was face," says Diehl.

Some argue the wisdom of spending $45 million on an ad campaign for a coin. But in 1997, Congress ordered a new dollar coin. So the mint held focus groups, resulting in a coin depicting Sacagawea, a Native American woman and a member of the Lewis and Clark expedition. Then came the distribution deal with Wal-Mart Stores Inc. and, now, the ad blitz about to hit.

> **The unmitigated failure of the Susan B. Anthony dollar has put pressure on the mint to do this coin right**

> ***Selling Sacagawea:*** **The mint's campaign includes tie-ins with Wal-Mart and Cheerios**

Critics think the mint has lost its bearings. Bankers, for example, feel snubbed by the Wal-Mart deal, since new coins have traditionally been theirs to release. Jerry Ursprung, vice-president of First Liberty National Bank in Liberty, Tex., says he was "caught off guard" when his local Wal-Mart had the first supply of the new dollar coins.

Others insist no amount of marketing will make the coin a success. They point out that the Canadian dollar coin, introduced in 1987, was a success because its paper counterpart was phased out. "With the dollar bill to fall back on, who needs the coin," says Donna Pope, a former director of the U.S. Mint.

Diehl argues that the right coin with the right marketing will work alongside a greenback. "This can be a 'hot' product," he says. Now he just has to convince everyone out there that he's right.

By Ellen Neuborne in New York and Richard S. Dunham in Washington, D.C.

Notes

Notes

Notes

Notes

Notes

Notes

Notes

Notes

Notes

Notes